Rethinking Gender, Crime, and Justice

Feminist Readings

Claire M. Renzetti
University of Dayton

Lynne Goodstein
University of Connecticut

Susan L. Miller
University of Delaware

New York   Oxford
OXFORD UNIVERSITY PRESS

Oxford University Press, Inc., publishes works that further Oxford University's
objective of excellence in research, scholarship, and education.

Oxford   New York
Auckland   Cape Town   Dar es Salaam   Hong Kong   Karachi
Kuala Lumpur   Madrid   Melbourne   Mexico City   Nairobi
New Delhi   Shanghai   Taipei   Toronto

With offices in
Argentina   Austria   Brazil   Chile   Czech Republic   France   Greece
Guatemala   Hungary   Italy   Japan   Poland   Portugal   Singapore
South Korea   Switzerland   Thailand   Turkey   Ukraine   Vietnam

For titles covered by Section 112 of the US Higher Education Opportunity Act,
please visit www.oup.com/us/he for the latest information about
pricing and alternate formats.

Published by Oxford University Press, Inc.
198 Madison Avenue, New York, New York 10016
http://www.oup.com

Oxford is a registered trademark of Oxford University Press

ISBN: 978-0-19-533030-4 (pbk)

Printed in the United States of America
on acid-free paper

Contents

Preface

In 2001, Lynne Goodstein and I edited a book entitled *Women, Crime, and Criminal Justice: Original Feminist Readings*. Each of the chapters was written specifically for that book, and each explored a different aspect of women's experiences in the criminal justice system, as offenders and as victims. Overall, we were pleased with the outcome of that effort but worried that the book, which was intended for use by undergraduate students, might be too difficult for many, especially those who had no previous exposure to criminology or criminal justice courses. Based on reviewers' feedback, our concerns were not unwarranted. The volume, we were told, was interesting and informative, but often too empirically-based for the typical undergraduate, putting it well beyond their intellectual reach.

When we were asked to prepare a second edition of the text, we decided essentially to start over with entirely new chapters—not just updates of those previously published—and with a new editor on board, Susan Miller. Susan's knowledge of the field, as well as her editing, writing, and teaching experience, have been welcome additions to the enterprise. The result of our labor is a completely new book, but one that retains its feminist framework; hence, the new title, *Rethinking Gender, Crime, and Justice: Feminist Readings*.

From the outset, our goal was student accessibility. Each chapter begins with a set of learning objectives that answers for the student the question, "Why should I read this chapter?" Moreover, contributors were asked to provide an overview of their topic that is appropriate for undergraduate students and covers the major themes, relevant literature, and basic research trends. Contributors were instructed to avoid jargon, to define specialized concepts clearly, and to avoid complex statistical analyses. We think that when you read the book you will agree that the authors took these requests to heart. In addition, authors provided three to five discussion questions derived from their chapter. These questions are designed to stimulate classroom discussion, encourage critical thinking, and help students delve more deeply into the issues raised in the chapter. They are also an important pedagogical tool that instructors may find useful for exam questions, take-home assignments, or papers.

Rethinking Gender, Crime, and Justice: Feminist Readings is the product of a collaborative effort not only among the editors but also among the contributors, who were willing to share their ideas with one another and to spend precious hours writing and revising their chapters in light of the editors' and reviewers' feedback. Obviously, the book would not exist without them, but more importantly, the book would not be as good without their commitment to the project and their collegiality. For this, we thank them. Thanks, too, to the individuals who spent their valuable time reviewing an early draft of the book: Peggy Bradford (Aurora University), Leanne Brecklin (University of Illinois at Springfield), Mary Bosworth (University of Oxford), Susan Cody (LaGrange College), Gloria Hamilton (Middle Tennessee State University), Hua-Lun Huang (University of Louisiana at Lafayette), Gwen Hunnicutt (University of North Carolina at Greensboro), and Marlyn Jones (California State University, Sacramento). We also extend our thanks to Phong Ho, Scott Carter, and Monica Gomez at Roxbury for guiding the book through production and to Claude Teweles, the Publisher at Roxbury, for supporting us in our decision to begin anew. Lynne Goodstein wishes to thank her coworkers at the University of Connecticut for their colleagueship and she thanks her husband, Peter Langer, and sons, Zachary and Aaron Shotland, for their understanding and support. Susan Miller extends her heartfelt thanks to Connor Miller and Nancy Getchell for their support during her various writing projects. She also sends special thanks to Nancy Quillen, secretary extraordinaire, in the Department of Sociology and Criminal Justice at the University of Delaware, for her capable assistance. And I wish to thank Denise Shaw, secretary in the Department of Sociology at St. Joseph's University, for keeping me organized, and I thank my new colleagues at the University of Dayton for welcoming me so warmly to their department and their campus. And I am, as always, grateful to my husband, Dan Curran, and my sons, Sean and Aidan Curran, for making me smile every day.

When we were asked to include our acknowledgements in this Preface, we each also wanted to say something about how we enjoyed working with one another. Collaborating on a book is often like performing a delicate dance, and it is easy to step on one another's toes. In this case, however, our friendship—and our toes—remain intact. It has been a rewarding experience for each of us and we are grateful to one another for that. ✦

About the Contributors

Terri Adams-Fuller is an assistant professor of administration of justice in the Department of Sociology and Anthropology at Howard University. Her areas of expertise include violent crime, women and crime, and Geographic Information Systems (GIS) technology. Her research primarily focuses on the examination of spatial patterns of violent crime and the impact of violent crime on women. She has worked as a research associate on various social science research projects at the American Sociological Association, the George Washington University's Institute for Crime Justice and Corrections, and the University of the District of Columbia's Institute for Public Safety and Justice. Dr. Adams-Fuller has also served as a consultant for the Urban Institute, the District of Columbia's Chapter of the Fraternal Order of Police, and the District of Columbia's Department of Corrections.

Gabrielle Alfieri earned her B.S. in criminal justice with a minor in sociology from Saint Joseph's University in 2002. She graduated *Cum Laude* and earned the annual departmental award given to the most outstanding graduating senior in criminal justice. She completed a year of master's work at Saint Joseph's in criminal justice before transferring to the State University of New York at Buffalo, where she is currently pursuing her master's degree in an interdisciplinary program that focuses on sociology and documentary film production.

Tammy L. Anderson is an associate professor in the Department of Sociology and Criminal Justice at the University of Delaware. She has conducted research and published numerous articles on drug abuse, gender, race, stigma, and health for more than ten years. She is currently engaged in an ethnographic study of club culture, drugs, crime, and victimization sponsored by her university and the National Institute of Justice. Dr. Anderson is the 2005–2006 Chair of the Section on Alcohol, Drugs and Tobacco of the American Sociological Association and past Chair of the Division on Drinking and Drugs of the Society for the Study of Social Problems (2003–2004).

Ronet Bachman is a professor in the Department of Sociology and Criminal Justice at the University of Delaware. Her research interests revolve primarily around issues of violence and victimization. Her recent coauthored books include *Murder American Style, The Practice of Research in Criminology and Criminal Justice, Statistics for Criminology and Criminal Justice,* and *Explaining Crime and Criminals*.

Joanne Belknap is a professor in the Department of Sociology at the University of Colorado. She received a Ph.D. in criminal justice and criminology from Michigan State University in 1986. Dr. Belknap has numerous scholarly publications, most of which involve violence against women and girls and female offenders. She is currently working on the third edition of her book *The Invisible Woman: Gender, Crime, and Justice* and a book on the court processing of domestic violence. Recent and forthcoming empirical publications are about college campus fraternity rapes, the court processing of woman battering cases, and institutionalized delinquent girls.

Susan Caringella is a professor in the Department of Sociology and in the Gender and Women's Studies Program at Western Michigan University. Her work has been recognized with national, state, and university honors, such as the American Society of Criminology's Division on Women and Crime Senior Scholar Award, and the Division on Critical Criminology (where she was founding chair) Lifetime Achievement Award. She is a deputy editor for the journal *Women and Criminal Justice* and on the editorial board of the journal *Violence Against Women.* Her most recent work is *Addressing Rape in Law and Practice,* forthcoming from Columbia University Press.

Patrick J. Carr is an assistant professor in the Department of Sociology at Rutgers University, and he is an associate member of the MacArthur Research Network on the Transitions to Adulthood and Public Policy. His research focuses on crime in urban communities, community responses to crime, youth violence, and the transition to adulthood. He has published a number of articles on informal social control and youth violence, and his manuscript, *Clean Streets: Controlling Crime, Maintaining Order, and Building Community Activism,* will be published by New York University Press in 2005.

Amy Desautels is a doctoral candidate in the Department of Sociology and Anthropology at Fordham University. Her research interests include the political economy of sex work, racial inequality, and policy issues pertaining to low-income Americans.

Jeanne Flavin is an associate professor in the Department of Sociology and Anthropology at Fordham University and has published in the area of gender and sentencing. Her current research examines race, punishment, and how the criminal justice system regulates women's reproductive freedom.

Lynne Goodstein is Associate Vice-Provost and Director of the Honors Program and a professor in the Department of Sociology at the University of Connecticut. Dr. Goodstein has co-authored or co-edited four books, including *Determinate Sentencing and Imprisonment: A Failure of Reform, The American Prison,* and *Women, Crime, and Criminal Justice: Original Feminist Readings,* and a number of book chapters and journal articles. She writes on correctional institutions, criminal sentencing, women and the criminal justice system, and higher education. She was honored as the 2001 recipient of the Herbert Bloch award from the American Society of Criminology.

Dian P. Gonyea holds a master's degree from the School of Criminal Justice, Michigan State University. She has conducted research on women and men who work in policing and is currently employed as a specialist in survey research.

Angela R. Gover is an associate professor in the Department of Criminology, Law and Society at the University of Florida. She received her Ph.D. from the University of Maryland's Department of Criminology and Criminal Justice. Her research interests include the victimization of women and children and their treatment by the criminal justice system. She is currently working with colleagues from the University of South Carolina on a project funded by the National Institute of Justice that examines violations and enforcement of no-contact orders for domestic violence offenders processed by the Lexington County Domestic Violence Court.

Robin N. Haarr is a Fulbright Senior Specialist who works with UNICEF, the Swiss Agency for Development and Cooperation on Violence Against Women, and the Organization for Security and Cooperation of Europe on Gender Mainstreaming in the Government of Tajikistan. She holds a Ph.D. in criminal justice and criminology from Michigan State University.

Stephanie A. Hays is a doctoral student in the Department of Criminology, Law and Society at the University of Florida. She has an MA in criminology with a minor in statistics from the University of Florida in addition to a master's degree in human relations from the University of Oklahoma. Her research interests focus on gender and crime, specifically the structural correlates of female offending, as well as rural crime.

Catherine Kaukinen is an assistant professor in the Department of Criminology and Criminal Justice at the University of South Carolina. She received her Ph.D. in 2001 from the Department of Sociology at the University of Toronto. Kaukinen's research interests include the social and developmental risk factors and long-term behavioral and mental health consequences of violent victimization and criminal offending. She is currently working with Dr. Angela Gover on an examination of the impact of intensive enforcement of court-imposed no-contact orders in criminal domestic violence cases. They will examine the effect of these orders on offender recidivism and victim well-being.

Christina Lanier is a doctoral student in sociology at the University of Delaware. She is a research assistant at the Center for Drug and Alcohol Studies. Her current research examines American Indian suicide, homicide, and accidents. Her interests include quantitative methods and binge drinking among adolescents and young adults.

Shana L. Maier is an assistant professor in the Department of Criminal Justice at Widener University. She received her Ph.D. in sociology from the University of Delaware in 2004. Her research interests include violence against women, the treatment of victims by the criminal justice and legal systems, the transformation of rape crisis centers, and the experiences and struggles of rape advocates. She is the co-author of articles appearing in the *International Review of Victimology* and *Women's Health and Urban Life*.

Susan E. Martin was formerly a health scientist administrator in the Prevention Research Branch at the National Institute on Drug Abuse (NIDA). Previously, she held a similar position at the National Institute on Alcohol Abuse and Alcoholism, conducted research at the Police Foundation, and was a study director at the National Research Council. She is author (with Nancy Jurik) of *Doing Justice, Doing Gender: Women in Law and Criminal Justice Occupations* as well as other books and articles on alcohol-related violence, women in policing, sexual harassment and hate crime. She has a B.A. from Swarthmore College and a Ph.D. from American University. She is currently an independent consultant living in Chevy Chase, MD.

Michelle L. Meloy is an assistant professor in the Department of Sociology, Anthropology, and Criminal Justice at Rutgers University–Camden. She received her Ph.D. in criminology from the University of Delaware. Her research interests include domestic violence, sexual violence, victimology, and crimi-

nal justice policy. She has just completed a book about male sex offenders (Northeastern University Press) and is currently completing a book on victim policies and politics, with Susan L. Miller (Oxford University Press).

James W. Messerschmidt is a professor of sociology in the Criminology Department at the University of Southern Maine. He is the author of numerous articles, chapters, and books on gender and crime, including *Capitalism, Patriarchy, and Crime, Masculinities and Crime, Crime as Structured Action, Nine Lives,* and most recently, *Flesh and Blood.* Currently, he is working on three research projects involving the sex-gender distinction and criminological theory; the gendered body and interpersonal violence; and global masculinities, political crimes, and the state.

Jody Miller is an associate professor in the Department of Criminology and Criminal Justice at the University of Missouri–St. Louis. She specializes in feminist theory and qualitative research methods. Her research focuses on situational aspects of gender, crime, and victimization, particularly among urban adolescents and youth gangs and in the commercial sex industry. Her current research includes a comparative study of the commercial sex industry in Sri Lanka, examining local and tourist markets as well as prostitution in war zone regions. She is author of *One of the Guys: Girls, Gangs, and Gender* (Oxford University Press, 2001) as well as numerous articles and chapters.

Susan L. Miller is a professor in the Department of Sociology and Criminal Justice at the University of Delaware. She received her Ph.D. in criminology from the University of Maryland. Her research interests include gender and crime as well as criminal justice policy related to domestic violence. Her books are *Crime Control and Women: Feminist Implications of Criminal Justice Policy* (Sage), *Gender and Community Policing: Walking the Talk* (Northeastern University Press), and two recent or forthcoming books, one on victim policies and politics, with Michelle L. Meloy (Oxford University Press) and *Victims as Of-*

fenders: The Paradox of Women's Violence in Relationships (Rutgers University Press).

Merry Morash is a professor at the School of Criminal Justice, Michigan State University. She received her Ph.D. in criminal justice and criminology from the University of Maryland. Her research focuses on gender, crime, and justice. In addition to data collection on women police in the United States, she is conducting research on women who work as police in South Korea.

Hillary Potter is an assistant professor in the Department of Sociology at the University of Colorado at Boulder. She was an assistant professor of criminal justice and criminology at Metropolitan State College of Denver from 1999 to 2004. She received her B.A. in sociology, with an emphasis in criminology, from the University of Colorado at Boulder in 1991 and her M.A. in criminal justice, with an emphasis in corrections, from the John Jay College of Criminal Justice at the City University of New York in 1996. Dr. Potter received her Ph.D. in sociology from CU–Boulder in 2004, where her dissertation focused on the experiences of battered black women. Her current research and teaching interests are race and crime, women and crime, feminist criminology, theories of crime causation, intimate partner violence, correctional systems, juvenile justice and delinquency, and qualitative and feminist research methods.

Jody Raphael is a senior research fellow at the Schiller DuCanto & Fleck Family Law Center at the DePaul University College of Law. The author of numerous research reports on violence against marginalized women, she is currently writing a trilogy describing the many ways that violence makes and keeps women poor in the United States. *Saving Bernice: Battered Women, Welfare, and Poverty* appeared in 2000, and the second volume, *Listening to Olivia: Violence, Poverty, and Prostitution*, was published in spring 2004, both in paperback by Northeastern University Press.

Claire M. Renzetti is a professor in the Department of Sociology, Anthropology, and Social Work at the University of Dayton in Dayton, Ohio. She is editor of the international, interdisciplinary journal *Violence Against Women*, co-editor of the Interpersonal Violence book series for Oxford University Press, and editor of the Gender, Crime, and Law book series for Northeastern University Press/University Press of New England. She previously co-edited the *Violence Against Women* book series for Sage Publications. She has authored or edited sixteen books as well as numerous book chapters and articles in professional journals. Her current research focuses on the violent victimization experiences of economically marginalized women living in public housing developments.

Cynthia Siemsen is an associate professor in the Department of Sociology at California State University–Chico. She holds a Ph.D. in sociology from the University of California, Santa Cruz. Her research focuses on the social psychological intersection between professional and personal identities in the legal setting and resulting emotional and ideological conflicts. Dr. Siemsen is the author of *Emotional Trials: The Moral Dilemmas of Women Defense Attorneys* (2004), an exploration of women criminal lawyers' careers. She is currently researching the careers of African American judges. Dr. Siemsen is a recent recipient of Chico State's Professional Achievement Honor, which recognizes excellence in teaching and scholarship.

Mary K. Stohr is a professor in the Department of Criminal Justice at Boise State University. She worked in corrections many moons ago and tends to consult with correctional agencies, serve on their boards and, from time to time, assist those who are suing to change agency or actor practices. Most of her publications are concerned with research on corrections, gender, or management topics.

Vernetta D. Young is an associate professor of administration of justice in the Department of Sociology and Anthropology at Howard University. Dr. Young has taught at American University and the University of Maryland at College Park. She completed her B.S. in sociology with a concentration in criminology at the University of Maryland, College Park and her Ph.D. in criminal justice at the State University of New York at Albany. She is co-editor of *African American Classics in Criminology and Criminal Justice* and co-author of *Women Behind Bars: Gender and Race in U.S. Prisons*. Her research interests include race, gender and crime, the history of juvenile justice, and victimization. ◆

1
Introduction

Rethinking Gender, Crime, and Justice

Lynne Goodstein

In this chapter you will learn the following:

- Why it is important to include gender in the study of crime and the criminal justice system
- The major focus of each of the chapters in this volume

Gender and Justice

As we move through the first decade of the twenty-first century, some might wonder whether another book on gender and crime is warranted. After all, it is has been almost 40 years since the second wave of the feminist movement in the United States inspired criminologists to turn their attention to women as offenders, victims, and professionals in the criminal justice system and to the issue of gender and crime. By now, one might think that the knowledge that has been amassed would have been integrated into the fabric of all criminology and criminal justice textbooks.

For the answer, student readers of this volume need look no further than the content of most courses in a criminal justice or criminology curriculum. Despite over 30 years of exciting and prolific scholarship on women, gender, and crime, many courses and texts continue to pay only cursory attention to women's experiences and to the role of gender in the creation of and response to criminal activity. The chapters in this book represent the superb work of scholars who have created a criminological and criminal justice literature that rectifies this longstanding imbalance and extends our knowledge into new domains. Much of the material here provides information not covered in mainstream criminology and criminal justice texts.

This goal—balancing the scales of knowledge by shining the light of inquiry directly on women's experiences in the criminal justice system—is a worthy one in and of itself. It was the primary focus of our earlier edited volume, *Women, Crime, and Criminal Justice: Original Feminist Readings* (Renzetti and Goodstein 2001). But the chapters in this volume go well beyond the purpose of filling gaps and rectifying imbalances. Its contents reflect the tremendous advancements made in the field of feminist criminology even in the five years since the publication of the previous volume. There is more comprehensive coverage on feminist theory, including theories on masculinities and crime, as well as feminist research methods. Another change is an attempt through a chapter on global prostitution and sex trafficking to reflect the importance of globalization in contemporary life. Several chapters devote increased attention to the intersecting effects of race and class as well as gender in understanding crime. There is also an expanded section on women who work in criminal justice professions.

The editors hope that readers will see not only how interesting it is to learn about women and the criminal justice system but also that feminist criminology invites us to rethink our assumptions about crime and the criminal justice system in general. Before research on women and gender began to be published to a greater degree, general assumptions about such topics as the causes of crime, best practices for incarcerating and rehabilitating offenders, and so on were based primarily—and often solely—on studies of men. The researchers in this book, and others, challenge those assumptions. For example, take the assumption that we can understand the mechanisms women use to adjust to prison based on our knowledge of male prisons. Research on women in prison has yielded many factors that differentiate women's from men's prison adjustment. For instance, because in our society women are assigned responsibility as primary caregivers to children, women inmates encounter stressors that are quite different from those of their male counterparts.

The editors of this volume have chosen to emphasize the term *feminist* in the title. The contributing scholars, mostly women but some men as well, integrate feminism into their work in ways that have changed how other criminologists think, conduct research, and write about women and men. The text's authors have also been instrumental in promoting methods of research that are consistent with a feminist approach to the topic at hand. Feminist researchers are committed to social equality based upon gender, certainly, but also to equality for all people who have been systematically disadvantaged due to their ethnicity, race, sexual orientation, or poverty. It is probably not an overstatement to claim that these authors have been agents of change in the organization of criminological knowledge and theory. Their scholarly efforts acknowledge that the field of criminology has been dominated by research on men and that most previous research was performed by men.

This book brings together scholarly observations and research findings of some of the most prominent scholars of gender, crime, and criminal justice in the world today. Each chapter was written expressly for publication here and with a focus on an advanced undergraduate and graduate student readership, although the content will be valuable to the scholarly community as well. The authors review the most up-to-date scholarship and highlight the importance of gender in our understanding of crime; of gender differences among offenders, victims, and professionals; and of gender issues that affect the criminal justice system's response. In the following chapters, the authors provide much documentation and analysis to answer two questions arising from the book's title: Why a book on gender and crime? Why are the readings considered feminist? They also tackle a question implied by the title: How does feminism help us to rethink our understanding of crime in general? By the time readers have completed the book, you will have acquired the factual and analytical tools to answer these questions authoritatively.

Feminist Approaches to Criminology

Chapters 2 through 4 lay the groundwork of the development and history of feminist criminology. Jeanne Flavin and Amy Desautels (Chapter 2) begin this conversation by recognizing that contemporary scholarship on women and crime is conducted at a much more sophisticated level than in the past. They show the importance of studying women as offenders, victims, and criminal justice system professionals, but they argue that criminologists must also examine the role of gender in the causes and consequences of all crime. As Flavin and Desautels write, "We can benefit from asking Why are men so overrepresented in crime? as well as asking Why are women so underrepresented?"

This theme is further developed in Chapter 3 by James Messerschmidt, "Masculinities and Crime." Messerschmidt provides a comprehensive history of criminological theory on gender and crime, beginning with Edwin Sutherland's emphasis on biologically-based sex roles and continuing through the contemporary, "gender inclusive" theories of criminologists such as Hagan and Agnew. Messerschmidt charges that most criminological work presumes a binary—male/female—differentiation in efforts to integrate sex and gender into an understanding of criminal behavior. He presents fascinating anthropological and biological research challenging this dualism and cites recent research arguing for an examination of *masculinities by women and girls* (and femininities by men and boys) and their relation to crime" (p. 39).

Intrinsically connected to discussions of feminist theories of criminal behavior are the methods researchers use to create new knowledge. In Chapter 4, Ronet Bachman and Christina Lanier review the rich literature on feminist research methods and how these critical concepts are applied to criminological and criminal justice research. They raise questions about the extent to which knowledge is determined by one's choice of research methods. Do scientists whose findings are based upon statistical data gleaned from surveys of thousands yield different understandings of crime than those whose findings come from in-depth interviews with a handful of individuals? Even more fundamentally, Bachman and Lanier argue that knowledge is shaped by the way questions are asked and who asks the questions. For instance, researchers frequently select topics to study, questions to ask, and methods to use that reflect in some way their own ethnicity, gender, class, or sexual orientation. And even when the topics and methods are "neutral," the experiences a researcher brings to the investigation inevitably influence her or his interpretations.

Bachman and Lanier are joined by Flavin and Desautels in discussions of feminist research methods. These authors argue that a researcher's inevitable subjectivity should not be viewed as a problem but simply as another factor to be considered in interpreting the researcher's findings. Moreover, those who use feminist research methods must continually remind themselves that their research has consequences for the lives of real people. Researchers have an ethical obligation to treat with respect those who provide them with information and to allow their voices to shine through in the work. Many feminist researchers also embrace their role as societal change agents through selecting projects that have the potential of reducing inequalities based upon gender, race, socioeconomic status, and sexual orientation.

Gender and Criminal Offending

Any reader with a television would probably hypothesize that most crime occurs in a world populated by men. In TV dramas, reality shows, and even on the news, the violent, antisocial tough guys—as well as the conniving, manipulative, and deceitful executives gone bad—are all most likely to be men. However, women are not immune from criminal impulses. The newspapers report periodically that women harm their young children or perhaps retaliate against an abusive husband by taking his life. Readers may have even seen recent accounts of an increase in violent crime and gang involvement among teenage girls.

As criminologists turn their attention to the task of analyzing both women and men as criminal offenders, they document the extent of involvement of girls and women in various types of crime, such as homicide, robbery, and aggravated assault. They also examine whether there were changes over time in women's criminal involvement. Finally, they develop theories to account for the differences between males and females in the extent, nature, and type of criminal offending.

It is important to keep in mind that, overall, women are less likely to engage in criminal activity than men. Women commit substantially less crime than men do in virtually every crime category except prostitution. This disparity in the extent to which women and men engage in crime, the gender ratio problem, has been a longstanding focus of study among feminist criminologists.

And yet, as Patrick Carr and Gabrielle Alfieri note in Chapter 6 on juvenile delinquency and gender, the ratio for female involvement in crime has been altered over the past two decades. While males still dominate in most areas of criminal activity, young women have closed the gap in some areas. Since the 1980s, the proportion of women being arrested and incarcerated for certain offenses relative to men has increased substantially.

Carr and Alfieri propose that one explanation for this relative increase in girls' and women's involvement in the types of criminal activity that were formerly considered part of the male domain may be that women's societal position has changed relative to men's. The past several decades have witnessed an expansion of women's involvement in the workforce and participation in fields that used to be predominantly or exclusively male. There are small hints that "liberation" of women from traditional roles, to use a term from the early years of the feminist movement, may be occurring in the criminological arena as well. A cursory look at crime statistics might suggest the merging of women's and men's roles in criminal activity, or at least a tendency to think that women offenders are beginning to behave more like men. Carr and Alfieri note an increase in girls' and women's involvement in gang activity as well as in property and violent crime. Based upon these simple findings, one might infer that the disparities traditionally found between male and female offenders are diminishing.

Although proportionately more women are becoming involved in certain types of crime, Claire Renzetti in Chapter 7 reminds us that males continue to be responsible for the vast bulk of serious criminal behavior, accounting for a significantly disproportionate number of murders, robberies, and aggravated assaults compared with women. Renzetti also cautions that looking only at differences between male and female crime rates provides an incomplete picture of the relationship between gender and crime. She shows that gender interacts with other factors, such as race, age, social class, and even the relationship between the victim and the offender, in accounting for differences between males and females in the rates both of commission of and victimization by criminal activity.

Renzetti also suggests that male and female offenders express their gender through the types of crimes they commit and the approaches they take in committing those crimes. In other words, women and men "do" crime differently. Carr and Alfieri's chapter on the involvement of girls and women in gang activity illustrates this point. Despite an increase in female gang involvement, gang women do not behave the way men do, especially with respect to violence and drug use.

For example, when young women join primarily male gangs, they typically do not take leadership roles, nor do they exhibit the same levels of violence as their male counterparts.

Renzetti offers a variety of explanations for gender differences in criminal behavior, ranging from the purely biological to the power of social conditioning. She and other authors in this volume point to the connection between female offending and women's status in society as generally subordinate to men. They point to patriarchal relations, in which there is unequal distribution of power and privilege on the basis of gender, to account for patterns of women's criminal behavior.

Another author who makes a similar point is Susan Martin, writing in Chapter 8 about women involved in the drug trade. She presents data suggesting that in drug distribution and sales organizations, women have the fewest opportunities for participation, occupy the lowest level positions, and are the most expendable. Martin cites normative differences in acceptable behavior for women and men as another factor that affects women's criminality. Masculinity involves a certain amount of aggressiveness, and men are valued for their dominance and risk-taking ability. These attributes are compatible with certain criminal activities that require boldness and the ability to dominate others. Martin portrays the illicit drug industry as one in which violence and the threat of violence are used to maintain organizational stability and as a strategic weapon in turf battles. She argues that the incompatibility between women's traditional social role of docility and the industry's requirement of toughness and bravado may result in women being perceived as less suited for leadership positions. Moreover, the likelihood of harassment or victimization in the context of this "culture of terror" deters some women from selling drugs.

Victimization and Offending

One consistent theme of the book is the interactive relationship between having been a victim of crime and future offending by girls and women. Several chapters document the conditions of poverty and physical and sexual violence in the lives of women offenders. Featured are survival strategies that sometimes involve drug and alcohol abuse, running away, or accepting offers for jobs or companionship that lead to unintended criminal activity. While the chapters cover the stories of women from vastly different backgrounds, the thread of victimization runs through many of the authors' analyses. The chapters also relate the interactivity of victimization and offending, showing that each may lead to the other.

This concept—that being the victim of violence, abuse, or neglect may lead one to engage in criminality—has also been used to account for male criminality, to be sure. However, again as a result of patriarchal conditions, especially those surrounding sexual norms and expectations, girls and women are thought to be more at risk (at least certain types of risk) than boys and men. The consequences of a life as a victim can sometimes inexorably lead a girl or woman down the pathway to a criminal lifestyle. Conversely, the very act of engaging in crime involves a significant risk of harm for women.

In Chapter 5, Catherine Kaukinen, Angela Gover, and Stephanie Hays provide ample evidence of the relationship between childhood abuse and subsequent delinquent or criminal behavior. The "pathways to crime" model holds that women and girls seeking to escape conditions of victimization and abuse frequently find themselves enmeshed in situations that lead to further abuse and criminality. The authors describe a scenario in which young women who run away from victimization in the home become criminally involved and also further victimized as they try to make their way on the street with few skills and job experience.

Susan Martin's chapter also discusses the opposite side of the recursive loop of the victimization-offending nexus. Martin emphasizes the dangers of criminal lifestyles for women involved in drug offenses and as sex workers. Not only are the lives of sex workers extraordinarily risky but also high proportions of these women are victimized by assault, rape, and other forms of physical violence in the context of their work.

Perhaps the most powerful chapter that covers the connection between victimization and offending is Jody Miller's account of global prostitution, sex tourism, and sex trafficking. In Chapter 10, Miller describes a multibillion dollar global business that takes advantage of some of the most powerless and vulnerable people on the planet—girls and women from the poorest regions of developing countries in Asia, Europe, and North America—by manipulating them into the prostitution industry. These girls and women are prey to deception, debt bondage, violence, disease, lack of control over their working conditions, and criminalization. The irony is that they may be prosecuted as criminals while those who reap financial benefits—recruiters, businesses, hotels, and even governments—experience no adverse consequences. Jody Raphael's discussion of prostitution in the United States in Chapter 9 echoes many of the same themes reflected in Miller's and other chapters on women offenders.

The ultimate example of the victimization-criminality nexus is the case of women who kill their abusers. Kaukinen, Gover, and Hays review the numerous studies of women found guilty of homicide of their spouses after having endured extensive, brutal, and humiliating violence from their intimate partner, often for years on end. Clearly, this is another area in which the roles of victim and offender are inextricably linked.

Several authors note that women commit other types of crime, such as accomplice to robbery, because of coercive relationships with powerful males. In some cases, male partners threaten to enact violence against the woman or her children if she fails to comply with his wishes. In others, simply the males' level of emotional control is strong enough for him to achieve the desired result.

Throughout the book, readers will find discussions of the connections between victimization and criminality among women.

Common to these analyses is violence against women within a societally condoned context of male power and control. The dominant social institutions of religion, kinship, the economy and the media normalize hierarchical gender relations and enforce male power and privilege, leading some males to exercise emotional and physical abuse. In a sense, physical and emotional abuse suffered by women at the hands of men represents a second victimization—the first being the relegation to second-class citizenship within a patriarchal culture. For the many women who fall into criminal activity as a result of abuse, the consequences of criminality may be viewed as yet a third level of victimization.

Sexual and Intimate Partner Abuse

Until the 1970s little was known about the crimes of sexual assault and intimate partner violence. Victimized women and girls were reluctant to come forward out of fear of stigmatization and rejection by family and friends. The laws that existed were themselves disincentives for women to report their victimization; the standards of proof were in some cases more stringent than those required for prosecuting other crimes. These offenses, perpetrated for the most part by people known to the victims, occurred primarily in the private sphere and did not fit traditional conceptions of "real" crime—crimes committed by strangers. Therefore, criminal justice professionals frequently viewed victims of rape or violence at the hand of a domestic partner as somehow responsible for their plight. Women who did report their abuse were often treated with suspicion by the very officials who should have helped them achieve justice.

As a result of the hard work of feminist activists and scholars advocating with the courts, legislators, and agents of the criminal justice system, the conditions for victims of sexual and intimate partner violence have changed in recent decades. Beginning in the 1970s for example, activism led to significant improvements in legal statutes and protocols for police and medical handling of sexual and violent crime. Behaviors that in the past may have been overlooked or ignored are now handled more consistently and professionally by the police and the courts. The legitimacy of women's victimization by acquaintances and spouses is today more adequately acknowledged.

Susan Caringella's research on sexual assault policy in Chapter 11 acknowledges the advancements that have been put in place, including changes in the legal terminology surrounding what constitutes a sexual offense, relaxation of corroboration requirements, and legal protections of victims in the courtroom. Much of her chapter focuses on the limitations of these reforms; research is inconclusive regarding the impact that changes in law or policy have yielded. Caringella also stresses that some of the gains achieved by the pioneering feminists who brought this issue to public attention have been eroded due to a backlash during the conservative political climate of the 1990s and beyond.

In Chapter 12, Joanne Belknap and Hillary Potter focus broadly on what they call "intimate partner abuse." Within this rubric they consider a wide range of types of abuse perpetrated against persons by intimates—physical, sexual, psychological, economic, and even against pets and property. In reviewing the responses of the "criminal processing system"—law enforcement and courts—to the problem of intimate partner violence over the past several decades, the authors draw many of the same conclusions as the previous chapter. They acknowledge the dismal conditions for battered women prior to the 1970s, characterized by the weakness of legal statutes and police and courts' resistance to taking victims seriously. Belknap and Potter recognize feminists' hard-won advancements in police and legal response to intimate partner violence, such as proarrest and no-drop policies, but also point to a concurrent backlash. For example, some scholars and practitioners claim "gender symmetry" in the dynamics of intimate partner violence—equal responsibility for men and women. This viewpoint has led to substantial numbers of women being arrested as the perpetrators of intimate partner abuse. Belknap and Potter present compelling evidence that the harms resulting from these types of offenses are not equally distributed by gender. Rather, while men may be victimized by their partners, in general they initiate the harm instead of using it in self-defense and, compared with women, male perpetrators use more serious levels of violence and cause more serious injury.

Gender and the Criminal Justice Response to Crime

Women's and men's crime is not only influenced by individual, interpersonal, and sociocultural influences, but the responses of the criminal justice system itself also have the potential to shape women's and men's criminal involvement. In recent years, for instance, an increasing proportion of women has been identified as criminal as a result of changes the system's policy regarding certain behaviors, particularly those related to the use, possession, and trafficking of illicit drugs. In turn, changes in drug policy and enforcement have had a profound and disproportionate impact on the number of women who have been arrested and sentenced to prison.

Susan Martin discusses in Chapter 8 how governmental policy regarding drug offenses has disproportionately affected women, especially women from underrepresented minority groups, in terms of increased prosecution and incarceration. In the 1980s, the federal government attempted to deal with what it viewed as an increasing problem with drug-related crime spurred by the "crack epidemic." In response to public concern for this highly potent and addictive form of cocaine, Congress passed laws increasing the penalties associated with relatively low-level drug offenses. In addition, many jurisdictions implemented mandatory prison sentences for

certain drug crimes, reducing judges' discretion to mete out alternative sanctions. Given women's greater responsiveness to this drug, coupled with the imposition of more serious penalties for the types of drug selling characteristic of women; the consequences have been particularly profound, even if perhaps unintended. Correctional incarceration rates have skyrocketed, especially for poor women of color.

Martin and others have noted that the crackdown on persons involved in lesser drug offenses has had a disproportionate effect on women of color, particularly women of African-American descent. The government's decision to impose significantly stiffer penalties for crack, as opposed to powdered cocaine, was viewed by many as an act of blatant racism that hit women especially hard. This was because the less expensive crack cocaine became the drug of choice among poor black women. Vernetta Young and Terri Adams-Fuller, in Chapter 13 on race and criminal justice system processing, highlight the problem of the extensive involvement of women of color. They document disproportionately high numbers of African-American women involved at every stage of the crime processing system, beginning with arrest and continuing through incarceration to parole. They argue that as offenders progress through the system, race or ethnicity should play no part in determining outcomes.

In Chapter 14, Tammy Anderson looks at issues facing women offenders and raises similar concerns. She joins other authors in arguing that policies implemented as part of the "war on drugs" have had a differentially adverse and unfair effect on women. Focusing on incarcerated women, Anderson questions the justice of "gender blindness," or sentencing female offenders exactly the same as male offenders. She suggests that given women's subordinate status and the different circumstances often surrounding their offending, fair and equitable treatment for women would require less severe sanctions than would be applied to males, such as diversion from correctional institutions.

Reviewing historical and contemporary trends in women's imprisonment, Anderson also points to the importance of gender in determining prison conditions. Early prison polices involved severe punishment of women for "moral" offenses that seldom resulted in arrests, much less punishment, of males. Anderson advocates designing women's treatment programs that are responsive to their particular situations and needs within the context not only of gender but also of race and class. Given the less serious nature of the offenses of many women, she argues for community alternatives to prison that speak specifically to women's economic needs, particular substance abuse problems, and societally prescribed roles as mothers and caregivers. She recognizes the victimization-criminality nexus for so many female offenders and emphasizes the need for programs to assist women offenders in dealing with past physical, sexual, and emotional abuse within culturally sensitive contexts.

Gender in the Criminal Justice Professions

The final four chapters in this volume turn the feminist lens in a different direction, toward women as workers in the criminal justice system. Merry Morash, Robin Haarr, and Dina Gonyea (Chaper 15) focus on women in policing; Cynthia Siemsen (Chapter 16) looks at gender in the legal profession; Michelle Meloy, Shana Maier, and Susan Miller (Chapter 17) discuss the judiciary; and Mary Stohr (Chapter 18) examines correctional officers. In this section of the book, as in earlier chapters on offenders and victims, issues of gender and race stratification weigh heavily in everyone's understanding of women and men in criminal justice professions.

Looking across the four professions under review, we see similar dynamics of women's struggles to create professional lives in these fields. There are predictable parallels in the histories of women's involvement in policing, corrections, law, and the courts. In the latter part of the nineteenth century, small numbers of women found their way into each of the professions, but their roles differed markedly from those of their male colleagues. Especially in policing and corrections, women professionals worked almost exclusively with female offenders, adopting roles more akin to social workers than enforcers of the law. Throughout much of the twentieth century, women's participation in all the professions remained low. For example, by the 1960s the proportion of U.S. practicing attorneys was about 4 percent, and this number was no higher in any of the other criminal justice fields.

As we have found in other sections of the book, the past three decades have witnessed significant change in women's involvement and status in the criminal justice professions. By the year 2000, women in all related fields were occupying more substantial positions, both in relative numbers and status. For example, women occupy positions as justices in the U.S. Supreme Court, state corrections commissioners, and police chiefs of major cities. Almost half of all students in law school are women, as are one-third of all practicing attorneys. At the same time, mirroring the authors' conclusions about women offenders and victims, what can be called "advancements" for women should in no way be construed as full success in overcoming all obstacles to equal status with men. Women in all four professions continue to struggle with variants of the same employment dynamics in what continues to be a male-dominated professional world.

The nature of the work and type of preparation for each of the four fields are unique. But corrections and policing draw from populations of high school and college graduates, while the legal and judicial professions, clearly regarded as offering higher social status, require postsecondary degrees. Nevertheless, the four chapters suggest some striking parallels in the challenges experienced by women attempting to succeed in these professions.

Despite the increased numbers of women entering criminal justice professions, women in general occupy positions at the lower end of the status hierarchy. For example, Siemsen notes that women attorneys are more likely than men to hold positions in small government and legal aid offices and deal with "society's downtrodden." These characteristics reflect lower-status work than male-dominated specialties such as elite corporate law. A similar point is made by Meloy, Maier, and Miller, who note that the relatively few women who have made it to the judiciary are clustered in family court work.

Across the four fields, factors account for women's difficulties in career advancement. In all cases, the authors point to a "gendered" organizational climate that is, at minimum, chilly or, at maximum, overtly hostile to the prospect of women as full participants. Stohr describes vividly some of the tactics used by male correctional officers to make their women colleagues feel unwelcome. Other authors identify certain behaviors, including sexual jokes, "putdowns," demeaning personal references, and blatant, unwelcome sexual advances, as challenges that women professionals have had to deal with. Women also encounter roadblocks to advancement due to the tendency of male colleagues to support "their own" through an informal mentoring network that often helps young professionals get ahead.

Another theme throughout the chapters on criminal justice professions is the issue of perceived differences of women and men in their personalities and behavior. Each chapter notes that women suffer from having to prove that they are physically and mentally tough enough to command the respect of their peers and the public. Women have to contend with the disconnect between conforming to the traditionally feminine role and the requirements for boldness, aggressiveness, and toughness associated with being a criminal justice professional. Showing too much weakness would be counterproductive, but women professionals in every field who demonstrate appropriate assertiveness may be characterized as overly brash.

Women may be hamstrung at times by this incompatibility between their traditional gender role and public expectations for behavior befitting the quintessential criminal justice professional. Yet this condition may also enable them to do their jobs differently, and some might say even better, than male counterparts. The four chapters review scholarly work that tries to determine whether women and men behave differently on the job. The jury is still out on the answer to this question but it does seem safe to make some conclusions. Women are more likely than men to approach their criminal justice work from the standpoint of client care, and they are usually more supportive of a human services model of professional performance.

Exploring Gender and Justice

As our world becomes more diverse and as women become more integrated into all aspects of society, it is all the more important for criminology and criminal justice students and scholars to be familiar with the new feminist scholarship. In this volume, some of the major researchers in the field have prepared chapters outlining the most up-to-date knowledge on their respective topics. The editors, Claire Renzetti, Susan Miller, and I, had a vision of a volume that would cover important contemporary topics in the field of gender, crime, and justice in a manner that is accessible to students without being watered down. The authors have worked hard to achieve this balance.

The topics covered mirror many of those featured in the companion volume published in 2001, yet the significant majority of the authors are new. Many have received their Ph.D.s within the past decade and represent the "younger" generation of feminist criminologists. These scholars received their educations in an environment in which feminist scholarship was more widely accepted and valued within the academy. Some of the authors have formally studied, or now teach, in women's studies programs or departments. The commitment of all of the authors in this volume to integrate feminist scholarship into the courses they teach and into their research, provides a force for continued advancement in the fields of criminal justice and criminology.

It is our hope that this volume will assist readers in gaining solid grounding in the important and thought-provoking work currently being produced in the area of gender and crime. As the field develops, and as the talented contributors to this volume continue to advance in their careers, no doubt new topics will garner attention. Perhaps readers of this volume will be able to locate gaps in what is known about gender, crime, and justice and feminist criminology. We hope they will pursue those gaps and join the ranks of scholars who will produce the work that is important to students of feminist criminology in years to come.

Study/Discussion Questions

1. Why do you think the field of criminology has given such little attention in the past to the study of women, gender, and crime? What are some consequences of the fact that until the 1970s, the field of women, gender, and crime was overlooked by criminology?

2. Why do you think the editors decided to use the word *feminist* in the title of this book? How might a feminist book differ from a nonfeminist one?

3. This chapter refers to themes that are repeated in many other chapters in this book. Can you think of two themes that are relevant both to women offenders and women police officers, judges, correctional offices, and lawyers?

4. Women victims and women offenders are frequently one and the same. Can you imagine and describe the lives of three hypothetical women that reflect this connection?

References

Renzetti, C. M., and Goodstein, L. (Eds.). (2001). *Women, crime, and criminal justice: Original feminist readings*. Los Angeles: Roxbury Publishing. ✦

2
Feminism and Crime[1]

Jeanne Flavin
Amy Desautels

In this chapter you will learn the following:

- What distinguishes feminist criminology from mainstream criminology

- Why an understanding of gender is critical to an understanding of criminal offending, victimization, and criminal justice responses

- What epistemology is and different types of feminist epistemologies

- What androcentrism is and how feminist criminological theory addresses it

- The defining characteristics of feminist research methodologies

- The major contributions of feminist criminologists to criminological theory, methodology, and public policy

Introduction

In 2003, the Nobel Peace Prize was awarded, for the first time in history, to a woman from the Muslim world. The prize recognized Shirin Ebadi's efforts for democracy and human rights and, in particular, her advocacy for the rights of women and children. In her acceptance speech, the Iranian human rights activist and feminist lawyer observed that

> Women constitute half of the population of every country. To disregard women and bar them from active participation in political,

social, economic, and cultural life would in fact be tantamount to depriving the entire population of every society of half its capability. The patriarchal culture and the discrimination against women, particularly in the Islamic countries, cannot continue forever. (Ebadi 2003, 1)

In criminology, women also have been disregarded. For most of the history of this male-dominated discipline, criminologists ignored women completely or viewed women's deviance in stereotypical ways. In the 1970s, for example, the typical article published in one of four major criminology journals used an all-male sample (Hannon and Dufour 1998). Criminologists' limited focus on the criminal man (rather than the criminal or conforming woman) meant that relatively little information was available about women's experiences. It also contributed to faulty and often stereotypical knowledge about both men's and women's experiences of crime and the criminal justice system.

Since sometime in the early 1970s, however, feminist criminologists have addressed the shortcomings in existing research and theorizing on women. Consequently, it is much harder for a criminologist to pass off a study of men as being generalizable to both men and women. Now, for instance, most articles published in these same journals include a sample of both men and women (Hannon and Dufour 1998). More important, and as we will see in this chapter, scholars are increasingly locating women and gender at the center of their research and theorizing about crime. Why is this development significant? Because when we take steps to ensure that women are recognized, valued, and not misrepresented in our research, our understanding of crime and justice benefits as a result.

Feminist contributions to our understanding of crime and justice have raised awareness of gender inequality and the ways in which both women and men are oppressed by current structural arrangements. This awareness, in turn, has led to dramatic policy changes. While feminists sometimes differ in

what we see as the source of the problem and what needs to be done, we share a view that gender inequalities exist in society and that these inequalities should be addressed.[2]

Feminism and *feminist criminology* refer to diverse perspectives that focus on women's interests, are overtly political, and strive to present a new vision of equality and social justice (Rafter and Heidensohn 1995).[3] No longer must criminologists "make do" with theories and models designed to explain men's experiences of crime, trying to fit them to women. Contemporary scholars ask new questions and reconsider the answers to old ones. The field is burgeoning with new findings and insights.

Judith Stacey and Barrie Thorne (1985) observed in a now-classic article, entitled "The Missing Feminist Revolution in Sociology," that while feminists have made important contributions to sociology, the discipline as a whole and its dominant paradigms have remained much the same (pp. 301–302). Similarly, we find that although feminism has made a considerable impact on the study and practice of criminal justice, some students do not understand even the most basic aspects of feminist criminological thought, much less feminism's relevance to criminal justice. Part of the problem is that many criminology professors were not widely exposed to feminist perspectives during their graduate education. Thus, they continue to assume incorrectly that feminism deals with women, while criminology deals with men (Naffine 1996, 1–2). A reviewer of an earlier version of this chapter observed that for those scholars or practitioners who have devoted their lives to either ignoring gender or to developing "gender neutral" theories, change may be too hard or too unsettling. As a result, many scholars, practitioners, and policy-makers have yet to understand, much less appreciate, the importance of gender and feminism's contribution to criminology and thus cannot adequately introduce students to feminism's principles and merits.

To address the problem, this chapter explains some of the major feminist insights in the interrelated areas of theory (including theories of knowledge), methodology, and policy. Before proceeding, three caveats are in order. First, this chapter provides an overview rather than a comprehensive treatment of feminist criminology; consequently, some concepts have been omitted from the discussion and some important distinctions have been glossed over. Second, we discuss epistemology, theory, methods and methodology, and policy separately here, even though they are intertwined. We have tried to make the overlap and interconnections apparent without being overly repetitious.

Last, our near-exclusive focus on feminist perspectives does not mean that only feminist perspectives have the answers or ask the right questions. Many feminist concerns are shared by other criminological approaches. For example, feminism generally shares a view with other critical approaches that the class, ethnic, and patriarchal relations that control our society are the major sources of crime, and that reducing crime and criminality requires structural and cultural change (DeKeseredy and Schwartz 1996; Thomas and O'Maolchatha 1989). With these caveats in mind, the rest of this chapter relates how feminism addresses gender in the study and practice of criminal justice, using examples that illustrate the diversity and richness of feminist contributions to the discipline.

Women and Gender in Criminology

Why do so many standard criminal justice texts give short shrift to gender? One common response is that women represent a small percentage of those involved in the criminal justice system. For example, according to official crime statistics, women comprise about 7 percent of prison inmates and 11 percent of jail inmates, 23 percent of those arrested, and almost 13 percent of sworn officers in police departments with a hundred or more officers (Bureau of Justice Statistics [BJS] 2003; Federal Bureau of In-

vestigation [FBI] 2002; National Center for Women and Policing 2002).

This justification for ignoring gender falls short on a number of fronts. First, while women are underrepresented as victims, offenders, and workers, the *number* of women involved in the criminal processing system is large and growing. Currently, females account for nearly 2.3 million of those arrested, including almost 450,000 arrests for Index crimes and almost 78,000 arrests for violent crimes (FBI 2002). Over 70,000 adult women were being held in local jails at the end of 2000 and, at the end of 2002, almost 98,000 adult women were imprisoned under the jurisdiction of state and federal authorities (BJS 2003). Around 250,000 women are employed as sworn officers or civilian employees in law enforcement agencies, and another 142,000 are employed in state, federal and private adult correctional facilities (BJS 2003; FBI 2002).

Second, policies and practices that disproportionately affect men have an impact on women as well. Money spent on the criminal justice system is not available to support low-income women and their children (Danner 1998). Frequently, it is women who shoulder the economic and emotional responsibilities of childcare when a male parent is incarcerated or released from prison (Flavin 2004). For example, upon release from prison, most people seek the support of a family member. This support is often provided by an adult female relative (broadly defined), be it a grandmother, mother, aunt, godmother, sister, wife, girlfriend, or female friend. Consequently, women find themselves managing a former prisoner's reentry into society more directly than their male counterparts as they stretch their resources to meet another family member's need for childcare, housing, food, employment, transportation, and so on.

Moreover, while the criminal justice system *is* overwhelmingly male, gender is relevant when we are discussing men's involvement in the system as well as women's. Gender is the strongest predictor of criminal involvement: Boys and men perpetrate more, and more seri-

ous, crimes than do girls and women. So we can benefit from asking Why are men so overrepresented in crime? as well as Why are women underrepresented? Furthermore, both men and women "do gender," that is, handle situations in such a way that the outcome is considered gender-appropriate. Studying how men and women accomplish masculinity and femininity prompts us to consider how social structures constrain and channel behavior (Joe-Laidler and Hunt 2001; Messerschmidt 1997; West and Fenstermaker 1995; West and Zimmerman 1987).

Discussing gender and crime is definitely easier now than it was 30 years ago. Since the 1970s, hundreds of books and articles have appeared that reflect the in-roads feminism has made into criminology and related fields. Feminism's influence, though, has been far from uniform. Most criminal justice scholarship, practice, and policymaking that consider women and gender can be grouped into one of three general approaches (Daly 1995; Goodstein 1992). Traditionally, most criminological scholarship focused on men or merely extended theorizing based on men's experiences to women without offering any reconceptualization (Daly 1995). Fortunately, more and more scholars recognize that women's criminal justice experiences are ignored or distorted when one simply "adds women and stirs." A second approach, then, focuses attention on aspects of crime and criminal justice that adversely affect women more than they affect men, such as domestic violence. This approach pays attention not only to the ways in which women's experiences differ from men's, but also to how women's experiences differ from each other based on characteristics such as race, ethnicity, class, age, and sexual orientation.

While addressing women's "invisibility" is better than simply adding women and stirring, scholarship in this category still tends to treat men as the norm and women as the anomalies. Such an approach interferes with efforts to achieve fairer treatment of men and women throughout the criminal justice system. If an entire field has been shaped by a male norm, then we must seriously question whether the issues deemed important to our understanding of victims, offenders, and workers include those that are also important for women. Our inherited ways of thinking obstruct our ability to imagine or comprehend new ways of viewing crime and criminal justice (Collins 1998; Daly 1995; Eichler 1988).

Recognizing the importance of studying women on their own terms, some feminist scholars are constructing core theoretical frameworks. For example, Beth Richie (1996) developed the idea of "gender entrapment" to explain the criminal behavior of battered African American women. Nearly all of the battered black women in Richie's study occupied a privileged status in their families growing up, receiving extra attention, opportunities, and material possessions. These women, however, also felt burdened by a responsibility to "make good" on their families' investments in their futures. As a result, their identities were closely aligned with meeting the needs of others, an identity that made them vulnerable to abuse as adults.

Dorie Klein (1997) contended that a social science based on women's realities should be built around blurred offender and victim definitions. Insisting on a clear victim-offender distinction distorts the interpretation of many women's and men's real experiences. Instead of assuming a clear division exists that distinguishes victims from offenders, we should recognize the predominance of histories of victimization in the lives of many people who commit crime.

In the future, theories and research will "reach beyond the current stereotypes of women, and beyond the current real lives of women, to think of women differently" (Naffine 1996, 143). Our knowledge base will be transformed to include a theoretical and analytical focus on the interacting relations of class, race, and gender as well as sexual orientation, age, and ethnicity. By acknowledging the limitations of mainstream approaches and considering feminist perspectives, feminist and nonfeminist scholars

hopefully can work together to advance our understanding of gender and crime.

Feminist Epistemologies

Epistemology refers to "theories of what knowledge is, what makes it possible, and how to get it" (Harding 1991, 308). The criminological tradition continues to be deeply embedded in the scientific method (Naffine 1996). Much of mainstream criminology is rooted in claims that science is value neutral and scientific methods protect against our scholarship being contaminated by subjectivity. Studies can be replicated, positivism assumes, because researchers produce knowledge in similar ways, rendering individual criminologists interchangeable with others.

Are some beliefs better supported by empirical evidence than others? Yes. Are there advantages to using traditional (i.e., quantitative) research methods? Absolutely. Does the use of certain research procedural safeguards mitigate against biased results? Of course. These points are not disputed here. What *is* challenged is the assumption that we can and should strive to achieve absolute objectivity and universally valid knowledge.

In a special issue of the *New York Times Magazine*, Richard Powers (1999) heralded the "vesting of authority in experiment" as the best idea of the millennium. Powers acknowledged, however, that thinkers "from Ludwig Wittgenstein to Thomas Kuhn and beyond" have expressed concern

> that fact and artifact may be closer than most empiricists are comfortable accepting. . . . That great empiricists have rejected initial data on hunches, until their observations produced more acceptable numbers. That scientists need pre-existing theory and supposition even to ask the questions that will lead to data. That the shape of a question produces the data that answer it. (p. 83)

These concerns lie at the heart of *feminist epistemology.*[4] The most conservative feminist epistemological program, *feminist empiricism,* basically accepts the value of the scientific method but points out that ignoring women or misrepresenting their experiences is poor methodology. Feminist empiricism tries to correct "bad science" through stricter adherence to existing norms of scientific inquiry. This approach has filled in gaps in our knowledge of women victims of violence, the criminal justice system's response to girls and women who offend, and the experiences of women criminal justice workers (Martin and Jurik 1996; Smart 1995).

By contrast, other feminist epistemologies—feminist standpoint theories, for example—go beyond critiquing empirical practice to challenge mainstream criminology's empirical assumptions. Many feminists consider knowledge, including our definitions of crimes, masculinity, and femininity, to be socially situated. They ask whether knowledge can ever be truly objective in a society that is so deeply stratified by gender, race, and class. As philosopher Sandra Harding (1991) observed, "[T]he subject of belief and of knowledge is never simply an individual, let alone an abstract, one capable of transcending its own historical location. It is always an individual in a particular social situation" (p. 59).

Feminist *standpoint theories* assume that the perspective of the researcher influences what is known. Standpoint feminists try to construct knowledge from the perspective of the persons being studied on the grounds that the perspective of the oppressed or marginalized tends to be less distorted. The powerful have more interest in obscuring the conditions that produce their privileges and authority than the dominated groups have in hiding the conditions that produce their situation (Harding 1991).

Another feminist epistemological approach, feminist postmodernism, criticizes standpoint feminists for assuming that women are a "clearly defined and uncontroversially given interest group" (Smart 1995, 10). While positivists and other modernists (including many feminists) claim that we can determine the truth if we all agree on responsible ways of going about it, post-

modern critics argue for multiple truths that take context into account (Collins 1998; Wonders 1999). Many criminologists recognize that "knowledge" or "truth" often reflects the perspective of those with more power (e.g., definitions of what actions we consider illegal, what constitutes a fair punishment). Postmodernists take this further, questioning whether *any* knowledge is knowable and rejecting the ideas that there is a universal definition of justice, that is, one that would be true for all people, all of the time (DeKeseredy and Schwartz 1996; Wonders 1999). Toward this end, postmodernism emphasizes the importance of alternative discourses and accounts and frequently takes the form of examining the effects of language and symbolic representation (e.g., how legal discourse constructs different "types of Woman," such as "prostitute" or "bad mother") (Smart 1998, 28–30).

Some charge that postmodernism basically amounts to a "call to inaction" (Tong 1989, 232). If justice is different for everyone depending on one's perspective, then what is the point of trying to pursue it? If we cannot be certain that the good quality knowledge we produce will provide useful insight (or a fair outcome), then as one student asked, "Why not just sit by the pool?" (Smart 1995, 212). This is an overly dismal view of the postmodern perspective, however. Postmodern and feminist scholars recognize a responsibility to work collectively across diversity *not* to arrive at a universal understanding of justice but, rather, "to do our best to make judgments that make the world a good place to be" for everyone (Wonders 1999, 122).

Regardless of where one falls on the "Knowledge is scientifically derived" to "Knowledge is socially produced" to "Knowledge is power/Power is knowledge" continuum, it is hard to imagine a criminal justice enterprise where epistemology is irrelevant. Yet, rarely does it receive even passing mention. Given that we routinely encounter totalitarianism, bureaucratization, psychopharmacology, and heteroskedasticity in academic publications, it is more than a matter of *epis-*

temology being a word that doesn't roll easily off the tongue. Yet, we rarely discuss it in our classes and our scholarship. The nature of the concept itself may contribute to our reluctance to address it. It is far easier to open a discussion by asserting "The following are some of the major theories of crime causation. . ." than by challenging whether we can ever claim to "know" why people commit crimes or any other class of so-called truths. Questioning how knowledge has been or ought to be produced can be unsettling, and the process of questioning—almost by definition—does not lead to straightforward, universally accepted answers. But recognizing the importance of epistemology and the biases of the scientific method lies at the core of transforming the study of crime. Gaining a better understanding of gender and crime demands that we not only fill in gaps in knowledge but also challenge the assumptions upon which existing knowledge is based.

Theoretical Contributions

Charges that criminology is male-centered (or *androcentric*) raise hackles among those who incorrectly reduce the criticism to an attack on the sex of the researchers. In reality, women are vulnerable to androcentric bias just as men are capable of overcoming it. Male dominance of the discipline contributes to androcentricity, but it is by no means the only source.

Ideally, theoretical development is grounded in a larger literature, building upon the contributions of past scholarship. Theorizing about the relationship between gender and crime has been seriously hampered by the fact that, as noted earlier, it often attempts to take explanations of men's experiences of crime and justice to see if they apply to women. By contrast, feminist scholarship has been invaluable in calling attention to the "generalizability problem" of many traditional theoretical approaches (Daly and Chesney-Lind 1988).

Traditional theories of crime (e.g., anomie theory, labeling theory, differential association, subcultural theory, and Marxism) cannot be adopted wholesale to explain female patterns of crime (see Leonard 1995/1973; Klein 1995/1973). For example, Robert Merton's (1938) theory holds that when people lack legitimate means (i.e., a job, a savings account) to achieve socially accepted goals (i.e., material and monetary success), they innovate (e.g., steal, write bad checks). His theory has been criticized, however, for assuming that financial success is as important a goal for women as it is for men. Further, his theory fails to address why women—who are overrepresented among the poor and thus arguably subjected to more strain than men—are less likely to deviate. Wendy Chan and George Rigakos (2002) criticized theories of risk taking and risk avoidance for assuming that all men and all women evaluate and respond to risk in similar ways, instead of recognizing that gender intersects with race and class to define risk and shape our responses to it.

Feminist scholars also have provided critiques and proposed modifications of popular criminological theories. Feminists have taken issue with gender-neutral theories that do not differentiate regarding the theory's applicability to men and women. For example, in *A General Theory of Crime*, Michael R. Gottfredson and Travis Hirschi (1990) attempted to be linguistically gender neutral in discussing victimization and parenting. In doing so, Susan Miller and Cynthia Burack pointed out that "[n]either socialization nor criminality occur in a vacuum, removed from social, political, cultural, and economic relations and institutions" (1992, 130). They overlooked the reality that violent victimization is *not* gender neutral (nor race nor class neutral, for that matter); more than half of men's violent victimizations are committed by a stranger, but over two-thirds of women's violent victimizations are committed by someone she knows (NCVS 2003). Elsewhere, Gottfredson and Hirschi (1990) asserted that mothers and fathers are interchangeable in their influence in the socialization process, apparently denying the gendered character of parenting. Miller and Burack (1993) criticized the theorists for "both their gender-neutral stance when inappropriate and by lack of gender specificity when appropriate" (p. 116).

Feminist scholars have examined the gendered nature of criminal justice organizations (see Miller 1999; Pierce 1995). More recently, Jill McCorkle (2003) asked whether purported gender-neutral policies challenge the existing theoretical model of gendered organizations. She found that even when women's institutions attempted to implement gender-neutral disciplinary practices (which were actually based on those found in male facilities), the policies still were shaped by perceived differences between male and female offenders.

Increasingly, feminist perspectives are serving as the basis for theories of crime and crime control. As noted earlier, Beth Richie's (1996) interviews with women inmates led her to develop the idea of "gender entrapment" as a means of understanding the criminal behavior of battered African-American women. For many of these women, Richie (1996) concluded, criminal behavior is a logical extension of "their racialized gender identities, their culturally expected gender roles, and the violence in their intimate relationships" (p. 4).

Masculinity has also been the focus of feminist criminological scholarship. "Crime, men and masculinity have an intimate relationship," Naffine (1996) observed, "so intimate that we often fail to see it, and so intimate that it can seem natural" (p. 6). Perhaps because men's involvement in the criminal justice system has been treated as the norm for so long, men's gender has been ignored. In recent years, scholars' willingness to reconsider what we "know" about men's experiences has led to studies of masculinities and crime. Much of this research relies on conceptualizations of "hegemonic masculinity" and "emphasized femininity," that is, the "dominant forms of gender to which other types of masculinity and femininity are subordinated or opposed"

(Messerschmidt 1997, 10; see also Chapter 3, this volume; and Connell 1987, 1995). In the United States, the dominant, culturally supported form of masculinity is based on white, middle-class, heterosexual men and emphasizes characteristics such as paid employment, subordination of women and girls, authority, control, and rationality (Pyke 1996). Crime provides one structurally permitted means of establishing a man's masculinity when other channels are blocked due to one's race, ethnicity, class, or age. Crime also provides a means of "doing" gender. For example, Jana Bufkin (1999) found that male bias crime offenders typically attack women, homeless people, people with disabilities, racial and ethnic minorities, homosexuals/bisexuals, and others who undermine the hegemonic masculine ideal. Jody Miller (1998, 2001) drew upon similar ideas to explain differences in the ways women and men commit robbery.

Much nonfeminist criminological theorizing tends to be *gender essentialist,* that is, it implies that there is a universal women's experience or men's experience that can be described independently of other facets of experience such as race, ethnicity, and class. Racial and ethnic minority women victims, offenders, and workers, however, are not simply subjected to "more" disadvantage than white women; their oppression is often of a qualitatively different kind. For instance, all women who are victims of domestic violence may fear that the police will ignore their complaints and not do enough to protect them against future violence. Many women of color, however, may be concerned that racially biased police officers may do too much and be overly zealous toward the minority men they arrest. Theories of crime and justice need to acknowledge that "black women experience sexual and patriarchal oppression by black men but at the same time struggle alongside them against racial oppression" (Rice 1990, 63).

In sum, overcoming male-centered theorizing involves more than simply extending theories designed to explain male criminality to women or presenting our theories in gender-neutral terms. It requires recognizing gender as a social process relevant to the actions of men as well as women. It demands that we consider the complex ways in which gender interacts with other social characteristics. When evaluating a theory's merits, we should include feminist critiques and consider whether gender is recognized as a central organizing factor in social life (Renzetti 1993). And, to ensure that androcentric and essentialist biases are overcome, feminist theoretical critiques and feminist theorizing should be fully integrated into our undergraduate and graduate curricula (for specific strategies, see Goodstein 1992; Wilson 1991; Wonders and Caulfield 1993).

Today, more research and policymaking efforts consider feminist theoretical contributions. By and large, however, feminist theories have not been fully integrated into the study and practice of criminal justice and thus have not received the same attention as varieties of strain theories, social control theories, or individualistic theories. As a result, the richness and insights of feminist perspectives have yet to be widely appreciated.[5]

Research Methodology and Methods

Feminists vary in their theoretical orientations and their views of how knowledge should be acquired. Feminism also offers not a distinctive methodology but, rather, a rich variety of perspectives on the research process (Taylor and Rupp 1991, 127). These themes relate to the choice of topic, choice of research methods, the subjective experiences of doing research, and the relationship between the researcher and the research subjects (Gelsthorpe 1990). Another area of feminist concern—the relationship between policy/action and research—is discussed in the next section. Many of the following methodological issues are not unique to feminism; they are shared by scholars of other orientations (particularly critical scholars). But because feminists have been at the fore-

front in calling attention to these issues, they are included here.

Choice of a Research Topic

Feminist criminological scholarship comprises a substantial and mature body of literature that poses "some of the more difficult and interesting questions about the nature of (criminological) knowledge" (Naffine 1996, p. 4). Feminist research encompasses a larger sphere of inquiry than just that "on, by, and for women" (McDermott 1992). For example, feminist scholarship includes research "on" gender, which includes men and masculinity; it recognizes that research conducted "by" a woman is not representative of all women's experiences nor does being biologically male disqualify one from working from a feminist perspective. And, though remaining committed to positions "for" women, feminism ultimately aims to benefit both men and women. While sharing a view that gender is central to our understanding of crime and justice, feminist criminological scholarship reflects considerable diversity and originality in the choice of topic. Feminists have addressed time-honored criminological questions as well as newer lines of criminological inquiry, such as the gendered nature of criminal justice organizations (c.f., Britton 2003; Miller 1999; Pierce 1995), the impact of sentencing policies on women (c.f., Raeder 1993), the blurred boundaries between victimization and criminalization (c.f., Daly and Maher 1998; Klein 1997), and the media's role in shaping perceptions of crime and justice (c.f., Chancer 1998, forthcoming; Danner and Carmody 2001), to name but a few.

Choice of Research Methods and Methodologies

One of the thorniest points of contention is the discussion surrounding the use of qualitative and quantitative research methodologies, a debate that has been described as "sterile and based on false polarization" (Jayartne and Stewart 1991, 85). Put simply, not all feminist research is qualitative, and not all studies that rely on qualitative methods are conducted from a feminist orientation. Briefly, findings from quantitative data drawn from large, representative samples may be more generalizable, and statistical techniques can handle more contextual variables and permit simultaneous evaluation of complex theoretical models and interaction terms. Quantitative methods have been criticized, though, for obscuring the experiences of women and contributing to a "dataset mentality" (that is, limiting research questions to those that can be answered by available variables).

By contrast, qualitative approaches (e.g., interviews, ethnographies, and life histories) permit women and men to articulate or conceptualize their experiences more completely and in their own terms, potentially providing more accurate and valid information. That subjective experience is part of science should not be confused with the belief that simply describing an individual's experiences or feelings in itself comprises a scientific treatment of a problem. Instead, many feminist scholars use narrative statements to identify important themes while at the same time giving their research a human face. For instance, see Belknap, Holsinger, and Dunn's (1997) study of incarcerated girls: "I've been here so long, I don't want to just be thrown out. I'm anxious" and "I was scared [to help an old lady cross the street] when I was on [a day] leave once. I felt like I had institution written all over me" (p. 396).

Despite their obvious advantages, and their roots in the Chicago School and the work of respected scholars such as W. I. Thomas and Robert Park, qualitative research methods have had to fight off a reputation as an oxymoron in mainstream criminal justice circles.[6] Qualitative methods are sometimes stereotyped as unsystematic and, therefore, unscientific and overtly biased (Jayartne and Stewart 1991). Also, because qualitative research may be very time consuming, the samples in a qualitative study tend to be relatively small and homogenous. Many feminist and nonfeminist researchers use a combination of quantitative and qualitative methods to compensate for the weaknesses in any one method by incorporating the strengths of another (c.f., Leonard 2002; Melton and Belknap 2003; Owen 1998).

Reflexivity

While many scholars acknowledge the limitations of a particular method or methodology, feminists also often stress the importance of critically examining the nature of the research process itself. *Reflexivity* refers to identifying the assumptions underlying the research endeavor and often includes the investigator's reaction to doing the research. "For the most part," Leon Pettiway (1997) observed,

> criminology is unreflective . . . many criminologists, in their search for neutrality, fail to consider their own identity in their investigative enterprises. Perhaps this is the aftershock of attempting to impose the strictures and methods of the physical sciences on criminology in our effort to make it more 'scientific.' (p. xv–xvi)

Reflecting on the research process calls attention to possible sources of bias as well as provides guidance to future researchers. Reflexivity also prompts examination of whether research can ever truly be said to be "objective." The identity of a researcher shapes even a deliberately noninterpretive research endeavor, such as presenting transcripts of taped interviews with women involved in drugs and crime given that the researcher frames the questions, focuses the interviews, and edits the transcripts for publication (Pettiway 1997). Not only do many feminists consider subjectivity as unavoidable but some also argue it may be a strength of a study. Barbara Owen (1998) reported that the relationships she formed with several prisoners led her to better appreciate the women's experiences from their own point of view. The result, she suggested, is a study that not only contributed to a scientific understanding of women prisoners, but to a political awareness of their marginalized status. So too, the authors of one article called attention to a power struggle between researcher and participants often inherent in the research process (Bosworth et al. 2005). The authors (four of whom had been prisoners) candidly admitted to this dynamic by including the frustrated words of a male inmate who wrote to lead author Bosworth, challenging her knowledge and legitimacy:

> "Just because you wrote that book, because you are an editor, a teacher at a university, so knowledgeable . . . none of that means a damn thing! How much time have you did? How many strip-searches? How many hours in chains? How many beatings? How many brutalities? You know nothing! All that you know (of the truth) is what we tell you! Are you listening? Are you really listening?" (p. 253)

In other words, reflexivity strengthens the research process by promoting greater honesty and awareness of the limitations and biases inherent in our research. It also provides a valuable guide to other researchers who may be considering undertaking similar research projects. Further, as is discussed next, reflexivity encourages us to think about the relationship between ourselves as researchers and the people who agree to be our research subjects.

Relationship Between Researcher and Subjects

Feminists have criticized researchers' objectification and exploitation of their subjects, particularly when information is gained through interviews or surveys. Objectification occurs when it is assumed that a radical difference exists between the roles of scientist and subject. In the most extreme positivist forms, studying human beings is treated, in principle, as no different from studying things (Gorelick 1996, 24). While conventional criminology assumes that scientific detachment requires emotional detachment, the quest for neutrality and objectivity can be a disadvantage when so much emphasis is placed on "maintaining distance" that we strip away context and the humanity of the research participants.

Advising interviewers to adopt an objective, noninvolved stance, to view interviews as minimally interactive, and to adhere to other standard guidelines for interviewing treats research as a one-way hierarchical process. When one assumes that the interviewer's role is to collect but never to provide information, the interviewee is reduced to mere data (Carty 1996). By contrast, a feminist methodological approach tries to minimize hierarchical relationships within the research process. Ideally, the research enterprise strives for a collaborative and reciprocal association between the researcher and the subject consistent with Ann Oakley's maxim: "No intimacy without reciprocity" (quoted in May 1993, 90).

Admittedly, there are difficulties and some drawbacks to minimizing the distance between interviewer and subject. Researchers responsible to funding agencies may not have total control over how their studies are conducted. The subjects themselves may not embrace the idea of collaboration. Particularly in criminal justice, it seems unlikely that offenders, victims, and even many criminal justice workers will see themselves on equal footing with academic researchers. Language, dress, age, and other cues may serve as constant reminders of the differences in roles and status between the researcher and the subjects. For instance, although juvenile justice professionals seemed to forget the presence of researcher-onlookers while participating in a focus group, many of the incarcerated girls in the same study checked out how the researchers responded to their own and their peers' comments (Belknap, Holsinger, and Dunn 1997).

Confidentiality and privacy issues—always a concern when a study involves human subjects—become even more important when researchers form rapport, ties, even friendships with the study participants. Women respondents may find it easier to reveal intimate details of their victimization or offending experiences when the interviewer is a woman. All researchers "must take extra precautions not to betray the trust so freely given" (Fonow and Cook 1991, 8) since we may not have complete control of how information will be used once we have gathered it from respondents. In spite of these obstacles, a number of specific actions may be undertaken to reduce the distance between researchers and subjects (see Chapter 4, this volume, for a discussion of specific strategies).

Mary Bosworth epitomizes feminists who value reciprocity and reflexivity. Having involved prisoners in her book about the U.S. federal prison system (Bosworth 2002), she followed up on the experience by writing an article about the collaborative experience with four prisoner-contributors. Specifically, Bosworth and her colleagues (2005) applied themselves to the following questions:

> How do the people who are interviewed in ethnographies or other pieces of research choose what to say, when to agree to participate and what to leave out in their stories? What is it like to be consulted about prison life? Is it empowering or disheartening? Is it an emotional experience similar to that of the researcher? Is it an escape? A chance to be validated? A chance to "keep it real"? To "kick it" with a professor? A way to open a dialogue, to learn, to grow, to reach out, to rehabilitate? Do participants feel as though their opinions are heard? How and why does anyone elect to help an academic? (n.p.)

In sum, the phrase "feminist research methods" is something of a misnomer. Many of the measures championed by feminist criminologists can be and have been adopted by researchers from mainstream orientations. Criminologists, however, need to give more thought to feminists' approaches to research not only in terms of giving qualitative methods their due but also in considering reflexivity and the relationship between researcher and

subject. Researchers frequently cite time and money in justifying their choice of methods. We also should consider how the subjects' race, gender, and class might influence the choice of research methods. Proposals should be critiqued not only on the basis of sample selection and measurements but also on how subjects were compensated for their participation in the study and what steps were taken to reduce the distance between researcher and subject. Attending to these aspects of the research process does not constitute subscribing to a feminist methodology per se. Rather, it reflects a commitment to good research practices designed to give greater visibility to the experiences of women (and other historically marginalized groups) and to increase subjects' involvement in the research process.

Policy and Action

Feminist scholars have informed criminal justice policies and contributed to the public debate about crime. Feminism always has placed a premium on policy and action; one of feminism's defining components is a standing and overt commitment to identifying "a set of strategies for change" (Daly and Chesney-Lind 1988, 502). Feminists are perhaps best known for raising awareness of violence against women and the need for laws and policies regarding not only stranger rape and woman battering but also marital rape, acquaintance rape, stalking, and other crimes that disproportionately involve women victims. The 1994 Violence Against Woman Act (VAWA, recently reauthorized in 2005) was the first piece of federal legislation in the United States designed to address domestic violence. It provides funding for police, prosecutors, battered women service providers, state domestic violence coalitions, and a national domestic hotline to improve services to victims, improve police department and prosecutor's office procedures, to educate and train communities and professionals about domestic violence, and to foster collaboration between advocates and the criminal justice system.

Feminists have also called for responses to women victims of crime that reflect an appreciation for the differences that exist among women. For example, a shortage of bilingual and bicultural criminal justice workers creates a system ill-prepared to address many battered Latinas' claims. Latinas and other racial and ethnic minority women must decide whether to seek assistance from an outsider who "may not look like her, sound like her, speak her language, or share any of her cultural values" (Rivera 1997/1994, 261). Some women also may encounter a failure on the part of their racial, ethnic, religious, and community leaders to recognize "a sexist problem within the community . . . as important as a racist problem outside of it" (Rasche 1995/1988, 257). In response to criticism of feminists and other advocates, VAWA 2000 made numerous improvements that expanded battered immigrant women's access to immigration relief and reduced abusers' ability to use immigration laws as a tool of control over immigrant victims.

Feminism's impact in the arena of domestic violence and other forms of violence against women has been substantial, but to confine our contribution to these issues is to sell feminism short. Feminists also engage in policy evaluation, asking What is this policy supposed to accomplish? How will it actually be implemented? Who wins and who loses if this policy is adopted? What can we do to improve on this? (S. Miller 1998; Renzetti 1998).

Women's stake in the war on crime is important, though often unrecognized. While the public construction of the criminal is male, "the hidden victims of many of the get-tough policies have been women, particularly women of color" (Chesney-Lind 1998, xi). Feminists have played an important role in calling attention to the unintended or unforseen consequences of purportedly gender-neutral policies. New sentencing policies have been implemented with the goal of treating women and men the same. With regard to the Federal Sentencing Guidelines, Myrna Raeder

(1993) suggested that we should consider sentencing fewer men to prison on the grounds that it would be more humane for men, women, and their children. Instead, we have increasingly incarcerated women, a shift that has been described as equality with a vengeance.

In addition to women being harmed by purportedly gender-neutral policies or policies aimed primarily at men, some policies have been targeted specifically at women and therefore are cause for concern. Specifically, reproductive rights are frequently reduced to the notion of having access to abortion. However, for many women, particularly poor women of color, these rights more often have been about the right to conceive, to be pregnant, and to raise one's children without unwarranted government interference than the right to terminate a pregnancy. For instance, according to a 1996 report prepared by the Center for Reproductive Law and Policy, at least 200 women in more than 30 states have been arrested for their alleged drug use or other actions during pregnancy. Courts have overturned many of these cases on the grounds that they violate women's rights to due process and privacy, are based upon exaggerated assessments of risk, and are contrary to sound public policy. Yet, as recently as March 2004, prosecutors charged Melissa Rowland, a mentally ill Utah woman, with murder for delaying a Cesarean section.

Whether motivated by paternalism or retribution, the criminal justice system can have a devastating and far-reaching impact on women's reproductive rights through its policies of increased surveillance, prosecution, punishment, or involuntary termination of parental rights (Flavin 2002; forthcoming). Feminist perspectives, by contrast, encourage us to recognize the harmful consequences of criminalizing pregnant women's behavior and the benefits of public health approaches that recognize that the vast majority of women share a desire for a healthy pregnancy.

Feminists have not limited their interests to policies aimed at or affecting women but have also challenged the masculine basis of many programs and policies. Feminists have been critical of correctional officer and police training programs for their overemphasis of physical strength, intimidation, and aggressiveness as a means for resolving disputes while devaluing interpersonal skills (Britton 2003). Similarly, feminist criminologists are among those critical of boot camps for being unnecessarily demeaning and abusive to inmates. The boot camp model embodies a distorted image of masculinity, one that emphasizes aggressiveness, unquestioned authority, and insensitivity to others' pain while de-emphasizing "feminine" characteristics, such as group cooperation and empathy. "Why," Merry Morash and Lila Rucker (1998/1990) asked, "would a method that has been developed to prepare people to go into war, and as a tool to manage legal violence, be considered as having such potential in deterring or rehabilitating offenders? . . .[T]he program elements of militarism, hard labor, and fear engendered by severe conditions do not hold much promise, and they appear to set the stage for abuse of authority."(p. 35, 38)

Feminism gives great weight to identifying strategies for social change and ending domination in all its forms. Feminist voices have influenced change in federal, state, and local policy. In addition to VAWA, for instance, another federal mandate, the Juvenile Justice and Delinquency Prevention Act of 1992, calls for funding to evaluate and improve gender-specific programs and services for juvenile offenders. On the state level, Hawaii, Connecticut, Florida, Minnesota, and Texas have each enacted policies to ensure access to comparable programming and to create "gender responsive" services to meet the specific needs of women. Such initiatives include improving access and quality of health care for incarcerated women; improving the quality and availability of drug treatment for women; developing advocacy services for imprisoned mothers and their children; and increasing public awareness about the negative impacts of incarcerating mothers.[7]

Feminists have made impressive headway in challenging existing assumptions about women and crime as well as suggesting specific avenues for change. Feminist perspectives remind us of not only our professional responsibilities but also our social responsibility to consider the implications of research on policies for women.

Conclusion

So at the end of the day, what does it mean to adopt a feminist approach to the study of crime and criminal justice? Feminism demands that we respect the complexities and diversity of people's lives and experiences and show this respect when we communicate with the people whose experiences we aspire to understand or improve. Feminism challenges us all to recognize and reject male-centered biases. It challenges us to be thoughtful in what we choose to study, how we study it, how we present our findings, and in the actions we recommend. Feminism encourages collaboration and the sharing of information among other students and scholars, and also with people outside the university setting, including members of our communities, practitioners, law makers, journalists, victims, people with criminal records, and advocates.

Feminism demands that we pursue lines of inquiry that have the potential to make a real, human impact. And there is no shortage of issues demanding our attention. At the time of this writing, the United States is engaged in a war in Iraq that has raised troubling questions about the lack of legal representation and fairness in judicial proceedings, brutal and inhumane conditions of confinement, and U.S. soldiers (including some women) sexually abusing both Iraqis and female troops serving in Iraq. These issues are at the heart of many feminist and other critical concerns. We do not claim here that women are morally superior to men. We do assert, however, that any understanding of criminal and social justice, both in the United States and internationally, must embrace women's contributions, including feminist perspectives and insights. Feminism invites all of us to recognize the existence of gender norms and sexism, to try to understand their sources, and to work toward identifying and overcoming all forms of discrimination that operate throughout the justice system, and beyond. To return again to the inspirational words of Nobel Prize winner and feminist activist, Shirin Ebadi (2003),

> If the 21st century wishes to free itself from the cycle of violence, acts of terror and war, and avoid repetition of the experience of the 20th century—that most disaster-ridden century of humankind—there is no other way except by understanding and putting into practice every human right for all [hu]mankind, irrespective of race, gender, faith, nationality or social status. (n. p.)

Notes

1. This chapter was originally published as "Feminism for the Mainstream Criminologist," *Journal of Criminal Justice* 29: 271–285, (2001). It has been revised and updated for inclusion in this volume.

2. The variety of feminist perspectives has prompted some to criticize feminists for their lack of consensus. This charge, however, could be leveled against any group of theorists who subscribe to a particular school of thought. Readers interested in a discussion of various feminist theories are urged to consult Tong (1998), Daly and Chesney-Lind (1988), hooks and Marable (2000), and Martin and Jurik (1996).

3. Readers interested in learning more about feminist approaches to criminology are urged to consult any number of the excellent texts on the subject, including Belknap (2000), Daly and Maher (1998), Gelsthorpe and Morris (1990), Heidensohn (1995), Naffine (1996), Price and Sokoloff (2003), and Smart (1976, 1995).

4. The present discussion of epistemology is grossly simplified in the interest of clarity and brevity. For excellent treatments of epistemology, empiricism, and criminology, readers are encouraged to consult Ngaire Naffine's *Feminism and Criminology* (1996) or Carol Smart's *Law, Crime, and Sexuality: Essays in Feminism*, (1995).

5. Many standard textbooks contribute to this problem. Early studies of introductory criminal justice and criminology textbooks conclude that women are typically ignored or depicted in stereotypical ways (Baro and Eigenberg 1993; Wright 1992). A nonrandom sampling of the texts on our bookshelves suggests the problem persists and the short shrift extends to feminist perspectives as well. For example, in discussing "other branches of conflict theory," Senna and Siegel (2002) cited only one feminist perspective—radical feminism—ignoring other major critical feminist perspectives, such as Marxist feminism, socialist feminism, and postmodern feminism.

6. Thomas' own work on female crime showed an appreciation for the interaction between society and the individual. He, however, saw women's physiology and biology as being at the root of their inferior position in society (see Klein 1995/1973).

7. One of the problems, however, is that many new policies and services focus on women's ties to young children while ignoring the needs of women who are not mothers. This focus on mothers diminishes the range of other functions women perform in families and communities in their roles as advisors, advocates, mediators, and financial managers.

Study/Discussion Questions

1. Feminist criminology has made contributions to mainstream criminology in the areas of epistemology, theory, methods, and policy. In your opinion, in which area has feminism's influence been most significant?

2. This chapter discusses feminism's contributions to mainstream criminology. How would you answer the question "What does mainstream criminology have to offer feminism?"

3. What specific strategies should be undertaken to ensure that feminist criminological insights are fully integrated into mainstream criminology? What role should men occupy in feminist criminology?

4. At heart, feminists share a view that gender inequalities exist in society and these inequalities should be addressed. Do you consider yourself a feminist? Why or why not? How important is it whether a person identifies himself or herself as feminist?

References

Baro, A., and Eigenberg, H. (1993). Images of gender: A content analysis of photographs in introductory criminology and criminal justice textbooks. *Women and Criminal Justice,* 5, 3–36.

Belknap, J. (2000). *The invisible woman: Gender, crime, and justice* (2nd ed.). Belmont, CA: Wadsworth.

Belknap, J., Holsinger, K., and Dunn, M. (1997). Understanding incarcerated girls: The results of a focus group study. *The Prison Journal,* 77, 381–404.

Bosworth, M. (2002). *The U.S. federal prison system.* Thousand Oaks, CA: Sage.

Bosworth, M., Demby, B., Campbell, B., Ferranti, S., and Santos, M. (2005). Doing prison research: Views from inside. *Qualitative Inquiry,* 11 (2): 249–264.

Britton, D. (2003). *At work in the iron cage: The prison as gendered organization.* New York: New York University Press.

Bufkin, J. L. (1999). Bias crime as gendered behavior. *Social Justice,* 26, 155–176.

Bureau of Justice Statistics (BJS). (2003). *Census of state and federal correctional facilities, 2000.* Washington, DC: U.S. Department of Justice.

Carty, L. (1996). Seeing through the eye of difference: A reflection on three research journeys. In H. Gottfried (Ed.), *Feminism and social change: Bridging theory and practice,* (pp. 123–142). Urbana, IL: University of Chicago Press.

Chan, W., and Rigakos, G. S. (2002). Risk, crime, and gender. *British Journal of Criminology,* 42 (4), 743–761.

Chancer, L. S. (1998). Playing gender against race through high-profile crime cases. *Violence Against Women,* 4, 100–113.

——. (forthcoming). *Provoking assaults.* Chicago: University of Chicago Press.

Chesney-Lind, M. (1998). Foreword. In S. L. Miller (Ed.), *Crime control and women* (pp. ix–xii). Thousand Oaks, CA: Sage.

Collins, P. H. (1998). *Fighting words: Black women and the search for justice.* Minneapolis: University of Minnesota Press.

Connell, R. W. (1987). *Gender and power: Society, the person, and sexual politics.* Stanford CA: Stanford University Press.

——. (1995). *Masculinities.* Los Angeles: University of California Press.

Daly, K. (1995). Looking back, looking forward: The promise of feminist transformation. In B. R. Price and N. J. Sokoloff (Eds.), *The criminal justice system and women* (2nd ed.). (pp. 443–457). New York: McGraw-Hill.

Daly, K., and Chesney-Lind, M. (1988). Feminism and criminology. *Justice Quarterly,* 5, 497–538.

Daly, K., and Maher, L. (1998). *Criminology at the crossroads: Feminist readings in crime and justice.* Oxford, UK: Oxford University Press.

Danner, M. J. E. (1998). Three strikes and it's women who are out: The hidden consequences for women of criminal justice police reforms. In S. L. Miller (Ed.), *Crime control and women* (pp. 1–14). Thousand Oaks, CA: Sage.

Danner, M. J. E., and Carmody, D. C. (2001). Missing gender in cases of infamous school violence: Investigating research and media explanations. *Justice Quarterly,* 18, 87–112.

DeKeseredy, W. S., and Schwartz, M. D. (1996). *Contemporary criminology.* Belmont, CA: Wadsworth.

Ebadi, S. (2003, December 10). *The Nobel lecture.* Unpaginated. *http://www.nobel.no/eng_lect_2003b.html* (last accessed July 21, 2004).

Eichler, M. (1988). *Nonsexist research methods: A practical guide.* Winchester, MA: Allen and Unwin.

Federal Bureau of Investigations (FBI). (2002). *Crime in the United States, 2002*. Washington, DC: Government Printing Office.

Flavin, J. (2004, March). Prisoner reentry: Giving family members their due. (Transition from Prison to Community Iniative) TPCI Review. March.*http://www.abtassociates.com/Page.cfm?PageID=12583&TPCI_Issue=2004_03&Article=1*. Date accessed, Nov. 17, 2005.

——. (Forthcoming). Reproducing race: Slavery's legacy in black women's struggle for reproductive rights. In M. F. Bosworth and J. Flavin (Eds.), *Regulating differences: Race, gender, and punishment in America*. Rutgers University Press.

——. (2002). A glass half full? Harm reduction among pregnant women who use cocaine. *Journal of Drug Issues, 32,* 973–998.

Fonow, M. M., and Cook, J. A. (1991). Back to the future: A look at the second wave of feminist epistemology and methodology. In M. M. Fonow and J. A. Cook (Eds.), *Beyond methodology* (pp. 1–15). Bloomington: Indiana University Press.

Gelsthorpe, L. (1990). Feminist methodologies in criminology: A new approach or old wine in new bottles. In L. Gelsthorpe and A. Morris (Eds.), *Feminist perspectives in criminology* (pp. 89–106). Buckingham, UK: Open University Press.

Gelsthorpe, L., and Morris, A. (1990). *Feminist perspectives in criminology*. Buckingham, UK: Open University Press.

Goodstein, L. (1992). Feminist perspectives and the criminal justice curriculum. *Journal of Criminal Justice Education, 3,* 165–181.

Gorelick, S. (1996). Contradictions of feminist methodology. In H. Gottfried (Ed.), *Feminism and social change: Bridging theory and practice* (pp. 23–45). Urbana, IL: University of Chicago Press.

Gottfredson, M. R., and Hirschi, T. (1990). *A general theory of crime*. Stanford, CA: Stanford University Press.

Hannon, L., and Dufour, L. R. (1998). Still just the study of men and crime? A content analysis. *Sex Roles, 38,* 63–71.

Harding, S. (1991). Whose science? Whose knowledge? Ithaca, NY: Cornell University Press.

Heidensohn. F. M. (1995). *Women and crime* (2nd ed.). New York: New York University Press.

hooks, b., and Marable, M. (2000). *Feminist theory: From margin to center*. Cambridge, MA: South End Press.

Jayartne, T. E., and Stewart, A. J. (1991). Quantitative and qualitative methods in the social sciences: Current feminist issues and practical strategies. In M. M. Fonow and J. A. Cook (Eds.), *Beyond methodology: Feminist scholarship as lived research* (pp. 85–106). Bloomington: Indiana University Press.

Joe-Laidler, K., and Hunt, G. (2001). Accomplishing femininity among the girls in the gang. *British Journal of Criminology, 41,* 656–678.

Klein, D. (1995/1973). The etiology of female crime: A review of the literature. In B. R. Price and N. J. Sokoloff (Eds.), *The criminal justice system and women* (2nd ed.) (pp. 30–53). New York: McGraw-Hill.

——. (1997). An agenda for reading and writing about women, crime, and justice. *Social Pathology, 3,* 81–91.

Leonard, E. (1995/1973). Theoretical criminology and gender. In B. R. Price and N. J. Sokoloff (Eds.), *The criminal justice system and women* (2nd ed.). (pp. 54–70). New York: McGraw-Hill.

——. (2002). *Convicted survivors: The imprisonment of battered women who kill*. New York: State University of New York Press.

Martin, S. E., and Jurik, N. C. (1996). *Doing justice, doing gender: Women in law and criminal justice occupations*. Thousand Oaks, CA: Sage.

May, T. (1993). Feelings matter: Inverting the hidden equation. In D. Hobbs and T. May (Eds.), *Interpreting the field: Accounts of ethnography* (pp. 69–97). Oxford, UK: Oxford University Press.

McCorkle, J. A. (2003). Embodied surveillance and the gendering of punishment. *Journal of Contemporary Ethnography, 32,* 41–76.

McDermott, M. J. (1992). The personal is empirical: Feminism, research methods, and criminal justice education. *Journal of Criminal Justice Education, 3,* 237–249.

Melton, H. C., and Belknap, J. (2003). He hits, she hits: Assessing gender differences and similarities in officially reported intimate partner violence. *Criminal Justice and Behavior, 30,* 328–348.

Merton, R. K. (1938). Social structure and anomie. *American Sociological Review, 3,* 672–683.

Messerschmidt, J. W. (1997). *Crime as structured action: Gender, race, class, and crime in the making.* Thousand Oaks, CA: Sage.

Miller, J. (1998). Up it up: Gender and the accomplishment of street robbery. *Criminology, 36,* 37–65.

——. (2001). *One of the guys: Girls, gangs, and gender.* New York: Oxford University Press.

Miller, S. L. (1998). Introduction. In S. L. Miller (Ed.), *Crime control and women* (pp. xv–xxiv). Thousand Oaks, CA: Sage.

——. (1999). *Gender and community policing: Walking the talk.* Boston: Northeastern University Press.

Miller, S. L., and Burack, C. (1993). A critique of Gottfredson and Hirschi's general theory of crime: Selective (in)attention to gender and power positions. *Women and Criminal Justice, 4,* 115–134.

Morash, M., and Rucker, L. (1998). A critical look at the idea of boot camp as a correctional reform. In S. L. Miller (Ed.), *Crime control and women* (pp. 32–51). Thousand Oaks, CA: Sage.

Naffine, N. (1996). *Feminism and criminology.* Philadelphia: Temple University Press.

National Center for Women and Policing. (2002). *Equality denied: The status of women and policing, 2001.* Los Angeles: Author.

National Crime Victimization Survey (NCVS). (2003). *Criminal victimization, 2002.* Washington, DC: Office of Justice Programs.

Owen, B. (1998). *In the mix: Struggle and survival in a woman's prison.* Albany: State University of New York Press.

Pettiway, L. E. (1997). *Workin' it: Women living through drugs and crime.* Philadelphia: Temple University Press.

Pierce, J. (1995). *Gender trials: Emotional lives in contemporary law firms.* Berkeley: University of California Press.

Powers, R. (1999, April 18). Eyes wide open. *New York Times Magazine,* pp. 80–83.

Price, B. R., and Sokoloff, N. J. (Eds.). (2003). *The criminal justice system and women: Offenders, victims, and workers* (3rd ed.). New York: McGraw-Hill.

Pyke, K. D. (1996). Class-based masculinities: The interdependence of gender, class, and interpersonal power. *Gender & Society, 10,* 527–549.

Raeder, M. S. (1993). Gender and sentencing: Single moms, battered women, and other sex-based anomalies in the gender-free world of the federal sentencing guidelines. *Pepperdine Law Review, 20,* 905–920.

Rafter, N. H., and Heidensohn, F. (1995). *International feminist perspectives in criminology: Engendering a discipline.* Buckingham, UK: Open University Press.

Rasche, C. E. (1995[1988]). Minority women and domestic violence. In B. R. Price and N. J. Sokoloff (Eds.), *The criminal justice system and women* (2nd ed.) (pp. 246–261). New York: McGraw-Hill.

Renzetti, C. M. (1993). On the margins of the malestream (or, they *still* don't get it, do they?): Feminist analyses in criminal justice education. *Journal of Criminal Justice Education, 4,* 219–234.

——. (1998). Connecting the dots: Women, public policy, and social control. In S. L. Miller (Ed.), *Crime control and women* (pp. 181–189). Thousand Oaks, CA: Sage.

Rice, M. (1990). Challenging orthodoxies in feminist theory: A black feminist critique. In L. Gelsthorpe and A. Morris (Eds.), *Feminist perspectives in criminology* (pp. 57–69). Buckingham, UK: Open University Press.

Richie, B. E. (1996). *Compelled to crime: The gender entrapment of battered black women.* New York: Routledge.

Rivera, J. (1997/1994). Domestic violence against Latinas by Latino males: An analysis of race, national origin, and gender differentials. In A. K. Wing (Ed.), *Critical race feminism: A reader* (pp. 259–266). New York: New York University Press.

Senna, J. J., and Siegel, L. J. (2002). *Essentials of criminal justice* (9th ed.) Belmont, CA: Wadsworth.

Smart, C. (1976). *Women, crime, and criminology: A feminist critique.* Boston: Routledge and Kegan Paul.

——. (1995). *Law, crime, and sexuality: Essays in feminism.* London: Sage.

——. (1998). The woman of legal discourse. In K. Daly and L. Maher (Eds.), *Criminology at the crossroads* (pp. 21–36). New York: Oxford University Press.

Stacey, J., and Thorne, B. (1985). The missing feminist revolution in sociology. *Social Problems,* 32, 301–316.

Taylor, V., and Rupp, L. J. (1991). Researching the women's movement: We make our own history, but not just as we please. In M. M. Fonow and J. A. Cook (Eds.), *Beyond methodology: Feminist scholarship as lived research* (pp. 119–132). Bloomington, IN: Indiana University Press.

Thomas, J., and O'Maolchatha, A. (1989). Reassessing the critical metaphor: An optimistic revisionist view. *Justice Quarterly,* 6, 143–172.

Tong, R. (1989). *Feminist thought: A comprehensive introduction.* Boulder, CO: Westview Press.

——. (1998). *Feminist thought: A more comprehensive introduction,* (2nd edition). Boulder, CO: Westview Press.

West, C., and Fenstermaker, S. (1995). Doing difference. *Gender & Society,* 9, 8–37.

West, C. and Zimmerman, D. H. (1987). Doing gender. *Gender & Society,* 1, 125–151.

Wilson, N. K. (1991). Feminist pedagogy in criminology. *Journal of Criminal Justice Education,* 2, 81–93.

Wonders, N. A. (1999). Postmodern feminist criminology and social justice. In B. A. Arrigo (Ed.), *Social justice/criminal justice* (pp. 111–128). Belmont, CA: West/Wadsworth.

Wonders, N. A,. and Caulfield, S. L. (1993). Women's work?: The contradictory implications of courses on women and the criminal justice system. *Journal of Criminal Justice Education,* 4, 79–100.

Wright, R. (1992). From vamps and tramps to teases and flirts: Stereotypes of women in criminology textbooks, 1956 to 1965 and 1981 to 1990. *Journal of Criminal Justice Education,* 3, 223–236. ✦

3
Masculinities and Crime

Beyond a Dualist Criminology

James W. Messerschmidt

In this chapter you will learn the following:

- How criminologists have historically studied masculinities and crime

- What it means to *reify* gender, and how the reification of gender has occurred in criminology

- The similarities and differences between pre-feminist and liberal feminist criminologies

- Why criminology may be considered a dualistic discipline as well as why and how criminology should move beyond dualism

- Why it is important to study gender similarities as well as gender differences in crime

Beginning in the early 1990s, numerous criminologists turned their research and theoretical interest to the topic of masculinities and crime. The result has been various individually authored books (Collier 1998; Hobbs 1995; Messerschmidt 1993, 1997, 2000, 2004; Polk 1994; Winlow 2001), edited volumes (Bowker 1998; Newburn and Stanko 1994; Sabo, Kupers, and London 2001), and special academic journal issues (Carlen and Jefferson 1996; *Theoretical Criminology* 2002). Criminologists writing on the relationship between masculinities and crime were influenced by second-wave feminism—originating in the 1960s—which challenged the masculinist

nature of the academy by illuminating the patterns of gendered power that, up to that point, social theory had all but ignored. In particular, feminism secured a permanent role for sexual politics in popular culture and moved analysis of gendered power to the forefront of much social thought. In addition, feminist research—within and without criminology—spotlighted the nature and pervasiveness of violence against women, crime by girls and women, the social control of girls and women, and women working in the criminal justice system (see Belknap 2000; Chesney-Lind and Pasko 2004; Daly and Maher 1998; Martin and Jurik 1996; Naffine 1995). The importance of this feminist work is enormous. It has contributed significantly to the discipline of criminology and has made a lasting impact. Not only is the importance of gender to understanding crime more broadly acknowledged within the discipline, but it has led, logically, to the critical study of masculinity and crime. Boys and men are no longer seen as the "normal subjects"; rather, the social construction of masculinities has come under careful criminological scrutiny.

Nevertheless, in approaching the relationship between masculinities and crime, criminologists have concentrated on men and boys and ignored women and girls. This should not be surprising since men and boys dominate crime. Arrest, self-report, and victimization data reflect that men and boys perpetrate more conventional crimes—and the more serious of these crimes—than do women and girls. Moreover, men have a virtual monopoly on the commission of syndicated, corporate, and political crime (Beirne and Messerschmidt 2005). Indeed, criminologists have consistently advanced gender as the strongest predictor of criminal involvement. Consequently, studying men and boys provides insights into understanding the highly gendered ratio of crime in industrialized societies. Concentrating exclusively on men and boys, however, neglects the fact that women and girls occasionally engage in masculine practices and crime and, therefore, constructs a transparent dualist criminology. As Robert Connell (2000) noted, "Unless we subside into defining masculinity as equivalent to men, we must acknowledge that sometimes masculine conduct or masculine identity goes together with a female body" (p. 16). It is, therefore, logically necessary that we also analyze how crime and violence committed by women and girls is related to masculinities.

What follows is an examination of past and current criminological thinking about gender, masculinities, and crime. Historically and contemporaneously, criminologists have conflated masculinity exclusively with men and boys, thereby collapsing gender into sex and (perhaps unintentionally) arguing that "the genders really do constitute coherent, uniform categories whose social and psychic consequence is a perfect homogenous binary" (Hood-Williams 2001, 39). Thus, criminology is dualist—it concentrates exclusively on gender differences in crime, eschewing an examination of gender similarities in crime (Messerschmidt 2004; Miller 2002).

Pre-Feminist Criminology

The earliest criminological theorists relied ultimately upon an essentialist "sex-role" framework to explain the relationship between masculinity and crime. That is, the presumption was that a "natural" distinction exists between men and women, a distinction that leads ineluctably to masculine men and feminine women. Accordingly, what unites criminologists who focus their specific theoretical attention on "sex roles" is that their frameworks ultimately ascribe to individuals certain innate characteristics. These form the basis of gendered social conditions—the male and female sex roles—that lead to specific sexed patterns of crime. In other words, biogenic criteria allegedly establish differences between men and women and society culturally elaborates the distinctions through the socialization of sex roles. These sex roles, in turn, determine the types and amounts of

crime committed by men and women, and by boys and girls. Thus, for sex-role theorists, the body enters criminological theory cryptically as biological differences between men and women. Consider a few notable pre-feminist theorists of this genre.

It was Edwin Sutherland who, in the 1930s, rejected biogenic perspectives on crime by arguing that through interaction and communication within certain intimate personal groups, individuals learn the techniques, motives, drives, rationalizations, and attitudes necessary to commit crime. For Sutherland, criminal behavior is learned in exactly the same way as conforming behavior. Thus, a particular person comes to engage in criminal behavior "because of an excess of definitions favorable to violation of [the] law over definitions unfavorable to violation of the law" (Sutherland 1947, 6).

In 1942, Sutherland first recognized the important criminological fact that nothing "is so frequently associated with criminal behavior as being a male" (p. 19). Yet Sutherland (1942), although not providing an explanation himself, added, "It is obvious that maleness does not explain criminal behavior" (p. 19). In other words, just as all lower working-class people do not commit crime—and, therefore, a simple causal analysis of poverty is problematic—so, not all men and boys engage in crime. Thus, a causal analysis of maleness is problematic.

It was not until 1947 that Sutherland attempted an explanation of why boys engage in crime more often than girls. Anticipating power-control theory (Hagan 1989), in the fourth edition of *Principles of Criminology*, Sutherland (1947, 100–101) argued that the higher rate of crime for boys could be explained by the differences in care and supervision of boys and girls. As Sutherland (1947) asserted, inasmuch as boys and girls live in the same poverty-ridden neighborhoods, social environment does not

explain the relatively high rate of boy delinquency and relatively low rate of girl delinquency. The significant difference is that girls are supervised more carefully and the behavior in accordance with social codes taught them with greater care and consistency than is the case with boys. From infancy girls are taught that they must be nice, while boys are taught that they must be rough and tough; a boy who approaches the behavior of girls is regarded as a "sissy." *This difference in care and supervision presumably rested originally on the fact that the female sex is the one which becomes pregnant.* The personal and familial consequences of illicit pregnancy lead to special protection of the girl not only in respect to sex behavior but in reference to social codes in general. (101, emphasis added)

Thus, boys are more likely to become delinquent because they are not controlled as strictly as girls and are taught to be "rough and tough." As is self-evident, Sutherland's explanation of boys' delinquency and girls' lack of delinquency rested on the assumption that socialization of sex roles is grounded ultimately in *biological and reproductive differences* between men and women—the body vaguely yet biologically entered Sutherland's explanation of gender differences in crime.

Sutherland's overall emphasis on biologically based sex roles must be understood in the intellectual context of the 1940s, when concepts of sex roles became fashionable in U.S. sociology. It was chiefly the work of Talcott Parsons (1902–1979) that popularized this concept, arguing that sex roles link men and women into a conjugal family unit that helps integrate the overall social system. Dichotomous sex roles structure the family: the *instrumental* role involves goal attainment, focusing on the relationship between the family and the wider society; the *expressive* role involves integration, concentrating on the internal structure and functions of the family. Men fulfill the instrumental role; women fulfill the expressive role. In turn, the family unit prepares children for adequate participation in society by teaching them the appropriate sex roles—masculine (instrumental) and feminine (expressive). Thus, when children are socialized into their proper sex role, society remains stable over generations.

Parsons reasoned that these dichotomous roles are based in *biological reproduction:* the fact that women bear and nurse children and men do not. Therefore, women are best fitted to perform expressive roles whereas men (absent from the reproductive biological functions previously noted above) are best adapted to instrumental roles. Accordingly, the family is structured in conformity with biological demands, functioning best for society when women's role is "anchored primarily in the internal affairs of the family, as wife, mother and manager of the household" and men's role is "anchored in the occupational world, in his job and through it by his status-giving and income-earning functions for the family" (Parsons and Bales 1955, 14–15). For Parsons, the relationship between men and women is one of harmony, and the connection between masculine and feminine sex roles is complementary. Thus, it is not surprising that Parsons (p. 103) suggests the "prohibition of homosexuality has the function of reinforcing the differentiation of sex roles" and, therefore, is necessary and functional for society.

Parsons employed his dichotomous functionalist perspective in the early 1940s to explain the greater delinquency of boys. He (1942) argued that in the family, "girls are more apt to be relatively docile, to conform in general according to adult expectations to be 'good,' whereas boys are more apt to be recalcitrant to discipline and defiant of adult authority and expectations" (p. 605). In the urban family, specifically, because the father is absent most of the time performing his "instrumental role," the mother is the emotionally significant adult, the role model for both boys and girls. For a girl, this is "normal and natural . . . because the functions of the housewife and mother are immediately before her eyes and are tangible and relatively easily understood by a child. Almost as soon as she is physically able, the girl begins a direct apprenticeship in the adult feminine role" (Parsons 1947, 171). But the boy does not have his father immediately available and, therefore, initially forms a feminine identification with the mother. He soon discovers that women are "inferior to men, that it would hence be shameful for him to grow up to be like a woman" (p. 171). The consequence of this "masculine anxiety" is the engagement of a compensatory "compulsive masculinity." As Parsons further stated, boys

> refuse to have anything to do with girls. "Sissy" becomes the worst of all insults. They get interested in athletics and physical prowess, in the things in which men have the most primitive and obvious advantage over women. Furthermore they become allergic to all expression of tender emotion; they must be "tough." This universal pattern bears all the earmarks of a "reaction-formation." It is so conspicuous, not because it is simply "masculine nature" but because it is a defense against a feminine identification. (p. 171)

In short, reaction-formation and resulting compulsive masculinity create a "strong tendency for boyish behavior to run in anti-social if not directly destructive directions, in striking contrast to that of . . . girls" (p. 172). Thus, for Parsons, masculinity is something that is internalized in adolescence and, resultingly, boys engage in more delinquency than girls; no conception exists that possibly girls may also engage in masculine practices.

Although Parsons' work is seriously flawed (which we consider further on), it is important because it was the first attempt to connect masculinity with the gendered nature of crime. However, it would take the later work of Albert Cohen before Parsons' perspective was developed into a full-fledged criminological theory.

In 1955, Albert Cohen synthesized the respective sex-roles arguments of Sutherland and Parsons into a theoretical formulation for understanding why gangs are dominated by boys. In *Delinquent Boys*, Cohen argued that a working-class delinquent subculture arises in reaction to discriminatory middle-class standards. Entering schools where teachers typically evaluate children in accordance with how their behavior approximates middle-class standards, boys socialized in working-class families are relatively unprepared for the challenge. Because working-class boys have internalized middle-class standards, they become "status-frustrated" and are "in the market for a solution" to their problems of adjustment (p. 119). The obvious solution is the collective repudiation of middle-class standards and adoption of their very antithesis—the public display of nonutilitarian, malicious, and negativistic delinquent behavior.

In a section of *Delinquent Boys* headed "What About the Sex Differences?" Cohen (1955) revealed his acceptance of Sutherland's and Parsons' idea of dichotomous, biologically based sex roles, by using himself and his wife as examples:

> My skin has nothing of the quality of down or silk, there is nothing limpid or flute-like about my voice, I am a total loss with needle and thread, my posture and carnage are wholly lacking in grace. . . . My wife, on the other hand, is not greatly embarrassed by her inability to tinker with or talk about the internal organs of a car, by her modest attainment in arithmetic or by her inability to lift heavy objects. (pp. 137–138)

Cohen went on to attempt, through a discussion of sex-role socialization, an explanation of why delinquency is dominated by boys. Enthusiastically following Parsons' idea that the actual socialization into the "male sex role" causes a compulsive masculinity, Cohen stated:

> Because of the structure of the modern family and the nature of our occupational system, children of both sexes tend to form early feminine identifications. The boy, however, unlike the girl, comes later under strong social pressure to establish his masculinity, his *difference from* female figures. Because his mother is the object of the feminine identification which he feels is the threat to his status as a male, he tends to react negativistically to those conduct norms which have been associated with mother

and therefore have acquired feminine significance. Since mother has been the principal agent of indoctrination of "good," respectable behavior, "goodness" comes to symbolize femininity, and engaging in "bad" behavior acquires the function of denying his femininity and therefore asserting his masculinity. This is the motivation to juvenile delinquency. (p. 164)

Thus, although the nature of "male sex-role" socialization is not a smooth process, simply joining the gang in the street can solve the problem of masculine anxiety in the home. For Cohen, gang activity is explicitly masculine in that it emphasizes achievement, exploit, aggressiveness, daring, active mastery, and pursuit. The delinquent gang acts in ways that reflect these aspects of the "male sex role." As Cohen stated, the delinquent response "is well within the range of responses that do not threaten his identification of himself as a male" (p. 140). Moreover, Cohen unmistakably applauded the masculine behavior of delinquent boys:

> The delinquent is the rogue male. His conduct may be viewed not only negatively, as a device for attacking and derogating the respectable culture; positively it may be viewed as the exploitation of modes of behavior which are traditionally symbolic of untrammeled masculinity . . . which are not without a certain aura of glamor and romance. (140)

Given that the most highly "ego-involved region" for the boy is his performance and achievement relative to other boys, the "corresponding highly ego-involved region" for a girl is establishing successful relationships with boys. Arguably then, the delinquent subculture is a "tailor-made" solution primarily to problems of the "male role" but is an inappropriate solution to adjustment problems of the "female role." The latter is so because the delinquent subculture is "irrelevant to the vindication of the girl's status as a girl" and threatens her in that status by reason of its "strongly masculine symbolic function" (pp. 140–144).

Sutherland, Parsons, and Cohen have been praised by many for allegedly rejecting biogenic, and firmly asserting sociogenic, perspectives on crime. Yet such praise is only partially deserved. When addressing the question of gender, biology cryptically entered into each of their theories. For all three, *biological differences* are the foundation of sex roles and, therefore, ultimately of differences in crime by men and women. Thus, these theorists were important historically in the construction of a dualist criminology that concentrates on the differences between males and females—while simultaneously ignoring the similarities—in the commission of crime.

Nevertheless, Sutherland, Parsons, and Cohen can be credited for putting masculinity on the criminological agenda. These theorists perceived the theoretical importance of gender and its relation to crime and acted upon that awareness. However, their conclusions demonstrate the limitations one would expect from any pre-feminist work. Indeed, essentialism was the accepted doctrine of the day and it took modern feminism to dismantle that powerful "commonsense" understanding of gender. Rather than being gender-blind, then, Sutherland, Parsons, and Cohen simply had a different conception of gender than exists among many social scientists today. They wrote in a social and historical context that maintained: (1) a relative absence of feminist theorizing and politics and (2) an assumed "natural" difference between men and women. Accordingly, it should not be surprising that they advanced the types of theories they did.

Liberal Feminist Criminology

Liberal feminism, which emerged in the industrialized world in the late 1960s, centers its analysis of gender inequality on a different type of sex-role perspective. Following the lead of the civil rights movement, the liberal feminist perspective identified as its major goal the extension of equal rights to women. Differing from Sutherland, Parsons, and Cohen, liberal feminist criminologists highlighted the social inequalities between men and women. According to liberal feminism, women are discriminated against on the basis of sex and, therefore, are deprived of the same opportunities as men and kept outside the mainstream of society (politics, business, finance, medicine, law, and so forth). Consequently, if "the problem is that women are in some sense 'out,' then it can be solved by letting them 'in'" (Ehrenreich and English 1978, 19). The goal of liberal feminism is to remove sexist stereotypes promoted through sex-role socialization in the family, school, media, and state, and thereby clear the way for "women's rapid integration into what has been the world of men" (p. 19).

Liberal feminist criminologists challenged the assumption by Sutherland, Parsons, Cohen, and others that gender inequality is rooted in biological sex differences. Although arguing that sex differences exist, for liberal feminists it is *society* rather than biology that primarily constrains women's abilities and, therefore, creates gender differences in crime. A central principle, then, of liberal feminist criminology is that gender differences are not fixed in the bodies of men and women. Indeed, liberal feminists minimize sex and emphasize gender; the former is understood as "natural" while the latter is "social." Thus, for liberal feminists, gender is not intrinsic to the species but is socially acquired. Assuming that linking inequality between men and women with unchanging natural bodily characteristics is erroneous, liberal feminist criminologists developed perspectives on gender differences in crime. Two of the most popular liberal feminist perspectives that appear to reject the alleged biological foundation of sex roles endorsed by Sutherland, Parsons, and Cohen, yet likewise exclusively concentrate on gender differences, are John Hagan's (1989) *power-control theory* and Robert Agnew's (1992) *general strain theory of delinquency.*

Hagan (1989) argued that in industrialized societies an instrument-object relationship exists between parents and children.

Parents are the instruments of control and their objects are children, and this relationship shapes the social reproduction of gender. However, these power relationships vary by class and by gender. In particular, as women increasingly enter the labor market, they gain "new power in the family" (p. 156).

Hagan identifies two family structures based on women's participation in the paid labor market, "patriarchal" and "egalitarian." In patriarchal families, the husband/father works outside the home in an authority position and the wife/mother works at home. Patriarchal families, through sex-role socialization, "reproduce daughters who focus their futures around domestic labor and consumption, as contrasted with sons who are prepared for participation in direct production" (p. 156). In egalitarian families, the husband/father and wife/mother both work in authority positions outside the home. These egalitarian families "socially reproduce daughters who are prepared along with sons to join the production sphere" (p. 157).

Thus, although in both types of families daughters are less criminal than sons because daughters are more controlled by their mothers, Hagan argued that daughters in patriarchal families are more often taught by parents to avoid risk-taking endeavors, whereas in egalitarian families, both daughters and sons are frequently taught to be more open to risk taking. It is this combination of the instrument-object relationship and corresponding socialization of risk taking that affects delinquency. According to Hagan (p. 158), patriarchal families are characterized by large gender differences in delinquent behavior, while egalitarian families maintain smaller gender differences in delinquency: "Daughters become more like sons in their involvement in such forms of risk-taking as delinquency" (p. 158). Thus, sons are for the most part ignored in this theory, and gender differences in crime are explained by a concentration on the characteristics of mothers and daughters.

In a recent statement of power-control theory, the emphasis remains exclusively on gender differences in crime, arguing that four conditions result in male overinvolvement in crime (Hagan, McCarthy, and Foster 2002):

> (1) a greater degree of freedom from the controls of parental agency; (2) more exposure to and support for master schemas that define activities as gender specific and legitimize male independence; (3) a greater preference for a risk-seeking approach to life; and (4) a stronger conviction that one is unlikely to experience negative consequences for engaging in risky activities. (p. 43)

Thus, for Hagan and his colleagues, gender similarities in crime are theoretically irrelevant.

Agnew (1992) identified three forms of "strain" that may lead to delinquency: the failure to achieve positively valued goals (such as disjunctions between expectations and actual achievements), the removal of positively valued stimuli from the individual (such as a loss of a girlfriend/boyfriend or death of a parent), and the presence of negative stimuli (such as child abuse/neglect or negative relations with parents). In examining strain in relation to gender and crime, Agnew (2001) concentrated on the question Why do males have a higher crime rate than females? His answer was that this is *not* due to boys and men having higher levels of strain than girls and women; in fact, females experience as much if not more strain than males. Instead, males experience different *types* of strain than females, and these are more likely to lead to crime. For example, Agnew argued that because of sex-role socialization, "males are more concerned with material success and extrinsic achievements, while females are more concerned with the establishment and maintenance of close relationships and with meaning and purpose in life" (p. 168). Such differences in strain, Agnew argued, explain the greater rate of property crime among males. Moreover, he noted important additional differences in social control and sex-role socialization:

> Females are more likely to experience strains like the excessive demands of family members and restrictions on their behavior, with females being more likely to be confined to the "private sphere." These types of strain involve a restriction of criminal opportunities and excessive social control. It is difficult to engage in serious violent and property crime when one spends little time in public, feels responsible for children and others, is burdened with the demands of others, and is under much pressure to avoid behaving in an aggressive manner. (p. 169)

Because men are more likely to be in public and, therefore, to experience conflict with others and criminal victimization, they are more likely to be involved in violence. Thus, the different types of strain men and women experience result in higher rates of crime by the former.

However, Agnew did not stop there, but added that males and females also differ in their emotional response to strain. Given that strain leads to certain negative emotions—such as anger—this in turn creates pressure to take corrective action. Although both males and females respond to strain with anger, they differ in their experience of anger. Female anger often is accompanied by emotions such as fear and depression whereas male anger more often is characterized by moral outrage. In explaining these differences, Agnew, like Hagan, concentrated on sex-role theory, arguing that by reason of differences in "the socialization process," women learn to blame themselves for negative treatment by others and view their anger as inappropriate and a failure of self-control; men blame others for their negative treatment and view their anger "as an affirmation of their masculinity" (p. 169). Consequently, men are more likely to commit violent and property crimes, whereas women are more likely to resort to self-destructive forms of deviance, such as drug use and eating disorders.

Liberal feminist criminology, then, is progressive but in a limited sense; there is at least an acknowledgment of gender inequality and an accompanying conditional focus on the social dimensions of behavior—that gendered behavior is learned through interaction in an unequal culture and such social conditions give rise to differences in control and types of strain experienced. In addition, the theoretical conceptualization of power-control and strain do present interesting insights on gender differences in crime, and these insights present an opportunity for a politics of reform. However, by concentrating on gender *differences* in crime, liberal feminists ignore gender *similarities* in crime and, thereby—like Sutherland, Parsons, and Cohen—construct a dualist criminology by collapsing gender into sex.

Reifying Gender

Let us more closely examine the serious problems with pre-feminist and liberal feminist theories of crime. Consider first the fact that research on *gender character traits* historically has found more similarities than differences between men and women. For example, meta-analysis of comparisons between men and women on "care" and "justice" finds no statistically significant difference (Jaffee and Hyde 2000). In addition, a recent summary of the most influential research on gender difference since the 1970s finds that "the concept of character dichotomy, as a basis of gender, is decisively refuted. Broad similarity between men and women is the main pattern" (Connell 2002, 46). Thus, the assumed differences in terms of sex roles are problematic for pre-feminist and liberal feminist criminological theories.

More than 25 years ago, Shover and Norland (1978, 115) showed that criminologists bring to their work on crime a set of gendered stereotypes and then proceed to discern empirical patterns and construct theoretical explanations consistent with their beliefs. All of the previously featured pre-feminist and liberal feminist criminologists assume *ab initio* that there exist only two "natural" sexes (male and female) and, therefore, but two genders (masculine and feminine). This as-

sumption is grounded in a specific cultural framework that views sex as strictly dichotomous and unchanging. And criminologists are not alone. In their critique of research on biology and gender, for example, Suzanne Kessler and Wendy McKenna (1978) reported that as natural scientists engage in the social practice of biological research, they always begin with a conception of *man* and *woman*. That is, natural scientists justify and appear to give grounds for "the already existing knowledge that a person is either a woman or a man and that there is no problem differentiating between the two" (p. 163).

Likewise, pre-feminist and liberal feminist criminologists begin with the assumption that there are only two sexes, and then proceed to find evidence supporting that assumption. These criminological theorists have addressed the problem of the gendered nature of crime through a theoretical lens that assumes that sex—and thereby gender—is exclusively dichotomous when no such dichotomy holds biologically, historically, cross-culturally, or even currently within such industrialized societies as the United States. For example, chromosomes are seen as a critical biological criterion for determining sex. If there is at least one Y chromosome, the individual is "male"; if there are no Y chromosomes, the individual is "female." Yet as Kessler and McKenna demonstrated, there exist people who are genetic mosaics (individuals with XO, XXY, or XXXX chromosomes, for example). So what is their sex? Chromosomal testing in the Olympic games provides the answer: All mosaics are declared men and may only participate in "male" events and the sex dichotomy is preserved (pp. 52–54).

Historical research likewise problematizes the notion of a natural unchanging sex dichotomy that is explicit in pre-feminist and liberal feminist criminologies. For example, in *Beyond the Natural Body*, Nelly Oudshoorn (1994) showed that conceptualizations of "sex" by natural scientists are, not surprisingly, read through gender. Oudshoorn examined the historic rise of endocrinology and how hormones were first "seen" by natural scientists as the material *truth* of sex difference. Not only did these scientists define hormones differently among each other—"the hormone of the biochemist is . . . quite different from the hormone of the biologists" (p. 36)—but Oudshoorn showed how "scientific facts" about sex hormones are constructed socially and then, in the not so distant future, dissolved socially. Natural scientists struggled incisively in the 1920s and 1930s to discover distinct sex hormones, only later to find "male hormones" in women's bodies and "female hormones" in men's bodies. In other words, despite differences among natural scientists, they were all similar, Oudshoorn argued, in beginning their research with a conception of sex differences and in persisting to search for and locate evidence of such difference, only to discern later that their "proof" is a frivolous social construction. Indeed, both testosterone and estrogen are present in all human bodies (many women have higher levels of the former than many men) "and after age fifty, men on average have higher levels of estrogen in their bloodstream than women" (Connell 2002, 33). Thus, we should not be surprised to find Anthony Giddens (1989) arguing that "[t]here is not a single physical characteristic, or even combination of physical characteristics, which cleanly and completely separates 'women' from 'men'" (p. 286). And as Kaplan and Rogers (1990) argued after a careful examination of biological studies on "sex," "The rigid either/or assignment of the sexes is only a convenient social construct, not a biological reality" (p. 214).

This does not mean, of course, that the body is not an existing biological phenomenon but, rather, that certain biological criteria are historically and socially "seen" and, therefore, constructed so as to buttress the sex dichotomy. As Williams and Bendelow (1998, p. 116) put it, what is conceptualized as "sex" is always "mediated by our existence as *social* beings and *historical* agents." Thus, the assumed sex dichotomy embedded in both pre-feminist and liberal feminist criminological theories does not hold biologically or historically.

Regarding cross-culture, anthropological evidence reveals that in other societies sex is not always dichotomous and not always assigned on biological criteria. Whereas in Western industrialized societies the ultimate criterion for sex assignment is *genitalia*, in several other societies it is strictly *social activities*. Martin and Voorhies (1975), for example, found that certain societies recognize more than two sex statuses and that in these societies, sex is not assigned on the basis of physical criteria (e.g., genitalia). In this regard, consider the following account of the Nuer of East Africa, which indicates that a woman who remains childless a certain number of years is considered sterile (Heritier-Auge 1989)

> [She] returns to her own family, where from then on she is considered a man—"brother" to her brothers, paternal "uncle" to her brothers' children. As an "uncle" she will be in a position to build up a herd, just like a man, from her share of the cattle paid as a bride price on her nieces. With this herd and the fruits of her personal industry, she will in turn be able to pay the bride price for one or several wives. She enters into these institutionalized matrimonial relations as the "husband." Her wives wait on her, work for her, honor her, show her the courtesies due a husband. She hires a [male] servant of another ethnic group, usually a Dinka, of whom she demands services including sexual services for her wife or wives. The children born of these relations are hers, call her "father" and treat her the way one treats a male father. (p. 294)

In other words, for the Nuer, a sterile woman becomes a "man" and thus it is *fertility* that determines "sex" in this particular society (p. 295).

Moreover, in the Sambia of Papua New Guinea, Gilbert Herdt (1994) found a "three-sex model" in which the "third sex" is neither male nor female, but labeled *kwolu-aatmwol*. The Sambia determine sex through genitalia; their third sex is what Western societies label the *intersexed* or *hermaphrodites*. Although a masculine dominated culture, the third sex is accepted into Sambian society and may even become, for example, distinguished shamans and warriors. As Herdt concluded: "The *kwolu-aatmwol* is not therefore rejected or frozen out of daily and normative social contacts and may indeed rise to distinction through special achievements" (p. 437).

In contemporary Western societies such as the United States, on the basis of *genitalia* alone there exist at least five sexes, three sexual orientations, five gender displays, six types of relationships, and ten self-identifications (Lorber 1994). As Robert Connell (2002) remarked in response to these variations: "Leaving aside the five sexes, that makes, if my arithmetic is correct, 900 different gender situations one can be in. So much for 'dimorphism'" (p. 36).

Some scholars have argued that possibly a third gender is being constructed today—what has been labeled a *transgenderist*—as a "social woman with a penis" or a "social man with a vagina" (Bolin 1993, 479). The transgenderist lives androgynously or may "pass," but either way challenges the pre-feminist and liberal feminist criminological paradigms that focus their analysis through a binary conception of sex as the *sine qua non* of gender. Indeed, the trangenderist "approximates the 'other' but never fully becomes the 'other'" (p. 485).

Societies, then, culturally construct varying definitions of sex and gender and, therefore, the latter does not develop naturally from biology. To be sure, "[o]ur conception of what is natural and of what natural differences consist is itself a cultural construct, part of our specific way of thinking about gender" (Connell 1987, 76). Furthermore, the social emphasis on physical sex difference ignores the fact that physical differences are considerably more pronounced *within* the sexes and that distributions between the sexes substantially *overlap*. As Connell pointed out:

> The members of either sex vary tremendously in height, strength, endurance, dexterity and so on [and] the distributions of the two sexes overlap to a great extent. Social practices that construct women and men as distinct categories by converting an average difference into a categorical difference—"men are stronger than women"—negate the major pattern of difference that occurs within sexes rather than between them. (p. 80)

In short, the resulting gross exaggeration of differences between men and women through gendered social practice occurs precisely because "the biological logic" is unable to "sustain the gender categories" (p. 81).

Pre-feminist and liberal feminist criminological theories, then, create an artificial dualist polarization, thereby distorting actual variability in gender constructions and reducing all masculinities and femininities to one normative standard case for each—the "male sex role" and the "female sex role"—and resultantly, they reify gender. Concentrating on the *differences* between men and women, these criminological theories ignore the *similarities* between men and women and disregard the differences *among* men and boys as well as *among* women and girls in the construction of masculinities, femininities, and crime. Not only are there differences cross-culturally but also, within each particular society, masculine and feminine practices by men and by women are constructed on the basis of class, race, age, sexuality, and particular social situation, such as the school, peer/leisure group, family, and workplace. The variations in the construction of masculinity and femininity are crucial to understanding the different types and amounts of crime. Pre-feminist and liberal feminist criminological theories require that we examine masculinity exclusively by men and boys and femininity by women and girls, thus ignoring *masculinities and femininities by people:* the way individuals construct gender differently.

Thus, pre-feminist and liberal feminist criminological theorists miss what must be acknowledged—women and girls also construct masculine practices that are related to crime. For example, when we examine different contexts—even within the same milieu—we can conceptualize situations where gender difference is highly salient when compared with those situations in which gender difference is relatively insignificant

(Thorne 1993). Pre-feminist and liberal feminist criminological theories overlook the salience and fluidity of gender and the diverse ways individuals construct gender in different situations. That is, these theories are capable only of "seeing" gender *differences* in crime (which is important), but thereby they are incapable of explaining gender *similarities* in crime. Consequently, sometimes commonalities across gender occur whereby women and girls through engagement in crime construct masculine conduct.

Finally, pre-feminist and liberal feminist criminological theories additionally describe men and women simply as "passive vessels" into which a variety of expectations are poured. In their reliance on sex-role theory, individuals resultantly display little if any creativity; their actions, including crime, are the result of their socialized sex role—gender is simply internalized and becomes resolute and unvarying. This reliance ignores the fact that men and women are active agents in their social relations, and it fails to account for the intentions of social actors, how social action is often—but not always—a meaningful construction in itself, and how individuals may reinterpret, resist, or subvert sex roles. In other words, the above theories "obscure the work that is involved in producing gender in everyday activities" (West and Zimmerman 1987, 127). Gender is not simply shaped and established beforehand; it is accomplished through social action and sometimes in ways that challenge culturally "appropriate" patterns (Thorne 1993). Indeed, individuals (men *and* women) actively negotiate specific types of masculinity out of the social settings—and subsequent resources at their disposal—in which they find themselves.

For all these reasons, then, pre-feminist and liberal feminist criminological theories are unsuitable to our task: They construct more enigmas than they resolve. In their concentration on a binary conception of gender and crime, they are haunted by the actual reality of diversity and occasional similarities by men and women in crime. In short, these theories construct a dualist criminology by reifying gender differences.

Beyond Dualism

A major result of an exclusive concentration on gender difference has been to direct theory in criminology away from issues that seriously complicate gender difference, such as when girls and women engage in what has traditionally been defined as "male crime." Accordingly, such approaches obscure a full and complete situational understanding of gender and crime: Where gender differences in crime are the exclusive focus, similarities in crime often are ignored or misrepresented. Abstracting gender from its social context and insensitive to issues of agency, such perspectives mask the possibility that gender patterns of crime may vary situationally and that, occasionally, girls/women and boys/men engage in similar types and amounts of crime. As Karlene Faith (1993) declared over ten years ago in a discussion of women and crime, to concentrate solely on crimes consistent with emphasized femininity "is to deny women's diversity and to promote gender-based objectification and stereotyping" (p. 57).

Given that masculinities and femininities are not determined biologically, it certainly makes sense to identify and examine possible *masculinities by women and girls* (and femininities by men and boys) and their relation to crime. Indeed, there remains a necessity in criminological research to uncover not only gender diversity among girls/women but also girls'/women's relations to crime and violence and whether or not such social action constructs masculinity or femininity.

Jody Miller (2001, 2002) has begun to move us in this direction, and her important book, *One of the Guys*, showed that certain gang girls identify with the boys in their gangs and describe such gangs as "masculinist enterprises": "To be sure, 'one of the guys' is only one part of a complex tapestry of gender beliefs and identities held by the gang girls I spoke with—and is rarely matched by gendered actions—but it remains significant nonetheless" (Miller 2002, 442). Miller pointed out that gender inequality such as male leadership, a double standard with regard to sexual activities, the sexual exploitation of some girls, and most girls' exclusion from serious gang crime is rampant in the mixed-gender gangs of which these girls were members. In this context, certain girls differentiated themselves from other girls through a construction of "one of the guys." In other words, the notion "one of the guys" is not fashioned by being *similar* to boys (because of inequalities) but, rather, certain girls being *different* from other girls.

Miller (p. 442) employed a modified version of Thorne's (1993) notion of "gender crossing"—whereby gang girls who "cross" (join male dominated mixed-gender gangs) exclusively embrace a "masculine identity"—to explain how certain girls differentiate themselves from other girls:

> Even within their gangs, status hierarchies among girls were evident and dictated in part how successfully girls could resist gender typecasting and cross into boys' terrain. Clearly, part of what young women were doing was constructing an identity in opposition to other normative constructs of femininity. But they were "crossing" gender to do so. . . . These girls' accounts do not simply reflect the construction of a "bad-girl" femininity that is differentiated from other femininities; instead, they reflect gender crossing, embracing a *masculine* identity that they view as contradicting their bodily sex category (that is, female). (p. 443)

Miller's research contributes to the process of discovering differences among gang girls, especially regarding how the distribution of male and female members within particular gangs may impact gender construction. Indeed, her work helps point scholars in an important direction for discovering these differences and how girls, like boys, can construct a masculine self.

Similarly, in my recent life-history study of adolescent assaultive violence (Messerschmidt

2004), I discovered numerous gender constructions by violent girls and that some girls "do" masculinity by in part displaying themselves in a masculine way, by engaging primarily in what they and others in their milieu consider to be authentically masculine behavior, and by outright rejecting most aspects of femininity. As an example, consider the case of Kelly whom I interviewed as part of this study.

Kelly was a short, stocky, 17-year-old who came to each interview without makeup, with her shoulder-length blonde hair pulled back in a ponytail, and wearing the same worker boots, baggy jeans, and sweatshirt with a hood. Kelly was on probation for assaultive violence when I interviewed her.

Kelly indicated that from an early age she actively rejected nearly all aspects of femininity because as a child she came to understand that "doing" femininity was painfully confining and required unexciting domestic labor. Accordingly, Kelly distanced herself from in-home emphasized feminine displays and practices (as represented by her sisters and mother). There were clear advantages, from Kelly's point of view, for eschewing femininity and practicing masculinity. The latter permitted Kelly to enjoy tranquil (rather than tumultuous) interaction with her extremely violent stepfather. Moreover, it sanctioned practices she conceptualized as "fun," for example, playing outside with boys. For Kelly, then, "doing" femininity restricted bodily mobility and freedom; "doing" masculinity offered a semblance of autonomous self-rule in the home when compared with the status of her sisters and mother. Kelly's interaction at home and alliance with her stepfather clearly was fraught with tension and fear—she allied with her stepfather in part to avoid succumbing to his violence, and Kelly enjoyed more privileges than mother and sisters, yet she remained subordinate to, and under the domination of, her stepfather.

By intimately attaching herself to her stepfather, then, Kelly reflexively opened the possibility to become accountably "Daddy's boy" and to reap the gendered benefits such embodied social action promised. Arguably, Kelly drew on the practices and subsequent discursive criteria at home, and she constructed a complicit (albeit subordinate) masculinity in this setting by benefiting from the oppression of her sisters and her mother. Kelly was accountable to—and wholly endorsed—her stepfather's in-home hegemonic masculine project. Yet she did not embody hegemonic masculinity at home. Rather, Kelly reflexively constructed a masculinity that included partial procurement of the in-home "patriarchal dividend" without "doing" the violence of its chief practitioner (Connell 1995, 79). Although Kelly gained from the subordination of her sisters and mother, she was not a "frontline trooper" (p. 79). In other words, Kelly subverted emphasized femininity while simultaneously perpetuating oppressive and dichotomous gender relations at home and, therefore, occupied a specific masculine presence and *place* in in-home gender relations.

From a young age, then, Kelly attempted in all aspects of home life to be accountably masculine. Accordingly, Kelly endorsed and defied certain practices of copresent interactants—her parents and sisters—in the specific milieu of home. The particular situational interaction at home resulted in Kelly becoming accountably masculine in this milieu yet simultaneously practicing nonviolence. Kelly's experiences at home highlight the time- and place-specific aspects of "doing gender" through embodied nonviolence. Kelly had no need to engage in violence at home because she constructed a complicit masculine self in-part sustained through the violence of her stepfather. Consequently, *as a girl* embodying a masculine self, Kelly interacted with and through her body in a specific way by *blurring gender difference* at home: She embodied gender nonconformity.

Kelly's masculine self was carried over to other settings, such as the school. In Kelly's negotiation of in-school gender relations among girls, she initially positioned herself as a "jock." Yet because of her masculine appearance and practice, eventually Kelly was ostracized and labeled a "dyke" (by girls) and a "wimp" (by boys). Although prudently avoiding boys physically larger than her—the vast majority of whom ignored Kelly anyway—she intentionally created situations where, in response to the verbal abuse, physical domination of boys would be seen by others as admirable. Her physical sense of masculinity at school was derived in part, then, from her ability to "fight back" against boys who verbally abused her. Indeed, Kelly specifically concentrated on beating up boys (similar in physical size) who verbally abused her at school, and she chose spaces (e.g., the hallway) where her assaultive violence would be confirmed as masculine by her peers. Kelly developed a "Don't-mess-with-me" reputation and, therefore, actually became accountably masculine at school. Kelly's motive for fighting at school was to exhibit embodied power over boys and, therefore, put an end to the verbal abuse. By exercising bodily power on and over certain boys, Kelly established a sense of embodied masculine presence at school, albeit a subordinate masculinity. To engage in such acts was to be accountably masculine at school because the particular gender relations in that setting gave meaning to this type of violence as gendered masculine. And as a result, although the boys (and girls) who verbally abused her eventually stopped, she remained marginalized at school as "Other."

In short, the task of contemporary criminologists is not to reify gender by concentrating research and theory solely on gender differences in crime. Rather, the goal should be to examine and explain both gender differences and gender similarities—that is, gender diversity—in the commission of crime.

Study/Discussion Questions

1. What are the major differences between pre-feminist and liberal feminist criminological theories? Why did such differences arise?

2. Explain what is meant by *reifying gender* and how it relates to a *dualist criminology*.

3. Summarize and evaluate the suggestions for moving criminology beyond dualism.

References

Agnew, R. (1992). Foundation for a general strain theory of crime and delinquency. *Criminology*, 30, 47–87.

——. (2001). An overview of general strain theory. In R. Paternoster and R. Bachman (Eds.), *Explaining criminals and crime: Essays in contemporary criminological theory* (pp. 161–174). Los Angeles: Roxbury Publishing.

Beirne, P., and Messerschmidt, J. W. (2005). *Criminology*. 4th Edition. Los Angeles: Roxbury Publishing.

Belknap, J. (2000). *The invisible woman: Gender, crime, and justice*. Belmont, CA: Wadsworth.

Bolin, A. (1994). Transcending and transgendering: Male-to-female transsexuals, dichotomy, and diversity. In G. Herdt (Ed.), *Third sex, third gender: Beyond sexual dimorphism in culture and history* (pp. 447–486). New York: Zone Books.

Bowker, L. (Ed.). (1998). *Masculinities and violence*. Thousand Oaks, CA: Sage.

Carlen, P., and Jefferson, T. (Eds.). (1996). *British Journal of Criminology, Special Issue, Masculinities and Crime*, 33 (6): 337–444.

Chesney-Lind, M., and Pasko, L. (2004). *The female offender: Girls, women, and crime*. 2nd Edition. Thousand Oaks, CA: Sage.

Cohen, A. (1955). *Delinquent boys: The culture of the gang*. New York: Free Press.

Collier, R. (1998). *Masculinities, crime and criminology: Men, hetrosexuality, and the criminal(ised) other*. London: Sage.

Connell, R. W. (1987). *Gender and power: Society, the person, and sexual politics*. Stanford: Stanford University Press.

——. (1995). *Masculinities*. Berkeley, CA: University of California Press.

——. Connell, R. W. (2000). *The men and the boys*. Sydney: Allen and Unwin.

——. (2002). *Gender*. Cambridge, UK: Polity Press.

Daly, K., and Maher, L. (Eds.). (1998). *Criminology at the crossroads: Feminist readings in crime and justice*. New York: Oxford University Press.

Ehrenreich, B., and English, D. (1978). *For her own good*. Garden City, NY: Anchor Press.

Faith, K. (1993). *Unruly women*. Vancouver: Press Gang Publishers.

Giddens, A. (1989). A reply to my critics. In D. Held and J. B. Thompson (Eds.), *Social theories of modern societies: Anthony Giddens and his critics* (pp. 249-301). New York: Cambridge University Press.

Hagan J. (1989). *Structural criminology*. New Brunswick, NJ: Rutgers University Press.

Hagan, J., McCarthy, B., and Foster, H. (2002). A gendered theory of delinquency and despair in the life course. *Acta Sociologica*, 45, 37–46.

Herdt, G. (1994). Mistaken sex: Culture, biology and the third sex in New Guinea. In G. Herdt (Ed.), *Third sex, third gender: Beyond sexual dimorphism in culture and history* (pp. 419–445). New York: Zone Books.

Heritier-Auge, F. (1989). Older women, stout-hearted women, women of substance. In M. Feher, R. Naddaff, and N. Tazi (Eds.), *Fragments for a history of the human body, Part III* (pp. 281–299). New York: Zone Books.

Hobbs, D. (1995). *Bad business: Professional crime in modern Britain*. New York: Oxford University Press.

Hood-Williams, J. (2001). Gender, masculinities and crime: From structures to psyches. *Theoretical Criminology*, 5, 37–60.

Jaffee, S., and Hyde, J. S. (2000). Gender differences in moral orientation: A meta-analysis. *Psychological Bulletin*, 126, 703–26.

Kaplan, G. T., and Rogers, L. J. (1990). The definition of male and female: Biological reductionism and the sanctions of normality. In S. Gunew (Ed.), *Feminist knowledge: Critique and construct* (pp. 205–228). New York: Routledge.

Kessler, S., and McKenna, W. (1978). *Gender: An ethnomethodological approach*. New York: John Wiley.

Lorber, J. (1994). *Paradoxes of gender*. New Haven, CT: Yale University Press.

Martin, M. K., and Voorhies, B. (1975). *Female of the species*. New York: Columbia University Press.

Martin, S. E., and Jurik, N. C. (1996). *Doing justice, doing gender: Women in law and criminal justice occupations.* Thousand Oaks, CA: Sage.

Messerschmidt, J. W. (1993). *Masculinities and crime: Critique and reconceptualization of theory.* Lanham, MD: Rowman & Littlefield.

——. (1997). *Crime as structured action: Gender, race, class, and crime in the making.* Thousand Oaks, CA: Sage.

——. (2000). *Nine lives: Adolescent masculinities, the body, and violence.* Boulder, CO: Westview.

——. (2004). *Flesh and blood: Adolescent gender diversity and violence.* Lanham, MD.: Rowman & Littlefield.

Miller, J. (2001). *One of the guys: Girls, gangs, and gender.* New York: Oxford University Press.

——. (2002). The strengths and limits of "doing gender" for understanding street crime. *Theoretical Criminology,* 6, 433–460.

Naffine, N. (Ed.). (1995). *Gender, crime, and feminism.* Brookfield, MA: Dartmouth.

Newburn, T., and Stanko, E. A. (Eds.). (1994). *Just boys doing business? Men, masculinities and crime.* London: Routledge.

Oudshoorn, N. (1994). *Beyond the natural body: An archaeology of sex hormones.* New York: Routledge.

Parsons, T. (1942). Age and sex in the social structure of the United States. *American Sociological Review,* 7, 604–616.

——. (1947). Certain primary sources and patterns of aggression in the social structure of the Western world. *Psychiatry,* 10, 167–181.

Parsons, T., and Bales, R. F. (1955). *Family, socialization, and interactional process.* New York: Free Press.

Polk, K. (1994). *When men kill: Scenarios of masculine violence.* New York: Cambridge University Press.

Sabo, D., Kupers, T. A., and London, W. (Eds.). (2001). *Prison masculinities.* Philadelphia: Temple University Press.

Shover, N., and Norland, S. (1978). Sex roles and criminality: Science or conventional wisdom? *Sex Roles,* 4, 111–125.

Sutherland, E. H. (1942). Development of the theory. In A. Cohen, A. Lindesmith, and K. Schuessler (Eds.), *The Sutherland Papers* (pp. 13–29). Bloomington: Indiana University Press, 1956.

——. (1947). *Principles of criminology.* Philadelphia: Lippincott.

Theoretical Criminology, (2002) 6 (1) 5–99.

Thorne, B. (1993). *Gender play: Girls and boys in school.* New Brunswick, NJ: Rutgers University Press.

West, C., and Zimmerman, D. H. (1987). Doing gender. *Gender & Society,* 1, 125–151.

Williams, S., and Bendelow, G. (1998). *The lived body: Sociological themes, embodied issues.* New York: Routledge.

Winlow, S. (2001). *Badfellas: Crime, tradition, and new masculinities.* New York: Berg. ✦

4
Liberating Criminology

The Evolution of Feminist Thinking on Criminological Research Methods

Ronet Bachman
Christina Lanier

In this chapter you will learn the following:

- The defining characteristics of feminist research methodology

- What distinguishes positivism from post-postivism and constructivism

- The differences between qualitative and quantitative research methods

- The ethical concerns of feminist methodologists and how they address these concerns

- The importance among feminist criminologists of connecting social research to social action

Introduction

Central to an emerging interdisciplinary feminist methodology are issues such as: Who gets to be a knower? What is knowledge? How are competing knowledge claims resolved? (Harding 1986, 191)

Although Sandra Harding was referring to social science research in general in the above quote, the questions she raises mirror those voiced by the revolution feminist scholars created in the criminology research field, regarding the ways in which the discipline

had traditionally produced "knowledge." But more important, the questions illustrate that what is distinctive about feminist methodology is not so much the methods themselves but researchers' thinking about the methods. As with most other scientific revolutions, the effects of feminism on criminological research can more realistically be seen as an evolution of thought rather than an agreed upon set of criteria that define feminist methods. For example, even after a group of academic feminists developed a program that would increase the availability of feminist research and teaching across disciplines, participants still could not come to a consensus on what feminist methodology was.[1] They stated, "Although its [feminist] methodologies were rooted in social activism, it could not be reduced to an easily defined set of propositions, theoretical claims, or research methods." (Hesse-Biber, Gilmartin, and Lydenberg 1999, 6). This pluralism is reinforced by literature reviews documenting the fact that feminist researchers are not homogeneous in their choice of methods but have employed virtually all available research methods (Reinharz 1992). As such, feminist methodology can be seen as more of a perspective than a method unto itself.

Even though there is no single feminist method, a substantial literature on "feminist methodology" exists that informs and guides us, although it may not always speak with one voice. This chapter outlines the evolution of feminist thought about methodology in the field of criminology and criminal justice. So that readers are oriented for the discussion of how feminist methodologies often compare with other notions of scientific inquiry, the first part of the chapter outlines the basic distinctions between the philosophies of positivism and constructivism. The second part of the chapter outlines the following main themes that infuse feminist concerns about how "doing research" is and should be different from a feminist perspective: (1) the process of methodology, (2) the selection of research topics, (3) ethical issues, including the interruption of power and control hierarchies in research and the acknowledgment of researcher subjectivity, and (4) the tie of research to social action.

Positivism and Constructivism

A researcher's choice of methods is not just a matter of matching the appropriate techniques to a particular research problem. Methodological preferences also reflect theoretical perspectives on reality and the role of the researcher. There are two general perspectives that serve as foundations for social science within the area of criminology: positivism and constructivism.

Positivism is the view that there is a reality that exists quite apart from our own perception of it. Researchers who perceive the world through a positivist lens believe that valid ideas about the empirical world can be observed and that these observations accurately reflect the natural world and processes within it, without distortion by the observer. The goal of the scientist, according to the positivist view, is to develop these ideas and continually test them against empirical evidence (Bachman and Schutt 2003). As Weber (1949) so succinctly put it, "The type of social science in which we are interested is an empirical science of concrete reality" (p. 72).

The positivist perspective has been modified by some philosophers of science who adopt a postpositivist or critical realist perspective (Guba and Lincoln 1994).

Postpositivism accepts the basic premise of an external, objective reality but recognizes that its complexity, and the limitations of human observers, precludes us from developing anything more than a partial understanding of it. Thus, the goal of science should be seen as seeking to achieve intersubjective agreement about the nature of reality rather than certainty about the nature of objective reality.

Criminologists are more likely to accept this postpositivist view than the original positivist perspective because of the special challenges posed by the scientific study of people.

First, human beings have the capacity to think and to reflect, to create mental interpretations of themselves and their world that have no concrete manifestation or necessary relation to subsequent individual action. Second, scientists themselves are human beings; and therefore when they study people, they are studying others like themselves, and they may project on them their own interpretations (Bachman and Schutt 2003).

Some researchers, including many feminist researchers, go further in their criticisms of the positivist perspective. In contrast to positivism, many feminist researchers adopt what is sometimes referred to as a *constructivist* perspective.

Constructivism is a theoretical perspective that challenges the notion of a concrete, objective reality that scientific methods help us to understand (Lynch and Bogen 1997). Constructivist perspectives also are sometimes called *interpretivist*. In the view of constructivists, scientists construct an image of reality that reflects their own preferences and prejudices and their interactions with others. From this standpoint, the goal of validity, actually measuring what we think we are measuring, becomes meaningless: "Truth is a matter of the best-informed and most sophisticated construction on which there is a consensus at a given time" (Schwandt 1994, 128). As Sandra Harding (1986) so eloquently asked, "Does science reflect the real world? Does it tell one true story that is readymade and is out there for reflecting by our glassy mirror minds? . . . [T]his peculiar notion of objectivity?" (p. E24).

For constructivists, the goals of research should be to discover what is meaningful to individuals and how and why they orient themselves to particular meaningful objects and values at particular times and places (Larson 1993). As Rubin and Rubin (1995) explained, "Searching for universally applicable social laws can distract from learning what people know and how they understand their lives. The interpretive social researcher examines meanings that have been socially constructed. . . . There is not one reality out there to be measured; objects and events are understood by different people differently, and those perceptions are the reality or realities that social science should focus on" (p. 35).

The resulting methodologies that emerge from these two perspectives are usually categorized into quantitative versus qualitative research methods.

Quantitative methods are designs, such as surveys and experiments, that record variation in social life in terms of categories that vary in amount, such as magnitudes of delinquency or of victimization. In contrast, *qualitative methods,* such as participant observation and intensive interviewing, are designed to capture social life as participants experience it rather than in categories predetermined by the researcher (Bachman and Schutt 2003).

An example may help illustrate the differences. Suppose you are a researcher interested in the effects of police intervention in cases of intimate partner violence. One way to explore this issue with a quantitative methodology may be to give women who report their victimization to police a self-administered questionnaire that asks them a number of questions with fixed responses about their experience. For example, one question might be: On a scale of one to ten with one being not at all satisfied and ten being extremely satisfied, how satisfied are you with the police response to your reported victimization? In contrast, a way to explore this issue with a qualitative methodology may be to conduct in-depth interviews with these women and allow them to provide you with the details of their experiences in their own words. When either methodology is utilized using a feminist lens, the researcher generally seeks to recontextualize what is being studied by underscoring the political, social, and personal worlds from which reality is being observed. From a feminist perspective, this generally includes the structures of patriarchy and the intersection of patriarchy and discrimination by gender, race, class, and sexual orientation. Next, we talk more about this contextualization.

What Makes Methodology Feminist?

A primary contribution of feminist scholars to criminological research has been to illuminate the fact that everything we consider to be knowledge, including such things as who are the offenders and victims, is socially situated. Moreover, most feminist researchers assume that "gender is not a natural fact but a complex social, historical, and cultural product," and that "gender and gender relationships order social life and social institutions in fundamental ways that result in constructs of masculinity and femininity that are not symmetrical but are based on an organizing principle of men's superiority and social and political-economic dominance over women" (Daly and Chesney-Lind 1988, 504).

As a result of this attention to context, feminist researchers generally begin with the assumption that the researcher will always influence knowledge and its creation. The goal of many feminist criminologists is to "construct knowledge from the perspective of the persons being studied on the grounds that the perspective of the oppressed or marginalized tends to be less distorted" (Flavin 2001, 274). Because the perspective and perceptions of the research participants are so important, many feminist researchers prefer qualitative research methods.

Feminism and Qualitative Methods

Qualitative research has several features that are synonymous with the goals of feminist researchers, such as: (1) a focus on previously unstudied processes and unanticipated phenomena, (2) an orientation to social context, to the interconnections between social phenomena rather than to their discrete features, (3) a focus on human subjectivity, on the meanings that participants attach to events and people give to their lives, (4) a focus on the events leading up to a particular event or outcome instead of general causal explanations, (5) reflexive research designs that consider or modify the research in response to new developments or to changes in some other component of the phenomena being researched, and (6) sensitivity to the subjective role of the research (Bachman and Schutt 2003).

Examples of feminist research that relies on qualitative methods abound and are far too numerous to list here. Jody Miller's analysis of interviews with female robbery offenders and how their motives and methods compared with their male counterparts is just one recent example. The in-depth interviews with the robbery offenders lasted one to two hours and included a range of questions about the respondents' involvement in robbery. "Respondents were asked to describe why they committed robbery, their typical approach when committing robbery, and the details of their most recent offenses. The goal was to gain a thorough understanding of the contexts of these events from the respondents' perspective" (Miller 2000, 31). Miller found that women's and men's motivations for committing robbery were similar; however, the ways in which they committed robbery were strikingly different.

Susan Miller (1999) adopted the role of complete observer when she conducted research on community policing. She was particularly interested in how gender affected the attitudes and behavior of neighborhood police officers (NPO), and her discussion of this choice captures well the benefit of qualitative methods for her feminist agenda:

> I was curious as to whether the interpersonal dynamics I observed with Officer Terry [a female officer] would be like those when a male NPO was involved. I wanted to delve into the heads and hearts of the NPOs to see for myself what worked in community policing and see what they felt did not. I wanted to examine how such a paradigm shift in the theory and practice of policing would affect the officers who desire street action, and how they assess their new "walk and talk" colleagues. (p. x)

The consciousness and self-perceptions of those being studied can also illuminate surprising results. For example, after interviewing female survivors of male violence about their self-descriptions, Michelle Fine (1989) and her colleagues were surprised to learn that the women often tried to distance themselves from the labels feminists often use to heighten public recognition to gendered violence, such as "battered woman." Fine noted one woman as stating, "Not me. I'm not a battered woman. Battered women have bruises all over their bodies. Two broken legs. And he's not a batterer, not like I see them. No, he just hits me too much" (p. 553).

Feminism and Quantitative Methods

Although many feminist scholars prefer qualitative methods, others investigating research questions in the area of criminology and criminal justice also rely on quantitative methods. At first blush, the tenets of positivism and its resulting methods would seem in stark contrast to the goals of feminist researchers. Perhaps that is why feminist methodology has often been stereotyped as being synonymous with qualitative methods. However, this is decidedly not the case. Again, what makes research feminist is not the method but the perspective taken by the researcher. When doing all research, including quantitative studies such as surveys or the use of official data, a feminist perspective encourages a critical questioning of the assumptions that underlie most positivist notions, particularly that objectivity can be attained and that there is a reality that exists apart from one's own perception of it.

One example of a major contribution by feminist researchers in the area of quantitative criminology has been the demand for more reliable surveys to estimate the magnitude of violence against women. Understanding the magnitude of a phenomenon is the starting point for social action and policies to prevent it. Because violence against women, particularly violence perpetrated by intimate partners, was not adequately measured in the United States, it remained off the radar screen of policy makers. Although the National Crime Victimization Survey (NCVS), funded by the Bureau of Justice Statistics, has made progress in redesigning its screening instrument to more accurately measure intimate partner violence against women and rape (Bachman and Taylor 1994), feminist scholars have pointed out the deficiencies that still remain (Bachman 2000; Koss 1992). Other feminist scholars have been instrumental in conducting large, nationally representative surveys that more adequately track the life histories of violence in women's lives; these include the National Violence Against Women Survey (NVAWS) (Tjaden and Thoennes 2000), a violence against college students survey (Fisher, Cullen, and Turner 2001), and the Violence Against Women in Canada Survey (Johnson 1996).

There are several important contributions these surveys have made to the state of knowledge regarding violence against women. First, they provide the only estimates of stalking available, both nationally and at the college level. In addition, since the NVAWS collects information about all previous victimizations women have experienced, it is the first of its kind in the United States to permit a glance at the interconnections among women's experiences with violence over a lifetime. Victimizations experienced by women, regardless of when they occur, can have a profound effect on perceived levels of safety and well-being. The one-year reference period used by the NCVS, while avoiding problems of memory recall, discounts the effects of victimizations that occurred beyond this time frame. In addition, the NVAWS used a greater range of questions with sensitive lead-ins, thereby increasing the willingness of women to disclose victimizations. As Johnson (1996) stated, this added information can "help place women's experiences of sexual assault and wife battering into a broader social context and can significantly enhance discussions about the correlates of women's fear" (p. 46).

The monitoring of women's growing rates of imprisonment is another important contribution feminist scholars have made using quantitative research. As Tammy Anderson notes in this volume, the rate of women under correctional authority has increased dramatically during the past two decades. In fact, the rate of women under the jurisdiction of state and federal correctional authorities has increased around 5 percent annually since 1995. In sum, since 1995, the number of women under federal correctional jurisdiction has increased 51 percent and the number of women under state correctional jurisdiction has increased 42 percent (Harrison and Beck 2003). Feminist scholars along with other advocates have been instrumental in illuminating these facts to the public using quantitative analyses.

Feminist scholars, like other researchers in our discipline, are beginning to acknowledge that the strengths and weaknesses of qualitative and quantitative methods are complementary. For example, the intensity of in-depth interviews produces detailed narratives that shed light on the perceptions and thoughts of those being interviewed. This type of information is almost impossible to obtain through a survey using a fixed-choice format for responses. However, the time demands involved in conducting intensive interviews almost preclude the ability to obtain a large sample that would be representative of the population. Although a survey may not be able to obtain detailed narrative information, it is possible to obtain a large random sample in which to distribute a survey and thereby increase the generalizability of the survey findings. The bottom line is that "both quantitative and qualitative methods can be used for the advancement of the feminist agenda, or they can both be used in anodrocentric objectifying ways" (Dankoski 2000, 12).

The Triangulation of Research Methods

Because of complementary strengths such as this, many feminist researchers have adopted research projects that include a combination of qualitative and quantitative methods. The use of multiple research methods to study one research question is called **triangulation**. The term suggests that a researcher can get a clearer picture of the social reality being studied by viewing it from several different perspectives. In fact, the term is actually derived from land surveying, where knowing a single landmark allows you to locate yourself only somewhere along a line in a single direction from the landmark. However, with two landmarks, you can take bearings along both lines and locate yourself at their intersection (Bachman and Schutt 2003).

Kathleen Daly's book (1994), *Gender, Crime, and Punishment*, used both statistical analyses of data and in-depth qualitative analysis to examine the sentencing outcomes of female and male felony defendants. In defense of her triangulated methods, she emphatically stated,

> I would like to think it is possible to find a truce between those whose representations of the social world are numerical and logico-scientific and those whose representations take a more narrative form. Such a truce will assume some bilingualism in the strengths of statistics and [some] storytelling in the creation of plausible truth claims (p. 13).

The Research Question: Deciding What and Whom to Study

The research process and selection of methods are propagated from a research question. At the dawn of feminist thinking in criminology, a resounding echo was heard across the discipline that asked Where are the women represented in this research? Prior to this, theories of criminality were developed from male respondents and subjects and validated on male respondents and subjects (Daly and Chesney-Lind 1988). The problem, of course, was that the findings were generalized to fe-

males as if there were no differences in the etiology of offending or in victimization between males and females. This is not the case, as a proliferation of research has shown. Two of the main contributions of feminist methods have been (1) to fill the knowledge gaps that exist in criminology regarding questions that affect women's lives, including violence against women, the treatment of female offenders by the criminal justice system, and the experiences of women who work in the domain of criminal justice (Martin and Jurik 1996; Naffine 1996; Smart 1995) and (2) to make these areas of inquiring a priority in criminological research.

More than this, the research questions asked by researchers with a feminist perspective don't simply examine the differences between males and females. Rather, they take as their reference point the fact that what is observed in society stems from the patriarchal nature of the power dynamics between men and women in society. As Gelsthorpe (1990) explained,

> For most this has meant choosing topics which are relevant or sympathetic to women and to the women's movement. In essence, it has meant choosing a topic which it is hoped will contribute to ending the oppression of women, that is, topics which have both political and practical import. (p. 90)

For example, when conducting research on female victims of intimate partner violence, some may ask, Why do battered women stay in abusive relationships? A researcher with a feminist perspective, however, may pose the question somewhat differently. What are the factors that prevent or impede a woman from escaping a battering relationship? (Gelsthorpe and Morris 1990) In short, the goal of feminist research is typically of doing research "for" rather than "about" women.

Research using a feminist lens often uncovers the gendered nature of violence that is often missed by the media and policy makers alike. The school shootings of the 1990s are a good example. The Columbine High School shootings in suburban Colorado that left 15 people dead, including the shooters, Eric Harris and Dylan Klebold, in 1999 were just one of the school shootings that occurred that academic year. Each of the shootings caused a media frenzy. How could such atrocities occur? Then President Clinton talked about hate, prejudice, community policing, parental responsibility, and violence in the culture. Charlton Heston, spokesman for the National Rifle Association, blamed the absence of armed security guards in schools, even though one was present at Columbine High.

It took feminist researchers to illuminate the gendered nature of the shootings: Statistically, 100 percent of the offenders were male and 59 percent of the victims were female (Danner and Carmody 2001). The consequences of ignoring the gendered nature of school violence are enormous and have profound implications for policy directed at preventing such violence. After performing a content analysis of newspaper articles covering school shootings, Danner and Carmody (2001) concluded that

> Existing research links sexual harassment and dating violence to other forms of violence against women, and connects bullying to male violence; yet the "experts" failed to emphasize these connections when approached by the media. . . . Until researchers make these connections clear, the media coverage of these events will remain skewed, and public policy aimed at increasing school safety will fail to protect the lives of all students. (pp. 110–111)

In addition to examining the gendered nature of violence and the different etiological explanations of violence against women and by women, feminist scholars have also moved beyond an examination of simple gender differences. This actually began in the 1980s when feminist scholarship that prioritized sexual differences between men and women began to be criticized explicitly for neglecting differences among women stemming from class, race, ethnicity, or sexual ori-

entation and for implicitly privileging a norm of womanhood as white, heterosexual, middle class, and Western. "New scholarship by black feminists, postcolonial critics, queer theorists, and others exposed this normative ideology as racist, ethnocentric, heterosexist, and elitist" (Hesse-Biber, Gilmartin, and Lydenberg 1999, 4).

Today, feminist scholars across all disciplines, including those in criminology, have begun to explore the diversity of perspectives among women that intersect with gender, including race, ethnicity, sexual orientation, and social class. For example, while researchers have noted the war on drugs' deleterious effects on African-American males, feminist researchers are now uncovering the tremendous incarceration rates for drug offenses by women in general and for black women in particular (Rolison, Bates, Poole, and Jacob 2002). Other researchers are filling the gaps in our understanding of other invisible groups, such as the reality of domestic violence in Chinese immigrant families (Yick 2001) and violence against indigenous women (Lucashenko 1996). Research examining subgroups of women such as these has found that the different cultural values often present within the context of violence against minority women necessitate that their social realities and viewpoints be given voice.

Ethics and Power

All research has an ethical dimension. Feminist research is concerned with the same ethical issues that concern other researchers, including voluntary participation, subject well-being, identity disclosure, deception, and anonymity and confidentiality. However, many feminist researchers add to their list of ethical concerns the power relationships that exist in many research settings as well as the subjective nature of the researcher. Perhaps more than other researchers, those using a feminist lens identify and take responsibility for the consequences of their research process. We will briefly discuss a few of these key ethical concerns.

The protection of respondents and research participants is paramount to all feminist scholars. Only if no identifying information about research participants is obtained can researchers guarantee true **anonymity**. In this way, no identifying information is ever recorded that could link respondents or participants to what they said or did. If identifying information is obtained, it is critical to protect participants' **confidentiality** by using pseudonyms in place of real names or geographic locations (Bachman and Schutt 2003). It is also important to keep all identifying information protected, such as storing it under lock and key and destroying it when the research is complete.

Voluntary participation in a study is not often a problem when researchers can obtain a signed, informed consent form from all participants. However, in participant observation studies, it can be more difficult, particularly when the researcher is covertly observing a setting. Even when the researcher's role is more open, interpreting the standard of voluntary participation still can be difficult. The issue becomes even more problematic when interviewing or observing minors. Feminist research, like all research, must grapple with these issues and ensure that committees, such as institutional review boards in universities, approve of their plan to protect human subjects from potential harm as well as to ensure their confidentiality and anonymity.

It is a given by the majority of feminist and nonfeminist researchers alike that if any potential harm could come to research participants, this should be disclosed fully. When most of us think of harm, we imagine egregious cases like the Tuskegee syphilis experiment. However, the protection of human subjects is not limited to experiments that may pose physical harm to participants but includes potential harm to survey respondents and other research participants.

We have already mentioned the surveys that solicit information about violent victimizations, such as the National Crime Victimization Survey (NCVS) and the National Violence Against Women Survey (NVAWS). Whenever sensitive subject matter such as rape and intimate-perpetrated assaults is investigated, particular attention should be given to the protection of respondents. As Johnson (1996) reminded us, "Researchers must never lose sight of the possibility that with every telephone call, respondent[s] could be living with an abusive [partner] and that their safety could be jeopardized should they learn of the content of the survey" (p. 52). In addition, by asking respondents to recall incidents of abuse and violence, there is always the possibility of causing victims serious emotional trauma. Feminist researchers would contend that researchers have the responsibility to provide safety should respondents need it. Although the NCVS does provide its respondents with confidentiality and anonymity, it is interesting to note that the U.S. Department of Justice does not extend these other safety protections to its survey respondents. In contrast, respondents in the NVAWS were given a toll-free number they could call if they needed to suddenly hang up during the course of the interview (e.g., if they felt danger). In addition, interviewers of the NVAWS were instructed to contact an attending supervisor at the first sign a respondent was becoming upset or emotionally distraught. These supervisors were provided with a sourcebook from the National Domestic Violence Coalition that listed rape crisis and domestic violence hotline numbers from around the country.

The power dynamics inherent in the research process also are of interest to feminist researchers. Feminist research, regardless of the methodology employed, generally seeks to minimize the power and control dynamics inherent in the research process (DeVault, 1999). For example, Ann Oakley (1981) argued that conventional interviewing techniques that include a one-way process, in which researchers define who is being "researched" and where there is no real social interaction, invalidate women's subjective experiences as women and as people. Inherent in this discussion are the notions of power and control. For example, when the interview process is a one-way street, those being interviewed are often treated as mere objects. Once the interview is over, they are sent on their way. This, of course, represents a hierarchical relationship with the researcher controlling the research participants (Stanley and Wise 1983).

Many feminist researchers, particularly those conducting qualitative research, strive to balance this power. For example, when conducting interviews with victims of intimate partner violence and with medical service providers to such victims, Williamson (2000) did several things to make the research process more collaborative. First, she sent those she interviewed a copy of the transcript of their first interview to ensure that they had the opportunity to revise and verify their testimonies. Williamson also maintained contact with the women after her project was complete. She explained,

> Attempting to establish a collaborative relationship between myself and the participants was the only way to ensure awareness of the process in which we were engaging. The only way I could attempt to establish such a relationship was to be honest about my own experiences, to answer questions about the research and my personal investment and rewards from it, to give advice when requested, and to acknowledge the power dynamics of the research process. (Williamson 2000, 142)

The assumed objectivity of researchers is also questioned by many feminist scholars and should be included in this discussion. Many believe objectivity to be a myth and contend that the subjectivity of the researcher must always be acknowledged (Oakley 1981). In reality, it is almost impossible to separate our own experience from what we are observing. Indeed, many of us select an area of inquiry based on our experiences. The important point, many believe, is to be open and honest about the research process and how our own experience informs our work.

Some scholars go even further in making our experiences a priority. For example, some feminist scholars believe that one's experiences not only should be noted but also should become the center of research attention as well. As Scott (1999) wrote, "Experience is not a word we can do without. . . . [I]t serves as a way of talking about what happened, of establishing difference and similarity, of claiming knowledge that is 'unassailable'" (p. 96). Scott (1999) also insisted that we must analyze our experiences and the political nature of their construction, not just accept them as is. "Experience is at once always already an interpretation and something that needs to be interpreted. What counts as experience is neither self-evident nor straightforward; it is always contested, and always therefore political" (p. 96). Of course, a rejection of the notion of objectivity does not mean a rejection of a concern for being accurate.

Linking Research and Activism

One of the fundamental threads that run through all feminist methodology is related to social activism. Specifically, most feminist scholars attempt to use their research to advance a feminist agenda by challenging and questioning constructions of gender and power imbalances in many forms, including those based on race/ethnicity, socioeconomic status, and sexuality (Dankoski 2000). Criminological research conducted through a feminist lens strives to raise public consciousness, mobilize political support to change unjust policy, and encourage structural reform.

Examples of feminist action-oriented research in the literature are far too numerous to discuss here. In fact, virtually every aspect of the criminal justice system as it affects women and women's lives has benefited from feminist action research, from illuminating the special needs of both female victims and female offenders to critically evaluating the legal statutes and procedures that pertain to women's lives. For illustrative purposes, we will highlight the reform of state and federal rape statutes that have been the product of action-oriented research by many groups, including feminist researchers.

For feminist researchers, the way rape offenders and rape victims were handled by the criminal justice system could not be separated from the perceptions and stereotypes of rape that were held by society. Such perceptions included the following: (1) the belief that rape was not a serious violent offense, (2) the notion that acquaintance rapes or rapes perpetrated by intimates were less serious than and different from those perpetrated by strangers, and (3) the various rape myths, which suggested, among other things, that rape victims were somehow partially to blame for their own victimization. For feminist researchers, then, very important consequences of rape law reform were to educate the public about the seriousness of all forms of sexual assault, to reduce the stigma experienced by victims of rape, and to neutralize rape myth stereotypes (Rose 1977).

In addition to these ideological and symbolic consequences, rape law reforms were also expected to have instrumental effects on the way rape cases were handled by the criminal justice system. Before reforms, rape offenders infrequently were arrested for their crimes because many victims were reluctant to report the offense. When they were arrested, many were not convicted or were convicted of a less serious offense because frequently the victim, rather than the offender, was put on trial. For example, the defense would use the victim's own sexual history to question her lack of consent (Horney and Spohn 1991). Further, feminist scholars contended that when a rapist was convicted of raping a victim he knew, incarceration was rare because the public did not view victimization by an acquaintance or intimate as "real rape" (Estrich 1987).

In short, the symbolic and instrumental effects of rape law reform were expected to increase rape reports by victims and rates of arrest, conviction, and imprisonment of offenders. Have rape reforms had the intended consequences? The results of the extant literature investigating the efficacy of reforms in various states are somewhat equivocal. Although some scholars have found modest increases in the number of arrests and conviction rates (Bachman and Smith 1994; Caringella-MacDonald 1984; Marsh, Geist, and Caplan 1982), others have found that (except for a few jurisdictions that experienced extremely zealous reforms), some jurisdictions have not had significant increases in either the reporting of rape cases or arrest and conviction rates for rape since reforms were instituted (Horney and Spohn 1991; Largen 1988; Loh 1980; Polk 1985).

Of course, the reform process of existing statutes is ongoing in nature. For example, even though most state-level reform statutes were enacted during the mid- to late 1970s, virtually every state's original statutes continue to undergo numerous revisions based on appellate court decisions. For this reason, monitoring the adjudication of rape by the criminal justice system continues to be on the research agenda of many feminist researchers.

Conclusion

Feminist voices have made important contributions to the ways in which researchers think differently about research, what constitutes knowledge, how to acquire it, and how it is used for social action and change. We started this chapter by noting that feminist methodology in the areas of criminology and criminal justice was not so much a method as it was a lens guiding many aspects of research, including the questions readers ask, how we go about answering them, and the application of our results to social action.

We want to underscore the fact that research using a feminist lens not only guides methodology, but also affects the way in which one interprets the empirical observations, be they of a qualitative or quantitative nature. We hope that you have learned that feminist thought regarding research methods has added tremendously to the discipline of criminology. As Simpson (1989) stated, "[Feminist theory] is best understood as both a world view and a social movement that encompasses assumptions and beliefs about the origins and consequences of gendered social organization as well as strategic directions and actions of social change" (p. 606). The infusion of a feminist voice into criminological research has helped transform society's antiquated notions and sexist stereotypes concerning victimization and offending committed by and against women.

Study/Discussion Questions

1. What defines a *positivist approach* versus a *constructivism approach* to research?

2. What general assumption do most feminist researchers begin with?

3. How do qualitative research methods contribute to a feminist approach to research?

4. What is *triangulation* and how has it been utilized in feminist research?

5. As noted, power dynamics in research are of interest to feminist researchers. Explain how this issue has been addressed within research.

6. How does a feminist approach/lens affect one's research methods?

Note

1. The program eventually emerged as the Graduate Consortium in Women's Studies at Radcliffe College. The program mandate was to bring together faculty from different fields to teach interdisciplinary courses on topics of interest to feminist graduate students from many disciplines.

References

Bachman, R. (2000). A comparison of annual incidence rates and contextual characteristics of intimate-partner violence against women from the National Crime Victimization Survey (NCVS) and the National Violence Against Women Survey (NVAWS). *Violence Against Women, 6,* 839–867.

Bachman, R., and Schutt, R. (2003). *The practice of research in criminology and criminal justice.* Thousand Oaks, CA: Pine Forge Press.

Bachman, R., and Smith, P. (1994). The adjudication of rape since reforms: Examining the probability of conviction and incarceration at the national and three state levels. *Criminal Justice Policy Review, 6,* 342–358.

Bachman, R., and Taylor, B. (1994). The measurement of rape and family violence by the redesigned National Crime Victimization Survey. *Justice Quarterly, 11,* 702–714.

Britton, D. M. (2000). Feminism in criminology: Engendering the outlaw. *Annals of the American Academy on Political and Social Sciences, 571,* 57–76.

Caringella-MacDonald, S. (1984). Sexual assault prosecution: An examination of model rape legislation in Michigan. *Women and Politics, 4,* 65–79.

Daly, K. (1994) *Gender, crime, and punishment.* New Haven, CT: Yale University Press.

Daly, K., and Chesney-Lind, M. (1988). Feminism and criminology. *Justice Quarterly, 5,* 497–538.

Danner, M. J., and Carmody, D. C. (2001). Missing gender in cases of infamous school violence: Investigating research and media explanations. *Justice Quarterly, 18,* 87–114.

Dankoski, M. E. (2000). What makes research feminist? *Journal of Feminist Family Therapy, 12,* 3–19.

DeVault, M. L. (1999). *Liberating method: Feminism and social research.* Philadelphia: Temple University Press.

Estrich, S. (1987). *Real rape.* Cambridge, MA: Harvard University Press.

Fine, M. (1989). The politics of research and activism: Violence against women. *Gender & Society, 3,* 549–558.

Fisher, B. S., Cullen, F. T., and Turner, M. G. (2001). *Sexual victimization of college women.* Washington, DC: U.S. Department of Justice, Bureau of Justice Statistics.

Flavin, J. (2001). Feminism for the mainstream criminologist: An invitation. *Journal of Criminal Justice, 29,* 271–285.

Gelsthorpe, L. (1990). Feminist methodologies in criminology: A new approach or old wine in new bottles? In L. Gelsthorpe and A. Morris (Eds.), *Feminist perspectives in criminology* (pp. 89–106). Philadelphia: Open University Press.

Gelsthorpe, L., and Morris, A. (Eds.). (1990). *Feminist perspectives in criminology*. Philadelphia: Open University Press.

Guba, E. G., and Lincoln, Y. S. (1989). *Fourth generation evaluation*. Newbury Park, CA: Sage.

———. (1994). Competing paradigms in qualitative research. In N. K. Denzin and Y. S. Lincoln (Eds.), *Handbook of qualitative research* (pp. 105–117). Thousand Oaks, CA: Sage.

Harding, S. (1986). *The science question in feminism*. Ithaca, NY: Cornell University Press.

Harrison, P., and Beck, A. (2003). *Prisoners in 2002*. Washington, DC: U.S. Department of Justice, Bureau of Justice Statistics.

Hesse-Biber, S., Gilmartin, C., and Lydenberg, R. (Eds.). (1999). *Feminist approaches to theory and methodology: An interdisciplinary reader*. New York: Oxford University Press.

Horney, J., and Spohn C. (1991). Rape law reform and instrumental change in six urban jurisdictions. *Law and Society Review*, 25, 117–153.

Johnson, H. (1996). *Dangerous domains: Violence against women in Canada*. Toronto, Canada: ITP, An International Thomson Publishing Company.

Koss, M. P. (1992). The underdetection of rape: Methodological choices influence incidence estimates. *Journal of Social Issues*, 48, 61–75.

Largen, M. A. (1988). Rape-law reform: An analysis. In A. W. Burgess (Ed.), *Rape and sexual assault II* (pp. 271–292). New York: Garland Press.

Larson, C. J. (1993). *Pure and applied sociological theory: Problems and issues*. New York: Harcourt Brace Jovanovich.

Loh, W. D. (1980). The impact of common law and reform rape statutes on prosecution: An empirical study. *Washington Law Review*, 55, 543–652.

Lucashenko, M. (1996). Violence against indigenous women: Public and private dimensions. *Violence Against Women*, 2, 378–390.

Lyncy, M., and Bogen, D. (1997). Sociology's asociological "core": An examination of textbook sociology in light of the sociology of scientific knowledge. *American Sociological Review*, 62, 481–493.

Marsh, J. C., Geist, A., and Caplan, N. (1982). *Rape and the limits of law reform*. Boston: Auburn House.

Martin, S. E., and Jurik, N. C. (1996). *Doing justice, doing gender: Women in law and criminal justice occupations*. Thousand Oaks, CA: Sage.

Miller, J. (2000). Feminist theories of women's crime: Robbery as a case study. In S. Simpson (Ed.), *Of crime and criminality: The use of theory in everyday life* (pp. 25–46). Thousand Oaks, CA: Pine Forge Press.

Miller, S. (1999). *Gender and community policing: Walking the talk*. Boston: Northeastern University Press.

Naffine, N. (1996). *Feminism and criminology*. Philadelphia: Temple University Press.

Oakley, A. (1981). Interviewing women: A contradiction in terms. In H. Roberts (Ed.), *Doing feminist research* (pp. 30–61). London: Routledge and Kegan Paul.

Polk, K. (1985). Rape reform and criminal justice processing. *Crime and Delinquency*, 3, 191–204.

Reinharz, S. (1992). *Feminist methods in social research*. New York: Oxford University Press.

Rolison, G. L, Bates, K. A., Poole, M. J., and Jacob, M. (2002). Prisoners of war: Black female incarceration at the end of the 1980s. *Social Justice*, 29, 131–143.

Rose, V. M. (1977) Rape as a social problem: A by-product of the feminist movement. *Social Problems*, 25, 75–89.

Rubin, H. J., and Rubin, I. S. (1995). *Qualitative interviewing: The art of hearing data*. Thousand Oaks, CA: Sage.

Schwandt, T. A. (1994). Constructionist, interpretivist approaches to human inquiry. In N. K. Denzin and Y. S. Lincoln (Eds.), *Handbook of qualitative research* (pp. 118–137). Thousand Oaks: Sage.

Scott, J. W. (1999). The evidence of experience. In S. Hesse-Biber, C. Gilmartin, and R. Lydenberg (Eds.), *Feminist approaches to theory and methodology: An interdisciplinary reader* (pp. 79–99). New York: Oxford University Press.

Simpson, S. S. (1989). Feminist theory, crime and justice. *Criminology*, 27, 605–631.

Smart, C. (1995). *Law, crime, and sexuality: Essays in feminism.* London: Sage.

Stanley, L., and Wise, S. (1983). Back into the personal, or our attempt to construct "feminist research." In G. Bowles and R. D. Klein (Eds.), *Theories of women's studies* (pp. 192–209). London: Routledge and Kegan Paul.

Tjaden, P., and Thoennes, N. (2000). *Extent, nature, and consequences of intimate partner violence: Findings from the National Violence Against Women Survey.* Washington, DC: U.S. Department of Justice, National Institute of Justice.

Weber, M. (1949). *The methodology of the social sciences.* New York: Free Press.

Williamson, E. (2000). Caught in contradictions: Conducting feminist action-oriented research within an evaluated research programme. In J. Radford, M. Friedberg, and L. Harne (Eds.), *Women, violence, and strategies for action* (pp. 136–148). Buckingham: Open University Press.

Yick, A. G. (2001). Feminist theory and status inconsistency theory: Applications to domestic violence in Chinese immigrant families. *Violence Against Women, 7,* 545–562. ◆

5
Age-Graded Pathways to Victimization and Offending Among Women and Girls

Catherine Kaukinen
Angela R. Gover
Stephanie A. Hays

In this chapter you will learn the following:

- How to study gender and crime from a life course or age-graded perspective

- That age is one of the most important predictors of life events and affects not only the type of victimization likely to be experienced by females but also the subsequent type of offending in which females are likely to engage

- How early victimization and offending may affect transitions to adolescence and adulthood

- The consequences of female victimization at various stages of the life course

- How age-graded pathways to victimization and offending vary by gender

- The relationship between victimization and offending among girls and women

Introduction

Traditionally criminological research has examined the causes of crime and delinquency among samples of boys and men.

Similarly, the criminal justice system's concentration on male offenders has resulted in the development of policies, programs, and treatment regimes that potentially ignore the unique problems and issues faced by girls and women who have contact with the law (Bloom and Covington 1998). The historic focus on boys and men has limited the examination and theoretical understanding of girls' and women's offending behavior. Although more recent research has explored offending behavior among girls and young women, many researchers have concluded that family, peer, and school factors that lead to criminality and the developmental processes by which these factors operate are similar for males and females. In contrast, some criminologists and feminist researchers suggest that the qualitatively unique nature of female victimization, differences in the extent of involvement in crime and the character of male and female criminality, and more recent increases in female offending provide a justification for treating women offenders as a separate and unique population (Scully-Whitaker 2000). This had led researchers to acknowledge and recognize factors that may uniquely affect the lives of girls and women, shaping their risk for criminal offending, including women's experiences as both victims and offenders.

While earlier research on women offending sometimes viewed victimized women as pushed into criminality through their interactions with criminal men, more recently some scholars have viewed female criminality as a phenomenon embedded in unique life course experiences. For example, since young children and adolescent girls are more likely to experience physical abuse and sexual violence at the hands of caregivers and dating partners, the behavioral outcomes and offending consequences of this abuse are unique to young girls and teenagers. An age-graded perspective of victimization experienced by girls and women suggests that violent experiences may culminate in unique life influences that can contribute to their risk of offending. In other words, the long-term impact of violent victimization and subsequent involvement in a variety of negative behavioral patterns may depend on the stage in the life course in which violence occurs. According to Kilpatrick, Saunders, and Smith (2003), specific types of violent victimization vary in terms of their relationship to offending, and some types of victimization are more important for predicting problems and behavioral outcomes for girls.

Previous researchers have drawn on a variety of theoretical perspectives to explore the impact of victimization experiences on behavioral outcomes. For example, some research conceptualizes victimization as one of many forms of marginalization that lead girls away from the protection of adolescence and toward a pathway of offending and future victimization (Gaardner and Belknap 2002; Hagan and Foster 2001). However, those drawing on derailment theory (Chesney-Lind 1989; Gilfus 1992) suggest that the relationship between victimization and offending is indirect. That is, victimized women and girls use a variety of survival tactics in dealing with the impact of victimization, and these in turn have the consequence of alienating them and potentially leading them into offending. Alternatively, some researchers suggest that women use violence as a direct response to their victimization, so offending behavior in these cases may be seen as a form of self-defense. Additionally, researchers have adopted several different methodological techniques and have used data from a variety of diverse samples that may have implications for exploring the connections between victimization and offending. Research using longitudinal data offers one of the best tests of a causal relationship between victimization and offending (Hagan and Foster 2001; Widom and Maxfield 2001). Other researchers have explored the connections between victimization and offending using clinical samples drawn from a variety of sources, including samples of domestic violence victims (Hattendorf, Ottens, and Lomax 1999; Stout 1991), women recruited from substance abuse programs (Austin 2003), and those living in correctional settings (Chesney-Lind and Pasko 2004; Gaarder and Belknap 2002).

This chapter reviews studies that examine victimization experiences that are more often experienced by girls and young women. An examination of such experiences provides a more in-depth understanding of specific types of female offending that are likely to occur during childhood, adolescence, and adulthood. By looking at the impact of child abuse and maltreatment, we explore the connection between sexual violence and maladaptive reactions to sexual trauma, such as drug use and abuse, running away, and delinquency. We further examine the effect of sexual violence on adolescent girls while also exploring the connection between offending and young women's experience with dating violence. Finally, we examine the research that identifies the long-term influence of victimization in the lives of women and discuss the immediate consequences of intimate partner violence for women's involvement in crime and violence.

Traditional Causes of Delinquency and the Role of Victimization

Criminologists who examine factors that motivate or protect adolescents from involvement in criminal activity have traditionally focused on the impact that family, peer, and school variables can have on both male and female offending. While many researchers have concluded that these factors similarly shape offending behavior for both girls and boys, some scholars suggest that girls are differentially exposed to such influences (Simons, Miller, and Aigner 1980; Smith and Paternoster 1987). According to these scholars, the processes by which parental, peer, and school factors operate are different for boys and girls (Johnson 1979). For example, Hagan (1989) suggested that maternal efforts to provide informal social control are more likely to focus on controlling daughters than sons. Girls are simply supervised more strictly and raised differently than boys. This control over the movements and activities of girls in turn shapes their opportunities to be influenced and pressured by their peers. Mears, Ploeger, and Warr (1998) suggested that girls' rates of offending are therefore different from boys because girls are both differentially exposed to delinquent peer groups and are more strongly socialized to be morally restrained. So while parents and peers are important factors that shape the risk of offending for both boys and girls, the operation of these factors differs markedly for boys and girls.

Given differences in the process by which traditional causes of crime operate in shaping girls' behavior and because of an increased focus on female offending more generally, researchers have been exploring whether additional factors heighten the risk for female criminality. This research has begun to identify factors that may be unique to female offending, including an examination of previous experiences with violent victimization in determining behavioral outcomes and shaping criminal trajectories. It is likely that qualitatively different experiences with violence may uniquely influence girls' lives and thereby contribute to their risk of offending. In this respect, more studies are now focusing on how early childhood sexual victimization contributes to girls' and women's offending later in the life course. Some researchers have suggested that the key to understanding differences between girls' and women's lives compared with boys' and men's lives involves increased attention to female victimization (Katz 2000).

Victimization and Offending as Age-Graded Events

Life course research suggests that age is one of the most important predictors of life experiences and events. Violent victimization and involvement in criminal offending are events that often occur early in the life course and have implications ranging from child and adolescent development to successful transitions to adulthood. More important, the qualitative nature of experiences with violence varies over the life course, and the meaning, significance, and long-term impact of violent victimization will be determined by the stage in the life course in which violence occurs (Macmillan 2001).

Opportunities for criminal offending and factors that shape the risk for offending similarly vary over the life course. Age restricts activities during childhood and adolescence while family, peer, and school factors play a prominent role in the lives of young girls and boys. Alternatively, adulthood presents both opportunities and economic strains that shape and determine the types of criminal involvement engaged in by adult women. Age therefore not only determines the type of victimization experienced by girls and young women but also determines the types of offending that may result as a consequence of victimization. For example, given that adolescent girls are more likely to experience physical abuse and sexual violence at the hands of caregivers and dating partners (Tjaden and Thoennes 2000), the impact and offending consequences of this abuse—such as running away, alcohol and drug use and abuse, and other delinquent behaviors that may be limited to adolescence—are unique to teenage girls. In contrast, some adult women have long histories of violent victimization in both childhood and adolescence, substantial involvement in a variety of criminal activities, and continuing experiences with violence and coercive control in intimate relationships. These prior life course experiences with violence and offending, often combined with women's economic dependence on their male partners, may heighten the risk that women will engage in violent behavior and, albeit less often, turn to potentially lethal violence in self-defense.

Childhood Victimization and Delinquency

During the past two decades, criminology researchers started focusing on specific issues related to girls' and women's offending (See Chesney-Lind and Pasko 2004, 14–15 for a discussion). Researchers started questioning the validity of research and theory based on boys and then simply applied to the behavior and lives of girls (See Daley and Chesney-Lind 1988 for a discussion). Additionally, more recent increases in girls' delinquent behavior and drug use and some modest increases in violent offending have spurred interest in the offending behavior of girls. For example, between 1988 and 1997, delinquent acts among females increased by 89 percent (Scahill 2000). During this same time, however, the number of females committed to a juvenile residential facility increased by 105 percent and the number of females placed on probation increased by 129 percent (Scahill 2000). Research suggests that increases of females in the criminal justice system are directly related to both increases in the actual commission of simple assault and changes in how the criminal justice system treats female offenders (Steffensmeier 1993).

Background

The Office for Victims of Crimes (2002) defines *child abuse* as "any act or conduct that endangers or impairs a child's physical or emotional health or development." Child abuse includes any damage done to a child that cannot be reasonably explained and is often represented by an injury or series of injuries appearing to be intentional or deliberate in nature. Child abuse therefore includes physical abuse, sexual abuse, emotional abuse, and neglect. *Physical abuse* includes behaviors directed at a child that cause both major and minor physical injuries. Examples of major physical injuries include bone fracture, dislocation/sprains, and internal injuries. Examples of minor physical injuries include bruises, welts, or similar injuries that do not place the child's life at risk. *Sexual abuse* includes the involvement of a child in any sexual act or situation, such as incest, exposure to indecent acts, exploitation, forcible or statutory rape, sexual assault, moles-

tation, involvement in child pornography, or sexual rituals. *Emotional abuse* can occur when an adult's behavior terrorizes a child and causes fear or anxiety and can include verbal abuse, belittlement, a lack of emotional availability, and behaviors on the part of the caretaker causes the child to have low self-esteem. This form of abuse includes harm inflicted on the victim's intellectual or mental capacity and inhibits normal functioning. *Neglect* is not one single action but rather a series of "inactions," such as failing to provide nourishment, clothing, shelter, health care, education, and supervision.

Both physical and sexual violence in childhood have a number of negative implications for child and adolescent development and later life course outcomes. Sexual violence in particular is associated with a number of unique and long-lasting consequences for both boys and girls (Kilpatrick, Saunders, and Smith 2003). These include delinquency, involvement in drug and alcohol abuse, and negative mental health outcomes. While the consequences of sexual violence influence the lives of both boys and girls, researchers (Kilpatrick, Saunders, and Smith 2003) point out that girls have a much greater risk of experiencing sexual violence as compared with boys (approximately 13 percent versus 3 percent for boys). Abused girls are typically victims of people they trust, such as members of their families and close family friends. Girls are also more likely to be abused earlier in life and for longer periods of time compared with boys (Simkins and Katz 2002). Studies have shown that up to 90 percent of incarcerated girls have experienced prior childhood abuse and sexual victimization (Calhoun, Jurgens, and Chen 1993). In addition, sexual violence is a phenomenon that primarily affects the lives and well-being of girls. The high prevalence of childhood and sexual victimization among inmates directs researchers to fully examine the connection between victimization and offending among girls. The following section provides an overview of the research findings specific to the relationship between physical abuse and sexual victimization, and delinquent and behavioral outcomes among girls.

Research Findings

Social science researchers have conducted hundreds of studies exploring the causes of childhood delinquency. Some of these studies examined the relationship between physical abuse experienced during childhood and subsequent delinquent behavior. Child development researchers (see Loeber and Hay 1997) clearly identify the role of early stressful life events in the development of negative behaviors. Unfortunately, many of the earlier studies looked only at the offending behavior of boys or did not conduct separate analyses for girls and boys.

In some of the most well-known studies on childhood abuse and crime, Cathy Spatz-Widom and her colleagues examined the connection between victimization and offending among girls. Using a longitudinal research design, they followed the lives of two groups of children from the same age cohort. One group consisted of children who were identified as victims of abuse, and the comparison group consisted of children who were not victims of abuse. This research clearly identified the connection between childhood abuse and neglect and delinquency (English, Widom, and Brandford 2001; Widom and Maxfield 2001). Interestingly, this research indicated that abused and victimized girls were at an increased risk for being arrested for violent offending, yet the same was not true for victimized boys. The likelihood of arrest among abused girls was almost two times that of the girls in the non-abused sample (English, Widom, and Brandford 2001; Widom and Maxfield 2001), but significant differences were not found between abused and non-abused boys.

More recently, researchers have also begun to explore the effect of corporal punishment on a variety of immediate behavioral outcomes among children (Brezina 1999), as well as the long-term implications for violence within intimate relationships of both victims and offenders (Simons, Lin, and Gordon 1998; Straus 2001). In outlining the most recent literature on the negative consequences of childhood corporal punishment for later behavioral and criminal outcomes, Straus (2001) argued for an examination of corporal punishment that calls into question the logic of spanking. He suggested that the difference between spanking and other disciplinary strategies is that when spanking does not work parents do not question its effectiveness as a disciplinary tool and generally believe other methods are less effective. So, when children repeat their misbehavior an hour or two later, parents often fail to perceive that spanking has the same high failure rate as other modes of discipline. Consequently, parents spank again and for as many times as it takes to ultimately secure compliance. Eventually, parents gain compliance through their consistent and persistent use of spanking. Yet, Straus pointed out that the same success could be achieved through the consistent and persistent use of non-physical punishments. Straus (2001) concluded that since "the benefits of avoiding corporal punishment are many, but they are virtually impossible for parents to perceive by observing their children," (p. 59) never-spank must be the message given to parents.

Dahlberg and Potter (2001) similarly suggested "that family environments that include harsh discipline, child maltreatment, spousal/partner violence, and a climate of conflict and hostility place children at increased risk for later violence" (p. 7). Research on the specific consequences of corporal punishment and spanking include an examination of the way in which physical punishment influences the risk for antisocial behavior, later child-to-parent violence, and dating violence. Research especially on the impact of corporal punishment for girls has included a focus on dating violence. For example, Foshee, Bauman, and Linder (1999) found that for both boys and girls, violence in the home increases the risk for the perpetration of dating violence. They suggested that an understanding of the connection between violence in the family of origin and dating violence is largely mediated through social learning (positive violence outcomes and aggressive conflict resolution strategies) as compared with social control processes (attachments to parents and conventional bonds).

Although researchers have devoted a tremendous amount of effort to examine and identify the impact of child abuse in general, few studies have used representative data to fully examine the behavioral outcomes associated with sexual victimization among girls. Recently, however, gender-specific research has focused on the consequences of sexual violence and its influence on offending among girls and women. For example, Siegel and Williams (2003) conducted a long-term follow-up of 411 girls who received medical treatment. Half of these girls were victims of sexual abuse. Twenty years later, researchers found that sexually abused females had higher rates of juvenile arrests, including violent offenses, property offenses, and running away. In fact, the sexually abused girls were significantly more likely than nonsexually abused girls to be arrested for violent offenses and running away. Fourteen percent of girls who were sexually abused were arrested for violent offenses. In comparison, only 5 percent of nonsexually abused girls were arrested for violent offenses. Additionally, Kilpatrick, Saunders, and Smith's (2003) analyses of the National Survey of Adolescents suggested that girls who are victims of sexual assault are five times more likely than girls who are not victims of sexual assault to have substance abuse problems and offend as juveniles.

Recent research suggests that female membership in gangs is higher than indicated by past official estimates, which has led to a research focus on female gang involvement. Some of this work has focused on how victimization during childhood and adolescence may lead girls to seek out support, comfort, and love from nonsocial and deviant influences in an attempt to find a "family." Gaarder and Belknap (2002) suggested that when girls, especially economically and racially disadvantaged girls, experience violence in the home, they may turn to a substitute family and, in particular, criminal influences on the street. This may lead girls into a variety of criminal pursuits, such as drug use, prostitution, and gang involvement. Gaarder and Belknap's (2002) qualitative research on girls in adult prison suggested that as a consequence of victimization experiences in the home and other difficulties at home and school, girls are more open to the opportunity to view gang involvement as an alternative socializing agent.

Other research on female gang participation suggests that females' risk of victimization within a gang is clearly shaped by gender roles. For example, membership in a gang increases a girl's risk of victimization from both retaliatory behavior associated with being in a gang and sexual and physical victimization from male gang members (Hunt and Joe-Laidler 2001; Miller 1998). For instance, Miller (1998) noted that young women adopting "masculine attributes" may increase their risk of victimization because they become more heavily involved in risky and delinquent behavior. At the same time their victimization experience (e.g., sexual victimization) may increase the likelihood that they are victimized in the future because they become viewed as "weaker" than their male gang counterparts (pp. 433–434). Female gang members may also be at risk of victimization through the experience of gang initiation, conflicts with rival gangs and conflicts with female gang members in their own and rival gangs (Hunt and Joe-Laider 2001). Yet, research points out that females often join gangs because they view the gang as a source of protection (Decker 1996; Joe and Chesney-Lind 1995; Miller 1998).

Research also reveals that girl gang members are victimized by their own gangs in ways that are unique to their gender role in the gang. For example, a number of studies show that in male-dominated gangs, girls are more likely to be sexually assaulted as a method of gang initiation (Fleisher 1995;

Miller 1998). Female gang members may be required to sleep with multiple male gang members as a method of initiation. Other research, however, suggests that the "sex object" concept does not play a major role in female gang involvement (Rosenbaum 1996). Sexual victimization in the gang may have more to do with the status of the particular female in the gang (Miller 1998). In general, both qualitative and quantitative research indicates that gang membership increases the risks of victimization for females. However, the risks are gendered in such ways that their overall risks of violent victimization are less than victimization risks for male gang members.

In addition to an increased risk of gang involvement and offending during adolescence, many victims of childhood abuse, and specifically sexual abuse, also suffer from a host of mental health consequences, including decreased self-esteem, psychological problems such as anxiety and depression, problems with trusting others, teen pregnancy, problems in schools, and other serious issues that girls face during adolescence (Garnefski and Arends 1998; Gover 2004a; Kilpatrick et al. 1987). For example, Kilpatrick, Saunders, and Smith (2003) found that sexually assaulted girls have a lifetime rate of posttraumatic stress disorder (PTSD) four times that of girls who have not been victims of sexual assault. Also, some victims of childhood sexual abuse run away from their abusive homes or use alcohol or other drugs as a way to cope with their emotional pain (Acoca 1995). These mental health and behavioral outcomes help to explain subsequent criminal involvement and violent offending as survival strategies while living on the street.

Overall, research clearly links early victimization experiences in childhood to later juvenile offending. Specifically, sexual violence may be a pivotal life course event that influences girls' risk for negative outcomes, including involvement in crime and delinquency. The following section examines dating violence and its relationship to female offending.

Dating Violence Vicimization and Offending

During the past two decades, dating violence in teen relationships has become an issue of heightened concern to the research, academic, and policy communities. Some research suggests that dating violence may serve as a potential link between childhood maltreatment and subsequent involvement in violent intimate partner relationships (Wolf and Foshee 2003). Hagan and Foster (2001) examined the impact and outcomes associated with adolescent victimization, including during dating. They suggested that adolescent victimization is a pivotal factor in "leading youth away from a protected adolescent role and into the vulnerabilities associated with adulthood" (Hagan and Foster 2001, 892). Similarly, Kessler and Magee (1994) suggested that adolescent victimization heightens the risk for emotional reactivity to interpersonal stress.

Background

The majority of adolescents experience their first dating relationship during high school (Jackson, Cram, and Seymour 2000) and many adolescents experience an episode of dating violence by the age of 15 (Henton et al. 1983). Researchers estimate that between 10 percent and 60 percent of high school and college students are involved in dating relationships as victims and/or offenders, with an average rate of 30 percent (Monson and Langhinrichsen-Rohling 2002; Neufeld, McNamara, and Ertl 1999; Shook et al. 2000). This large variation in the incidence of violence and abuse is a function of the types of physical aggression used as indicators of violence in dating relationships. For example, physical assault occurs in approximately 29 percent of all college dating relationships, while severe assaults (i.e., physical assaults resulting in injuries) occur in less than 7 percent of all dating relationships (Straus 2004). Despite the variation in estimates, research suggests that adolescents and college women are vulnerable to dating violence because it is during this age period that romantic relationships begin.

Some dating violence research indicates that violence perpetration may be more prevalent among women compared with men (Silverman et al. 2001; Straus 2004; Wolf and Foshee 2003). A common explanation for adolescent women's greater perpetration of violence is that women and girls are acting in self-defense (Harned 2001). Other studies, however, find similar victimization rates between young men and women (Chase, Treboux, and O'Leary 2002; Harned 2001; Katz, Kuffel, and Coblentz 2002; Straus 2004). It is important to note nevertheless, that the most severe types of violence resulting in injuries are more often inflicted by males on their female partners (Johnson 1995; Straus 2004). Additionally, women and adolescent girls are more likely than males to officially report their experiences with partner violence to the police and social service providers (Kaukinen 2002b). Women and adolescent girls are also more likely to report their violence perpetration to survey researchers (Jackson 1999). Jackson (1999) suggested that young men seem to be less inclined than young women to report their own perpetration of violence because it is not socially appropriate for men to physically hurt women. While studies have clearly established that adolescent girls and young women are both victims and perpetrators of violence in dating relationships, recent research has focused on the different causes of female-perpetrated versus male-perpetrated intimate violence, and other studies have examined the mental health and behavioral consequences of dating violence for girls' transitions to adulthood. The section that follows reviews the recent studies involving adolescent and college women as both victims and offenders within the context of dating violence.

Research Findings

As noted, some research suggests that adolescent girls are as equally or more likely than boys to be the perpetrators of violence within a dating relationship. For example, Wolf and Foshee's (2003) recent study of eighth and ninth graders found that 28 percent of adolescent girls reported perpetrating violence in a previous dating relationship compared with 15 percent of adolescent boys. Among the girls who perpetrated violence against their boyfriends, many experienced violence themselves and/or as a child witnessed spousal violence between their parents. In contrast, a study involving university undergraduates found comparable rates of victimization for males and females (Katz, Kuffel, and Coblentz 2002). However, female perpetrators engaged in higher rates of "moderate" violence compared with males, while both males and females sustained low levels of severe violence.

Research on dating violence points to important overlaps in both perpetration and victimization. For example, a recent survey of undergraduate women at a university found that approximately one-third were involved in a violent relationship as either a victim or perpetrator, or both (Lewis, Travea, and Fremouw 2002). The young women in this study who were both the victims and perpetrators of violence had lower self-esteem and were more likely to have witnessed their fathers victimize their mothers during their childhood, compared with females who were not involved in violent relationships.

While most research on adult women suggests that they are actually less likely than men to engage in the most severe forms of intimate partner violence (Johnson 1995), adolescent girls appear to have a heightened risk for violence perpetration within dating relationships often greater than that of boys. Given these facts, it is important to identify the causes of this violent behavior during adolescence among girls and, at the same time, to examine differences in the context of male-perpetrated and female-perpetrated violence. Monson and Langhinrichsen-Rohling's (2002) study of male and female university students found that young women were less likely than men to perpetrate sexual victimization. At the same time, these university women were more likely than university men to perpetrate non-sexual violence against a dating partner. As compared with the male perpetrators, young women who engaged in dating violence were more likely to have been the victims of childhood sexual abuse and were less likely to have psychological problems. Consistent with prior research, violence perpetrated by these young women was less severe than violence perpetrated by young men (Archer 2000; Johnson 1995). Dating violence at the hands of male perpetrators has been found to increase fear and concerns for safety among young women (Monson and Langhinrichsen-Rohling 2002).

With respect to the risk of victimization, Cleveland, Herrera, and Stuewig's (2003) analyses of data from the National Longitudinal Study of Adolescent Heath found that the protective factors that insulate girls from the risk of violence include a good relationship with their mother, a high GPA, and being attached to school. In contrast, alcohol use and depression among high school girls increased the likelihood of experiencing dating violence. Similarly, lifestyle choices and health-related risk-taking behaviors heighten high school girls' risk for dating violence (Gover 2004b).

While these studies underscore that female adolescents are at risk for being both victims and perpetrators of dating violence, it is also crucial to identify the life course outcomes associated with adolescent violence. Researchers have clearly identified a number of long-term psychological consequences of violence, including reduced self-esteem, negative self-identity, and increased feelings of helplessness (Horowitz et al. 1980; Janoff-Bulman 1979; Janoff-Bulman and Frieze 1983; Margolin and Gordis 2000). Violence during adolescence has also been associated with a number of early adolescent role exits, including running away, teenage pregnancy, and dropping out of school (Hagan and Foster 2001). Victims of violence may also use and abuse alcohol and drugs as a maladaptive coping strategy (Banaji and Steele 1989; Flannery et al. 1998; Runtz and

Schallow 1997) or as a form of self-medication to alleviate the symptoms associated with victimization (Fischbach and Herbert 1997; Jasinski, Williams, and Siegel 2000; Widom, Ireland, and Glynn 1995). Each of these behavioral outcomes may be particularly problematic for adolescent development and may have implications on one's successful transition to adulthood. At the same time, some research suggests that there are important race differences in the short- and long-term impact of violence. For example, while depression is often an outcome associated with violence among white and Latina women (Kaukinen and DeMaris 2005), African Americans are often less likely to experience depression as a consequence of sexual assault, and are more likely to respond to violence by withdrawing and/or through anger and aggression (Bell and Jenkins 1991; Sanders-Philips et al. 1995).

Our examination of adolescent dating violence and other violence perpetrated by girls has highlighted the nature of adolescent girls' involvement in violence and the continuity of violence and negative outcomes over the life course. We have also shown a connection between early childhood victimization experiences of girls and their predisposition to becoming both perpetrators and victims of dating violence during adolescence and the influence that these prior experiences may have on their transition to adulthood. The next section examines the relationship between life course experiences with violent victimization and adult criminality among women.

Violent Victimization and Adult Criminality

Over the past several decades, women's presence in the criminal justice system has dramatically increased (Beck 2000; Chesney-Lind 2000). Regardless of this fact, the combination of women and crime has continued to be relatively overlooked within criminological literature. While overall incarceration rates have been increasing during the past several years, rates for females have been growing at a faster pace compared with rates for males (Beck 2000). In addition, the number of women placed in community corrections has also increased.

Background

Despite their increased involvement in crime, women have been viewed by criminologists as posing a minimal threat to society and participating in criminal acts at low levels (Smart, 1976). Common characteristics among women offenders include being young, poor, of a minority race, undereducated, single and responsible for children, and having a history of violent victimization (Greenfield and Snell 1999; Snell 1994). Women offenders are not typically incarcerated for participating in serious violent crime (Chesney-Lind 1994). Instead, women, and in particular racially and economically marginalized women, are usually incarcerated for their involvement in nonviolent property crimes, such as forgery, embezzlement, larceny, or theft, and a considerable number of offenses related to drugs and prostitution (American Correctional Association 1990; Chesney-Lind and Pollock 1995).

In examining the connections among girls' experiences with violence, offending, and incarceration, Gaarder and Belknap have pointed to a continued need for feminist scholarship that investigates the "interlocking systems of race, class, and gender oppression." These areas of oppression not only place minority women at greater risk for experiencing victimization but also increase the risk that their offending will be viewed and treated as deviant (2002, 487). In their analysis of the life histories of girls who are later transferred to the adult system, these researchers examined the complex connection between women's experience with violence, abuse, and criminal offending and the responsibility they take for their involvement in crime and their current treatment within an adult women's prison. Gaarder and Belknap concluded that the interlocking oppressions associated with gender, race, class, and sexuality have brought

them to the "blurred domain of victimization and offending" (2002, p. 509). For women offenders, the boundaries between victim and offender are not as "clear cut" as they seem. Women often turn to crime as a survival response after experiencing violence at an early age. Women often engage in crimes such as prostitution, theft, and drug dealing as a means of surviving on the street. As with adolescent girls who are victimized, women may also use and abuse drugs and alcohol as a coping strategy to escape the emotional pain of their experiences.

Research Findings

Initial research on the connections between women's experiences with violence and offending conceptualized abused women as being driven into crime. More recent work has attempted to view offending and victimization as overlapping and reciprocal events in the lives of women. While victimization heightens the risk for substance abuse and offending, involvement in crime in turn increases the risk of subsequent victimization. Studies that have focused on the overlap of victimization and offending in the lives of women include research on both arrested and incarcerated samples of women.

To examine the relationship between victimization and offending, researchers have interviewed women who have been arrested for crime. Using both cross-sectional and longitudinal analyses, women who had previously experienced physical and/or sexual abuse during childhood were found to be twice as likely as non-abused women to be arrested during adulthood (English, Widom, and Brandford 2001; Siegel and Williams 2003; Widom and Maxfield 2001). Compared to women in the general population, women confined to correctional institutions are two to three times more likely to have histories of childhood sexual abuse (Harlow 1999). For example, Chesney-Lind and Rodriguez's (1983) interviews with women in prison suggested that early victimization experiences have an impact on pathways to crime. Similar to women in studies that examine victimization and offending relationships during childhood and adolescence, the women they interviewed who were physically and sexually abused during adulthood became involved in drug use, prostitution, and other criminal involvement. Involvement in criminal pursuits on the street in turn also heightened the risk for subsequent victimization. Similarly, Gilfus' (1992) interviews with incarcerated women suggested that most women have experienced and witnessed multiple types of violence, abuse, and neglect during childhood and that delinquent and criminal behaviors served them as survival strategies.

Compared with male offenders, female offenders are disproportionately victims of violence and abuse during childhood and later during the life course in intimate relationships. Incarcerated women are more likely than incarcerated males to be the victims of childhood violence and abuse (Langworthy, Barnes, and Curtis 1998). Chesney-Lind and Pasko's (2004) research suggested that 12 percent of incarcerated men experienced some form of prior abuse compared with 43 percent of women in prison. Overall, researchers have explored the relationships between victimization and offending using a variety of methodological techniques and data from a variety of sources (i.e., clinical samples and samples of incarcerated women). Together, the literature indicates that prior and current experiences with victimization are a prevalent reality for adult female offenders. This body of work suggests that victimization early in the life course is a key ingredient to understanding pathways to offending and victimization over the life course for females.

Women's experience with violence and abuse within their intimate relationships is particularly relevant to explaining why a small number of women, when faced with limited options and alternatives, kill their intimate partners. The following section examines the relationship between victimization and offending among women who kill their intimate partners.

Intimate Partner Violence and Women Who Kill Their Batterers

Over the past 20 years, research and policy has increasingly focused on victimization among intimates, which includes current or former spouses and current or former boyfriends and girlfriends. Females are five to eight times more likely than males to be victimized by an intimate partner (Greenfield et al. 1998). Each year between 1992 and 1996, more than 960,000 incidents of intimate partner violence were committed against women (Greenfield et al. 1998). Similar to non-lethal forms of intimate partner violence, the vast majority of intimate partner homicide victims are women. In 2000, 1,247 women compared with 440 men were killed by an intimate partner (Rennison 2003). Recent statistics indicate that intimate partner homicide accounts for 33 percent of all the women who are murdered and 4 percent of the men who are killed (Rennison and Welchans 2000).

It is interesting to examine rates and trends in intimate partner homicide over time. Between 1976 and 1998, with the exception of white females, the number of homicides committed by an intimate partner declined substantially (Greenfield et al. 1998). Specifically, rates of African American females killed by intimates dropped 53 percent, white males by 54 percent, and African American males by 77 percent (Rennison and Welchans 2000). However, between 1997 and 1998 the intimate partner homicide rate increased 8 percent among women and 15 percent among white women (Greenfield et al. 1998; Rennison and Welchans 2000).

Background

In looking at the risks and consequences of intimate partner violence, Johnson (1995) identified four distinct patterns of violence between intimate partners. The distinctions between these different forms of violence relate to the role of power and coercive control in violent relationships as well as women's active or passive involvement as perpetrators. Johnson identified *common couple violence* as less severe acts of violence that are likely to be mutually perpetrated between partners (gender symmetric). Similarly, *mutual violent control* is a pattern of violence in which both male and female partners are controlling, emotionally abusive, and physically violent. In contrast, *patriarchal terrorism* is part of a general pattern of violent and emotional control by men that includes severe forms of violence as well as coercive control and emotional abuse that escalates over time (Hornung, McCullough, and Sugimoto 1981). This violence serves to subordinate, isolate, and increase women's emotional and financial dependence on their male partners (Hamby and Sugarman 1999). Finally, *violent resistance or self-defense* is, for the most part, perpetrated by women in response to victimization by their intimate partner. It is this type of self-defensive violence by women that may help to explain both gender differences in spousal homicide and the factors that lead to women killing their abusive partner (Serran and Firestone 2004).

In contrast, researchers suggest that male proprietariness best explains the dynamics of intimate relationships that influence homicidal behavior in men that is targeted at both their wives and children (Serran and Firestone 2004; Wilson and Daly 1993). In support of this assertion, research (Polk and Ranson 1991; Wilson and Daly 1993) has identified sexual jealousy and adultery as primary motives in the murder of female spouses. Relationships in which the spousal homicide of women occurs are characterized by long histories of coercive control, possessiveness, and sublethal violence.

Research Findings

While women are more often the victims of the most severe forms of intimate partner violence and spousal homicide (Dobash et al. 1992; Hornung, McCullough, and Sugimoto 1981; Johnson 1995; Johnson and Ferraro 2000), they are also occasionally the perpetrators of violence against their partner. Women commit 11 percent of all murders and more than 60 percent of these homicides are against an intimate partner or other family member (Greenfield and Snell 1999). It is important, however, to remember that men are more at risk of being victims of acquaintance or stranger homicide. Women who kill their intimate partner have often experienced long histories of intimate partner violence, emotional abuse, and coercive control, and for many of these women the abuse in the home also includes violence against their own children (Hattendorf, Ottens, and Lomax 1999; Stout 1991). Given moderate to high levels of posttraumatic stress disorder (PTSD) immediately prior to the killing of a battering partner, these women may perpetrate homicide in such situations as a way to escape violence when other alternatives appear to be blocked or unavailable, according to researchers (Hattendorf, Ottens, and Lomax 1999). Women who murdered their abusive partner often had experiences with intimate partner violence that included sexual assault within a short time period before the murder. Although many of the women who murder their partner do not have a prior record of violence, research indicates that as many as half of them will receive a life sentence of incarceration without the possibility of parole.

A number of unique personal, social, partner, and relationship characteristics have been identified among women who kill their battering partner as compared with abused women who remain in their abusive relationship or seek social service assistance and shelter. Women who kill are older, have been in a longer relationship with their batterer, have had a longer history of severe violence that included weapons and threats of death, and were less likely to have previous arrests as compared with other abused women (Browne 1987; Grant and Curry 1993; O'Keefe 1997).

Research also shows important differences between women who kill and non-offending battered women with respect to social class and other economic factors. For example, Roberts (1996) found that women who kill were more likely to have dropped out of high school, be on public assistance, and not be married to their partner. Grant and Curry (1993) found that battered women who killed their partners were less educated than battered women in a non-offending group.

In contrast, Browne (1987) found that women who kill were from a higher economic and social standing. These differences may be a function of the comparisons made between women who kill and battered women who do not. While some non-offending battered women stay with their abusive partner without seeking help, others utilize social services and seek shelter from abuse. For example, compared to non-offending battered women in a shelter, battered women who killed their partners were somewhat older and from a higher social class (Browne 1987).

This is consistent with the *marital dependency* perspective, which suggests that traditional economic status arrangements favoring men potentially place women at greatest risk for intimate partner violence (Hotaling and Sugarman 1986, 1990; Straus et al. 1980). In addition to increasing the risk of violence, this perspective suggests that given women's dependence on marriage and often inferior earning ability, they may be limited in identifying ways to end violent relationships (Kalmuss and Straus 1990). Similarly, research suggests that income, employment, and access to family resources are relatively powerful predictors of police reporting, social service utilization, and other help-seeking behavior (Bennett and Wiegand 1994; Birkbeck, Gabaldon, and LaFree 1993; Kaukinen 1997; Straus and Gelles 1990).

In contrast to the marital dependency perspective, Lenore Walker's *learned helplessness theory* (1979) suggests that it is the violence and control women experience by men over time that reduce a woman's will to leave, as the cycle of violence repeats itself over time. Perhaps less important are the so-cial, economic, and cultural reasons why a woman may be less likely to flee an abusive relationship. Walker argued that repeated victimization experiences combined with feelings of helplessness, financial dependence, and sheer differences in physical strength come together to explain why many women may be less able to put an end to a violent relationship. She also suggested that women's reasons for staying are likely to reflect fear of retaliation by the abuser to both herself and her children and a failure to recognize how truly dangerous this violence might ultimately become.

The nature of violence in intimate relationships and in women's previous experiences with violent victimization varies among women who kill and non-offending battered women. Women who murdered their partner experienced more frequent and severe forms of physical and sexual violence, and they were more likely to believe their lives were in imminent danger. Browne (1987) compared battered women incarcerated for killing their partners with women staying in a shelter. Incarcerated battered women were more likely to believe their partner could or would kill them and were more likely to have never previously called the police. In addition, both battered women who kill and their batterers were more likely to have used and abused alcohol as compared with those couples in which the battered woman did not kill her partner (Blount and Silverman 1994; Browne 1987). Similar studies report that battered women who kill their partners were more likely to have been sexually, physically, and emotionally abused during childhood and adolescence (Leonard 2002, 2001; Roberts 1996). Many women who had killed previously attempted suicide as a means of coping with their lifetime experiences with violence and victimization. Altogether, the research on the commission of homicide by women against an intimate partner indicates that these individuals had violent childhoods, experienced long-term physical violence by their intimate partner, including sexual abuse, and have children who witnessed the battering.

Conclusions

After examining the intersection between victimization and offending for children, adolescents, and adults, we can conclude that girls' and women's victimization is an important component to understanding their later involvement in crime and violent offending over the life course (Katz 2000). Many victimized girls come to the attention of social service agencies and the juvenile justice system because they are acting out against many years of violence, abuse, and neglect. Since the juvenile justice system does not place an emphasis on recognizing how prior victimization is related to a number of negative behavioral outcomes in girls, the system is not currently adequately equipped to address their needs. It therefore often focuses exclusively on girls' deviant and unlawful behavior.

Successful interventions should be dedicated to identifying and ending violence and providing appropriate treatment to abused girls to prevent initial contacts with the juvenile justice system. However, since the juvenile justice system does not fully recognize the role of victimization in the lives of girls and young women, future programming efforts need to tie identifiable risk factors, such as prior victimization experiences, into intervention services. Preventing the abuse and neglect of girls would reduce the risk of future involvement in drug use and delinquency during childhood, dating violence during adolescence, and domestic violence during adulthood. More so than for boys and young men, a more thorough understanding of the pathways to offending over the life course for girls and women requires a focus on the role of prior victimization experiences.

Study/Discussion Questions

1. What does the term *age-graded event* mean with respect to victimization and offending?

2. Why is violent victimization of girls such a traumatic event, (compared with boys), having implications for subsequent offending?

3. What are the consequences of violent victimization during childhood and adolescence?

4. What factors are important in understanding girls' and young women's perpetration of dating violence?

5. How would you explain why battered women kill their husbands compared with men who kill their intimate partners?

References

Acoca, L. (1995). Breaking the cycle: A developmental model for the assessment and treatment of adolescents with alcohol and other drug problems. *Juvenile and Family Court Journal, 46*, 1–48.

American Correctional Association. (1990). *The female offender: What does the future hold?* Washington, DC: St. Mary's.

Archer, J. (2000). Sex differences in aggression between heterosexual partners: A meta-analytic review. *Psychological Bulletin, 126*, 651–680.

Austin, A. (2003). Does forced sexual contact have criminogenic effects? An empirical test of derailment theory. *Journal of Aggression, Maltreatment & Trauma, 8*, 41–66.

Banaji, M., and Steele, C. (1989). Alcohol and self-evaluation: Is a social cognition approach beneficial? *Social Cognition, 7*, 137–151.

Beck, A. J. (2000). *Prison and jail inmates at midyear 1999* (NCJ 181643). Washington, DC: U.S. Department of Justice, Bureau of Justice Statistics.

Beckman, L. J. (1994). Treatment needs of women with alcohol problems. *Alcohol Health and Research World, 18*, 206–211.

Bell, C. C., and Jenkins, E. J. (1991). Traumatic stress and children. *Journal of Health Care for the Poor & Underserved, 2*, 175–185.

Bennett, R., and Wiegand, R. (1994). Observations on crime reporting in a developing nation. *Criminology, 32*, 135–148.

Birkbeck, C., Gabaldon, L., and LaFree, G. (1993). The decision to call the police: A comparative study of the United States and Venezuela. *International Criminal Justice Review*, 3, 25–43.

Bloom, B., and Covington, S. (1998, November). *Gender-specific programming for female offenders: What is it and why is it important?* Paper presented at the Annual meeting of the American Society of Criminology, Washington, DC.

Bloom, B., and McDiarmid, A. (2000). Gender-responsive supervision and programming for women offenders in the community. In National Institute of Corrections, *Topics in community corrections: Annual issue 2000: Responding to women offenders in the community* (pp. 11–18). Washington, DC: U.S. Department of Justice, National Institute of Corrections.

Blount, W. R., and Silverman, I. J. (1994). Alcohol and drug use among women who kill, abused women who don't, and their abusers. *Journal of Drug Issues*, 24, 165–177.

Brezina, T. (1999). Teenage violence toward parents as an adaptation to family strain: Evidence from a national survey of male adolescents. *Youth & Society*, 30, 416–444.

Browne, A. (1987). *When battered women kill.* New York: Free Press.

Calhoun, G., Jurgens, J., and Chen, F. (1993). The neophyte female delinquent: A review of the literature. *Adolescence*, 28, 461–471.

Chase, K. A., Treboux, D., and O'Leary, K. D. (2002). Characteristics of high-risk adolescents' dating violence. *Journal of Interpersonal Violence*, 17, 33–49.

Chesney-Lind, M. (1989). Girl's time and a woman's place: Toward a feminist model of female delinquency. *Crime and Delinquency*, 55, 5–29.

——. (1994). Rethinking women's imprisonment: A critical examination of trends in female incarceration. In B. R. Price and N. J. Sokoloff (Eds.), *The criminal justice system and women* (pp. 105–117). New York: McGraw-Hill.

——. (2000). Women and the criminal justice system: Gender matters. In National Institute of Corrections, *Topics in community corrections: Annual issue 2000: Responding to women offenders in the community* (pp. 7–10). Washington, DC: U.S. Department of Justice, National Institute of Corrections.

Chesney-Lind, M., and Pasko, L. (2004). *The female offender: Girls, women, and crime*, (2nd ed.). Thousand Oaks, CA: Sage.

Chesney-Lind, M., and Pollock, J. (1995). Women's prisons: Equality with a vengeance. In A. Merlo and J. Pollock (Eds.), *Women, law, and social control* (pp.155–175). Needham Heights, MA: Simon and Schuster.

Chesney-Lind, M., and Rodriguez, N. (1983). Women under lock and key: A view from the inside. *The Prison Journal*, 63, 47–65.

Cleveland, H. H., Herrera, V. M., and Stuewig, J. (2003). Abusive males and abused females in adolescent relationships: Risk factor similarity and dissimilarity and the role of relationship seriousness. *Journal of Family Violence*, 18, 325–339.

Dahlberg, L., and Potter, L. (2001). Youth violence, developmental pathways and prevention challenges. *American Journal of Preventive Medicine*, 20, 3–14.

Daly, K., and Chesney-Lind, M. (1988). Feminism and criminology. *Justice Quarterly*, 5: 497–538.

Decker, S. (1996). Collective and normative features of gang violence. *Justice Quarterly*, 13, 243–264.

Dobash, R. P., Dobash, R. E., Wilson, M., and Daly, M. (1992). The myth of sexual symmetry in marital violence. *Social Problems*, 39, 71–91.

English, D. J., Widom, C. S., and Brandford, C. B. (2001). *Childhood victimization and delinquency, adult criminality, and violent criminal behavior: A replication and extension, final report* (NCJ 192291). Washington, DC: U.S. Department of Justice, National Institute of Justice.

Fischbach, R. L., and Herbert, B. (1997). Domestic violence and mental health: Correlates and conundrums within and across cultures. *Social Science and Medicine*, 45, 1161–1176.

Flannery, D., Singer, M., Williams, L., and Castro, P. (1998). Adolescent violence exposure and victimization at home: Coping and psychological trauma symptoms. *International Review of Victimology*, 6, 29–48.

Fleisher, M. S. (1995). *Beggars and thieves: Lives of urban street criminals.* Madison: University of Wisconsin Press.

Flowers, R. B. (1995). *Female crime, criminals, and cellmates: An exploration of female criminality and delinquency.* Jefferson, NC: McFarland.

Foshee, V. A., Bauman, K. E., and Linder, G. F. (1999). Family violence and the perpetration of adolescent dating violence: Examining social learning and social control processes. *Journal of Marriage and the Family,* 61, 331–342.

Gaarder, E., and Belknap, J. (2002). Tenuous borders: Girls transferred to adult court. *Criminology,* 40, 481–517.

Garnefski, N., and Arends, E. (1998). Sexual abuse and adolescent maladjustment: Differences between male and female victims. *Journal of Adolescence,* 21, 99–107.

Gilfus, M. E. (1992). From victims to survivors to offenders: Women's routes of entry and immersion into street crime. *Women and Criminal Justice,* 4, 63–89.

Gover, A. R. (2004a). Childhood sexual abuse, gender, and depression among incarcerated youth. *International Journal of Offender Therapy and Comparative Criminology,* 48, 683–696.

——. (2004b). Risky lifestyles and dating violence: A theoretical test of violent victimization. *Journal of Criminal Justice,* 32, 171–180.

Grant, B., and Curry, G. D. (1993). Women murderers and victims of abuse in a southern state. *American Journal of Criminal Justice,* 17, 73–83.

Greenfield, L. A., Rand, M. R., Craven, D., Klaus, P. A., Perkins, C. A., Ringel, C., Warchol, G., Maston, C., and Fox, J. A. (1998). *Violence by intimates: Analysis of data on crimes by current and former spouses, boyfriends, and girlfriends* (NCJ 167237). Washington, DC: Department of Justice, Bureau of Justice Statistics.

Greenfield, L. A., and Snell, T. L. (1999). *Women offenders* (NCJ 175688). Washington, DC: U.S. Department of Justice, Bureau of Justice Statistics.

Hagan, J. (1989). *Structural criminology.* Piscataway, NJ: Rutgers University Press.

Hagan, J., and Foster, H. (2001). Youth violence and the end of adolescence. *American Sociological Review,* 66, 874–899.

Hamby, S. L., and Sugarman, D. B. (1999). Acts of psychological aggression against a partner and their relation to physical assault and gender. *Journal of Marriage and the Family,* 61, 959–970.

Harlow, C. W. (1999). *Prior abuse reported by inmates and probationers* (NCJ 172879). Washington, DC: U.S. Department of Justice, Bureau of Justice Statistics.

Harned, M. S. (2001). Abused women or abused men? An examination of the context and outcomes of dating violence. *Violence and Victims,* 16, 269–285.

Hattendorf, J., Ottens, A. J., and Lomax, R. G. (1999). Type and severity of abuse and post-traumatic stress disorder symptoms reported by women who killed abusive partners. *Violence Against Women,* 5, 292–312.

Henton, J., Cate, R., Koval, J., Lloyd, S. A., and Christopher, S. (1983). Romance and violence in dating relationships. *Journal of Family Issues,* 4, 467–482.

Hornung, C. A., McCullough, B. C., and Sugimoto, T. (1981). Status relationships in marriage: Risk factors in spouse abuse. *Journal of Marriage and the Family,* 43, 675–692.

Horowitz, M., Wilner, N., Marmar, C., and Krupnick, J. (1980). Pathological grief and the activity of latent self-images. *American Journal of Psychiatry,* 137, 1157–1162.

Hotaling, G. T. and Sugarman, D. B. (1986). Analysis of risk markers in husband to wife violence: The current state of knowledge. *Violence and Victims,* 1, 101–124.

——. A risk marker of analysis of assaulted wives. *Journal of Family Violence,* 5, 1–13.

Hunt, G., and Joe-Laidler, K. (2001). Situations of violence in the lives of girl gang members. *Health Care for Women International,* 22, 363–384.

Jackson, S. M. (1999). Issues in the dating violence research: A review of the literature. *Aggression and Violent Behavior,* 4, 233–247.

Jackson, S. M., Cram, F., and Seymour, F. W. (2000). Violence and sexual coercion in high school students' dating relationships. *Journal of Family Violence,* 15, 23–36.

Janoff-Bulman, R. (1985). Criminal versus noncriminal victimization: Victims' reactions. *Victimology,* 10, 498–511.

Janoff-Bulman, R., and Frieze, I. H. (1983). A theoretical perspective for understanding reactions to victimization. *Journal of Social Issues,* 39, 1–17.

Jasinski, J. L., Williams, L. M., and Siegel, J. (2000). Childhood physical and sexual abuse as risk factors for heavy drinking among African-American women: A prospective study. *Child Abuse & Neglect*, 24, 1061–1071.

Joe, K. A., and Chesney-Lind, M. (1995). "Just every mother's angel:" An analysis of gender and ethnic variations in youth gang membership. *Gender & Society*, 9, 408–431.

Johnson, M. P. (1995). Patriarchal terrorism and common couple violence: Two forms of violence against women. *Journal of Marriage and the Family*, 57, 283–294.

Johnson, M. P., and Ferraro, K. (2000). Research on domestic violence in the 1990s: Making distinctions. *Journal of Marriage and the Family*, 62, 948–963.

Johnson, R. (1979). *Juvenile delinquency and its origins*. Cambridge: Cambridge University Press.

Kalmuss, D., and Straus, M. (1990). Wife's marital dependency and wife abuse. In M. Straus and R. Gelles (Eds.). *Physical violence in American families: Risk factors and adaptations to violence in 8,145 families* (pp. 369–379). New Brunswick, NJ: Transaction.

Katz, J., Kuffel, S. W., and Coblentz, A. (2002). Are there gender differences in sustaining dating violence? An examination of frequency, severity, and relationship satisfaction. *Journal of Family Violence*, 17, 247–271.

Katz, R. S. (2000). Explaining girls' and women's crime and desistance in the context of their victimization experiences. *Violence Against Women*, 6, 633–660.

Kaukinen, C. E. (1997). *An examination of the reporting of domestic abuse to a variety of help sources*. Paper presented at the Annual Meeting of the American Society of Criminology, San Diego, CA.

——. (2002a). The help-seeking of women violent crime victims: Findings from the Canadian Violence Against Women Survey. *International Journal of Sociology and Social Policy*, 22, 5–44.

——. (2002b). The help-seeking decisions of violent crime victims: An examination of the direct and conditional effects of gender and the victim-offender relationship. *Journal of Interpersonal Violence*, 17, 432–456.

Kaukinen, C. E., and DeMaris, A. (2005). Age at first sexual assault and current substance use and depression. *Journal of Interpersonal Violence*, 20, 1244–1270.

Kessler, R. C., and Magee, W. J. (1994). Childhood family violence and adult recurrent depression. *Journal of Health and Social Behavior*, 35, 13–27.

Kilpatrick, D., Saunders, B., and Smith, D. (2003). *Youth victimization: Prevalence and implications*. Washington, DC: National Institute of Justice.

Kilpatrick, D. G., Saunders, B. E., Veronen, L. J., Best, C. L., and Von, J. M. (1987). Criminal victimization: Lifetime prevalence, reporting to police, and psychological impact. *Crime & Delinquency*, 33, 479–489.

Langworthy, R., Barnes, A., and Curtis, R. (1998). Inmate histories: Evidence of childhood abuse. *Alaska Justice Forum*, 15, 6–8.

Leonard, E. D. (2001). Convicted survivors: Comparing and describing California's battered women inmates. *The Prison Journal*, 81, 73–86.

——. (2002). *Convicted survivors: The imprisonment of battered women who kill*. Albany: State University of New York Press.

Lewis, S. F., Travea, L., and Fremouw, W. J. (2002). Characteristics of female perpetrators and victims of dating violence. *Violence and Victims*, 17, 593–606.

Loeber, R., and Hay, D. (1997). Key issues in the development of aggression and violence from childhood to early adulthood. *Annual Review of Psychology*, 48, 371–410.

Macmillan, R. (2001). Violence and the life course: The consequences of victimization for personal and social development. *Annual Review of Sociology*, 27, 1–22.

Margolin, G., and Gordis, E. B. (2000). The effects of family and community violence on children. *Annual Review of Psychology*, 51, 445–579.

Mears, D., Ploeger, M., and Warr, M. (1998). Explaining the gender gap in delinquency: Peer influence and moral evaluations of behavior. *Journal of Research in Crime and Delinquency*, 35, 251–266.

Miller, J. (1998). Gender and victimization risk among young women in gangs. *Journal of Research in Crime and Delinquency*, 35, 429–453.

Monson, C. M., and Langhinrichsen-Rohling, J. (2002). Sexual and nonsexual dating violence perpetration: Testing an integrated perpetrator typology. *Violence and Victims*, 17, 403–428.

Neufeld, J., McNamara, J. R., and Ertl, M. (1999). Incidence and prevalence of dating partner abuse and its relationship to dating practices. *Journal of Interpersonal Violence,* 14, 125–137.

Office for Victims of Crime. (2002). *Help series—Child abuse victimization* (BC 000669). Washington, DC: Author.

O'Keefe, M. (1997). Incarcerated battered women: A comparison of battered women who killed their abusers and those incarcerated for other offenses. *Journal of Family Violence,* 12, 1–19.

Polk, K., and Ranson, D. (1991). The role of gender in intimate homicide. *The Australian and New Zealand Journal of Criminology,* 24 (1), 15–24.

Rennison, C. M. (2003). *Intimate partner violence, 1993–2001* (NCJ 197838). Washington, DC: U.S. Department of Justice, Bureau of Justice Statistics.

Rennison, C. M. and Welchans, S. (2000). *Intimate partner violence* (NCJ 178247). Washington, DC: U.S. Department of Justice, Bureau of Justice Statistics.

Roberts, A. R. (1996). Battered women who kill: A comparative study of incarcerated participants with a community sample of battered women. *Journal of Family Violence,* 11, 291–304.

Rosenbaum, J. L. (1996). A violent few: Gang girls in the California Youth Authority. *Journal of Gang Research,* 3, 17–23.

Runtz, M., and Schallow, J. (1997). Social support and coping strategies as mediators of adult adjustment following childhood maltreatment. *Child Abuse & Neglect,* 21, 211–226.

Sanders-Philips, K., Moisan, P. A., Wadlinton, S., Morgan, S., and English, K. (1995). Ethnic differences in psychological functioning among Black and Latino sexually abused girls. *Child Abuse & Neglect,* 19, 691–706.

Scahill, M. (2000). *Female delinquency cases, 1997* (FS 200016). Washington, DC: U.S. Department of Justice, Office of Juvenile Justice and Delinquency Prevention.

Scully-Whitaker, M. (2000). Responding to women offenders: Equitable does not mean identical. In National Institute of Corrections, *Topics in community corrections: Annual issue 2000: Responding to women offenders in the community* (pp. 4–6). Washington, DC: U.S. Department of Justice, National Institute of Corrections.

Serran, G., and Firestone, P. (2004). Intimate partner homicide: A review of the male propriet-

ariness and the self-defense theories. *Aggression and Violent Behavior,* 9, 1–15.

Shook, N. J., Gerrity, D. A., Jurich, J., and Segrist, A. E. (2000). Courtship violence among college students: A comparison of verbally and physically abusive couples. *Journal of Family Violence,* 15, 1–22.

Siegel, J. A., and Williams, L. M. (2003). The relationship between child sexual abuse and female delinquency and crime: A prospective study. *Journal of Research in Crime and Delinquency,* 40, 71–94.

Silverman, J. G., Raj, A., Mucci, L. A., and Hathaway, J. E. (2001). Dating violence against adolescent girls and associated substance use, unhealthy weight control, sexual risk behavior, pregnancy, and suicidality. *Journal of the American Medical Association,* 286, 572–579.

Simkins, S., and Katz, S. (2002). Criminalizing abused girls. *Violence Against Women,* 8, 1474–1499.

Simons, R. L., Lin, K., and Gordon, L. C. (1998). Socialization in the family of origin and male dating violence: A prospective study. *Journal of Marriage and the Family,* 60, 467–478.

Simons, R. L., Miller, M. G., and Aigner, S. M. (1980). Contemporary theories of deviance and female delinquency: An empirical test. *Journal of Research in Crime and Delinquency,* 17, 42–53.

Smart, C. (1976). *Women, crime, and criminology: A feminist critique.* London: Routledge & Kegan Paul.

Smith, D. A., and Paternoster, R. (1987). The gender gap in theories of deviance: Issues and evidence. *Journal of Research in Crime and Delinquency,* 24, 140–172.

Snell, T. L. (1994). *Women in prison* (NCJ 145321). Washington, DC: U.S. Department of Justice, Bureau of Justice Statistics.

Steffensmeier, D. (1993). National trends in female arrest, 1960–1990: Assessment and recommendations for research. *Journal of Quantitative Criminology,* 9, 411–441.

Stout, K. D. (1991). Women who kill: Offenders of defenders? *Affilia,* 6, 8–22.

Straus, M. (2001, September/October). New evidence for the benefits of never spanking. *Society,* pp. 52–60.

——. (2004). Prevalence of violence against dating partners by male and female university students worldwide. *Violence Against Women, 10,* 790–811.

Straus, M. A., and Gelles, R. J. (1990). *Physical violence in American families: Risk factors and adaptations to violence in 8,145 families.* New Brunswick, NJ: Transaction Publishers.

Straus, M. A., Gelles, R. J., and Steinmetz, S. K. (1980). *Behind closed doors: Violence in the American family.* New York: Anchor Press.

Tjaden, P. and Thoennes, N. (2000). *Full report of the prevalence, incidence, and consequences of violence against women: Findings from the national violence against women survey* (NCJ 183781). Washington, DC: U.S. Department of Justice.

Walker, L. E. (1979). *The battered woman.* New York: Harper & Row.

Widom, C. S, Ireland, T., and Glynn, P. J. (1995). Alcohol abuse in abused and neglected children followed-up: Are they at increased risk? *Journal of Studies on Alcohol, 56,* 207–217.

Widom, C. S., and Maxfield, M. G. (2001). *An update on the "cycle of violence"* (NCJ 184894). Washington, DC: U.S. Department of Justice, National Institute of Justice.

Wilson, M., and Daly, M. (1993). Spousal homicide risk and estrangement. *Violence and Victims, 8,* 3–16.

Wolf, K. A., and Foshee, V. A. (2003). Family violence, anger expression styles, and adolescent dating violence. *Journal of Family Violence, 18,* 309–316. ✦

6
Juvenile Delinquency and Gender

Young Women, Criminal Behavior, and Gang Involvement

Patrick J. Carr
Gabrielle Alfieri

In this chapter you will learn the following:

- The extent of girls' involvement in juvenile delinquency and how that involvement has changed over the past thirty years

- What offenses young women most often commit

- Some of the more popular explanations for female delinquency

- What we know about young women in youth gangs and the ways in which female gang members behave similarly to their male counterparts

- How, taken side-by-side, male and female delinquency compares and why female delinquency should be considered as distinct from male delinquency

Introduction

On average, young women are less likely to engage in delinquent behavior than young men (DeKeseredy 2000; Empey, Stafford, and Hay 1999; Scahill 2000; Steffensmeier and Allan 1996). While the rate of female involvement in delinquency increased during the 1990s, as evidenced by arrest rates (Budnick and Shields-Fletcher 1998; Snyder 1996), detention rates (Harms 2003), and self-reports (Snyder and Sickmund 1999), that for young men remained static for violent crime and actually declined for property crime over the same period. Perhaps the most significant recent trend in female juvenile delinquency, and the one that has certainly gained the most media attention, is the reported increase in arrest and detention of young women for violent crimes (see Poe-Yamagata and Butts 1996). However, while female delinquency has increasingly mirrored that of males, there are important distinctions between the genders in terms of causes, behaviors, and future dispositions.

In this chapter, we assess the current state of knowledge about female juvenile delinquency. We begin by outlining the trends over the past two decades, relying on official, self-report, and victimization data. We then examine the major veins of research on female juvenile delinquency, and we identify the predominant theoretical explanations for female delinquency. Next we consider the phenomenon of young women in gangs, both female members and auxiliaries of predominantly male gangs and those who join all-female gangs. Finally, we conclude by illustrating the similarities and discontinuities between female and male delinquency, and we argue that delinquent behavior by young women ought to be considered analytically and theoretically distinct.

Female Delinquency: What Do Young Women Do and How Often?

A recent bulletin on juvenile arrests in the United States (Snyder 2003) indicated that in 2001 a little over one quarter of all juvenile arrestees were female. Moreover, the arrest rate of young women has increased by over 30 percent since 1980, peaking for property crime in 1994 and for violent crime a year later. Certainly, more attention has been focused on the female juvenile population (Hoyt and Sherer 1998; Sondheimer 2001), but a knowledge gap remains in terms of what we know about female delinquents in comparison with their male counterparts. For example, there is the widely reported incidence of young women being arrested in greater numbers for violent offenses. When one examines the time series data for juvenile female arrests for violent offenses between 1980 and 2001, the increase in the arrest rate overall between the two time points is 58 percent. However, upon closer examination of the trend, one can see that in 1995 the arrest rate was over twice that in 1980 for violent offenses, but it has since declined. Male juvenile arrest rates for violent crime have actually declined between 1980 and 2000, by over 20 percent. However, juvenile males are still over four times as likely as females to be arrested for a violent offense. There is a similar trend with respect to property crime. Female juvenile arrests for property crime have changed little in the past two decades, while that for males has declined by over 50 percent. Again, young men are twice as likely as young women to be arrested for property crime.

The upshot of the official arrest statistics is that over the past two decades, young women have been arrested at a higher rate than heretofore, and for violent as well as property crime. These rates peaked in the mid-1990s and have declined since. The main point of contrast between the arrest rates of young men and women is with respect to the rate of increase. Simply put, in terms of arrests, the rate of increase has been greater for young women than for young men, though young men are still more likely to be arrested overall, and for violent and property crimes (see Sondheimer 2001).

A number of theories have been advanced to account for the sudden rise in female juvenile arrests. *Organizational theory* holds that as the criminal justice system seeks to cope with a reduction in crime, one way to stay busy is to arrest and process females more than hitherto (McCluskey, McCluskey, and Huebner 2003).

A second explanation utilizes the *liberation hypothesis* (Adler 1975) and argues that the reason for the increase in female arrests is that young women are liberated and female delinquents have been "masculinized." Young women thus mirror young men and are engaging in more delinquent behavior, which in turn is being reflected in the arrest rate increases. The liberation hypothesis debate echoes a discussion from an earlier era (e.g., Berger 1989; Curran 1984) that provided little support for the notion of women becoming more like men in terms of delinquent and criminal behavior. One can speculate that perhaps norms have changed for young women and with respect to the criminal justice system. A third set of theories that can be utilized to explain increases in female delinquency center around the structural effects of poverty and disadvantage (for example, Bowker and Klein 1983; Hannon and Defronzo 1998; Steffensmeier and Haynie 2000). In these explanations, increases in female delinquency and crime are due to increased economic marginalization and inequality. Steffensmeier and Haynie (2000) found that structural disadvantage variables—poverty, income inequality, joblessness, female-headed households, and percentages of blacks—significantly affect female rates of homicide and robbery, with more moderate effects on aggravated assault, burglary, and larceny. Simply put, female offending rates are higher when poverty levels are high. It might become more apparent as to what mechanism is driving increased arrests when we examine what young delinquent females do.

What do young women get arrested for? The 2001 arrest statistics illustrate that the top three arrest categories for juvenile females are larceny-theft; being a runaway, which is a status offense; and simple assault. The runaway offense is the only one for which females are arrested at a higher rate than males, and a number of scholars have argued that this is because of an inherent gender bias in the juvenile justice system that punishes young women more often for status offenses (Chesney-Lind 1987, 1989; Chesney-Lind and Shelden 1992).[1]

Of course, official statistics are only part of the picture with respect to delinquency. Arrests tell us about who gets processed by the juvenile justice system, not necessarily who is engaging in delinquent acts. Self-report data are often used as a validity check on official statistics to ascertain who engages in delinquency but does not appear in the official record. In other words, just because you do something delinquent doesn't mean you are going to get caught. Thus, many young women (and men) who engage in delinquent behavior never appear in the official statistics. To help round the picture out researchers use self-report studies in which they ask respondents to report the activities that they have engaged in. Unsurprisingly, there are many more youth engage in delinquency than is apparent from official arrest statistics.

Canter (1982) utilized self-report data and argued that the gender gap in terms of offending is much less than what emerges from the official arrest data. However, other self-report studies, such as the National Youth Survey or the Rochester Youth Study, have indicated marked differences in terms of participation in delinquent behavior and frequency of offending between juvenile males and females (see Elliott, Huizinga, and Menard 1989; Jang and Krohn 1995). Research by LeBlanc and Bouthiller (reported in Lanctot and LeBlanc 2002), using self-reports on incarcerated juveniles, also demonstrates that juvenile males engage in a wider variety of delinquent behaviors. Research that utilizes samples of incarcerated youth is significant because, in theory, adjudicated male and female adolescents should be similar in terms of their misbehavior (assuming that they are being treated equally by the justice system) than if one were to sample the general population. So it is important to note that at the level of processed delinquents, there is a marked gender difference.

The census of juveniles in residential placement for 2001 shows that 14.5 percent of the more than 100,000 juveniles in placement are female (Sickmund, Sladky, and Kang 2004). The demographic profile of incarcerated juveniles illustrates that 46 percent of the females are white, 35 percent are black, and 13 percent are Hispanic, compared with 38 percent White, 39 percent Black, and 18 percent Hispanic for the males. The vast majority of incarcerated females are aged 14 and over. Harms (2003) indicated that cases in which females have been detained increased by 50 percent between 1990 and 1999, while that for males increased by only 4 percent. The increase in female delinquency cases entering detention is accounted for by the increase in females charged with person offenses, which increased 102 percent from 1990 to 1999. The placement statistics reinforce the trends reported earlier in the arrest data.

The juvenile incarceration data show that there seems to be a difference in terms of race with respect to which groups end up in the criminal justice system. As illustrated in the statistics for the 2001 census of incarcerated juveniles, African Americans are often overrepresented in the incarcerated population, though recent research posits that Hispanics are the minority group most harshly treated in terms of sentencing (Steffensmeier and Demuth 2001). Brennan (2002) studied women sentenced to jail in New York City in 1989 and found that the key factors in predicting a sentence are prior record and the type and severity of the charge. Since the African-American females in her sample were more likely to have records, open cases, and more severe charges than their white and Hispanic counterparts, they have an increased risk of receiving a jail sentence. There has been a great deal of ink spilled on the relationship between race and delinquency (for example, Bruce 1999; Cernkovich and Giordano 1992; Sampson and Lauritsen 1997), and there is a great deal of disagreement as to whether the overrepresentation of minorities in the criminal justice system is due to sociobehavioral differences between racial and ethnic groups (see Covington 1999 for a discussion of racial inequality theory), inherent bias against minorities in the criminal justice system (Warner 2000), or the peculiar structural and ecological circumstances of minority populations (Bruce 2004; Sampson and Wilson 1995).

Victimization research represents a third set of data commonly utilized to describe differences between populations. Each year, the National Crime Victimization Survey (NCVS) interviews a large sample of men and women age 12 and older and revealed, for example, that in 1998 women accounted for 14 percent of all violent offenses (Chesney-Lind 1999b). Dugan and Apel (2003) in their exploratory analysis of the NCVS, illustrated that violent victimization of women varies greatly by race/ethnicity and situational context. They found that Native American women have the highest risk of victimization, and that the risk for white and Asian women increases with employment, while for Hispanics, risk is increased by living in public housing. They advocated further research to examine the mechanisms that increase the likelihood of victimization for women. Given that there is a well-documented relationship between prior victimization of females and subsequent offending behavior, such research will enhance theory about the causation and etiology of delinquent behavior for young women.

Overall, the general picture of female delinquency in the United States is one in which young women figure prominently in arrest data and self-reports, and they are more likely than two decades ago to be arrested and incarcerated for person or violent offenses. The time series data indicate that the delinquency rates peaked in the mid-1990s and have declined subsequently. However, the overall rate of increase for young women is significantly greater than that for young men. Whether this is an artifact of increased attention and prosecution of cases involving young females, or the result of an actual increase, is an interesting and vexing question. However, as Acoca (1998, p. 562) argued, "the numbers alone demand attention."

Current Research on Female Delinquency

The so-called malestream bias (that is, the almost exclusive focus on males) in criminology generally, and in delinquency research in particular, has declined over the past three decades. One could speculate that if Al Cohen (1955) were writing today the title of his work might read delinquent "youth" instead of delinquent "boys." However, as Lanctot and LeBlanc (2002) cautioned, we should not assume that, because young women are included increasingly in research samples, they occupy a central place in theorizing juvenile delinquency. Rather, as Hannon and Dufour (1998) pointed out, gender is more often used as a control variable, and thus the opportunity for explaining why young women engage in delinquent behavior is often lost.

There is a body of research about the influence of peers on female delinquent behavior (for example, Aseltine 1995; Claes and Simard 1992; Giordano, Cernkovich, and Pugh 1986; Pleydon and Schner 2001). Some studies have characterized delinquent friendships between young women as being disturbed in terms of low trust and high conflict (Brownfield and Thompson 1991; Giordano, Cernkovich, and Pugh 1986), while other studies have noted high levels of attachment between female delinquent peers (Bowker and Klein 1983; Claes and Simard 1992; Elliott, Huizinga, and Ageton 1985; Giordano 1978). Pleydon and Schner (2001) focused their research on best friends and peer groups of delinquent and nondelinquent females, the latter group drawn from a high school sample and the former, an incarcerated group. In the self-reports, the delinquent group was more likely than the high school group to engage in delinquency. More important, the delinquent group experienced higher levels of peer pressure and less communication in their peer group than the nondelinquents. Contrary to previous findings, Pleydon and Schner (2001) found no difference between delinquent and nondelinquent friendships in terms of attachment, closeness, trust, help, and security. Delinquent females are also more likely to belong to a mixed-gender peer group.

Some recent studies (Fergusson, Horwood, and Lynskey 1993; Pajer 1998) have noted that levels of conduct disorder and delinquency among adolescent girls are comparable with those of male counterparts. Additionally, Hartwig and Myers (2003) noted that conduct disorder problems have consequences beyond adolescence in terms of criminal behavior, dysfunctional relationships, and mental health issues (see also Caspi and Elder 1988; Nagin, Pogarsky, and Farrington 1997; Robins and Price 1991). In terms of addressing female delinquency, Hartwig and Myers (2003) argued for a wellness paradigm that addresses the multiple problems that female delinquents face, not simply the manifestation of offending behavior.

Other veins of research focus on the risk factors for female delinquency (e.g., Johnson 1998), among which are direct experience with violence, early experience with stressful life events, association with delinquent peers and gangs, and substance abuse in the home. Mullis and colleagues (2004) argued that for young females, neighborhood context working together with personality development can shed light on both risk factors and resilience to offending. Blum and Ireland (2003) found in their analysis of the National Longitudinal Study of Adolescent Health that independent of gender, victimization predicts juvenile violence.

In addition to the research that seeks to isolate risk factors, there is a growing body of research on incarcerated females. Because larger numbers of young women are in the juvenile justice system than ever before, problems abound because the system and the various treatments it sponsors are tailored to young males (Chesney-Lind 1999a; Lederman and Brown 2000). A number of studies have illustrated that placing young women in programs designed for boys does little to either recognize the causal role that victimization plays in female delinquency (see also Gaarder and Belknap 2002; Miller and Trapani 1995; Widom 2000) or address the problems co-occurring with delinquency, such as depression (Obeidellah and Earls 1999). Other research on incarcerated young women (Corrado, Odgers, and Cohen 2000)

found evidence to suggest that delinquent girls are incarcerated more often for minor offences than violent offenses; however, much of this was because of a paternalistic attitude on the part of criminal justice professionals. The girls themselves did not view their sentences as punitive, rather they conceptualized their incarceration in terms of an opportunity to temporarily escape from the victimization, drug use, and general abuse that characterized their lives.

Recent research by Ness (2004) and Jones (2004) has attempted to make sense of female youth violence. Both researchers drew on ethnographic work in Philadelphia and they argued that for young women in disadvantaged neighborhoods violence is often used strategically (Jones 2004) and can be viewed as normative for the social context in which these young women live (Ness 2004). Jones (2004) further argued that young women who engage in violence utilize their reputation as a fighter among their peers to navigate the dangerous terrain of their neighborhoods. While young women may fight for many of the same reasons that young men do (Leitz 2003; Ness 2004; Phillips 2003), this new vein of research takes seriously the gendered dynamics of interpersonal violence. At the heart of much of the discussion of female violence is the contention that even as young women employ violence to gain respect (Leitz 2003; Jones 2004), they do so in gender-specific ways. Other discussions of violence have emphasized how the social construction of a masculine identity underpins much violent behavior (Bourgois 1996; Totten 2003; Wilkinson 2003), often in ways that brutally reproduce patriarchal relations.

In sum, then, the landscape of current research on female delinquency is quite diverse. A body of work seeks to better isolate risk and protective factors for female juveniles, while other research focuses on continuities and discontinuities between male and female delinquency patterns. For example, a central question in the research is whether peer influence operates in the same manner for young women as it does for young men.

On balance, the preponderance of research seems to indicate that it is different for girls, insofar as when there are similar correlates for male and female delinquency, even these are experienced in gender specific ways. In addition, a great deal of work indicates that some causes and correlates of delinquency are most often specific to female experience.

Next we look at gang research, one area in which there has been a recent effort to explain better the roles and behavior of young women.

Girls in the Gang: Female Gang Involvement and Crime

Classic studies and accounts of gangs (Asbury 1929; Thrasher 1927) did not really explore the role of young women in gangs. While both Asbury and Thrasher mentioned that there were women present in the gangs they document, only six of Thrasher's 1,313 gangs were female. When it came to gang research, females were invisible (Cloward and Ohlin 1960) or, if they were present, they were seen in their relation to male gang members. There were other sporadic dispatches about female gangs (Brown 1977; Miller 1975) but, for the most part, these tended to view the incidence of girl gangs as anomalous and exotic. The increased attention that focused on gangs generally in the 1990s also brought females in gangs to prominence. The media coverage (see Chesney-Lind 1993; Chesney-Lind, Shelden, and Joe 1996) and popular journalistic accounts (for example, Sykes 1997) have accentuated the outlandish and violent behavior of some of these young women in gangs, and this has distorted the overall picture of young women in gangs. Thankfully, enough meticulous scholarly attention has been devoted to females in gangs and this has redressed the imbalance somewhat (see the essays in Chesney-Lind and Hagedorn 1999). There are several current estimates of the extent of involvement of young women in gangs. Deschenes and Esbensen (1999) report that while official

statistics estimate that 10 percent of gang members are female, self-report studies have found that between 20 percent and 46 percent of members are young women.

Three decades ago, Walter Miller (1975) constructed an influential typology of female gangs, illustrating that young women in gangs could be classified as being in mixed gender gangs, autonomous female gangs, or as auxiliary members of male gangs. However, the basis of Miller's conceptualization is that female gangs can only be conceptualized in terms of their relation to male gangs. Anne Campbell's pioneering (1984) work did much to dispel this perception of females in gangs. Campbell's carefully crafted ethnography of girl gang members in New York illustrated both the variability in the female gang experience and the social context of membership for young women. For Campbell, female gangs can be avenues for resistance and liberation for their members (see also Campbell 1990), a point that is echoed by Lauderback, Hansen, and Waldorf (1992) in their portrait of a female gang in San Francisco. Brotherton (1996) showcased the agency of female gang members, and argues that the degree of autonomy obtained by young women in gangs is shaped by their success as criminal entrepreneurs. However, a number of other authors (for example, Miller 1998: Moore 1991) have illustrated the very real hazards of gang involvement for young women, for instance, victimization and exploitation.

Despite some of the theoretical issues with Walter Miller's (1975) typology, it has remained influential in terms of how researchers assess the involvement of young women in gangs. For example, Curry (1998) reported on a study of female gang members in three cities. He found that only 6.4 percent of the young women were in single-sex or autonomous female gangs, whereas 57.3 percent said that they were in mixed-gender gangs and 36.4 percent described their gang as being affiliated with a male gang. Jody Miller (2001) stated that the majority of the young women in her study were in mixed-sex gangs as opposed to the other two categories of female-only or auxiliary. Further, she indicated that three quarters of the women in mixed-sex gangs were in gangs that were mostly male, and one-third were in gangs where four-fifths of the members were male. The modal experience for women in mixed gender gangs would seem to be situations in which they are numerically in the minority (see also Miller and Brunson 2000).

The gender structure of the gang also seems to have implications for the type of gang activity in which young women engage. Some studies illustrate that girl gang members seem to be either serious offenders or petty delinquents (Fagan 1990; Miller 2001), but other studies note that young women in gangs contrast markedly with young men, especially with respect to violent behavior (Joe and Chesney-Lind 1995). Simply put, violence is not as normative for women in gangs as it is for men. Jody Miller (2001) noted that the young women she interviewed who were in majority female gangs, or gangs in which there was a substantial female membership, emphasized the importance of gangs in terms of the friendships and solidarity they experienced there (also noted by Campbell 1990; Joe and Chesney-Lind 1995).

As the research on young women in gangs begins to proliferate, it is increasingly evident that the female experience in gangs is not reducible to categories that mirror experiences of young men. For example, Hunt, Joe-Laidler, and Evans (2002) reported from an ongoing study of gangs in San Francisco that drug use by female gang members indicates that the young women in question use drugs in a highly gendered way. Specifically, female gangs members' drug use is mediated by group setting and subject to controls by males and females. Female gang members learn to distinguish recreational drug use from "out-of-control" use, and they develop gendered codes that attempt to counteract the prevailing construction of female drug use as unfeminine (see also Joe-Laidler and Hunt 2001). Joan Moore's work (1991, 1994) provided a nuanced portrait of drug use by Latina gang members, and she concluded that the young women she studied are not passive and emotionally damaged users but actively shape their social world as both users and dealers.

A related point to the specificity of the female gang experience is how race and ethnicity structure gang involvement and experience. Much of the work on females in gangs (for example, Chesney-Lind, Shelden, and Joe 1996; Joe and Chesney-Lind 1995; Moore and Hagedorn 1999) offers a nuanced and sophisticated portrait of how gender and race structure the gang experience for these young women, including the likelihood of joining gangs and engaging in serious delinquent behavior. Moore and Hagedorn (1999) explored the different experiences of Latina and African-American gang girls. They showed how gender expectations and ethnicity intersect with respect to the expected role of females, which, they said, is more traditional in the Mexican-American than in the African-American communities. Implicit here is the notion that Latina gang members journey farther against the grain when they decide to become gang members. Moore and Hagedorn (1999) also found that the young women are aware of the consequences of their actions, the Latinas are more pessimistic about the long-term effects of gang membership for their general life chances. Joe and Chesney-Lind (1995) also elaborated on how race and ethnicity in many cases prefigure gang involvement for young women in Hawaii. Specifically, they illustrated how the stress of immigration, economic marginalization, and encounters with an alien culture can lead to gang involvement for Samoan youth, while Filipino girls are influenced by their immigrant experience and a native culture that accords them a secondary status. Joe and Chesney-Lind (1995) further pointed out that Hawaiian youth closely resemble urbanized Native Americans and African Americans, who have "accommodated to poverty by normalizing early motherhood; high rates of school dropout; and welfare dependency for girls" (p. 418). Chesney-Lind, Shelden, and

Joe (1996) stated in a searching critique of the field that "girls' participation in gangs needs to be placed within the context of the lives of girls, particularly young women of color on the economic and political margins" (pp. 202–203).

One of the more intriguing approaches to examining young women in gangs is that pursued by Peterson, Miller, and Esbensen (2001), where they consider the effect of gender composition on the norms and behavior of gangs. The authors were interested not only in what this means for young women but also for the overall gang. Drawing on theories from organizational sociology, the authors examined whether gender composition affects what male and female gang members do, or whether such behavior is molded more by gender norms. They found that sex composition of gangs has an effect on the delinquent behavior of males and females. Specifically, they found that girls in gangs with a minority of female members have the highest rates of delinquency, as do the boys in such gangs. Simply put, sex composition influences gang members' behavior. For example, in gangs where there is a gender balance—equal or almost equal numbers of males and females—the males are more likely to engage in delinquent behavior than the female gang members. Peterson, Miller, and Esbensen (2001) explained that the males in the group feel that their position is threatened and they respond by "narrowing girls' opportunities for involvement in 'masculine' activities such as delinquency" (p. 432). In contrast, when the gang is mostly male, there is no perceived threat and so males and females engage in similar amounts of delinquency.

To summarize, the gang research on females has advanced greatly in the past decade, though areas exist in which there is still a paucity of scholarship. For instance, Chesney-Lind and Hagedorn noted in the introduction to their edited volume (1999) that very little is known about female prison gangs or interventions designed to deal with young women. Despite some reservations on our part, the body of work on female gang members has improved considerably in the past decade both in terms of volume and sophistication.

One of the areas in which gang research has contributed to the overall study of female delinquency is in terms of the advancement of theory. Hagedorn and Devitt (1999) alluded to two main camps in terms of conceptualizing gangs. First, the liberation view holds that changing gender roles has impacted girls and gangs, and that this has had the effect of increasing the number of females in gangs and influencing them to engage in serious crime, including violence and drug dealing (Taylor 1993). Second, the social injury hypothesis (Joe and Chesney-Lind 1995) however, argues that gender roles have not changed all that much and what is more important in terms of females in gangs is the serious harm gang membership can cause. A third perspective (Hagedorn and Devitt 1999) argues that gangs are social constructions and gender plays a role here in how gangs are constructed from the young people's point of view. Hagedorn and Devitt (1999) concluded by arguing that it is time to abandon the Walter Miller typology of auxiliary, independent, and mixed gang types. Instead we need to focus on the socially constructed and variable nature of gangs. The gang literature also seems to arrive at the conclusion that while female experiences in gangs share some commonalities with male experiences, separate categories and concepts are needed to explain girls in gangs.

Theories of Female Delinquency

The story of theories of female delinquency is very similar to that for women and crime generally. Up until the early 1970s, female delinquency was rarely theorized, and so, it was done in relation to theories that were constructed to explain male delinquency. The so-called malestream criminological theorizing began to be questioned in the early 1970s (for example, Adler 1975; Simon 1975). Daly and Chesney-Lind (1988) argued that the two main issues in terms of how criminology views women are a generalizability problem and a gender ratio problem. The generalizability problem is the assumption that theories about males can be applied to females. The gender ratio problem derives from the fact that women commit fewer and less violent crimes than men.

Feminist theory is one approach that seeks to amend the generalizability problem. Feminist theory, broadly conceived, has attempted to redress the male-centered conceptualization of delinquency (for example, Bessant 1994; McRobbie 1991; Schwartz and Milovanovic 1996). The central thrust of the feminist critique is that not only are prevailing discourses about delinquency focused more on the male experience, but also the way adolescence is socially constructed has implications for how any departure from the norm is treated. For young men, adolescence is something they will mature out of, and so any violation of norms is part of this process. However, young women are treated differently when they defy norms because they are violating predominant notions of femininity. This double standard implies that adolescence is not a terrain where experimentation can be as easily done by young women as by young men.

The notion that patriarchal relations, or the systematic domination of females by males, shape delinquent and criminal behavior has received some support in the research. For example, several studies have illustrated that street crime is a highly gendered space, and this serves often to limit or exclude women from criminal networks (for example, Joe-Laidler and Hunt 2001; Maher 1997; Maher and Daly 1996; Miller 2001). However, women do negotiate and enter criminal networks, and thus there is a certain degree of female agency. Mullins and Wright (2003) presented findings from their study of male and female burglars, and they argued that gender matters most in terms of initiation into offending and with respect to information gathering about potential targets. One can find more similarities than differences in terms of offense commission, a point echoed by Miller (1998) in her study of active robbers, but the experience overall is differentiated in terms of gender. These studies also engage directly with the gender-ratio problem, in that they explain differences in rates of offending as being caused by patriarchal relations that exclude many women from criminal networks.

Any theory of female delinquency has to take into consideration the gender-specific pathways through adolescence taken by young women. Miller and Trapani (1995) pointed out that the preponderance of research on female adolescence illustrates that females experience more depression, lower self-esteem, more suicide, and lower resilience than males. Gender differences also exist with respect to moral development and independence, which in turn impact the incidence of deviant and risk-taking behavior. The latter point draws on the work of developmental psychologist Carol Gilligan (see, for example, 1982), who argued that young women's moral development in adolescence is developmentally distinct from that of young men. Overall, young women are more advanced with respect to moral maturity than young men, even though they are generally not accorded as much independence. Both of these factors are said to reduce the probability of engaging in delinquency.

One fruitful way of conceptualizing female delinquency is to examine intersectionality, that is, how social structures such as race, class, and gender intersect in the lives of young women. In important ways, feminist theory has been at the forefront of intersectional analysis of race, class, and gender (for example, Mirza 1992), and Knaak (2004) has argued that gender should be reconceptualized as a social construction so as to better research and theorize the many ways in which it operates in conjunction with class and race. Risman (2004) also argued that gender is socially constructed, and she championed intersectional analysis that pays careful attention to the exact ways in which each system of domination operates (see also Brah and Phoenix 2004). To date, few studies of female delinquency have employed intersectional analysis, though the approach has been used to a limited extent to examine race and crime in Canada (Wortley 2003) and to domestic violence in the United States (Benson et al. 2004). As underused as it is, intersectional analysis has potential to shed light on several crucial questions in criminology, among them the overrepresentation of minorities in the justice system.

Belknap and Holsinger (1998) advanced another feminist-influenced theory of delinquency, in which they argued for a victim-to-offender theory of female delinquency, which is also known as a *"pathways to crime"* model (see also Arnold 1990; Daly 1992; Gaarder and Belknap 2002; Gover 2004; Richie 1996). This model holds that childhood traumas, such as physical and sexual abuse, are not only defining features in the lives of females, they also increase the likelihood that young women will engage in criminal behavior. Belknap and Holsinger (1998) argued that what underscores this relationship between victimization and delinquency is the fact that the criminal justice system criminalizes several survival strategies employed by girls. Acoca (1998) utilized this perspective in her study of girl offenders in California, where she demonstrated that prior sexual, emotional, and physical victimization is a precursor to involvement in the criminal justice system. Once in the criminal justice system, these young women are victimized further, which has the effect of compounding existing problems. Victimization can take many forms for young women. They can be exposed to marital violence, or they may be the victims of physical or sexual abuse. Of the three forms of abuse, childhood sexual abuse is the most important predictor of subsequent delinquency (Herrera and McCloskey 2003; Siegel and Williams 2003). This body of research strongly supports the victim-to-offender theory.

While feminist theories, including the victim-to-offender approach, seek to stake out a new terrain for theorizing female delinquency, other scholars have attempted to apply existing criminological theories to female behavior. Hay (2003) used Agnew's (1992) general strain theory in an examination of delinquency rates of males and females (see also Broidy and Agnew 1997). The general theory of strain holds that delinquency is caused by negative relationships and life events, and the theory posits that these events cause anger, which finds an outlet in delinquent behavior. Agnew's theory also details how individuals cope with strain and how only some of these mechanisms can lead to delinquency. Hay was interested in how this theory may help explain why males are more involved in delinquency than females, or the gender ratio problem. In terms of strain theory, he posited that males may be more subject to the types of strain that cause delinquency, such as physical punishment. A second possible explanation could be that males have different emotional responses to strain. Finally, strain experienced by males may lead to delinquency more often because of reduced social control (control theory) or access to delinquent role models (learning theory). Hay found that certain types of strain, such as physical punishment and parental rejection, are more likely to lead to delinquency and are also more likely to be experienced by males. Further, he found no gender difference in how strain produces anger but that young women are much more likely to feel guilty, which in turn has a negative effect on delinquency. Last, Hay finds that the magnitude of the positive effect of strain and anger on delinquency is greater for males than for females. Thus, the gender gap in delinquency could be due to how young men and women experience family strain.

Box (1981) believed that control theory is the most applicable to female delinquency, specifically that the amount of control experienced by the young person can explain the gender ratio. Simply put, young women have stronger social bonds, as evidenced by stronger attachment to family, school, and positive peer associations, high levels of involvement in prosocial activities, and high levels of commitment, all of which result in lower levels of delinquency than male counterparts. The question remains as to why young women develop stronger social bonds. Perhaps differences in sex-roles or development account for the propensity of young women to form more stable bonds than young men. Alternatively, it could be that different routine activities (Cohen and Felson 1979) account for differences in the strength of social bonds for young men and young women. The empirical support for control theory's ability to explain the gender ratio question has been mixed. For example, Sokol-Katz, Dunhan, and Zimmerman (1997) found no evidence that control theory was applicable to girls, while Smith and Paternoster (1987) and Torstensson (1990) found that some elements of the social bond influence delinquency in girls.

Giordano, Cernkovich, and Rudolph (2002) examined desistance from crime, and they argued that existing theories on what causes desistance from crime (Laub and Sampson 2003; Sampson and Laub 1993) do not seem to explain what happens to women.[2] Specifically, Giordano, Cernkovich, and Rudolph (2002) argue that their theory of cognitive transformation, which posits that, in addition to social controls normally seen as important for desistance—a good marriage, stable employment, or childbirth, for example—the role of how people decide to change, which influences how people actually seek out change, is very important. Giordano, Cernkovich, and Rudolph (2002) use the term "cognitive shifts" to identify the process of people seeking out change for themselves. Desistance is not simply a matter of entrance into prosocial bonds but rather a set of decisions that a person makes. It is also how a person constructs and describes this transformation in narrative terms, what Giordano, Cernkovich, and Rudolph (2002) labeled as "hooks for change." The theory of cognitive transforma-

tion is applicable across gender, but importantly it enables us to examine the different ways in which women explain desistance. While the focus of this work is on adult women, the approach of integrating theory to provide an explanatory framework that can account for both male and female behavior and their similarities and variations is promising and has applicability to the study of delinquency as well as adult crime.

All told, there have been significant advances in the theorizing of female delinquency. The broadly feminist approaches of the victim-to-offender pathways and the concept of intersectionality seem to hold the most promise for the field. Next we summarize the main points of this chapter.

Conclusion

In this chapter, we have explored the topic of juvenile delinquency and gender. In doing so, we have examined some of the recent trends and outlined current research in female delinquency. We have explored the topic of girls in gangs and summarized some of the main theories that seek to explain female delinquency.

Female delinquency has increased over the past few decades as evidenced by official and self-report data (Snyder 1996; Snyder and Sickmund 1999). The rate of increase for young women is greater than that for young men, though women are still less likely overall to engage in delinquent behavior and, it seems, more likely to engage in a smaller range of activities (Elliott, Huizinga, and Menard 1989; Jang and Krohn 1995; Sondheimer 2001). Even as young women are increasingly visible in arrests and incarceration statistics, there remains a distinct difference in their experience, both in the kinds of delinquency they engage in and how they are treated when they encounter the criminal justice system. A broad similarity exists between what young men and young women do—they steal, they rob, they beat each other up. However, it would be foolish to assume that it is possible to treat female delinquency as being the same as male delinquency. To do so would be to fall into the trap of malestream criminology, which denied that women were even worth considering in terms of delinquent and criminal behavior.

There are two major questions with respect to delinquency and gender (see for example, Lanctot and LeBlanc 2002), regarding the gender ratio of delinquent acts and whether the causes for female delinquency are the same as those for males. In light of the review we have presented here, we would suggest that the most fruitful approach to these questions is to theorize the difference between male and female delinquency. The research and theory that emphasizes the gendered pathways into delinquency (for example, Arnold 1990; Daly 1992; Gaarder and Belknap 2002; Gover, in this volume) offer an approach that has the potential to explain female delinquency in its own terms, and in relation to the larger issue of juvenile misbehavior. Under specific circumstances, young women may behave in ways that are similar to young men, but they do so under qualitatively different and, it must be said, gendered circumstances. On the whole, it is different for girls, and future research and theory about female delinquency should be mindful of this maxim.

Notes

1. A status offense is an activity that is illegal when engaged in by a juvenile but permissible for adults. Examples of status offenses are being truant, breaking curfew, or running away from home.

2. It should be noted that the respondents used by Sampson and Laub in the data set were male.

Study/Discussion Questions

1. Describe the trends in female delinquency over the past 20 years. Why do you think that the official rates of female delinquency have risen faster than those for males?

2. What are some of the main findings of recent research on female delinquency? Is there a consensus in this body of work as to the main causes of female delinquency?

3. What does the research tell us about girls in gangs? Do females experience gang membership in the same ways as males? How are the experiences the same or different?

4. What is the state of current theory about female delinquency? Evaluate the theories, such as "pathways to crime," and discuss whether female delinquency is theoretically distinct from male delinquency.

References

Acoca, L. (1998). Outside/inside: The violation of American girls at home, on the street, and in the juvenile justice system. *Crime and Delinquency*, 44 (4): 561–590.

Adler, F. (1975). *Sisters in crime: The rise of the new female criminal.* New York: McGraw-Hill.

Agnew, R. (1992). Foundation for a general strain theory of crime and delinquency. *Criminology*, 30, 47–87.

Arnold, R. A. (1990). Women of color: Process of victimization and criminalization of black women. *Social Justice*, 17, 153–166.

Asbury, H. (1929). *The gangs of New York.* New York: Paragon.

Aseltine, R. H. (1995). A reconsideration of parental and peer influences on adolescent deviance. *Journal of Health and Social Behavior*, 36, 103–121.

Belknap, J., and Holsinger, K. (1998). An overview of delinquent girls. In R. T. Zaplin (Ed.), *Female offenders: Critical perspectives and effective interventions* (pp. 31–64). Gaithersburg, MD: Aspen.

Benson, M. L., Wooldredge, J., Thistlethwaite, A. B., and Fox, G. (2004). The correlation between race and domestic violence is confounded with community context. *Social Problems*, 51, 326–342.

Berger, R. J. (1989). Female delinquency in the emancipation era: A review of the literature. *Sex Roles*, 21, 375–399.

Bessant, J. (1994). Making young female offenders visible. *Youth Studies Australia,* 13 (2), 45–51.

Blum, J., and Ireland, M. (2003). Gender differences in juvenile violence: A report from add health. *Journal of Adolescent Health,* 32, 234–240.

Bourgois, P. (1996). In search of masculinity: Violence, respect, and sexuality among Puerto Rican crack dealers in East Harlem. *British Journal of Criminology,* 36, 412–427.

Bowker, L. H., and Klein, M. W. (1983). The etiology of female juvenile delinquency and gang membership: A test of psychological and social structural explanations. *Adolescence,* 18, 739–751.

Box, S. (1981). *Deviance, reality, and society.* London: Holt, Rinehart and Winston.

Brah, A., and Phoenix, A. (2004). Ain't I a woman: Revisiting intersectionality. *Journal of International Women's Studies,* 5, 75–86.

Brennan, P. K. (2002). *Women sentenced to jail in New York City.* New York: LFB Scholarly Publishing.

Broidy, L., and Agnew, R. (1997). Gender and crime: A general strain theory perspective. *Journal of Research in Crime and Delinquency,* 34, 275–306.

Brotherton, D. C. (1996). "Smartness," "toughness," and "autonomy": Drug use in the context of gang female delinquency. *Journal of Drug Issues,* 26, 261–277.

Brown, W. K. (1977). Black female gangs in Philadelphia. *International Journal of Offender Therapy and Comparative Criminology,* 21, 221–228.

Brownfield, D., and Thompson, K. (1991). Attachment to peers and delinquent behavior. *Canadian Journal of Criminology,* 45–60.

Bruce, M. A. (1999). Inequality and delinquency: Sorting out some class and race effects. *Race and Society,* 2, 133–148.

——. (2004). Contextual complexity and violent delinquency among black and white males. *Journal of Black Studies,* 35, 65–98.

Budnick, K. J., and Shields-Fletcher, E. (1998). *What about girls?* Washington, D.C.: U.S. Department of Justice, Office of Justice Programs.

Campbell, A. (1984). *The girls in the gang.* New York: Oxford University Press.

——. (1990). On the invisibility of the female delinquent peer group. *Women and Criminal Justice,* 2, 41–62.

Canter, R. J. (1982). Sex differences in self-report delinquency. *Criminology,* 20, 373–393.

Caspi, A., and Elder, G. H. (1988). Childhood precursors of the life course: Early personality and life disorganization. In E. M. Hetherington, R. M. Lerner, and M. Perlmutter (Eds.), *Child development in life-span perspective* (pp. 115–142). Hillsdale, NJ: Lawrence Erlbaum.

Cernkovich, S. A., and Giordano, P. C. (1992). School bonding, race, and delinquency. *Criminology,* 30, 261–291.

Chesney-Lind, M. (1987). Family relationships and delinquency. *Criminology,* 25, 295–321.

——. (1989). Girl's crime and woman's place: Toward a feminist model of female delinquency. *Crime and Delinquency* 35 (1), 8–10.

——. (1993). Girls, gangs, and violence: Anatomy of a backlash. *Humanity and Society,* 17, 321–344.

——. (1999a). Challenging girls' invisibility in juvenile court. *Annals of the American Academy of Political and Social Science,* 564, 185–202.

——. (1999b). *The female offender: Girls, women, and crime.* Thousand Oaks, CA: Sage.

Chesney-Lind, M., and Hagedorn, J. M. (Eds.). (1999). *Female gangs in America: Essays on girls, gangs, and gender.* Chicago, IL: Lake View Press.

Chesney-Lind, M., and Shelden, R. G. (1992). *Girls, delinquency, and juvenile justice.* Pacific Grove, CA: Brooks/Cole.

Chesney-Lind, M., Shelden, R. G., and Joe, K. A. (1996). Girls, delinquency, and gang membership. In. C. R. Huff (Ed.), *Gangs in America* (2nd Edition) (pp. 185–204). Newbury Park, CA: Sage.

Claes, M., and Simard, R. (1992). Friendship characteristics of delinquent adolescents. *International Journal of Adolescence and Youth,* 3, 287–301.

Cloward, R., and Ohlin, L. (1960). *Delinquency and Opportunity: A Theory of Delinquent Groups.* Glencoe, IL: Free Press.

Cohen, A. (1955). *Delinquent boys: The culture of the gang.* Glencoe, IL: Free Press.

Cohen, L. E., and Felson, M. (1979). Social change and crime rate trends: A routine activity approach. *American Sociological Review,* 44, 588–608.

Corrado, R. R., Odgers, C., and Cohen, I. M. (2000). The incarceration of female young offenders: Protection for whom? *Canadian Journal of Criminology, 42,* 189–208.

Covington, J. (1999). African-American communities and violent crime: The construction of race differences. *Sociological Focus, 32,* 7–24.

Curran, D. J. (1984). The myth of the "new" female delinquent. *Crime and Delinquency, 30,* 386–399.

Curry, G. D. (1998). Female gang involvement. *Journal of Research in Crime and Delinquency, 35,* 100–118.

Daly, K. (1992). Women's pathways to felony court: Feminist theories of lawbreaking and problems of representation. *Southern California Review of Law and Women's Studies, 2,* 11–52.

Daly, K., and Chesney-Lind, M. (1988). Feminism and criminology. *Justice Quarterly,* 5: 497–535.

DeKeseredy, W. (2000). *Women, crime, and the Canadian criminal justice system.* Cincinatti, OH: Anderson.

Deschenes, E. P., and Esbensen, F. (1999). Violence and gangs: Gender differences in perceptions and behavior. *Journal of Quantitative Criminology, 15,* 63–96.

Dugan, L., and Apel, R. (2003). An exploratory study of the violent victimization of women: Race/ethnicity and situational context. *Criminology, 41* (3), 959–977.

Elliot, D. S., Huizinga, D., and Ageton, S. (1985). *Explaining delinquency and drug use.* Beverly Hills, CA: Sage.

Elliot, D. S., Huizinga, D., and Menard, S. (1989). *Multiple problem youth: Delinquency, substance use, and mental health problems.* New York: Springer.

Empey, L. T., Stafford, M. C., and Hay, C. H. (1999). *American delinquency: Its meaning and construction.* Belmont, CA: Wadsworth.

Fagan, J. (1990). Social processes of delinquency and drug use among urban gangs. In C. R. Huff (Ed.), *Gangs in America* (2nd Edition) (pp. 39–74). Newbury Park, CA: Sage.

Fergusson, D. M., Horwood, L. J., and Lynskey, M. T. (1993). Prevalence and co-morbidity of DSM-III-R diagnoses in a birth cohort of 15-year-olds. *Journal*

of the American Academy of Child and Adolescent Psychiatry, 32, 1127–1134.

Gaarder, E., and Belknap, J. (2002). Tenuous borders: Girls transferred to adult court. *Criminology, 40* (3): 481–517.

Gilligan, C. (1982). *In a different voice: Psychological theory and women's development.* Cambridge, MA: Harvard University Press.

Giordano, P. C. (1978). Girls, guys, and gangs: The changing social context of female delinquency. *Journal of Criminal Law and Criminology, 69,* 126–132.

Giordano, P. C., Cernkovich, S. C., and Pugh, M. D. (1986). Friendship and delinquency. *American Journal of Sociology, 91,* 1170–1202.

Giordano, P. C., Cernkovich, S. C., and Rudolph, J. L. (2002). Gender, crime, and desistance: Toward a theory of cognitive transformation. *American Journal of Sociology, 107,* 990–1064.

Gover, A. (2004). Risky lifestyles and dating violence: A theoretical test of violent victimization. *Journal of Criminal Justice, 32,* 171–180.

Hagedorn, J. M., and Devitt, M. L. (1999). Fighting female: The social construction of female gangs. In M. Chesney-Lind and J. Hagedorn (Eds.), *Female gangs in America.* (pp. 256–276). Chicago: Lake View Press.

Hannon, L., and Defronzo, J. (1998). The truly disadvantaged, public assistance, and crime. *Social Problems, 45,* 383–392.

Hannon, L., and Dufour, L. R. (1998). Still just the study of men and crime? A content analysis. *Sex Roles, 38,* 63–71.

Harms, P. (2003). *Detention in delinquency cases, 1990–99.* Washington DC: United States Department of Justice, OJJDP Fact Sheet.

Hartwig, H. J., and Myers, J. E. (2003). A different approach: Applying a wellness paradigm to adolescent female delinquents and offenders. *Journal of Mental Health Counseling, 25,* 57–76.

Hay, C. (2003). Family strain, gender, and delinquency. *Sociological Perspectives, 46,* 107–135.

Herrera, V. M., and McCloskey, L. A. (2003). Sexual abuse, family violence, and female delinquency: Findings from a longitudinal study. *Violence and Victims, 18,* 319–334.

Hoyt, S., and Sherer, D. G. (1998). Female juvenile delinquency: Misunderstood by the juvenile justice system, neglected by social science. *Law and Human Behavior*, 22, 81–104.

Hunt, G. P., Joe-Laidler, K., and Evans, K. (2002). The meaning and gendered use of getting high: Gang girls and drug use issues. *Contemporary Drug Problems*, 29, 375–415.

Jang, S. J., and Krohn, M. (1995). Developmental patterns of sex differences in delinquency among African-American adolescents: A test of the sex invariance hypothesis. *Journal of Quantitative Criminology*, 11, 195–222.

Joe, K., and Chesney-Lind, M. (1995). "Just every mother's angel": An analysis of gender and ethnic variations in youth gang membership. *Gender & Society*, 9, 408–430.

Joe-Laidler, K., and Hunt, G. P. (2001). Accomplishing femininity among girls in the gang. *British Journal of Criminology*, 41, 656–678.

Johnson, S. (1998). Girls are in trouble. *Corrections Today*, 60 (7), 136–141.

Jones, N. (2004). "It's not where you live, it's how you live": How young women negotiate conflict and violence in the inner city. *Annals of the American Academy of Political and Social Science*, 595, 49–62.

Knaak, S. (2004). On the reconceptualizing of gender: Implications for research design. *Sociological Inquiry*, 74, 302–317.

Lanctot, N., and LeBlanc, M. (2002). Explaining deviance by adolescent females. In M. Tonry (Ed.), *Crime and justice*, Vol. 29 (pp. 113–202). Chicago: University of Chicago Press.

Laub, J. H., and Sampson, R. J. (2003). *Shared beginnings, divergent lives: Delinquent boys to age 70*. Cambridge, MA: Harvard University Press.

Lauderback, D., Hansen, J., and Waldorf, D. (1992). "Sisters are doin' it for themselves": A Black female gang in San Francisco. *The Gang Journal*, 1, 57–70.

Lederman, C., and Brown, E. (2000). Entangled in the shadows: Girls in the juvenile justice system. *Buffalo Law Review*, 48, 909–925.

Leitz, L. (2003). Girl fights: Exploring females' resistance to educational structures. *International Journal of Sociology and Social Policy*, 23, 15–46.

Maher, L. (1997). *Sexed work: Gender, race, and resistance in a Brooklyn drug market*. Oxford, UK: Oxford University Press.

Maher, L., and Daly, K. (1996). Women in the street-level drug economy: Continuity or change? *Criminology*, 34, 465–492.

McCluskey, J. D., McCluskey, C. P., and Huebner, B. (2003). Juvenile female arrests: A holistic explanation of organization functioning. *Women and Criminal Justice*, 14 (4): 35–51.

McRobbie, A. (1991). *Feminism and youth culture*. London: Macmillan.

Miller, D., and Trapani, C. (1995). Adolescent female offenders: Unique considerations. *Adolescence*, 30, 429–436.

Miller, J. (1998). Up it up: Gender and the accomplishment of street robbery. *Criminology*, 36, 37–66.

———. (2001). *One of the guys: Girls, gangs, and gender*. New York: Oxford University Press.

Miller, J., and Brunson, R. K. (2000). Gender dynamics in youth gangs: A comparison of males' and females' accounts. *Justice Quarterly*, 17, 419–448.

Miller, W. B. (1975). *Violence by youth gangs and youth groups as a crime problem in major American cities*. Washington, DC: Government Printing Office.

Mirza, H. S. (1992). *Young, female, and black*. London: Routledge.

Moore, J. (1991). *Going down to the barrio: Homeboys and homegirls in change*. Philadelphia: Temple University Press.

———. (1994). The chola life course: Chicana heroin users and the barrio gang. *International Journal of the Addictions*, 29, 1115–1126.

Moore, J., and Hagedorn, J. (1999). What happens to the girls in the gang? In M. Chesney-Lind and J. Hagedorn (Eds.), *Female gangs in America* (pp. 177–186). Chicago: Lake View Press.

Mullins, C. W., and Wright, R. (2003). Gender, social networks, and residential burglary. *Criminology*, 41, 813–839.

Mullis, R. L., Cornille, T. A., Mullis, A. K., and Huber, J. (2004). Female juvenile offending: A review of characteristics and contexts. *Journal of Child and Family Studies*, 13, 205–218.

Nagin, D. S., Pogarsky, G., and Farrington, D. P. (1997). Adolescent mothers and the criminal behavior of their children. *Law and Society Review*, 31, 137–162.

Ness, C. D. (2004). Why girls fight: Female youth violence in the inner city. *Annals of the American Academy of Political and Social Science,* 595, 32–48.

Obeidellah, D. A., and Earls, F. J. (1999). *Adolescent girls: The role of depression in the development of delinquency.* Washington, DC: National Institute of Justice.

Pajer, K. A. (1998). What happens to "bad" girls? A review of adult outcomes of antisocial adolescent girls. *American Journal of Psychiatry,* 155, 862–870.

Peterson, D., Miller, J., and Esbensen, F. (2001). The impact of sex composition on gangs and gang members. *Criminology,* 39, 411–440.

Phillips, C. (2003). Who's who in the pecking order? Aggression and "normal violence" in the lives of girls and boys. *British Journal of Criminology,* 43, 710–728.

Pleydon, A. P., and Schner, J. G. (2001). Female adolescent friendship and delinquent behavior. *Adolescence,* 36, 189–206.

Poe-Yamagata, E., and Butts, J. A. (1996). *Female offenders in the juvenile justice system.* Washington, DC: Office of Juvenile Justice and Delinquency Prevention (OJJDP).

Richie, B. (1996). *Compelled to crime: The gender entrapment of battered black women.* New York: Routledge.

Risman, B. J. (2004). Gender as a social structure: Theory wrestling with activism. *Gender & Society,* 18, 429–450.

Robins, L. N., and Price, R. K. (1991). Adult disorders predicted by childhood conduct problems: Results from the NIMH Epidemiology Catchment Area Project. *Psychiatry: Journal for the Study of Interpersonal Processes,* 54, 116–132.

Sampson, R. J., and Laub, J. H. (1993). *Crime in the making: Pathways and turning points through life.* Cambridge, MA: Harvard University Press.

Sampson, R. J., and Lauritsen, J. L. (1997). Racial and ethnic disparities in crime and criminal justice in the United States. In M. Tonry (Ed.), *Ethnicity, crime, and immigration: Comparative and cross-national perspectives* (pp. 311–374). Chicago: University of Chicago Press.

Sampson, R. J., and Wilson, W. J. (1995). Toward a theory of race, crime, and urban inequality. In J. Hagan and R. D. Peterson (Eds.), *Crime and inequality* (pp. 37–54). Stanford, CA: Stanford University Press.

Scahill, M. (2000). *Female delinquency cases.* Washington, DC: U.S. Department of Justice, OJJDP Fact Sheet.

Schwartz, M. D., and Milivanovic, D. (Eds.). (1996). *Race, gender, and class in criminology: The intersection.* New York: Garland.

Siegel, J. A., and Williams, L.M. (2003). The relationship between child sexual abuse and female delinquency and crime: A prospective study. *Journal of Research in Crime and Delinquency,* 40, 71–94.

Sickmund, M., Sladky, T. J., and Kang, W. (2004). *Census of Juveniles in Residential Placement Databook.* Available online at *http://www.ojjdp.ncjrs.org/ojstatbb/cjrp.*

Simon, R. J. (1975). *Women and crime.* Lexington, MA: Lexington Books.

Smith, D. A., and Paternoster, R. (1987). The gender gap in theories of deviance: Issues and evidence. *Journal of Research in Crime and Delinquency,* 24, 140–172.

Snyder, H. N. (1996). *Juvenile Arrests.* Washington, DC: Office of Juvenile Justice and Delinquency Prevention, United States Department of Justice, Juvenile Justice Bullentin.

——. (2003). *Juvenile arrests 2001.* Washington, DC: OJJDP.

Snyder, H. N., and Sickmund, M. (1999). *Juvenile offenders and victims: 1999 national report.* Washington, DC: Department of Justice, OJJDP.

Sokol-Katz, J., Dunham, R. G., and Zimmerman, R. (1997). Family structure versus parental attachment in controlling adolescent deviant behavior: A social control model. *Adolescence,* 32, 199–215.

Sondheimer, D. L. (2001). Young female offenders: Increasingly visible yet poorly understood. *Gender Issues,* 19, 79–90.

Steffensmeier, D., and Allan, E. (1996). Gender and crime: Toward a gendered theory of female offending. *Annual Review of Sociology,* 22, 459–487.

Steffensmeier, D., and Demuth, S. (2001). Ethnicity and judges' sentencing decisions: Hispanic-black-white comparisons. *Criminology,* 39, 145–178.

Steffensmeier, D., and Haynie, D. (2000). Gender, structural disadvantage, and urban crime: Do macrosocial variables also explain female offending rates? *Criminology, 38,* 403–438.

Sykes, G. (1997). *8 ball chicks: A year in the violent world of girl gangs.* New York: Anchor Books.

Taylor, C. S. (1993). *Girls, gangs, women, and drugs.* East Lansing: Michigan State University Press.

Thrasher, F. (1927). *The gang.* Chicago: University of Chicago Press.

Torstensson, M. (1990). Female delinquents in a birth cohort: Tests of some aspects of control theory. *Journal of Quantitative Criminology, 6,* 101–115.

Totten, M. (2003). Girlfriend abuse as a form of masculinity construction among violent, marginal male youth. *Men and Masculinities, 6,* 70–92.

Warner, D. E. (2000). Race and ethnic bias in sentencing decisions: A review and critique of the literature. In M. W. Markowitz and D. D. Jones-Brown (Eds.), *System in black and white: Exploring the connections between race, crime and justice* (pp. 171–180). Westport, CT: Praeger.

Widom, C. S. (2000). Childhood victimization and the derailment of girls and women to the criminal justice system. In B. E. Richie, K. Tsenin, and C. S. Widom (Eds.), *Research on women and girls in the justice system: Plenary papers of the 1999 Conference on Criminal Justice Research and Evaluation* (pp. 27–36). Washington, DC: National Institute of Justice.

Wilkinson, D. L. (2003). *Guns, violence, and identity among African American and Latino youth.* New York: LFB Scholarly Publishing, LLC.

Wortley, S. (2003). Hidden intersections: Research on race, crime, and criminal justice in Canada. *Canadian Ethnic Studies, 35,* 99–117. ✦

7

Gender and Violent Crime

Claire M. Renzetti

In this chapter you will learn the following:

- About differences in patterns of violent offending and victimization by gender, race, and age

- How the offender-victim relationship is important for understanding gender differences in violent crime

- Why it is necessary to study the intersection of social class, race, and gender to get a more complete picture of violent crime in the United States

- What a hate or bias crime is, the characteristics and motivations of the majority of hate crime perpetrators, and the characteristics of the majority of hate crime victims

- The strengths and weaknesses of various theoretical explanations of gender and violent crime

The June 13, 2005, issue of *Newsweek* magazine carried a story, entitled "Bad Girls Go Wild," that presents data showing that between 1980 and 2003 the number of girls arrested for aggravated assault rose 96 percent, while the number of boys arrested for aggravated assault rose just 13 percent. Moreover, the article pointed out that the typical victims of the girls' assaults are other girls their own age (Scelfo 2005). The alarming claims of the article, however, are hardly new to criminologists. They are reminiscent of popular and academic writings from the early 1970s that argued that female crime

was not only increasing in frequency—in fact, at a faster pace than male crime—but also that it was increasing in severity, becoming more violent in nature (see, for example, Adler 1975). These publications were criticized for distorting the picture of men's and women's relative involvement in crime (see, for instance, Chesney-Lind 1997; Smart 1982; Steffensmeier 2001). For one thing, these reports focused only on rate changes rather than also considering the absolute base numbers from which the rates were calculated. This is a significant oversight because if a base number is small, even a slight increase will appear quite large; conversely, if a base number is large, a sizable increase may nevertheless appear to be minor. But the *Newsweek* article goes a long way in reviving the concerns raised in the 1970s. Are women and girls becoming more violent? Are they committing more violent crime than they have in the past? Does gender matter when it comes to violent crime, or has it become irrelevant? That is, are women now as violent as men?

In this chapter, we discuss gender differences in violent crime as well as some of the explanations that have been developed to explain these differences. We will begin by examining crime data that allow us to compare violent offending by sex and by race and age. We will also look at victimization data to determine who is most likely to be violently victimized by male and female offenders. We then consider theories of violent offending that take gender as well as other social locating variables, such as race, age, and social class, into account.

First, though, it is important to clarify what we mean by violent crime. A *violent crime* is a crime that results in the physical injury or death, or has the potential to result in the physical injury or death, of another person. The Federal Bureau of Investigation identifies four of these crimes as the most serious and groups them into the *Violent Crime Index*. The Violent Crime Index includes homicide, forcible rape, robbery, and aggravated assault. These crimes—with the exception of forcible rape, since it is examined elsewhere in this book (see Caringella)—is the focus of this chapter.

Gender Differences in Rates of Violent Crime

Table 7.1 shows arrest data for the ten-year period 1994–2003 for males and females for violent Index crimes. Looking at the data for murder and non-negligent manslaughter, we find that during this period homicide arrests of both males and females decreased substantially. Although it appears at first glance that the rate of decrease for women was somewhat lower than that for men (a 36.9 percent decline for males vs. a 30.1 percent decline for females), the base numbers on which these percentages are calculated indicate that regardless of the relative size of the decrease, men continue to be significantly more likely than women to kill someone. A similar pattern emerges with regard to robbery. Both males and females experienced a decrease in arrests for robbery between 1994 and 2003; the rate of decline for men was more than twice as large as the rate of decline for women (26.2 percent and 12.4 percent, respectively). Yet, as the actual numbers of arrests show, men still commit nearly eight times more robberies than women commit (55,851 vs. 6,696 in 2003, respectively).

It is perhaps the crime of aggravated assault that has many observers so concerned about changes in female crime. Looking again at Table 7.1, we see that while males experienced a 17.3 percent drop in arrests for aggravated assault between 1994 and 2003, arrests of females for aggravated assault increased by 14 percent during this period. Still, the numbers themselves do not appear to signal that the United States is in the midst of a female violent crime wave. Indeed, we must keep in mind the lesson learned from the mistakes of the 1970s studies: Consider not only the rate changes but also the absolute numbers from which those changes are calculated. In 2003, 55,426 women were arrested for aggravated assault compared with 212,913 men arrested for the same offense. While the number of arrests of women for aggravated assault rose by more than 7,800 between 1994 and 2003, men were almost four times more likely than women to be arrested for aggravated assault in 2003. Moreover, despite the *Newsweek* statistic that arrests of girls for aggravated assault increased 96 percent between 1980 and 2003 compared with just a 13 percent increase for boys during this time, the ten-year arrest trends show declines in arrests of both males and females for this offense. The rate of decline for females under 18 years old was substantially more modest than that for males under 18 (1.9 percent vs. 31 percent), but the number of girls arrested for aggravated assault in 2003 was just 8,298 compared with 26,923 boys arrested for aggravated assault the same year (Federal Bureau of Investigation 2005).

Table 7.1
Ten-Year Arrest Trends for Violent Index Crimes by Sex, 1994–2003

Offense charged	Male			Female		
	1994	2003	Percentage change	1994	2003	Percentage change
Murder and non-negligent manslaughter	9,931	6,268	−36.9	1,068	747	−30.1
Forcible rape	18,910	14,651	−22.5	215	212	−1.4
Robbery	75,729	55,851	−26.2	7,640	6,696	−12.4
Aggravated assault	257,370	212,913	−17.3	48,613	55,426	+14.0

Source: Federal Bureau of Investigation 2005.

Of course, the increase in arrests of women for aggravated assault between 1994 and 2003 warrants explanation. But before we turn to various explanations of gender differences in violent criminal offending, let us consider how other factors intersect with gender to affect particular outcomes. As other authors in this book emphasize, the categories male and female are not homogeneous groups. Gender intersects with other social locating factors, such as age, race, and social class to affect particular outcomes. Consider homicide, for example. Researchers who specialize in the study of violent crime point out that homicide "is of interest not only because of its severity but also because it is considered by experts to be a fairly reliable barometer of violent crime. At the national level, no other crime is measured as accurately or precisely" (Fox and Zawitz 2004, 1). The homicide data tell us that males are most often the perpetrators of homicide; in 2002, they were ten times more likely than females to commit murder (Fox and Zawitz 2004). When we consider race and age as well as gender, however, we discover that black males 18 to 24 years old have the highest rate of homicide offending of any age, race, or gender group (see Table 7.2). In contrast, while the homicide offend-

ing rate of black females in all age groups is significantly higher than that of white females, both white and black females in all age groups have rates of homicide offending lower than those of white males and substantially lower than those of black males. For all groups, these rates have declined significantly since the 1990s but appear to have stabilized in recent years.

There are, of course, different types of homicides. One way to classify homicides is in terms of the relationship between the offender and the victim. This results in two major homicide categories: stranger and nonstranger. Within the category of nonstranger homicide, offenders and victims may be intimates (that is, current or former spouses or boyfriends/girlfriends), related in some other way, or acquaintances. The homicide data indicate that patterns of homicide victimization parallel patterns of homicide offending for males. Males are more likely than females not only to commit murder but also to be the victims of murder, be it at the hands of a stranger, an acquaintance, or an intimate. However, when women are victimized, they are more likely to be killed by a man than by a woman, and they are more likely to be killed by someone they know, including an intimate partner.

Table 7.2
Homicide Offending Rates per 100,000 Population by Race, Gender, and Age 1990–2002

| | Race, Gender, Age | | | | | | | | | | | |
| | White Male | | | Black Male | | | White Female | | | Black Female | | |
Year	14–17	18–24	25+	14–17	18–24	25+	14–17	18–24	25+	14–17	18–24	25+
1990	22.0	30.9	9.2	194.0	290.0	70.3	1.5	2.8	1.1	6.9	19.1	10.1
1991	22.8	32.9	8.8	213.6	364.1	68.8	1.3	2.6	1.0	10.5	22.0	10.2
1992	23.3	31.8	8.0	208.5	325.3	65.6	1.4	2.3	.9	11.2	17.2	8.8
1993	22.8	32.7	7.9	253.0	361.6	60.7	1.3	2.3	1.1	9.2	20.1	8.1
1994	24.8	32.7	7.5	235.1	337.5	55.1	1.6	2.2	1.0	9.6	17.7	7.8
1995	22.0	32.0	7.2	176.6	300.3	51.2	1.3	2.1	.9	7.6	13.0	6.3
1996	18.3	31.6	6.4	142.8	281.5	47.1	1.8	2.7	.9	8.9	15.7	6.2
1997	16.3	29.5	5.9	116.7	251.9	45.1	1.5	2.8	.8	4.5	15.9	5.3
1998	14.1	29.7	6.1	80.2	226.2	39.6	1.2	2.5	.9	5.3	13.3	5.1
1999	10.5	24.8	5.4	68.3	212.1	36.3	1.4	2.4	.8	6.1	10.7	4.3
2000	8.0	24.6	5.4	63.2	210.3	38.1	1.2	2.0	.8	5.3	11.5	4.1
2001	8.2	26.0	5.4	60.8	206.6	38.8	1.0	2.2	.7	5.2	12.6	4.2
2002	9.2	24.9	5.5	54.5	191.1	40.9	.9	2.0	.7	0.7	11.0	0.7

Source: Bureau of Justice Statistics 2005.

While 3 to 4 percent of male murder victims were killed by an intimate in 2002, about one-third of female murder victims were killed by an intimate that year. The proportion of male murder victims killed by an intimate has declined significantly since 1976, but the proportion of female murder victims killed by an intimate remained fairly stable from 1976 to the mid-1990s, when it began to increase; the proportion of female murder victims killed by an intimate has stabilized in recent years (Bureau of Justice Statistics 2005; see also Kaukinen, Gover, and Hays, this volume). When race is taken into account, we find that white and black men and women have experienced a decline in intimate homicides since 1976, but the rates of decline vary dramatically across these groups. Black males experienced the greatest decrease (81 percent) in intimate homicide victimization between 1976 and 2002; the decline for white males during the same period was 56 percent. Between 1976 and 2002, black females experienced a decline in intimate homicide victimization of 49 percent, but the decline for white females during this period was only 9 percent (Bureau of Justice Statistics 2005). Again, these findings do not support the claims that women are committing more violent crime than in the past or that when they do commit a violent crime, they typically victimize other women. To recap the data discussed so far, men are significantly more likely than women to engage in violent crime and to be the victims of violent crime. However, when women are violently victimized, they are more likely to be victimized by a man, especially a man they know.

Data on other types of violent crime lead to conclusions similar to those derived from the homicide data. Since we have already examined arrest statistics for robbery and aggravated assault, we turn now to the victimization data for these crimes. Looking at Table 7.3, we again see that gender and race intersect to affect victimization rates. For instance, while males are more likely than females to be the victims of a robbery, black males are nearly twice as likely as white

males to be robbery victims. Black males are also significantly more likely than white males and both white and black females to be injured during a robbery. With regard to aggravated assault, race appears to have a greater impact than gender. Although white males are almost twice as likely as white females to be the victims of aggravated assault, there is only a 1.3 percent difference between the aggravated assault victimization rates of black males and black females. And while white males are nearly twice as likely as white females to be threatened with a weapon during an aggravated assault, there is little difference in the likelihood of black males and Black females being threatened with a weapon during an aggravated assault. In fact, black females have a .2 percent greater rate of being threatened with a weapon during an aggravated assault than black males do.

Again, the offender-victim relationship is telling, although we have these data for gender only. Male robbery victims are most often victimized by strangers (74 percent), whereas female robbery victims are most often victimized by someone they know (55 percent), including intimate partners (19 percent). Only 4 percent of male robbery victims report that the offender was an intimate partner (Maguire and Pastore, 2004). Assuming that most victims are involved in heterosexual relationships and that few robbery arrests involve female perpetrators, we may conclude that female robbery victims are most often victimized by men as are most male robbery victims.

The pattern for aggravated assault is more difficult to discern from the available data. Male victims of aggravated assault are most likely victimized by a stranger (60 percent). Male victims of aggravated assault report that the assailant was someone they knew in 39 percent of cases. However, in only 2 percent of cases is this known assailant an intimate partner; in 32 percent of cases, the known assailant is a friend or acquaintance. In contrast, female victims of aggravated assault are most likely victimized by someone they know (58 percent). In 19 percent of cases, the known assailant is an intimate

Table 7.3

Estimated Number and Rate (per 1,000 persons age 12 and older) of Personal Victimization, Selected Violent Crimes by Sex and Race of Victim, 2001

Type of Crime	Male				Female			
	White		Black		White		Black	
	Number	Rate	Number	Rate	Number	Rate	Number	Rate
Crimes of Violence	2,537,870	27.2	398.090	30.8	2,144,890	21.9	488,110	31.6
Completed violence	701,890	7.5	165,910	12.8	735,500	7.5	175,480	11.4
Attempted/threatened violence	1,835,970	19.6	232,190	18.0	1,409,380	14.4	312,630	20.2
Robbery	321,400	3.4	82,970	6.4	183,100	1.9	20,270	1.3
Completed/property taken	199,110	2.1	67,130	5.2	133,450	1.4	11,190	0.7
With injury	87,170	0.9	19,250	1.5	56,470	0.6	7,840	0.5
Without injury	110,940	1.2	47,880	3.7	76,980	0.8	3,360	0.2
Attempted to take property	123,290	1.3	15,840	1.2	49,650	0.5	9,070	0.6
With injury	43,920	0.5	3,750	0.3	13,800	0.1	3,780	0.2
Without injury	79,370	0.8	12,090	0.9	35,850	0.4	5,290	0.3
Assault*	2,199,860	23.5	308,790	23.9	1,778,150	18.2	441,910	28.6
Aggravated	600,660	6.4	114,370	8.8	365,990	3.7	116,450	7.5
With injury	196,480	2.1	48,530	3.8	102,660	1.0	35,190	2.3
Threatened w/weapon	404,180	4.3	65,840	5.1	263,330	2.7	81,250	5.3

*includes simple assault

Source: Maguire and Pastore 2004, p. 197.

partner. Like male victims, however, 32 percent of female victims are assaulted by a friend or acquaintance (Maguire and Pastore 2004). If we assume that most victims are involved in heterosexual relationships, we can safely conclude that the majority of intimate aggravated assaults are committed by men.

We are on much shakier ground in drawing conclusions about the sex of perpetrators in stranger aggravated assaults against men and women and in aggravated assaults committed by friends and acquaintances. Given the arrest data we examined earlier, it would appear that most are men. However, arrest data reflect crimes reported to the police, and the victimization data we have been discussing come from the National Crime Victimization Survey, which has found that only about half of all violent crimes committed are reported to the police (Siegel 2003). Consequently, we must refrain from inferring the sex of the perpetrator for these specific offenses.

Before turning to explanations of gender—and race and age—differences in violent crime, two other issues deserve mention. First, we have not discussed the relationship of social class and violent crime. As other authors in this text have pointed out, those arrested and convicted of crimes are most likely to be poor; and poor, young, black men and women are overrepresented among the U.S. prison population (see Anderson, this volume; Young and Adams-Fuller, this volume). The available data on violent criminal victimization show an inverse relationship between social class and being the victim of a violent crime. That is, as social class increases, the likelihood of being a violent crime victim steadily decreases. In 2001, for example, 46.6 out of 1,000 people with annual incomes less than $7,500 were victims of a violent crime compared with 18.5 out of 1,000 people with annual incomes of $75,000 or more (Maguire and Pastore 2004). Given that we know that racial minorities are significantly more likely than whites to be poor, and the data we have examined show that racial minorities are more likely than whites to be the victims of violent crimes, we can perhaps better understand why it is necessary to examine the intersection of race and social class along with gender to get a more complete picture of the violent crime problem in the United States.

Second, we need to keep in mind that some violent crimes are hate crimes. A *hate crime* or bias crime is a crime motivated by an offender's bias against the race, ethnicity, religion, disability, or sexual orientation of the victim.[1] Thus, a hate crime is not a separate type of crime, but rather a crime against a person (a violent crime) or the person's property (a property crime) that is distinguished by the offender's motivation for committing the crime. The vast majority of violent hate crime perpetrators are male (83 percent); 60 percent are white men, while 21 percent are black men and 2 percent are men of another race (Strom 2001). According to data reported by the Bureau of Justice Statistics, 61 percent of hate crime incidents are motivated by race, 14 percent by religion, 13 percent by sexual orientation, 11 percent by ethnicity, and 1 percent by disability. As we have seen with other types of violent crimes, not only are most perpetrators of violent hate crimes male, most victims of such crimes are also male (65 percent): 40 percent of victims are white men, 23 percent are black men, and 2 percent are men of another race (Strom 2001). One might intuitively expect that most victims of violent hate crimes are victimized by strangers. However, the Bureau of Justice Statistics data indicate that 38 percent of victims report that their attackers were acquaintances. Victims were attacked by strangers in 26 percent of the violent hate crimes and by intimates, relatives, or friends in 7 percent, but in 30 percent of the cases the relationship between the offender and the victim was either unknown or unreported (Strom 2001). Unfortunately, the data on the victim-offender relationship are not broken down by sex. However, Strom (2001) reported that age is associated with the victim-offender relationship. Specifically, younger victims are more likely to be victimized by someone they know. For instance, 67 percent of victims of violent hate crimes who were 12 years old or younger were victimized by acquaintances compared with 46 percent of victims aged 13 to 15 and 21 percent of victims aged 21 or older.

In sum, the data we have examined show significant differences in both violent offending and violent victimization for males and females as well as across racial and age groups. An important question that remains is, How can we account for these gender, race, and age differences? Criminologists offer several competing answers to this question, which we'll consider next.

Gender and Violent Crime: Theoretical Explanations

Historically, criminologists ignored women as offenders. In their view, crime was something women just didn't do. Among the few criminologists who discussed female criminality, the emphasis was on the natural depravity of female offenders, especially violent female offenders. The rationale was that since "normal" women are passive or docile, women who commit violent crimes must be "sick" or "abnormal" (Stanko 2001). The notion that *natural differences* between males and females are responsible for gender differences in behavior has not disappeared. Some criminologists and other social scientists continue to argue that gender differences in violent criminal offending are the product of biological differences between the sexes (Putallaz and Bierman 2004). For example, hormonal differences between males and females have been attributed as the source of gender differences in violent or aggressive behavior. Although both males and females produce the same sex hormones, they secrete them in different amounts, with males secreting more testosterone and other androgens and females producing more estrogen and progesterone. The hormone *testosterone* has been associated with aggressive and violent behavior.

Initially, the evidence linking testosterone to aggression came primarily from animal studies. In these experiments, laboratory animals injected with testosterone showed a significant increase in fighting behavior, regardless of their sex. In other experiments, newborn animals were castrated with the result that they matured into docile adult animals. Critics have urged caution in generalizing the findings from animal studies to humans. However, in research with humans, findings do indicate that high levels of circulating testosterone are correlated with edginess, competitiveness, and anger in both men and women. For instance, in one recent study, female athletes who had taken synthetic testosterone during training were more easily irritated and more quickly angered than women who had not used testosterone (Van Goozen, Frijda, and Van de Poll 1994). However, it is difficult to pinpoint the relationship between testosterone and aggressive or violent behavior because research indicates that testosterone levels rise and fall *in response* to environmental stimuli (Angier 1999; Blum 1997). For example, one study showed that testosterone rose in male tennis players before a match, dropped as the match was played, and then rose dramatically in players who won the match, but it dropped just as dramatically in players who lost (Booth et al. 1989; see also Mazur, Booth, and Dabbs 1992).

It is also difficult for scientists to pinpoint the relationship between testosterone and human violence because testosterone is only one of many chemicals interacting in the body that affect behavior. *Neurotransmitters*, for example, are chemical compounds found between nerve cells that send messages or signals from one neuron to another. Our bodies produce many different neurotransmitters, but only about 50 of them have been extensively studied. The available research shows that neurotransmitters have a direct impact on behavior, emotions, moods, and learning. Among the neurotransmitters that have been associated with aggressive and violent behavior are norepinephrine, a "watchdog" chemical involved in responses to threats of danger; dopamine, a chemical involved in feelings of pleasure and reinforcement or re-

ward; and serotonin, a chemical that regulates impulsivity (Niehoff 1999). However, similar to the research on testosterone, much of the research on neurotransmitters has been done on animals, so caution is needed in generalizing these findings to men and women. In addition, many studies of neurotransmitters' effects have produced contradictory results, leading some researchers to speculate that the relationship between a particular neurotransmitter and a specific behavioral outcome such as violence—like the relationship of testosterone to violent behavior—is not one of direct cause and effect but rather a *reciprocal interaction effect*, where fluctuations contribute to certain behaviors; but engaging in certain behaviors or having particular experiences also produce fluctuations in the neurotransmitter (Niehoff 1999).

Indeed, few criminologists and other social scientists believe that human social behavior is determined solely by biological factors. Decades of research clearly demonstrate that human social behavior is highly amenable to the situation or context in which it occurs and this, in turn, may override or alter the potential effects of biology. Consequently, many criminologists have sought explanations for gender differences in violent offending in the different socialization experiences of males and females in Western industrialized societies (Zahn-Waxler and Polanichka 2004). Put quite simply, in societies such as the United States, males are taught from an early age that aggression and even violence are expected of them, and they are rewarded for such behavior; however, females are taught from an early age to be passive, dependent, and compliant, and aggressive or violent behavior by girls is strongly discouraged and even punished. Children receive these messages from parents, teachers, and peers as well as the media. Boys are given toy guns and other toy weapons to play with, but girls are given dolls, miniature plastic appliances, and pretend beauty products (Renzetti and Curran 2003). Research shows that most boys and girls learn their respective gender lessons quickly, with boys even as preschoolers exhibiting a preference for rough-and-tumble play and a greater willingness to fight than girls.

Yet, despite the power of socialization to shape gendered behavior, human beings are not empty vessels into which socialization messages are poured so that we are indelibly molded into masculine males and feminine females. What makes us distinctively human is our ability to reflect on our social circumstances, to give them meaning, and to actively participate in the shaping of our own identities through social interaction. Some feminist theorists have recently developed this idea further in an effort to explain a wide variety of gender differences in behavior, including violent offending.

Sociologist Candace West and her colleagues (West and Fenstermaker 1995; West and Zimmerman 1987) borrow the ethnomethodological concept of *situated action* or *situated accomplishment* to reframe gender as something women and men do in response to contextualized norms of masculinity and femininity, rather than as a static social role externally imposed on them by others or by "society." Males and females "do gender" in various situations, making choices—albeit choices constrained by structural conditions and normative expectations—of how they will establish their masculinity and femininity, respectively. Thus, gender changes over time and varies from situation to situation depending on normative demands as well as an individual's resources and perceptions of others' evaluations of him or her. Even more important perhaps is the recognition that doing gender intersects with doing race/ethnicity, social class, age, and sexual orientation, producing a "multitude of masculinities and femininities—each shaped by structural positioning—rather than one static set of gender roles" (J. Miller 2002, 435).

Drawing on these ideas, some feminist criminologists theorize that violence constitutes a means for accomplishing gender in certain contexts. For example, James Messerschmidt (1993, 2000, this volume) has studied males' conscious decisions to use certain actions in specific situations and the meanings they give to these actions. His data show that violent crime, such as robbery and assault, are a means for young, urban, poor and working-class males to construct a type of masculinity that he calls "the hardman." In the social settings in which these young men live their everyday lives, many other resources for accomplishing masculinity are blocked; violent crime is an available option. Similarly, Bufkin (1999) and Perry (2001) applied the notion of gender as situated accomplishment in their analyses of hate crimes. In considering the characteristics of typical hate crime perpetrators and their victims—recall the statistics we examined earlier—as well as the characteristics of the crimes themselves (e.g., language used by perpetrators, the group nature of many hate crimes, the use of alcohol by perpetrators), both Bufkin and Perry theorize that committing hate crimes is a means of accomplishing a particular type of privileged masculinity. This type of masculinity is called *hegemonic masculinity*: white, Christian, able-bodied, heterosexual masculinity.[2]

This theoretical perspective is sometimes called *structured action theory* (see Messerschmidt 1997, this volume), and it has been applied primarily to violence by men and boys. But several criminologists have recently used structured action theory to explain some types of violent offending by women and girls. For instance, Messerschmidt (1995, 1997, 2002, this volume) studied girl gang members' violent offending. He reported that when girl gang members engage in violence, such as when they assault rival gang members to protect the "hood," they are not behaving like boys but rather are engaging in normatively appropriate femininity—femininity endorsed by gang members and that intersects with racial, class, sexual, and generational norms in the social context of the gang. He refers to this normative gang femininity as "bad girl femininity," and he emphasizes that when gang girls brag about their violence, they do not describe themselves as masculine, but as "bad."

Messerschmidt's analysis is especially important for pointing out that when girls and women engage in violence, they are not behaving "like men." Jody Miller (2002), another contributor to this text and a criminologist who has applied structured action theory to gang girls' violence, argued for more nuanced analyses of doing gender through violence and urged criminologists to stop thinking of gender in dualistic terms—that is, as masculinity *or* femininity. She stated that theories of gendered violence must account for the complexity and flexibility of social actors' agency coupled with the structural, institutional, and intersubjective constraints on their behavior. She showed, for instance, how in some violent situations gang girls may describe themselves as behaving "like boys," "embracing a *masculine* identity that they view as contradicting their bodily sex category (that is female)" (Miller 2002, 443). This does not mean, of course, that this self-identity construction is permanent or that they see themselves this way in other situations, even other violent situations. She highlighted, for example, situations such as robberies, in which crime is not a resource for women to accomplish gender but rather gender is used as a resource for women to accomplish crime. In her study of robbery, Miller (1998) found that men typically use guns, physical coercion, and violence in male-on-male robberies—"clearly a reflection of the masculine ideologies shaping men's robberies" (p. 50). In contrast, her study showed that women usually rob other women, whom they perceive as vulnerable and easy to intimidate. But when women rob men, Miller found, they play on gender stereotypes of women as weak and sexually available to manipulate their targets into situations in which the robbery is more easily completed.

Jody Miller (2002) also described situations in which other social locating factors, such as race, can have primacy over gender. For instance, she pointed out that whereas the African-American gang girls she studied saw violence as normative and status-enhancing, research with Asian-American gang girls indicates that violence is not "celebrated and normative" but rather a "consequence of and response to the abuse . . . that characterizes their lives at home" (Joe and Chesney-Lind 1995, 428). This latter point is important in that recent research, such as that discussed by Kaukinen and her colleagues in Chapter 5 of this text, shows that violent victimization is a more salient contributing factor to violent offending for girls and women than it is for boys and men.

Feminist criminologists, in fact, have focused a great deal of attention on the violent crime that they feel mainstream criminology neglected most: men's violence against women (see Belknap and Potter, this volume; Caringella, this volume). Although some criminologists have criticized feminists for referring to men's violence against women as an "epidemic" (see, for example, Felson 2002), empirical data on the frequency and severity of this violence—some of which we examined in this chapter—prompted feminists to develop a theoretical model for explaining it.

At the risk of oversimplifying the theory and to avoid redundancy with other chapters in this text, suffice it to say here that feminist criminology sees men's violence against women as a means of preserving and reinforcing men's dominance and women's subordination in a patriarchal society (Yllo 1993). Men's violence against women is an outgrowth of gender inequality. In *patriarchal societies*, men have greater access to resources (e.g., income) than women do, and greater resources translate into greater power—that is, the ability to control others and get them to comply with one's wishes. Women's economic dependence on men is one control tactic men can use to preserve their dominance; violence (or the threat of violence) may be seen as the ultimate control tactic to ensure women's subordination. Gender norms shore up these unequal gender relations to such an extent that men's superiority is taken for granted by many people, male and female. It is hardly surprising to feminists that women are more likely to be violently victimized by men they know, because gender norms bestow a sense of entitlement on men: entitlement to women's bodies, services, and deference, especially the bodies, services, and deference of "their" women. A substantial body of research with male offenders documents their sense of entitlement as well as their motives for using violence to punish and control women (see, for example, Barnett, Lee, and Thelan, 1997; Scully and Marolla 1985).

Critics of feminist theory have argued that in patriarchal societies, and particularly among men who adhere to "traditional" gender norms such as "men are superior to women" and "women are weak," there is strong support for chivalry, which serves to protect women from violence, not make them more vulnerable to it (Felson 2002). The overwhelming majority of people, these critics claim, abhor the idea of a man behaving violently toward a woman, which helps to explain why when men do violently victimize women, "they prefer to do it when no one is watching" (Felson 2002, 73). While this argument has some common-sense appeal as well as some empirical research to support it, feminist criminologists respond that it overlooks an important caveat: Chivalry protects women against men's violence *only if* the women conform to patriarchal standards of "true womanhood." Studies consistently show that a sizable minority of women and men believe it is acceptable for a man to hit a woman or force her to have sex with him under "certain circumstances," which typically can be subsumed under the following heading: "She did something to deserve it"; for example, she behaved promiscuously or "led him on," she used alcohol or drugs, she was unfaithful to him, or she is a lesbian. Standards of "true womanhood" are based on white, middle-class ideals of femininity, and research documents the elevated risk of violent victimization among women who "deviate" from these norms (see, for example, Crenshaw 1994; Perry 2001). But despite the shocking frequency of male violence against women, it is the case, as our statistics indicate, that relatively few men batter, assault, or in other ways violently victimize women. As Yllo (1993) asked, "Why is a subordinate, cowering wife pleasing [or rewarding] to some men, but

not others?" (p. 57). Herein lies the potential value for the further development of a *feminist* theory of structured action.

The notion of chivalry raises another interesting hypothesis that some criminologists have offered to explain gender differences in violent offending, at least as they are reflected in arrest rates. Specifically, it has been hypothesized that when women commit violent crimes, they are less likely than male violent offenders to be arrested, convicted, and sentenced to prison because of gender stereotypes of women as weak and passive. In this case, the argument goes, gender stereotypes work in women's favor by keeping them out of the criminal justice system. There is, however, little empirical evidence that supports this hypothesis. For example, one recent study that took into account such factors as type of offense and prior convictions showed that offense severity and prior record have the largest effect on sentencing for both male and female offenders; when men and women appear in court under similar circumstances—that is, charged with similar crimes and coming from similar backgrounds—they are treated alike (Steffensmeier, Kramer, and Streifel 1993; Steffensmeier, Ulmer, and Kramer 1998). However, other studies show that the perceived "respectability" of the offender, male or female, in terms of conformity to traditional gender norms does affect criminal justice outcomes (Spohn and Holloran 2000; Steffensmeier, Ulmer, and Kramer 1998). Again, "chivalry" is extended only to those women who conform to the traditional model of "true womanhood," and women who come into contact with the police and the judicial system rarely compare well to this model.

One area in which police decisions to arrest have had a significant impact on women's arrest rates is intimate partner violence. Since the late 1980s, there has been a nationwide trend in the United States toward preferred and mandatory arrest policies in cases of intimate partner violence. These policies were instituted to eliminate or substantially decrease police discretion to arrest in intimate partner violence cases, requiring officers, who are typically the first to arrive at such crime scenes, to arrest aggressors, the intent being to increase victims' safety (das Dasgupta 2002). An unintended consequence of such policies, however, has been a significant increase in dual arrests—that is, the arrest of both the male and the female partners in heterosexual intimate relationships—as well as the arrest of women as sole perpetrators (Hirschel and Buzawa 2002). In many states with mandatory and preferred arrest policies for intimate partner violence cases, the number of women arrested has increased dramatically; for example, in Connecticut, the percentage of women arrested on domestic violence charges rose from 11 percent to 18 percent between 1987 and 1997; in Boulder County, Colorado, women's representation among domestic violence arrestees went from 12 percent in 1997 to nearly 25 percent in just the first six months of 1999 (das Dasgupta 2002). Although analyses of the efficacy of mandatory arrest policies and the harm arrest does to victims of intimate partner violence are both beyond the scope of this chapter (see S. Miller 2005 for these analyses), it is very likely that such policies have contributed to the increase in women's arrest rates for aggravated assault shown in Table 7.1. Moreover, as Susan Miller (2005) pointed out, women are less likely than men to rely on their physical strength and may resort to weapons to equalize the force if they are defending themselves against an abuser. But the use of a weapon in such cases elevates the charges filed against them to felonies, whereas men, who may use their physical strength alone against women, would be charged only with misdemeanors.

Conclusion

We return to the questions that opened the chapter. Are women and girls becoming more violent? None of the data we have examined in this chapter point us to an affirmative answer. In fact, the data show a decline in violent crime for both males and females. Are women and girls committing more violent crime than in the past? Again, the answer appears to be no. With the exception of aggravated assault, females' already low rates of violent crime have gone even lower in recent years. The moderate increase in arrests for aggravated assault appear to pertain to adult women and may be explained, at least in part, by increases in women's arrests for domestic violence as a result of the adoption of mandatory and preferred arrest policies in domestic violence cases in many states.

Does gender matter when it comes to violent crime, or has it become irrelevant? The data we reviewed in this chapter show that gender is an important factor not only in violent criminal offending but also in violent victimization. In fact, one of the most consistent findings across studies and over time is that females are significantly less likely than males to engage in violent crime and to be violent crime victims. When women do commit a violent crime, it is usually against someone they know. And when women are violently victimized, they are more likely than men to be victimized by someone they know.

But we have also learned that gender is not the only social locating factor that matters when it comes to violent crime. Race, age, and social class intersect with gender in influencing violent offending and victimization rates. Specifically, young, poor, black men have the highest rates of violent offending and victimization.

Criminologists, we have seen, have developed a variety of theories to explain these differences in violent crime. The theory of structured action, in particular, suggests that we analyze gender—as well as race, age, social class, and sexual orientation—as multidimensional and fluid, varying across situations, individuals, and groups. Feminist tests and revisions of structured action theory hold tremendous promise for leading us to a more complex, but also more comprehensive, understanding of how doing certain forms of gender—and race, age, class, and sexual orientation—maybe accomplished through violent crime.

Notes

1. In a few states, such as Texas, gender is also a bias category in the hate crime statute. However, research indicates that prosecutors are often unaware of this aspect of the hate crime legislation and, even when made aware of it, do not think it can be used in a successful prosecution (McPhail and DiNitto 2005).

2. Although feminist criminologists so far have neglected to study terrorist violence, the concept of hegemonic masculinity may be helpful in explaining why there appear to be so few women in terrorist organizations, particularly those tied to fundamentalist religious or conservative political groups, which tend to adhere strongly to norms of gender segregation and inequality.

Study/Discussion Questions

1. If the data do not show that women and girls have become more violent, why do you think this idea has received so much attention and seems to be widely believed?

2. Other than increases in arrests of women for domestic violence due to mandatory and preferred arrest policies, what other factors might be contributing to the rise in women's arrests for aggravated assault?

3. Two types of gendered identities researchers have studied with respect to gang behavior are "the hardman" and "bad girl femininity." Can you think of any other types of gendered identities that may be associated with violent offending? What are some of the specific characteristics of these identities? How do race, age, social class, and sexual orientation come into play with each of these gendered identities?

References

Adler, F. (1975). *Sisters in crime*. New York: McGraw-Hill.

Anderson, T. L. (2006). Issues facing women prisoners in the early twenty-first century. In C. M. Renzetti, L. Goodstein, and S. L. Miller (Eds.), *Rethinking gender, crime, and criminal justice: Feminist readings* (pp. 200–212). Los Angeles: Roxbury Publishing.

Angier, N. (1999). *Women: An intimate geography*. New York: Anchor.

Barnett, O. W., Lee, C. Y., and Thelan, R. (1997). Gender differences in attributions of self-defense and control in interpartner aggression. *Violence Against Women*, 3, 462–481.

Belknap, J., and Potter, H. (2006). Intimate partner abuse. In C. M. Renzetti, L. Goodstein, and S. L. Miller (Eds.), *Rethinking gender, crime, and criminal justice: Feminist readings* (pp. 168–184). Los Angeles: Roxbury Publishing.

Blum, D. (1997). *Sex on the brain*. New York: Viking.

Booth, A., Shelley, G., Mazur, A. Tharp, G., and Kittock, R. (1989). Testosterone and winning and losing in human competition. *Hormones and Behavior*, 23, 556–571.

Bufkin, J. (1999). Bias crime as gendered behavior. *Social Justice*, 26, 155–176.

Bureau of Justice Statistics (2005). *Homicide trends in the United States*. Retrieved on July 26, 2005 from *www.ojp.usdoj.gov/bjs/homicide/homtrnd.htm*.

Caringella, S. (2006). Sexual assaults reforms: Thirty years and counting. In C. M. Renzetti, L. Goodstein, and S. L. Miller (Eds.), *Rethinking gender, crime, and criminal justice: Feminist readings* (pp. 155–167). Los Angeles: Roxbury Publishing.

Chesney-Lind, M. (1997). *The female offender*. Thousand Oaks, CA: Sage.

Crenshaw, K. W. (1994). Mapping the margins: Intersectionality, identity politics, and violence against women of color. In M. A. Fineman and R. Mykitiuk (Eds.), *The public nature of private violence* (pp. 93–119). New York: Routledge.

das Dasgupta, S. (2002). A framework for understanding women's use of nonlethal violence in intimate heterosexual relationships. *Violence Against Women*, 8, 1364–1389.

Federal Bureau of Investigation. (2005). Crime in the United States, 2004. Retrieved on July 26, 2005 from *http://www.fbi.gov/ucr*.

Felson, R. B. (2002). *Gender and violence reexamined*. Washington, DC: American Psychological Association.

Fox, J. A., and Zawitz, M. W. (2004). *Homicide trends in the United States: 2002 update*. Washington, DC: U.S. Department of Justice.

Hirschel, D., and Buzawa, E. (2002). Understanding the context of dual arrest with directions for future research. *Violence Against Women*, 8, 1449–1473.

Joe, K. A., and Chesney-Lind, C. (1995). "Just every mother's angel": An analysis of gender and ethnic variation in youth gang membership. *Gender & Society*, 9, 408–430.

Kaukinen, C., Gover, A. R., and Hays, S. A. (2006). Age-graded pathways to victimization and offending among women and girls. In C. M. Renzetti, L. Goodstein, and S. L. Miller (Eds.), *Rethinking gender, crime, and criminal justice: Feminist readings* (pp. 57–75). Los Angeles: Roxbury Publishing.

Maguire, K., and Pastore, A. L. (Eds.). (2004). *Sourcebook of criminal justice statistics 2002*. Washington, DC: U.S. Department of Justice.

Mazur, A., Booth, A., and Dabbs, J. M. Jr. (1992). Testosterone and chess competition. *Social Psychology Quarterly*, 55, 70–77.

McPhail, B. A., and DiNitto, D. M. (2005). Prosecutor perspectives on gender-bias hate crimes. *Violence Against Women*, 11, 1162–1185.

Messerschmidt, J. W. (1993). *Masculinities and crime*. Lanham, MD: Rowman & Littlefield.

——. (1995). From patriarchy to gender: Feminist theory, criminology, and the challenge of diversity. In N. H. Rafter and F. Heidensohn (Eds.), *International feminist perspectives in criminology* (pp. 167–188). Philadelphia: Open University Press.

——. (1997). *Crime as structured social action: Gender, race, class, and crime in the making*. Thousand Oaks, CA: Sage.

——. (2000). *Nine lives: Adolescent masculinities, the body, and violence*. Boulder, CO: Westview.

——. (2002). On gang girls and a structured action theory: A reply to Miller. *Theoretical Criminology*, 6, 461–475.

——. (2006). Masculinities and crime: Beyond a dualist criminology. In C. M. Renzetti, L. Goodstein, and S. L. Miller (Eds.), *Rethinking gender, crime, and criminal justice: Feminist readings* (pp. 29–43). Los Angeles: Roxbury Publishing.

Miller, J. (1998). Up it up: Gender and the accomplishment of street robbery. *Criminology*, 36, 37–66.

——. (2002). The strengths and limits of "doing gender" for understanding street crime. *Theoretical Criminology*, 6, 433–460.

Miller, S. (2005). *Victims as offenders: The paradox of women's violence in relationships*. New Brunswick, NJ: Rutgers University Press.

Niehoff, D. (1999). *The biology of violence*. New York: Free Press.

Perry, B. (2001). *In the name of hate: Understanding hate crime*. New York: Routledge.

Putallaz, M., and Bierman, K. L. (Eds.). (2004). *Aggression, antisocial behavior, and violence among girls: A developmental perspective*. New York: Guilford Press.

Renzetti, C. M., and Curran, D. J. (2003). *Women, men, and society: The sociology of gender* (5th ed.). Boston: Allyn and Bacon.

Scelfo, J. (2005, June 23). Bad girls gone wild. *Newsweek*, pp. 66–67.

Scully, D., and Marolla, J. (1985). Riding the bull at Gilley's: Convicted rapists describe the rewards of rape. *Social Problems*, 32, 251–263.

Siegel, L. J. (2003). *Criminology* (8th ed.). Belmont, CA: Wadsworth.

Smart, C. (1982). The new female offender: Reality or myth? In B. R. Price and N. J. Sokoloff (Eds.), *The criminal justice system and women* (pp. 105–116). New York: Clark Boardman.

Spohn, C., and Holleran, D. (2000). The imprisonment penalty paid by young, unemployed Black and Hispanic male offenders. *Criminology*, 38, 281–306.

Stanko, E. A. (2001). Women, danger, and criminology. In C. M. Renzetti and L. Goodstein (Eds.), *Women, crime and criminal justice* (pp. 13–26). Los Angeles: Roxbury.

Steffensmeier, D. (2001). Female crime trends, 1960–1995. In C. M. Renzetti and L. Goodstein (Eds.), *Women, crime, and criminal justice* (pp. 191–211). Los Angeles: Roxbury Publishing.

Steffensmeier, D., Kramer, J., and Streifel, C. (1993). Gender and imprisonment decisions. *Criminology*, 31, 411–446.

Steffensmeier, D., Ulmer, J., and Kramer, J. (1998). The interaction of race, gender, and age in criminal sentencing: The punishment cost of being young, black, and male. *Criminology*, 36, 763–797.

Strom, K. J. (2001). *Hate crimes reported in NIBRS, 1997–99*. Washington, DC: U.S. Department of Justice.

Van Goozen, S., Frijda, N., and Van de Poll, N. (1994). Anger and aggression in women: Influence of sports choice and testosterone administration. *Aggressive Behavior*, 20, 213–222.

West, C., and Fenstermaker, S. (1995). Doing difference. *Gender & Society*, 9, 8–37.

West, C., and Zimmerman, D. H. (1987). Doing gender. *Gender & Society*, 1, 125–151.

Yllo, K. A. (1995). Through a feminist lens: Gender, power, and violence. In R. J. Gelles and D. R. Loseke (Eds.), *Current controversies on family violence* (pp. 47–62). Newbury Park, CA: Sage.

Young, V. D., and Adams-Fuller, T. (2006). Women, race/ethnicity, and criminal justice processing. In C. M. Renzetti, L. Goodstein, and S. L. Miller (Eds.), *Rethinking gender, crime, and criminal justice: Feminist readings* (pp. 185–199). Los Angeles: Roxbury Publishing.

Zahn-Waxler, C., and Polanichka, N. (2004). All things interpersonal: Socialization and female aggression. In M. Putallaz and K. L. Bierman (Eds.), *Aggression, antisocial behavior, and violence among girls: A developmental perspective* (pp. 48–68). New York: Guilford Press. ✦

8

Female Drug Offenders and the Drug/Crime Subculture

Gender, Stigma, and Social Control[1]

Susan E. Martin

In this chapter you will learn the following:

- That the relationship between gender, drug use, and criminal behavior is not fixed but varies with the following changes: (a) women's opportunities and social expectations, (b) the availability and type of drug of abuse, and (c) the laws regarding illicit drug possession and distribution and their enforcement

- About women's limited "career" opportunities and roles in the "drug economy," which have increased with the rise of crack. Nevertheless, women still face discrimination and barriers in the underworld parallel to those in the legitimate economy

- About the gender differences in the pathways into and out of drug abuse and criminal activities as well as differences in patterns of drug-related crime

- That female drug users face greater stigma than do male users; that they are labeled failures as women and mothers; and that they encounter more social controls over their behavior that arise from both formal control mechanisms (e.g., criminalization of pregnancy) and infor-

mal ones (e.g., violent victimization by male partners and clients)

Close your eyes and picture a female drug offender. Most likely the image that comes to mind is of an inner city woman of color who uses crack-cocaine, frequently trades sex for crack, and has one or more "crack babies." News coverage of the crack epidemic of the 1980s and early 1990s, often including such sensationalistic presentations, resulted in this stereotype (Chavkin 2001; Vidaeff and Mastrobattista 2003). However, drug use among women is not new or primarily a problem of women of color, although women of color currently are disproportionately arrested, convicted, and incarcerated for drug offenses.[2] The stereotype distorts both the past and the present drug use of women of color, stigmatizes both the mother and the child who was exposed to cocaine in utero, and ignores the structural and cultural factors that contribute to and shape the nature of criminal activity and drug use among women and girls.

To understand female drug offenders, it is important to take a longer-term view of the United States' drug-related policies and how they affect drug use and users, and to explore the sociocultural and contextual factors that shape the lives of the women and girls in the drug-crime subculture. In the past century, there have been major changes in the availability and popularity of various drugs, in social norms regarding drug use and women's behavior in society, and in the laws controlling drug possession and sale as well as their enforcement by officials of the criminal justice system. There also has been a major change in the economic and social position of women in American society. Nevertheless, as will be more fully detailed, female drug offenders past and present tend to grow up in troubled families living in impoverished and disorganized neighborhoods and subsequently face multiple psychological, social, and economic problems. As their criminal behavior and addiction escalate, they encounter multiple stigma as "failed" women who have stepped out of "proper female roles" as lawbreakers and addicts, and they also are perceived as sexually promiscuous and incompetent mothers. In addition, they are burdened and socially marginalized for being poor and frequently women of color.

This chapter examines the social and economic factors that contribute to participation in the drug-crime subculture, the sexism that pervades that subculture, and the social and health consequences for these women and girls, as well as the costs to the broader society. The chapter first traces changes in drug use, the drug economy, and social control policies and examines how these are related to drug abuse and crime. It next examines the pathways to drug abuse, criminal behavior, and participation in the drug-crime subculture for female drug offenders. The third section presents a review of women's roles in the drug economy as users and dealers as well as alternative illegal sources of income, including prostitution or sex work and nondrug crimes or "hustles." The next section examines the legal and health consequences of serious drug use and crime for these women and their children. The concluding section addresses the gendered nature of the social response to this severely disadvantaged group of women and the implications for public policy.

It is important to note that one group of women who abuse drugs is excluded from the discussion largely because their behavior is rarely linked to crime: women who abuse and/or are addicted to prescription drugs. As will be noted, in the late nineteenth century, opium was legal and over-prescribed, particularly for women. Kandall (1998a) observed that, "a significant component of the problem of female addiction has come and still comes from the inappropriate and excessive medication of women by physicians and pharmacists and through self-medication" (p. 72). Because women are deemed as less able to bear physical and psychic discomfort, they receive "special treatment" (Kandall 1998a).

Currently, women are more likely than men to be given medications for depression, stress, and weight control that may result in addiction. Among men and women who use either a sedative, anti-anxiety, or hypnotic drug, women are almost twice as likely to become addicted (NIDA 2001). Such women, however, possess the drug legally and are rarely visible to the public or involved in the criminal justice system.

In this chapter, the term *female drug offender* is used ro refer to the subset of girls and women in the user population who are criminally involved with use and sale of illicit drugs and also are involved in other criminal activities. The term *drug use* refers primarily to the use of illicit substances, including marijuana, cocaine, heroin, and polydrug use. Because possession and sale of these drugs is illegal but there is a demand for them, an underground market or *drug economy* has developed to provide them. The drug economy also is part of and supports a subculture or social world in which heavy users and addicts as well as many professional criminals who use drugs participate. This is termed the *drug/crime subculture*.

Women and Drug Control Policies: Continuities and Change

Drug laws and public policies are shaped by and reflect social attitudes and norms. At the same time, laws alter not only norms and social perceptions of those who violate them but they also change opportunities for drug use and for those who would profit from it. This section briefly examines changes in drug control policies and their effects on women.

Social Change and the Evolution of Drug Control Policies

Women in the United States have long been major consumers of both legal and illegal drugs. In the mid- and late-nineteenth century, substances such as cocaine and opiates were generally accepted as medicines and were legally sold over the counter as well as frequently prescribed by physicians for an assortment of physical ailments particularly for women. At the beginning of the twentieth century, women—most of whom were white and middle class—comprised the majority of the opiate addict population due to overuse of opiate-containing medications (Kandall 1998a). This suggests that there is no necessary connection between drug use and crime and that the precise nature of that relationship is elusive and changing. Among the factors that affect the drug use-crime link are shifts in the availability and popularity of "new" drugs (e.g., LSD in the 1960s and crack-cocaine in the late 1980s), scientific evidence regarding the medical consequences of the drug's use, and policy responses to it—all of which contribute to public reaction and the extent of stigma of the drug and its users (McBride, VanderWaal, and Terry-McElrath 2003).

Three major social forces led to the curtailment of drug use in the United States in the early part of the twentieth century. First, physicians and pharmacists became aware of the dangers of certain drugs. Second, the sociodemographic changes in the American population led to a shift in the public perception of the drug addict from genteel white women to poor urban, minority, and immigrant males (particularly Mexican and Chinese workers) who were made the scapegoat for racist concerns about white women's innocence (Paltrow 2004). Third, the United States faced international pressures to control the flow of drugs. Together, these contributed to legislative initiatives that resulted in the passage of the Harrison Anti-Narcotic Act of 1914 (Kandall 1998a).

That Act and a number of subsequent laws and court decisions shifted the control of narcotic drugs from physicians and pharmacists to policy makers and the law enforcement community. From the 1920s through the 1940s, the severity of federal laws concerning the sale and possession of opium and cocaine gradually increased. In 1937, marijuana was placed under govern-

ment control as well (White and Gorman 2000, 7, 8). Because demand for these drugs continued, an underground drug economy developed to provide illicit drugs, accompanied by an underworld drug/crime subculture among users.

In the 1950s, drug abuse referred primarily to heroin addiction. It was primarily regarded as a man's disease and was associated with violent crime. By the end of that decade, women comprised only about 20 percent of the total drug-addicted population (Kandall 1998b). At the same time, female addicts, like their male counterparts, increasingly came from lower socioeconomic, more marginalized groups and their addiction became more and more interwoven with the drug/crime subculture. Because drug-using women relied on prostitution as well as theft as a means of support, their drug use and sexuality became closely linked; less visible but also linked to addiction in women were poverty, subservience to men, and social isolation.

The ferment in American society in the 1960s was reflected in its ambivalent attitude toward drug use and drug control policy. New lifestyles and new drugs emerged. Along with the free speech, civil rights, women's liberation, and anti-Vietnam war movements, and rise of the youth counterculture, came widespread experimentation with drugs, primarily marijuana and LSD. In the inner cities, in addition to marijuana, heroin use rapidly increased through the 1960s and 1970s (White and Gorman 2000).

These changes resulted initially in growing tolerance of recreational use of drugs, recognition that drug addiction is a disease, and questioning of America's punitive approach. However, increasing social disorder and rising crime rates led to growing fear of crime-committing addicts. In 1972, President Nixon declared a "war on drugs" focusing on heroin and marijuana, and Congress passed more punitive measures to control drug use that continued to climb through the 1970s.

The 1980s brought a renewed emphasis on "zero tolerance" and an exponential rise in drug arrest and incarceration rates for both men and women. The increase in drug arrests and prosecutions fundamentally changed the composition of the imprisoned population. By the early 1990s, 60 percent of federal prisoners were incarcerated for drug-related crime (White and Gorman 2000).

In the 1980s, as the use of heroin declined, cocaine reemerged as the drug of choice, first among the wealthy (who "snorted" it through the nose in powder form) and, shortly afterward, in the form of crack-cocaine (known simply as crack), which could be smoked. Crack gained popularity in part because it was cheap; a smokable "rock" could be purchased in street drug markets for as little as $5. In this form, cocaine can be rapidly absorbed by the body and causes an instantaneous intense "high" that lasts about 10 to 20 minutes, followed by depression and restlessness relieved by smoking more crack. Users typically smoke for as long as they have crack or the means to purchase it, often going on several day binges, as "pursuit and use of the drug outweighs other concerns" (Fullilove, Lown, and Fullilove 1992, 276). As this form of cocaine moved across the country from large cities on each coast, the number of users and dealers mushroomed, spawning competition and violence in many neighborhoods. The media labeled the new phenomenon a "crack epidemic."

Crack cocaine led to a substantial increase in the female proportion of the drug using population. Whereas women had represented a relatively stable 20 to 25 percent of the addicted population prior to 1960, that figure rose to about 33 percent during the 1980s (Butynski 1991), and following the appearance of crack, 40 percent of patients seeking admission for cocaine treatment between 1988 and 1992 in New York were women (Frank and Galea 1992). Urinalysis data from arrestees in 29 large cities across the United States indicate that in 2002, 63 percent of the women and 64 percent of the men tested positive for recent drug use, with cocaine being the most prevalent drug found among women (Taylor, Newton, and Brownstein 2003).

Policy makers responded to the new "crack epidemic" with large increases in punishment for drug-related offenses. In 1986 and 1988, Congress passed laws significantly increasing the penalties associated with crack-cocaine (but not powder cocaine) and adopted mandatory minimum sentences of five years for possession of relatively small amounts of crack, which were designed to deter "drug traffickers" (House Report 99845, Part 1, pp. 11–12, Sept. 19, 1986). In addition, as the media and scientific community labeled drug-exposed infants "crack babies," a number of states adopted an unprecedented policy, the prosecution of pregnant addicts under a variety of state criminal statutes, such as child endangerment or delivery of a dangerous weapon, thereby "selectively target(ing) pregnant women who use cocaine for sanctions even more punitive than those imposed on women who use other illicit substances" (Frank et al. 2001, 1621).

The impact of the sentencing legislation, regardless of the lawmakers' intent, has been skyrocketing correctional populations, with a particularly marked increase in incarceration rates for poor women of color charged with simple possession. In 1979, 10 percent of the women in U.S. prisons were doing time for drug offenses; by 1997, that figure was close to 40 percent, and more than two out of three of these women prisoners now are women of color (Greenfeld and Snell 1999).

In sum, the U.S. response to drug use, which initially was a problem of middle-class, primarily white women, was to make possession of certain substances illegal and to punish their use and sale with increasing harshness. This led to development of an underground drug economy and related drug/crime subculture and a growing number and proportion of women involved in them and under control of the criminal justice system. Nevertheless, as is documented in the next three sections, women's involvement in the drug/crime culture and underground economy has resulted in little benefit for themselves; rather, they experience continued oppression in that economy, low status and exploitation in the subculture, and a vast expansion of rates of imprisonment for drug use.

Pathways to Drug Use and Crime

Although many adolescents experiment with illegal drugs or commit minor crimes, or both, most "age out" of such behavior as they enter adulthood (Elliott, Huizinga, and Menard 1989). A few persist in criminal behavior and drug use, often escalating from alcohol and marijuana use to "hard" or narcotic drugs, such as heroin and cocaine, and become increasingly enmeshed in the drug/crime subculture. This section examines the characteristics of those individuals, the individual and environmental risk factors that propel them to lives of addiction and crime, and the nature of the association between criminal activity and drug abuse as well as differences between male and female pathways into drug use and crime.

Causal Associations: How Are Crime and Drug Use Related?

Many studies (see White and Gorman 2000 for citations) have sought to untangle the causal association between criminal activity and drug abuse; only a few of these have focused on girls and women. There are three possible positions with respect to the direction of causality between drug use and crime: drug use leads to or causes crime; criminal behavior is an antecedent of narcotic use; and both crime and drug use are the result of a third factor or set of factors. Studies that have examined the temporal sequence of drug use and crime have produced inconsistent results. Some studies have shown that criminal behavior in women addicts begins to emerge prior to serious drug use. For example, Inciardi, Pottieger, and Faupel (1982) found that the typical sequence is first criminal involvement, juvenile arrest, drug use, narcotic addiction, and first adult arrest, suggesting a progression from delinquency to drug use to addiction and

increased adult crime among heroin users. Similarly, among 708 sex-trading cocaine-using women in Miami, Florida, studied at several points in time during the 1990s, marijuana use began at age 15, criminal activity at 18, trading sex for drugs at 21, and use of crack-cocaine at age 24. Thus, the women's illicit drug use begins prior to the initiation of reported criminal activity, but the women's criminal careers were established before the use of crack-cocaine.

In contrast, Inciardi and Pottieger (1986) found that experimental drug use and criminal activity first occurred at the same ages in women who subsequently became addicted. This suggests that drug use and crime both are the result of the same adolescent antisocial developmental sequence, and subsequent use of narcotics several years later implied a continuation of the development of antisocial behavior.

Studies comparing changes in the level of criminality before and after initiation of narcotic use, however, clearly indicate that following addiction there are significant increases in crime (Anglin and Hser 1987; Fagan 1994; Inciardi, Lockwood, and Pottieger 1993). As criminal involvement and drug use intensify, the effects of each on the other become bi-directional and complex. Increased crime to help finance greater drug involvement occurs. At the same time, if criminal activity proves more profitable than anticipated, this permits an increase in drug intake, and the cycle continues (Inciardi, Lockwood, and Pottieger 1993). This consistent association of drug use and crime was found for both heroin and crack users (Fagan 1994; Inciardi, Lockwood, and Pottieger 1993) who became frozen into more intense patterns of criminality than they would have been without drugs.

Structural Characteristics and Common Problems of Women in the Drug/Crime Lifestyle

Studies conducted in inner-city neighborhoods in Chicago (Ouellet et al. 1993), New

York (Bourgois and Dunlap 1993; Fullilove, Lown, and Fullilove 1992; Maher and Curtis 1992), San Francisco (Rosenbaum 1981), Detroit (Mieczkowski 1994) and Miami (Inciardi, Lockwood, and Pottieger 1993; Inciardi and Surratt 2001) as well as a recent examination of women in small towns in the South (Evans, Forsyth, and Gauthier 2002) consistently have found that girls and women who become drug offenders and criminals confront numerous problems. These include poverty, parental substance abuse, violent victimization, a lack of education and marketable skills, gendered expectations and obligations, physical health risks, and psychological problems. Many have children and face economic pressures and homelessness that contribute to drug abuse. They also experience high rates of comorbid mental disorders including depression and post-traumatic stress disorder (PTSD) as a consequence of personal traumas, such as childhood abuse and neglect, rape, and partner violence. Thus, a mixture of individual, family, neighborhood, and social/environmental factors contribute to the pathways of drug use and crime for girls and women.

While there are many similarities in men's and women's pathways into and patterns of crime and drug use, there also are gender differences. Females report first drug use at a later age than males and have a briefer transition from first use to addiction, experiencing the adverse physiological effects of drug abuse more quickly than men (Weiss, Kung, and Pearson 2003). They are more likely to be initiated into drug use by a male partner (Amaro and Hardy-Fanta 1995), while male initiation into drug use is more likely to occur in the context of interactions with male friends (Maher and Curtis 1992). Women drug users also are more likely than men users to have a substance abusing spouse or domestic partner (Westermeyer and Boedecker 2000) and to have more life problems related to poverty, child care, and mental health (e.g., higher rates of comorbid addictive disorders and PTSD) (Bloom, Owen, and Covington 2003).

Family and neighborhood factors affect women's pathways to drug abuse. As children,

the women grew up in neighborhoods of extreme poverty and experienced chaotic family lives, including substance abusing and criminal family members. For example, Peugh and Belenko (1999) found that 40 percent of drug-using women in prison had parents who abused alcohol or drugs and half had a close family member who was incarcerated.

A study of parenting practices among crack-using individuals in one inner-city multi-generational household (Johnson, Dunlap, and Maher 1998) found that adults typically modeled various deviant behaviors. The women in the household were not expected to either raise or financially support the children born to them. Nor did the adults provide the children either emotional support or supervision. The children in these households came to regard drug abuse, sexual exploitation, and violence as normal. With little opportunity to learn conventional norms, they are likely to become juvenile delinquents, criminals, drug abusers, and prostitutes through the intergenerational transmission of drug use and criminal behavioral norms.

Sexual and physical abuse as well as emotional and physical neglect are common childhood experiences among female drug offenders (Browne, Miller, and Maguin 1999; Fullilove, Lown, and Fullilove 1992; Surratt et al. 2004) and contribute to the high rate of post-traumatic stress disorder (PTSD) in these women. For example, Surratt and colleagues (2004) found that half of the sex workers that they interviewed reported sexual abuse and 62 percent reported emotional abuse during childhood. In addition, as a result of the "compelled sexual contact" some girls in inner-city, multigenerational households experienced as part of their development processes, they learned that their sexual favors are a commodity that can be exchanged for what they want or need, easing the course into subsequent prostitution (Dunlap, Golub, and Johnson 2003).

Given childhood experiences in chaotic households within isolated and economically distressed neighborhoods where drugs and violence are the norm, it is not surprising that many girls and women self-medicate, using drugs not for "excitement" as is characteristic of males but as a coping mechanism for dealing with situational factors, life events or general psychological distress (Hser, Anglin, and Booth 1987; Inciardi, Lockwood, and Pottieger 1993; Novacek, Raskin, and Hogan 1991).

As adults, women addicts are frequent victims of violence by domestic partners. Studies have found that as many as 70 percent of women in drug treatment have experienced domestic violence (Dunn, Dunn, and Ryan 1998; El-Bassel et al. 2000). A study of drug-addicted welfare recipients observed that place of residence and neighborhood environment affected the frequency of exposure to drugs and the women's social network. Both of these, in turn, influenced experiences with both substance abuse and domestic violence (James, Johnson, and Raghavan 2004). Thus, both family and neighborhood factors contribute to continuing and sometimes escalating drug abuse.

Women in the Drug Economy

Drug dealing (i.e., selling or sharing drugs) is the most pervasive crime in the drug underground economy and the most lucrative way of making money among serious drug users (Hunt 1990). It also is a male-dominated activity in which women are limited to stereotypically gendered roles and activities. Like most (male) drug addicts, women may distribute drugs or drug services in exchange for money or drugs at some point in their criminal careers. However, most rely on a mix of sources to provide income, including theft, prostitution, and legal sources such as low wage work and welfare. This section examines the organization of the drug economy, women's varied roles in it, and the drug/crime subculture of the street drug abuser.

Drug Dealing and Women: The Persistence of Institutionalized Sexism

Prior to the rise of crack-cocaine in the 1980s, women were immersed in the street drug subculture and networks, but their roles in the street-level drug economy were very restricted since selling drugs traditionally was a highly gendered activity (Adler 1985; Johnson et al. 1985). The few women involved in dealing were consigned to peripheral roles, such as holders and lookouts, while men did the violent work associated with the criminal enterprise (Goldstein 1979). Women who sold drugs had low-status, short-lived, and sporadic selling involvement usually mediated by an intimate relationship with a man (Rosenbaum 1981). To support themselves and their drug habit, even those women who sold drugs relied on more stereotypically female activities, such as hustling (non-drug property crime) and prostitution. Some also drew on legal sources of income, including welfare and dependence on men for money and drugs (Hunt 1990; Rosenbaum 1981).

Steffensmeier (1983) explained women's limited roles in the drug economy and drug-selling networks as the result of "institutionalized sexism in the underworld" (p. 1013). He argued that male lawbreakers prefer to work, associate, and do business with other men; they view women as lacking the physical and mental attributes considered essential to working in an uncertain and violent context.

The rise of crack-cocaine in the mid-1980s brought a profound change to patterns of the distribution and consumption of illicit drugs in the United States (Bourgois 1989, 1995; Curtis et al. 1995; Fagan 1994; Hamid 1990; 1992; Johnson et al. 1994). These changes in the social and economic contexts in which drugs were bought and sold also led to significant shifts in women's drug involvement. The extent to which the shifts affected women's disadvantaged position in drug markets, however, is a matter of some debate (Fagan 1994; Maher 2004; Maher and Daly 1996).

Changes in the context of drug markets that affected women are related to three factors (Fagan 1994). Increased availability of inexpensive crack-cocaine made possible serious drug use without risk of injection and opened new opportunities for drug selling.

At the same time, structural shifts in the social and economic compositions of inner cities altered the social organization of drug use and selling. A loss of manufacturing jobs in large cities decreased legal income in inner-city neighborhoods and weakened informal neighborhood controls. With limited job skills and little hope for legitimate employment, inner-city youth were motivated to participate in the growing informal economy to generate income. As the demand for crack-cocaine outstripped the capacity of existing drug distribution systems, it created new marketing opportunities not previously available in family-centered heroin distribution organizations. Because crack could be sold in amounts as small as five dollars, it required little capital investment for a potential seller and yielded substantially more income than low-wage jobs or most other criminal activities. Many youth took advantage of these new opportunities in the drug economy.

Initially, many of the new crack entrepreneurs acted as "freelance" sellers who worked with loosely organized groups. Gradually, this organizational pattern has been replaced by a hierarchical system of organization and control (Johnson, Hamid, and Sanabria 1992). At the bottom rung of the drug economy hierarchy are street-level sellers and associates who act as lookouts, steerers or touts who solicit customers, holders who handle either drugs or money (but not both), and enforcers who intervene in cases of trouble (Johnson, Hamid, and Sanabria 1992). Street-level operatives are supplied and managed by crew bosses or managers who are conduits between them and the drug business "owners."

Women Drug Dealers in the Crack Era

Although there has been an increase in female participation in drug dealing in recent years, women either are freelance sellers or remain at the lowest levels of drug organizations with limited opportunities for partici-

pation. One three-year observation and interview study of women crack users in the Bushwick section of Brooklyn found only 19 of the 45 women had any role in the drug economy and none was an owner or manager (Maher and Daly 1996). Those women who participated in drug selling were overwhelmingly concentrated at the lowest levels and used as temporary workers when men were arrested or refused to work because it was "hot" due to police presence. Other women worked at low-level ancillary jobs, including "copping" (i.e., purchasing) drugs for others, typically white men, in return for small amounts of money or drugs; selling drug paraphernalia; or acting as lookouts, holders, gofers at crack houses, and "street docs" (persons who inject others).

Based on interviews with women from two northern Manhattan neighborhoods with high concentrations of crack use and selling, Fagan (1994) found that 36 percent of the women were involved in drug selling, either individually (20 percent) or as part of drug selling organizations (16 percent). The women sellers also were involved in high rates of nondrug crimes, predominantly shoplifting and fencing stolen goods but were able to greatly reduce the role of prostitution in generating income. Similarly, Inciardi, Lockwood, and Pottieger (1993) found that crack dealing was important in the criminal careers of female as well as male delinquents and adult women crack users in Miami. While the proportion of women who report some dealing does not differ greatly across these studies, interpretation of the findings regarding the availability of "new opportunities" for women does. Maher and Daly (1996) argued that women's opportunities for high income in drug sales continue to be limited by "the gender-stratified labor market and associated beliefs and practices that maintain it" (p. 485).

Studies of successful women drug dealers and the factors that contribute to their success (Denton and O'Malley 2001; Dunlap and Johnson 1996; Dunlap, Johnson, and Manwar 1994) suggested that these women operate differently from male dealers primarily in limiting their market activities and avoiding violence. Factors that contribute to their success include ability to draw on a significant reservoir of cultural, emotional, and material resources in childhood (e.g., strong emotional attachments) as well as skills and knowledge obtained in the conventional world as adults that provide tools for success and the ability to use them. Nevertheless, the social capital available to these working class women is not widely available in inner-city black neighborhoods.

Violence and Victimization of Women in the Drug Economy

Violence and the threat of violence are endemic to the operation of crack and other drug markets (Goldstein 1985). Because of the nature of the organization, violence is used to maintain organizational stability and as a strategic weapon in turf battles. Drug organizations recruit dealers who are violent and ruthless individuals, and who have little regard for loyalty or trust. In the context of this "culture of terror" (Bourgois 1989) characterized by male-dominated street networks, women who use the streets to sell or buy drugs are subject to constant harassment and are regularly victimized. Such violence deters some women from selling drugs (Maher 2004). Among women sellers, victimization was a more likely violence experience than was commission of a violent act. For example, in Fagan's (1994) New York study, over half the group of sellers and nearly one in four women overall were victims of crime in the course of drug transactions (Fagan 1994).

To avoid victimization, women who engage in drug selling employ several self-protective strategies. Some adopt a "gangsta bitch" or "crazy" stance, cultivating a "self-protective reputation of craziness" to survive (Maher and Daly 1996). Despite their tough posture and rhetoric, however, these women are widely perceived as less likely to possess the attributes associated with successful manag-

ers and street-level sellers. Men continue to be reluctant to work with women because they are seen as too emotional, unreliable, and lacking in the "heart" and physical capacity for violence that is an integral component of the street-level drug economy (Denton and O'Malley 2001; Waterston 1993). Therefore, they rarely gain reputations as ruthless sellers and do not move up in distribution organizations.

Other strategies for avoiding harassment by male sellers and arrest by police include being less conspicuous and staging performances in keeping with gender expectations. Some women sellers deliberately wear "ladylike" clothing or dress down to fit in with other neighborhood residents. They camouflage drug sales by arranging to meet customers at local restaurants, stores, or clubs, where they appear to be shopping or socializing (Jacobs and Miller 1998). They also maintain good relations with neighbors through greetings and small gifts to avoid having them complain to the police (Dunlap, Johnson, and Manwar 1994). But forgoing the "swaggering toughness" that male sellers display to maintain turf and adopting a less assertive stance that is more in keeping with gender expectations also restrict female sellers' clientele (Jacobs and Miller 1998), while violence remains an ever-present danger for women who sell drugs.

Non-Drug Crimes: Prostitution, Trading Sex-for-Crack, and Property Offenses

Women who are heavy drug users employ a shifting mix of "hustling" activities to survive on the street, including drug dealing, prostitution, theft, and fencing stolen goods. The media assume that women are forced to begin prostitution by drug enslavement (i.e., an existing addiction) and portray prostitutes as "fallen women," continuing the tradition of interpreting women's drug experience through the lens of cultural assumptions about substance abuse and sexuality. Researchers, however, have found a different pattern of the association of drug use and entry into prostitution and question the assumed causal links between drug addiction and sexuality.

Several studies indicate that drug use (usually use of alcohol and marijuana) and other criminal behavior (usually property offenses) begin prior to initiation into prostitution. However, prostitution usually occurs prior to initiation of narcotic drug use (i.e., heroin or crack) (Anglin and Hser 1987; Inciardi and Surratt 2001). Nevertheless, prostitution and sex trading (i.e., participating in sex-for-crack exchanges) are common at a later point in the crime/drug careers of heavy drug users given the expense of drugs and the lifestyle of users. Goldstein and colleagues' (1991) interviews with 133 women offenders in lower Manhattan found that during the eight-week study window 39 percent engaged in prostitution activities but 79 percent of those who were regular drug users did so. A recent study of 851 Miami cocaine-dependent women criminals found that 83 percent of the women reported having traded sex for money or drugs at least once during their last 30 days on the street (Inciardi and Surratt 2001). During that same 30-day period, however, nearly two-thirds (65 percent) of the offenses the women committed were drug sales or other drug-business offenses and just over a quarter were episodes of prostitution/sex trading. Prostitution activities also have been found to significantly increase during periods of heavy drug use (Anglin and Hser 1987).

The crack epidemic has negatively affected both the earning capacity and working conditions of street-level women sex workers and sex traders in low-income areas (Maher 2004; Murphy and Rosenbaum 1997). In inner-city neighborhoods, a barter system developed in which sex rather than money is exchanged for drugs. This system feeds on the particular nature of crack use in that the drug is consumed in binges. This pattern of drug use has created the "crack ho"—a prostitute who trades sex for extremely small amounts of money or drugs. Associated with this form of prostitution and crack houses are bizarre sexual practices and the degradation of women within the crack culture (Inciardi, Lockwood, and Pottieger 1993; Maher and Daly 1996).

Sex workers and sex traders are at high risk for assault, rape, and other forms of physical violence from drug dealers, pimps, police, "dates," and men who frequent freakhouses and crackhouses (Inciardi, Lockwood, and Pottieger 1993; Inciardi and Surratt 2001; Maher and Daly 1996). Their vulnerability is heightened by drug abuse, childhood abuse and neglect, and homelessness. Nearly half (42 percent) of the women in a recent study had experienced a violent encounter while engaging in prostitution in the previous year, including 29 percent who had a customer forcibly take back money paid for sex and 25 percent who were beaten by a "date" (Surratt et al. 2004).

Drug using sex workers and sex traders also frequently encounter violent victimization at the hands of men with whom they live, including their intimate partners (El-Bassel et al. 2000; Maher and Daly 1996). Violence by partners and others is viewed by the women as both expected and inevitable, deepening the patterns of violence and abuse many experienced in childhood (Surratt et al. 2004).

Homelessness, reported by 45 percent of women sex workers in Miami and a frequent condition among impoverished crack-abusing women in New York, contributes to women's victimization, sexual exploitation, and powerlessness (Inciardi and Surratt 2001; Maher and Daly 1996). Some women sleep on the street and in commercial establishments with high risks of theft and violent victimization; others find older males who take them in as companions or houseguests but exploit them in other ways, creating a new form of the commodification of women's sexuality in exchange for drugs and shelter while amplifying existing gender inequalities.

In sum, despite changes in the drug economy and drug/crime subculture, the former continues to be a gender-stratified labor market and the latter is dominated by sexist beliefs and practices. Thus, institutionalized sexism in the underworld continues to powerfully shape women's experiences. The new opportunities for drug dealing that emerged with the expansion of crack markets have demanded masculine qualities and capacities and been filled by men with the exception of sporadic short-lived opportunities for women in low-level distribution roles. With few exceptions, women continue to be relegated to marginal status in the drug business and in the street subculture. They use a mixture of income-producing strategies to finance their drug use including prostitution and other criminal "hustles" along with limited drug dealing activities. Even successful women dealers generate money by committing a wide variety of property offenses that is "the mark of the successful drug user/dealer" (Denton and O'Malley 2001). However, success in dealing generally reduces reliance on prostitution (Fagan 1994). Although the balance of drug-using women's criminal activities shifts with the availability of drugs, police pressure on drug dealing or street crime, and the amount and frequency of drug use of the woman, gender inequality is a constant. It continues to structure the opportunities for women in the drug economy and the cultural meanings that attach to female drug use.

Consequences for Women Drug Offenders

Gendered social expectations related to drugs have resulted in different social outcomes for male and female heavy drug use. This section identifies the legal, social, and health consequences for female drug offenders.

Patterns of Drug-Related Arrests, Prosecution, and Incarceration

Although crime, including drug offending, continues to be dominated by men, there have been significant changes in patterns of arrest and incarceration of women over the past four decades (Steffensmeier and Schwartz 2004).

First, the female proportion of total arrests across all criminal offenses doubled from 10 percent in 1965 to 20 percent in 2000 mostly due to sharp increases in the numbers of women arrested for minor property crimes, many of which are related to drug use. Second, between 1965 and 2000, there has been an exponential increase in rates of arrests for drug offenses of both men and women. The arrest rate of females for drug offenses per 100,000 women in the population quadrupled, going from 14 in 1965 to 68 in 1980. In the next decade, it increased by 300 percent, reaching 186 per 100,000 in the general population in 1990 and climbing to 240 in 2000. Comparable figures for men arrested for drug offenses per 100,000 men in the population were 92, 520, 1,005, and 1,175 in 2000. Thus, women's arrest rate for drug offenses grew 17-fold, compared with men's 12-fold increase so that by 2000, women comprised 17 percent of all persons arrested for drug offenses. Third, the proportion of women's arrests that was for drug-related offenses doubled from 5 percent in 1980 to 10.1 percent in 2000 (Steffensmeier and Schwartz 2004). In 2000, this translated into nearly 158,000 arrests of women for drug abuse violations as well as nearly 28,000 for prostitution and more than 250,000 for theft. Between 2000 and 2002, drug abuse arrests of juvenile and adult males decreased, those of adult females remained virtually unchanged, but arrests of females under age 18 climbed by nearly 6 percent (U.S. Department of Justice 2003).

The mandatory minimum sentencing policies adopted in 1986 and 1988 during the crack epidemic have had dire consequences for women. Prior to the war on drugs, although drug abuse was not uncommon, it was unusual for women to be incarcerated for offenses related to drug use. However, the number of women incarcerated in state prisons for drug offenses increased by 433 percent between 1986 and 1991 in comparison with a 283 percent increase for men during the same time period (Bush-Baskette 2000, 922). In 1979, 10 percent of women in prison were doing time for drugs; by 1999, drug offenders account for 38 percent of the female prison population (Greenfeld and Snell 1999). These figures led Chesney-Lind (1997) to suggest that the war on drugs had become a war on women. Bush-Baskette (2002) added that it disproportionately targets women of color. Between 1986 and 1991, the number of black women incarcerated in state prisons for drug offenses increased by 828 percent, the number of Hispanic women rose by 328 percent, while the number of white non-Hispanic women grew by 241 percent (Mauer and Huling 1995). In 1998, women of color comprised more than two out of three women in state and federal prisons (Greenfeld and Snell, 1999).

The toll on women is largest in the federal system, in which the passage of the 1986 law increased mandatory minimum sentences for federal crimes coupled with sentencing guidelines intended to reduce race, class, and other unwarranted disparities in sentencing have operated to the distinct disadvantage of women. In 1981, a quarter of the female prisoners were there for drug offenses; by 1991, that figure had risen to nearly two out of three (63.9 percent) women incarcerated in federal institutions being held for drug offenses, and by 1998 that had again risen to 72 percent (Greenfeld and Snell 1999). With mandatory minimums, the length of time served by women drug offenders also increased despite the fact that most of these women have little or no prior criminal record (Chesney-Lind 1997).

Drug-using women also have been stigmatized, blamed, and punished with additional charges for drug use during pregnancy as the media and scientific community labeled drug-exposed infants "crack babies." States adopted the unprecedented policy of prosecuting pregnant addicts under a variety of state criminal statutes, such as child endangerment, delivery of controlled substances to minors, and assault with a deadly weapon. By 2000, approximately 200 women had been arrested based on their status as pregnant drug-using women, and thousands of others had been affected by state laws that equate a pregnant woman's drug use with evidence of civil child neglect (Paltrow 2004). These prosecutions against maternal drug users have further marginalized these women when the crack baby served as "the poster child" in two politically charged controversies: the war on drugs and the struggle over abortion (Chavkin 2001). In the war on drugs, the crack baby was a useful symbol implying that a woman selfish enough to irreparably damage an innocent child for the sake of a quick high deserves retribution, making it easier to advocate a simplistic punitive response than to adopt a public health approach to address the complex causes of drug use (Chavkin 2001). The crack baby also is a symbol in the struggle over abortion, used by opponents of abortion in the name of fetal personhood who have advocated charges brought against new mothers.

Rising rates of incarceration affect not only the women themselves but also their children. An estimated 2 out of 3 women in state prisons have on average 2.38 minor children, and about two-thirds of these women were their primary caretakers, leaving more than 100,000 children with mothers serving time in state prison (Greenfeld and Snell 1999).

Health Risks and Other Consequences of Drug Addiction

Drug addiction is a major health problem for women offenders as well as a risk factor for other illnesses. Data on arrestees collected in 29 cities found that on average 42 percent of women arrestees were at risk for drug dependence compared with 37 percent of the men (Taylor, Newton, and Brownstein 2003). Among women in state prison, 50 percent described themselves as daily users of drugs, 40 percent were under the influence of drugs at the time of the offense, and nearly one-third said they had committed the offense that brought them to prison in order to obtain money to support their need for drugs (Greenfeld and Snell 1999).

Incarcerated women have much higher rates of psychiatric disorders compared with a group of women in the community. Jordan and colleagues (1996) found women in prison were 5 to 25 times more likely to suffer from a substance use disorder (including alcoholism). Teplin, Abram, and McClelland (1996) identified drug abuse disorders in 64 percent of female juvenile jail detainees, including 34 percent with PTSD. They also are vulnerable to malnutrition, hypertension, eating disorders, extreme feelings of guilt, anxiety, depression, dissociation and suicidal thoughts (El-Bassel et al. 1997; Najavits, Weiss, and Liese 1996).

Drug addiction also magnifies women's vulnerability to a variety of health risks that arise from poverty, malnutrition, exposure to violence, and lack of medical attention. It also greatly increases the risk of exposure to sexually transmitted diseases (STDs), including syphilis, gonorrhea, herpes simplex virus and HIV/AIDS. Nearly one-third of women sex traders in Miami had histories of injecting drugs and half reported having shared injection equipment. Their risks for STDs through sexual contacts were even higher given the large number of sexual contacts and inconsistent condom use (Inciardi and Surratt 2001).

AIDS cases among women have risen substantially along with the crack epidemic. In 1999, nearly one-fourth of all new AIDS cases were among women (Centers for Disease Control 2000); in Miami crack-using women have reported HIV prevalence rates ranging from 24 percent for nonsex traders to 38 percent among sex traders (Tortu et al. 1998). By the end of 1995, 4 percent of women inmates were HIV positive, making them twice as likely as male prisoners and 14 times as likely as the general population to be HIV-positive (Henderson 1998).

Discussion: Gender, Stigma, and Social Control

Women have always made up a significant portion of America's drug users and addicts, but until the past several decades their drug problems have largely been ignored. Focusing on minority and immigrant male addicts, Congress sought initially to control use of narcotic drugs. As drug control policies made possession and sale of many drugs illegal, a drug-crime link developed. With the growth of an underground economy to meet the demand for illicit drugs, drug addicts turned increasingly to crime as a source of income, and a drug/crime subculture or lifestyle emerged. Women drug users were increasingly stigmatized and marginalized from conventional society but also were offered only gender-related roles in the drug/crime underworld. Women criminal offenders also were rarely studied until the 1970s, so that knowledge about them and their drug use and criminal behavior still is limited and often based on a male model.

In contrast to popular stereotypes, women addicts come from a variety of racial, socioeconomic, and geographic backgrounds. They share a common bond of low self-esteem and societal blame as well as lives dominated by poverty and sexism, which have forced them to live in the margins of society. In addition, their addiction is stereotypically linked to sexuality, most recently represented by the image of the "crack ho" who trades sex for crack, reinforcing the association of the addicted woman with ethnic/racial minority status, HIV transmission, and "drug babies."

Problematic substance use is regarded as deviant and stigmatized behavior for both males and females; however it is often compatible with gender expectations for men but not women. A man gains status for being able to "hold his liquor," and experimentation with illicit drugs is a type of risk-taking tolerated in males. Such behavior in females violates gender expectations and is stigmatized and additionally interpreted as implying other violations of norms, particularly those of sexual misbehavior and emotional instability. Women who use illicit drugs on the street experience additional stigmatization and are most likely to be arrested and under criminal justice control because of their high visibility. According to Inciardi, Lockwood, and Pottieger (1993), "the stigma associated with socially problematic drug use by women is both the most consistent and most consequential similarity in the experience of drug-involved women" (p. 24).

These cultural stereotypes emerge from and rest on socially structured inequality. An emphasis on prison sentences suggests the view that the problems of drug addiction are the result of guilty individuals, distracting attention from the structural problems of poverty, crumbling communities, cutbacks in education and social services, and racism and sexism.

Gendered social expectations related to drugs also pervade the drug economy, resulting in different opportunities for males and females. The institutionalized sexism that pervaded the heroin trade has continued into the crack era and beyond. While there now are more women involved in drug dealing, they are confined to independent selling or limited work at the lowest level of the drug economy, mistrusted by male dealers and bosses, viewed as emotional and unreliable when confronted with violence, and vulnerable to victimization by clients and other dealers. To support themselves and their drug use, most women drug users rely on a shifting mixture of nondrug "hustles," including prostitution and property crime, along with minor dealing. They endure high rates of homelessness, violence, and other types of victimization in their struggle to survive on the streets.

Their lifestyle comes with high social costs to the women, their children, and society. Increasingly punitive sentencing policies have filled the prisons and jails with drug-abusing women, the majority of whom are women of color. Society pays not only the high economic costs of their imprisonment but also the longer-term psychosocial effects on their children of their mother's incarceration and the likelihood that, without drug treatment and other interventions, the women will return to crime and drugs once they are released.

Providing drug-abuse treatment is a necessary but insufficient first step because of the unique problems of women offenders. The challenge is designing gender-sensitive comprehensive interventions that address such basic issues as low self-esteem, comorbid mental disorders, absence of education and job skills, lack of parenting skills, homelessness, health problems, and the burden of multiple stigma as females, persons of color, drug addicts, and criminals.

At the same time, there is a need for structural social changes to level the playing field for women offenders while addressing larger social issues. Such changes might include modification of sentencing laws and social policies that consistently disadvantage poor and minority women and are costly to their children and the general public. For example, expanding the number and availability of treatment programs both in the community and within the criminal justice system might be less costly and more effective in the long run than current policies in reducing women drug offenders' recidivism rates. Finally, the growing inequality of income and opportunity that leads to poverty and hopelessness for inner-city residents as well as the intergenerational transmission of antisocial norms need to be addressed. This is a tall order, but without such changes the alternative costs in terms of the lives of these women and the next generation will be even greater.

Notes

1. The views expressed in this chapter are those of the author and do not necessarily represent the official position or policies of the National Institute on Drug Abuse, National Institutes of Health, or the Department of Health and Human Services.

2. A 1998 estimate of percentages of women 14 to 44 years of age using any illicit drug in the past year was 14.2 percent for white non-Hispanic women, 14 percent for black non-Hispanic women, and 10 percent for Hispanic women. Similar figures for cocaine use in the past year

were, respectively, 2.4, 2.2, and 1.6 percent (NIDA 2003, 53–54).

Study/Discussion Questions

1. Trace and discuss the changing characteristics and representation of women drug abusers in the general population and criminal justice populations in the past century.

2. How have changes in laws and policies affected the rates of arrests, convictions, and incarceration of women drug offenders?

3. Describe women's activities, opportunities, and barriers to success in the "drug economy."

4. How are women's drug use and criminal behavior related? Compare and contrast the etiology (origin) of drug use and criminal behavior of female and male drug offenders.

5. Discuss the stereotypic and actual links between sexuality and drug abuse.

References

Adler, P. A. (1985). *Wheeling and dealing: An ethnography of an upper-level drug dealing and smuggling community.* New York: Columbia University Press.

Amaro, H., and Hardy-Fanta, C. (1995). Gender relations in addiction and recovery. *Journal of Psychoactive Drugs,* 27, 325–337.

Anglin, M. D., and Hser, Y. (1987). Addicted women and crime. *Criminology,* 25, 359–397.

Baskin, D., Sommers, I., and Fagan, J. (1993). The political economy of violent female street crime. *Fordham Urban Law Journal,* 20, 401–407.

Bloom B., Owen, B., and Covington, S. (2003). *Gender responsive strategies: Research, practice, and guiding principles for women offenders.* Washington, DC: National Institute of Corrections.

Bourgois, P. (1989). In search of Horatio Alger: Culture and ideology in the crack economy. *Contemporary Drug Problems,* 16, 619–649.

———. (1995). *In search of respect: Selling crack in el barrio.* New York: Cambridge University Press.

Bourgois, P., and Dunlap, E. (1993). Exorcising sex-for-crack: An ethnographic perspective from Harlem. In M. S. Ratner (Ed.), *Crack pipe as pimp: An ethnographic investigation of sex-for-crack exchanges* (pp. 97–132). New York: Lexington Books.

Browne, A., Miller, B. A., and Maguin, E. (1999). Prevalence and severity of lifetime physical and sexual victimization among incarcerated women. *International Journal of Law and Psychiatry,* 22, 301–322.

Bush-Baskette, S. (2000). The war on drugs and the incarceration of mothers. *Journal of Drug Issues,* 30, 919–928.

Butynski, W. (1991). Drug treatment services: Funding and admissions. In R. W. Pickens, C. G. Leukefeld, and C. R. Schuster (Eds.), *Improving drug abuse treatment.* National Institute on Drug Abuse Research Monograph 106. DHHS Pub. No (ADM91-1754). Washington, DC: Government Printing Office.

Center for Disease Control and Prevention. (2000). *HIV/AIDS Surveillance Report,* 12(1), 1–12.

Chavkin, W., (2001). Cocaine and pregnancy: Time to look at the evidence. *Journal of the American Medical Association,* 285, 1626–1628.

Chesney-Lind, M. (1997). *The female offender: Girls, women, and crime.* Thousand Oaks, CA: Sage.

Curtis, R., Friedman, S. R., Neaigus, A., Jose, B., Goldstein, M., and Ildefonso, G. (1995). Street-level drug markets: Network structure and HIV risk. *Social Networks,* 17, 229–249.

Denton, B., and O'Malley, P. (2001). Property crime and women drug dealers in Australia. *Journal of Drug Issues,* 31, 465–486.

Dunlap, E. B., Golub, A., and Johnson, B. D. (2003). Girls' sexual development in the inner city: From compelled childhood sexual contact to sex-for-things exchanges. *Journal of Child Sexual Abuse,* 12, 73–96.

Dunlap, E. B., Golub, A., Johnson, B. D., and Wesley, D. (2002). Intergenerational transmission of conduct norms for drugs, sexual exploitation and violence: A case study. *British Journal of Criminology,* 42, 1–20.

Dunlap, E. B., and Johnson, B. D. (1996). Family and human resources in the development of a female crack-seller career: Case study of a hidden population. *Journal of Drug Issues,* 26, 177–200.

Dunlap, E. B., Johnson, B. D., and Manwar, A. (1994). A successful female crack dealer: Case of a deviant career. *Deviant Behavior*, 15, 1–25.

Dunn, G. E., Dunn, C. E., and Ryan, J. J. (1998). Cultural differences on three measures of dissociation in a substance abuse population. *Journal of Clinical Psychology*, 54, 1109–1116.

El-Bassel, N., Gilbert, L., Schilling, R. F., and Wada, T. (2000). Drug abuse and partner violence among women in methadone treatment. *Journal of Family Violence*, 15, 209–228.

El-Bassel, N., Schilling, R. F., Irwin, K. L., Faruque, S., Gilbert, L., VonBargen, J., Serrano, Y., and Edlin, B. R. (1997). Sex trading and psychological distress among women recruited from the streets of Harlem. *American Journal of Public Health*, 87, 66–70.

Elliott, D. S., Huizinga, D., and Menard, S. (1989). *Multiple problem youth: Delinquency, substance use, and mental health problems*. New York: Springer-Verlag.

Evans, R. D., Forsyth, C. J., and Gauthier, D. K., (2002). Gendered pathways into and experiences within crack cultures outside of the inner city. *Deviant Behavior*, 23, 483–510.

Fagan J. (1994). Women and drugs revisited: Female participation in the cocaine economy. *Journal of Drug Issues*, 24, 179–225.

Frank, B., and Galea, J. (1992). *Current drug use trends in New York City*. Albany: New York State Office of Alcoholism and Substance Abuse Services.

Frank, D. A., Augustyn, M., Knight, W. G., Pell, T., and Zuckerman, B. (2001). Growth, development, and behavior in early childhood following prenatal cocaine exposure. *Journal of the American Medical Association*, 285, 1613–1625.

Fullilove, M. T., Lown, E. A., and Fullilove, R. E. (1992). Crack 'hos and skeezers: Traumatic experiences of women crack users. *Journal of Sex Research*, 29, 275–287.

Goldstein, P. J. (1979). *Prostitution and drugs*. Lexington, MA: Lexington Books.

——. (1985). The drugs/violence nexus: A tripartite conceptual framework. *Journal of Drug Issues*, 15, 493–506.

Goldstein, P. J. Bellucci, P. A., Spunt, B. J., and Miller, T. (1991). Volume of cocaine use and vio-

lence: A comparison between men and women. *Journal of Drug Issues*, 21, 345–267.

Greenfeld, L., and Snell, T.L. (1999). *Women offenders*. Bureau of Justice Statistics Special Report (NCJ 175688). Washington, DC: U.S. Department of Justice.

Hamid, A. (1990). The political economy of crack-related violence. *Contemporary Drug Problems*, 17, 31–78.

——. (1992). The developmental cycle of a drug epidemic: The cocaine smoking epidemic of 1981–1991. *Journal of Psychoactive Drugs*, 24, 337–348.

Henderson, D. J. (1998). Drug abuse and incarcerated women: A research review. *Journal of Substance Abuse Treatment*, 15, 579–587.

Hser, Y. I., Anglin, M. D., and Booth, M. (1987). Sex differences in addict careers. 3: Addiction. *American Journal of Drug and Alcohol Abuse*, 13, 231–251.

Hunt, D. (1990). Drugs and consensual crimes: Drug dealing and prostitution in J. Q. Wilson and M. Tonry (Eds.), *Drugs and crime* (pp. 159–202) Chicago: University of Chicago Press.

Inciardi, J. A., Lockwood, D., and Pottieger, A. E. (1993). *Women and crack-cocaine*. New York: MacMillan.

Inciardi, J. A., and Pottieger, A. E. (1986). Drug use and crime among two cohorts of women narcotics users: An empirical assessment. *Journal of Drug Issues*, 16, 91–106.

Inciardi, J. A., Pottieger, A. E., and Faupel, C. (1982). Black women, heroin and crime: Some empirical notes. *Journal of Drug Issues*, 12, 241–250.

Inciardi, J. A., and Surratt, H. L. (2001). Drug use, street crime and sex-trading among cocaine dependent women: Implications for Public health and criminal justice policy. *Journal of Psychoactive Drugs*, 33, 379–389.

Jacobs, B. A., and Miller, J. (1998). Crack dealing, gender, and arrest avoidance. *Social Problems*, 45, 550–569.

James, S. E., Johnson, J., and Raghavan, C. (2004). 'I couldn't go anywhere': Contextualizing violence and drug abuse: A social network study. *Violence Against Women*, 10, 991–1014.

Johnson, B. D., Dunlap, E., and Maher, L. (1998). Nurturing for careers in drug use and crime:

Conduct norms for children and juveniles in crack-using households. *Substance Use & Misuse, 33,* 1511–1546.

Johnson, B. D., Goldstein, P. J., Preble, E., Schmeidler, J., Lipton, D. S., Spunt, B., and Miller, T. (1985). *Taking care of business: The economics of crime by heroin abusers.* Lexington, MA: Lexington Books.

Johnson, B. D., Hamid, A., and Sanabria, H. (1992). Emerging models of crack distribution. In T. M. Mieczkowski (Ed.), *Drugs and crime: A reader* (pp. 56–78). Boston: Allyn and Bacon.

Johnson, B. D., Natarajan, M., Dunlap, E., and Elmoghazy, E. (1994). Crack users and non-crack users: Profiles of drug use, drug sales, and nondrug criminality. *Journal of Drug Issues, 24,* 117–141.

Jordan, B., Schlenger, W., Fairbank, J., and Cadell, J. (1996). Prevalence of psychiatric disorders among incarcerated women: II. Convicted felons entering prison. *Archives of General Psychiatry, 53,* 739–754.

Kandall, S. R. (1998a). Women and addiction in the United States—1850 to 1920. In C. L. Wetherington and A. B. Roman (Eds.), *Drug addiction research and the health of women.* (pp. 53–80). Rockville, MD: National Institute on Drug Abuse.

———. (1998b). Women and addiction in the United States—1920 to the present. In C. L. Wetherington and A. B. Roman (Eds.), *Drug addiction research and the health of women.* (pp. 81–104). Rockville, MD: National Institute on Drug Abuse.

Maher, L. (2004). A reserve army: Women and the drug market. In B. R. Price and N. J. Sokoloff (Eds.), *The criminal justice system and women: Offenders, prisoners, victims, and workers* (3rd edition) (pp. 127–146). New York: McGraw-Hill.

Maher, L., and Curtis, R. (1992). Women on the edge of crime: Crack cocaine and the recent changing contexts of street-level sex work in New York City. *Crime, Law, and Social Change, 18,* 221–258.

Maher L., and Daly, K (1996). Women in the street-level drug economy: Continuity or change. *Criminology, 34,* 465–491.

Mauer, M., and Huling, T. (1995). *Young black Americans and the criminal justice system: Five years later.* Washington, DC: Sentencing Project.

McBride, D. C., VanderWaal, C. J., and Terry-McElrath, Y. M. (2003). The drugs-crime wars: Past, preset, and future directions in theory policy and program interventions. In #NCJ194616, *Toward a drugs and crime research agenda for the twenty-first century* (pp. 97–163). Washington, DC: U.S. Department of Justice.

Mieczkowski, T. (1994). The experiences of women who sell crack: Some descriptive data from the Detroit crack ethnography project. *Journal of Drug Issues, 24,* 227–248.

Murphy, S., and Rosenbaum, M. (1997). Two women who use cocaine too much. In C. Reinarman and H. Levine (Eds.), *Crack in America: Demon drugs and social justice* (pp. 98–112). Berkeley: University of California Press.

Najavits, L. M., Weiss, R. D., and Liese, B. S. (1996). Group cognitive behavioral therapy for women with PTSD and substance use disorder. *Journal of Substance Abuse Treatment, 13,* 13–22.

National Institute on Drug Abuse (NIDA). (2001). *Prescription drugs: Abuse and addiction.* (NIH Publication No. 01-4881). Bethesda, MD: Author.

———. (2003). *Drug use among racial/ethnic minorities* (Revised). (NIH Publication No. 03-3888). Bethesda, MD: Author.

Novacek, J., Raskin, R., and Hogan, R. (1991). Why do adolescents use drugs: Age, sex, and user differences. *Journal of Youth and Adolescence, 20,* 475–492.

Ouellet. L. J., Wiebel, W. W., Jimanez, A. D., and Johnson W. A. (1993). Crack-cocaine and the transformation of prostitution in three Chicago neighborhoods. In M. S. Ratner (Ed.), *Crack pipe as pimp: An ethnographic investigation of sex-for-crack exchanges* (pp. 69–96). New York: Lexington Books.

Paltrow, L. M. (2004). The war on drugs and the war on abortion. In B. R. Price and N. J. Sokoloff (Eds.), *The criminal justice system and women: Offenders, prisoners, victims, and workers* (3rd Edition) (pp. 165–184). New York: McGraw-Hill.

Peugh, J., and Belenko, S. (1999). Substance-involved women inmates: Challenges to providing effective treatment. *Prison Journal, 79,* 23–44.

Rosenbaum M. (1981). *Women and heroin.* New Brunswick, NJ: Rutgers University Press.

Sommers, I., Baskin, D., and Fagan, J. (1996). The structural relationship between drug use, drug dealing, and other income support activities among women drug sellers. *Journal of Drug Issues,* 26, 975–1006.

Steffensmeier, D. (1983). Organization properties and sex-segregation in the underworld: Building a sociological theory of sex difference in crime. *Social Forces,* 61, 1010–1032.

Steffensmeier, D., and Schwartz, J. (2004). Trends in female criminality: Is crime still a man's world? In B. R. Price and N. J. Sokoloff (Eds.), *The criminal justice system and women: Offenders, prisoners, victims, and workers* (3rd Edition) (pp. 95–112). New York: McGraw-Hill.

Steffensmeier, D., and Terry, R. (1986). Institutional sexism in the underworld: A view from the inside. *Sociological Inquiry,* 56, 304–232.

Surratt, H. L., Inciardi J. A., Kurtz, S. P., and Kiley, M. C. (2004). Sex work and drug use in a subculture of violence. *Crime and Delinquency,* 50, 43–59.

Taylor, B. G., Newton, P. J., and Brownstein, H. H. (2003). Drug use among adult female arrestees. *Annual report 2000: Arrestee drug abuse monitoring.* Washington, DC: National Institute of Justice.

Teplin, L., Abram, K., and McClelland, G. (1996). Prevalence of psychiatric disorders among incarcerated women: I. Pretrial jail detainees. *Archives of General Psychiatry,* 53, 505–512.

Tortu, S., McCoy, H. V., Beardsley, M., Deren, S., and McCoy, C. B. (1998). Predictors of HIV infection among women drug users in New York and Miami. *Women and Health,* 27, 191–204.

U.S. Department of Justice, Federal Bureau of Investigation. (2003). *Crime in the United States, 2002.* Washington, DC: Government Printing Office.

Vidaeff, A. C., and Mastrobattista, J. M. (2003). In utero cocaine exposure: A thorny mix of science and mythology. *American Journal of Perinatology,* 20, 165–172.

Waterston, A. (1993). *Street addicts in the political economy.* Philadelphia: Temple University Press.

Weiss, S. R., Kung, H. C., and Pearson, J. L. (2003). Emerging issues in gender and ethnic differences in substance abuse and treatment. *Current Women's Health Reports,* 2, 245–253.

Westermeier, J., and Boedecker, A. E. (2000). Course, severity, and treatment of substance abuse among women versus men. *American Journal of Drug and Alcohol Abuse,* 26, 523–535.

White, H. R., and Gorman, D. M. (2000). Dynamics of the drug-crime relationship. In *Criminal Justice 2000* (Volume VI) (pp. 151–218). Washington, DC: National Institute of Justice. ✦

9
Compensating for Abuse

Women's Involvement in the Sex Trade in North America

Jody Raphael

In this chapter you will learn the following:

- How and why so many poor girls and girls and women of color become attracted to the lifestyle of prostitution

- How the sex trade industry exposes these girls and women to violence and drug addiction, and why these girls become trapped in the prostitution lifestyle

- How the criminal justice system responds to further punish and marginalize these needy girls already harmed by racism and poverty

- What, based on the facts about women and girls in prostitution, are the arguments, pro and con, for decriminalization of prostitution

- What criminal justice responses would be most beneficial to women and girls in prostitution

The number of girls and women in prostitution in the United States is not insignificant. A 2002 study in Chicago (O'Leary and Howard 2001) found a minimum of 25,000 women and girls involved in any given year. Given the difficulty of researching a clandestine industry, national figures can only be estimates, but they range from 250,000 to 500,000 women involved in the sex trade industry in the United States (Miller and Jayasundara 2001). Experts are in agreement, however,

that only 10 to 20 percent of women in prostitution solicit customers on the street (Miller and Jayasundara 2001), and the rest are involved in off-street venues, including stripclubs, escort services, and brothels. Certainly the Internet has enhanced the ability of the industry to advertise indoor locations in what is now said to be a $16 billion global operation (Altman 2001).

During the past 20 years, the "crime" of prostitution has split feminist circles into two camps. For some feminists, prostitution is the ultimate expression of sexual freedom, representing as it does women's choices to use their bodies and their sexuality in ways contrary to patriarchy's prescriptions (Cornell 1998). For others, (Dworkin 1997), prostitution is the ultimate expression of patriarchy, a process in which women become only their bodies for the use and enjoyment of men. The first group wants to legalize prostitution, the other to abolish it; one advocates for women's right to trade sex for money, while the other argues that state support for the institution of prostitution itself constitutes a human rights violation.

The general public views women and girls in prostitution in two distinct ways. In some circles, they are demonized as strange, deviant, and hopeless drug-addicted burnt-out cases, unworthy of our attention and in need of being swept off our streets. Others view the women as plucky entrepreneurs who are voluntarily selling their bodies and should be respected and allowed to do so. Both stereotypes promote disinterest and inattention to the women; neither characterization captures the life trajectories of the real women and girls in the sex trade, which this chapter describes.[1]

Prostitution Entry

Pathways to prostitution for women and girls fall within several distinct categories, but several themes are common to all of them: early age of entry, high prevalence of sexual assault and abuse as children and other family dysfunction, running away from home, and early alcohol and drug use. Research unequivocally shows how the industry, through its various agents, entices young and economically and emotionally needy girls into its portals.

In her sophomore year of high school, the biracial Olivia (Raphael 2004) left a home, dominated by her alcoholic parents and a father who brutally beat her mother, for a residential Job Corps program, and at age 16 she found herself stripping in a downtown club. By the time she ran off, Olivia already had a serious alcohol habit, fueled by her need to drown out the sounds of her mother's distress. The attention, the glamour, and the money for the 16-year-old made the stripclub an attractive refuge. Olivia began to use more and more alcohol to enable her to get up there and take off her clothing and, later, to engage in prostitution in the club's back rooms.

> You learn to put up with a few things, and every time you do an act, it better prepares you to do a little bit more next time. You kind of desensitize yourself to what is really happening, and you are using more and more alcohol. I soon knew what the guys were looking for, and it didn't take long to figure out the scene. How did I do it? I was always in an altered state of mind before I got there. I came in drunk. I'd be half blasted before I arrived. (p. 5)

Looking back at it now, Olivia sees that the job remained attractive because she enjoyed all the attention from the men. Trading on her extroverted personality and strong verbal communication skills, Olivia felt a sense of power from the whole set up, although now she sees it as a false sense of power.

> It met some need that I was not even aware of at the time. I had no idea that I had other needs that were being met or even needing to be met. I was really caught up in it. I had control of these guys. I could make them eat out of my hand. And the beauty of it, the wearing of the pretty costumes. The chang-

ing of my name. I could be anybody I wanted to be. (p. 55)

The club owners and customers exploited this teenager, who yearned for approval and validation and worked so hard to please. But, over time, the party started to wind down as Olivia became addicted to the heroin she took to be able to perform the acts that were requested by men in the back rooms. Olivia's stripclub involvement led to 19 years in prostitution, the bulk of it as a heroin-addicted woman on the streets.

The story of Lucretia, a young African-American woman, provides an example of coerced prostitution, similar to tales of parents selling their young girls into sexual slavery in underdeveloped countries.

> My mom had a drug addiction, which I didn't understand then, and my mom sold me to one of her regular tricks—she introduced me to my first pimp at age 13. She came into my life and took me to a trick house, gave me my first drink, and took me over to one of her regulars, because he wanted a young girl. From there she introduced me to pimps. Every time she came to take me out, it was around a bunch of pimps.

> For me that was kind of hard, especially as a kid, me being excited to meet her. As a child you don't know who to go to, especially when it is your own mother doing this. You don't know who to tell. I wanted a relationship with my mom so bad to where I wouldn't tell my adopted mother, that is just how bad I wanted to be my mom's daughter. I felt that this is what I needed to do to be her daughter, and that's what I did.

Brenda, an African-American woman who was in prostitution for 25 years, had a slightly different pathway into the sex trade, but it also occurred when she was a young teen. Brenda's father was an abusive alcoholic. When she was 8 or 9 years old, however, older cousins consistently sexually molested her. Because she was ashamed and embarrassed to tell anybody, Brenda grew up with that secret. She became promiscuous at 13 or 14 years old and ran away from home a lot.

> I met a different type of person in the street. These people would give me false hope, tell me lies, I love you, come do this, and we will have the world, and they told me they loved me, and that's what I wanted to hear, because I didn't get it from home. So when they told me they loved me, I believed them. They introduced me to drugs and alcohol, and I wanted to fit in, so I did whatever it took to fit in, and I soon became addicted to the drugs and alcohol. Then I had to support my habit, and the only way I knew to support my habit was to steal or sell my body. I didn't want to prostitute too much, so I stole a lot, but going back and forth to jail, getting caught, after awhile I wasn't good at it, so the next thing I needed to do was I had to sell my body. It wasn't hard for me, I looked at it as, I was doing it anyway, but now I am doing it and getting paid for it.

Sasha, a white woman who was in the sex trade for 16 years, mostly in stripping and escort service work, also left home early due to sexual molestation; she consciously engaged in prostitution as a way of being compensated for earlier abuse. In the beginning, she traveled with an older man. They were both using drugs. Initially, said Sasha, it was exhilarating.

> It felt like everything was broken down into males and females, sex and money, it was a game, it felt like I could be powerful. I could be powerful and I could outwit these men. [For] most women [who] get involved in prostitution there is a history of sexual abuse or different types of sexual abuse, it is a kind of natural thing to feel. I felt that it was right that I should be compensated for the abuse that has been happening to me anyway. It was the first time that I had ever had a sense of power over that abuse. That is how I started on the streets. It was a game to me. I felt like I was working my way up through it, and the more I could take from someone, I felt like I had more control and that I was more powerful.

Olivia, Brenda, and Sasha all left home at early ages due to sexual assault and other family dysfunction. Olivia was attracted to stripping because of the money and the attention, Sasha to the sense of power and control, Brenda to the money it provided, and Lucretia—well, Lucretia had no choice. But even Lucretia acknowledged the sense of power that the activity gave her as a teen:

> Yes, there is a sense of control, and it is a lot of control for a teenager to know that I can make this grown man give me whatever I want him to give me, and all I have to do is spend 20, 25 minutes with him. Yes, it is a sense of control, and I liked that; I liked the fact that I could pick up the phone and say "Well, I need $500, when can you meet me"; the fact that this man had a wife and was sneaking to come and see me, and give me his money. This is the way I was thinking as a teenager, not knowing that it would hurt me in the long run.

Research data confirm that the experiences of Olivia, Brenda, Sasha, and Lucretia are typical. For example, studies with women and girls in prostitution in North America find that large percentages begin as teens. Fifteen percent of the women in the sex trade surveyed in the Cook County Chicago Jail (Chicago Coalition for the Homeless 2002) began in the sex trade before the age of 13, and 21 percent, between the ages of 14 and 17. Mean ages of 16 and 17 are common in other research studies (Benoit and Millar 2001; Cler-Cunningham 2001; Mary Magdalene Project 2001; Norton-Hawk 2002). In a sample of 222 women in prostitution interviewed in Chicago (Raphael and Shapiro 2002), about 3 percent reported they first exchanged sex for money before they were 11 years of age, and of these, several, like Lucretia, were used by parents or guardians to make money. Almost 33 percent of the sample first exchanged sex for money between the ages of 12 and 15, and 26 percent, between 16 and 17.

As in Lucretia's case, the involvement of other family members in the sex trade may well influence prostitution entry, but most research studies have neglected to ask about it. When they do, the results are dramatic: Almost a third of the women in the Chicago sample of women in prostitution (Raphael and Shapiro 2002) said there was someone in the household in their youth who regularly exchanged sex for money, and a large percentage of these traders were biological mothers. One young woman stated family members had threatened her with expulsion at age 13 if she did not cooperate in family prostitution endeavors. Another explained that her mother's partner, a drug dealer, turned her and her sisters to prostitution between the ages of 12 and 15. He drank, shot cocaine and heroin, and gave the girls the drug ecstasy.

Over and over again, research studies have demonstrated that 50 to 80 percent of women in prostitution have experienced physical and sexual abuse while growing up (Benoit and Millar 2001; Dalla, Xia, and Kennedy 2003; Norton-Hawk 2002; Valera Sawyer, and Schiraldi 2001). In one major study of jail detainees (McClanahan et al. 1999), childhood sexual assault nearly doubled the odds of entry into prostitution during the lifetime of the respondent. Not all incest victims proceed into the sex trade, but it is not difficult to divine the connection between childhood sexual abuse and prostitution. Incest teaches the child that love, attention, and financial rewards follow from sex; by rewarding incest, sexually abused children learn to use sexual behavior as a strategy for manipulating others to get their needs met (Finkelhor 1988). And as we have seen, although a woman's sense of control has disappeared through sexual assault, she can reclaim power by using the sexual allure she can exert over men. Remaining in the sexual arena to grab back power, women in prostitution, the majority of whom are incest victims, end up developing personal power only in relationship to men and sex (Wesely 2002).

Prostitution research samples have measured childhood household alcohol and drug use, finding from 58 percent to 81 percent of parents drinking excessively and 40 to 65 percent using illegal substances (Norton-Hawk 2002; Silbert and Pines 1982; Sweet and Tewksbury 2000). The substance abuse of parents appears to influence early experimentation with drugs and alcohol for the girls themselves. Women in the sex trade in one study used marijuana and alcohol at ages 8 and 10, and by age 12 they were trying cocaine and heroin (Inciardi et al. 1991). In two other studies (Kuhns, Heide, and Silverman 1992; Nadon, Koverola, and Schludermann 1998), the mean ages of alcohol intoxication, initiation of daily drinking, and experimentation with drugs other than alcohol were lower for girls involved in prostitution than for other arrestees.

Running away from home is now thought to be an important predictor of prostitution involvement. Some experts (Estes and Weiner 2001) believe that as many as 70 percent of street youth engage in prostitution to meet daily needs. Research confirms a correlation: The overwhelming majority of women in prostitution samples ran away from childhood homes and many permanently at extremely early ages. In a sample in a northeastern U.S. city, for example, 15 percent had left permanently between the ages of 10 and 13 and 49 percent, by the age of 16 (Norton-Hawk 2002). The average age that the women began living without a legal guardian was 16 years, and 11 percent were living on their own before the age of 14 in a Victoria, B.C., sample (Benoit and Millar 2001). Research with jail detainees in Chicago (McClanahan et al. 1999) found that women with a history of having run away entered prostitution at a younger age than those who did not, and those who reported ever having run away from home were significantly more likely than nonrunaways to have ever been in the sex trade (almost 45 percent compared with almost 30 percent) and to have engaged in routine prostitution (almost 36 percent, compared with 22 percent).

The sex trade industry employs diverse strategies to hook these needy teen girls. Advertisements for exotic dancers are important, playing into young girls' dreams for money and independence. One advertisement, on a popular Chicago radio station catering to teens, recruiting cocktail waitresses at what is a nude strip club with lap dancing, promotes the large amounts of cash for fun and independence and asks the girls if they are tired of depending on a man for their income (Shenoy 2003). The girls' intimate partners also serve as recruitment agents. Social service providers are troubled by the older men in teen girls' lives who entice them into a dating relationship and later emotionally coerce them into prostituting for them. One counselor explained,

> The guy takes control of the relationship really quickly. He is going to take care of her, he buys her things, and then after awhile he is going to say, "You owe me, you have to help me." Oh, if I had a dime for every time I have heard that story. They say, "They bought me an outfit, they buy me food," and then the guy says, "You owe me, what did you think, that was for free?"
>
> The girls don't want to lose the relationship. They've run away from home. They don't want to steal or shoplift, or sell drugs; it's dangerous and violent. (Raphael 2004, 43)

Sadly, research is verifying the fact that some men claim a special ability to identify vulnerable victims, the needy and unloved, children who have been victims before. Social service providers in the Chicago metropolitan area report that males congregate outside group homes and institutions housing girls who are wards of the child protective service, recognizing that these homes are sources of needy girls who can be recruited for prostitution (Raphael 2004). Many girls being helped in a prostitution recovery program in the United Kingdom are from group homes or foster care whom pimps have targeted. Police linked one London pimp, named Maris Malone, to 22 girls aged 12 to 28 whom he recruited from those in the child welfare system (Stickler 2001). As one research team explained:

Low self-esteem ensures that sex trade workers are easy "prey" for those who tell them what they most need to hear: that they are loved, that they are appreciated, they are understood and that they will be taken care of. No child or youth who has lived with a crippling lack of self-esteem could refuse such an apparent sanctuary. (Kingsley and Mark 2001, 31)

Research documents the pimp-as-boyfriend recruitment tactic. In the Canadian National Juvenile Prostitution Survey, 17 percent of the females indicated they had turned to prostitution to please another person who was likely a pimp (Brock 1998), and Chicago researchers found that 20 percent of the respondents entered regular prostitution through the urgings of a boyfriend (Raphael and Shapiro 2002). Coercion is also present, although the numbers of women involved are lower. In a western Canadian sample of women, all of whom began in prostitution as teens, 19 percent reported being coerced into the sex trade by intimate partners (Nixon et al. 2002), and in a fairly large sample of individuals in prostitution in Victoria, B.C., 12.5 percent said their involvement in prostitution had been forced (Benoit and Millar 2001).

Altogether, current data about early entry into the sex trade industry, childhood sexual assault, early use of drugs, and running away from home call into question characterizations of prostitution activity as freely chosen. The concept of choice indeed appears to be misplaced, for it is certainly a decision made at an early age under severely restricted circumstances, even under coercion.

Violence in Prostitution

We are only just now understanding the degree of violence experienced by women and girls in the sex trade in both indoor and outdoor prostitution venues. While stripping, Olivia experienced continual verbal and physical abuse from customers.

> They reach up and put money in your G-string and they ram their fingers into you.

A lot of groping. Within 30 days the awful reality sets in. There are 50,000 hands touching me, you begin to feel dirty, the guys are smelly, they are usually drunk. (Raphael 2004, 53)

As for prostitution in the club's back rooms, Olivia found that the back rooms were the site of a lot of violence from customers, many of whom were inebriated.

> This is where you would get the guys who would want to burn you with cigarettes. Sometimes in a frenzy, but some just do it as a kind of humiliation to degrade you. You try to resist it, but you get grabbed and held, you're half-drunk anyway, these guys are always bigger and stronger than you, and you walk away with scars and marks on you. (Raphael 2004, 75–76)

Although there has been acknowledgement that violent customers are a fact of life in street prostitution, women in indoor prostitution venues such as stripclubs and escort services have generally been believed to be immune and safer (McElroy 1998; Weitzer 2000). Historically, there were gentlemen's clubs where only dancing occurred, but the public has not caught on to the transformation of the stripclub business, in which lap dances involving tactile contact and backrooms in which anything goes are the norm. Recent memoirs of ex-strippers (Burana 2001; Eaves 2002) have documented the changes: "Stripping usually involves prostitution and always involves sexual harassment and abuse" (Holsopple 1996, online). Sasha, who worked for 16 years in indoor prostitution venues, confirmed that violence from customers is usual in indoor locations.

> I've been raped, I've been beaten, I've been kidnapped or confined and not able to leave. I've been confined and unable to leave situations and had escort services demand that I pay for the time that I was being raped or being held against my will, because I didn't call to check in and say it was over. The escort service is not there to protect you, they just want to make sure they get their money.

Gradually, Sasha realized that the act of selling her body always involved violence in one form or another, because she was allowing a stranger to penetrate her most private parts:

> Prostitution, the act of performing the sexual act for someone in exchange for money, in itself is violent. Just by the very nature of it. Your body is being invaded, you are being penetrated by a foreign object, whether it is a part of his body or something else. That in itself is violent. It is a violent act, and the things that you have to do to leave your body, in order to be able to cope with that.

Significantly, researchers are now understanding that women in the private rooms of stripclubs and in escort service work may be even more isolated from the public and at greater danger of abuse than women in the streets (Farley and Kelly 2000). Violent rapes involving drawn guns and knives in these venues raise troublesome thoughts about some of the men who are involved in the sex trade as customers. Research in Chicago (Raphael and Shapiro 2002), corroborated by a number of other studies (Holsopple 1999; Maticka-Tyndale et al. 2000; Wesely 2002), found that 21 percent of women in escort services in the sample had been raped more than 10 times, the same percentage for women in the streets, and 11 percent 5 to 10 times. Almost 19 percent of the strippers had been threatened with rape more than 10 times, and 19 percent had been threatened with a weapon between 5 and 10 times, with customers perpetrating most of the violence. These data indicate the difficulty some women have in controlling some customers, especially those who may be inebriated. A booklet for call girls in London recommends having mirrored walls to enable the women to see whether the customer has a knife behind his back (Jeffreys 2002). The memoirs of several ex-strippers (Burana 2001; Eaves 2002) detail the verbal abuse and degrading and often violent encounters with customers, many of whom are seeking more invasive sexual encounters at the clubs than some women are prepared to offer.

Thus, it should not be surprising that many women in indoor sex trade venues are plagued with alcohol and drug problems. Every woman, for example, in Chicago research involved in escort service prostitution stated she sometimes used drugs or alcohol, and only about 5 percent of women in exotic dancing said they had never abused these substances. Many of the women in escort services (43 percent) reported they took more drugs more frequently. Strippers reported that they drank heavily in order to continue to dance (Raphael and Shapiro 2002). All of the women in another sample (Maticka-Tyndale et al. 2000) reported drinking alcohol before their first stage performance and for an extended time period or throughout their dancing. One woman, for example, said she consumed between 5 and 19 drinks each evening shift. Holsopple (1999), an ex-stripper herself, reported from her research with exotic dancers that "[w]omen drink while getting ready to go to work, and they drink while doing their hair and make-up in the dressing room. Women who work at nude juice bars that do not serve alcohol or at bars that do not allow women to buy their own drinks report that they stop at another bar on their way in and 'get loaded'" (p. 261).

Other researchers (DeGraaf et al. 1995; Lever and Dolnick 2000; Pyett and Warr 1999) found that large percentages of women in escort services and clubs drank alcohol and used drugs during their involvement in the industry. Men's recommendations and ratings of escort services and stripclubs on the Internet frequently mention women's drug problems. One man wrote recently, "Finding a consistant [*sic*] escort is very hard [in] these days of drug addicts etc . . ." (Raphael 2004, 88). Women in a Victoria, B.C., study stated that they were able to hide their drug use from the management but rued the fact that concealment was unnecessary because the owners seemed totally unconcerned and would intervene only if the girls were unable

to attract customers (Benoit and Millar 2001). This lack of oversight from management, solely concerned with increasing profits by maximizing the number of customers per evening, also translates into managers who fail to shield the women from aggressive clients due to fear of police involvement that might result in closure of the business.

Women in prostitution in the streets are also subject to violence from customers at often alarming rates. Rapes, gang rapes, cuts with knives, and brutal and uncaring sex unfortunately come with the territory. Although the women try to size up the customers and avoid danger, they never really know when they will be subject to this kind of violence. The women reported that often the men used the violence to take back the money they had paid for the sexual encounter (Miller 1993). The contempt of some men for the women and their acting out of this hatred on the woman in prostitution is apparent. As Olivia explained:

> You're giving a blow job, and all of a sudden he is ramming your head against the car. He rips off your clothes, or tells you to take your clothes off and pushes you out of the car and laughs as he drives away. You are lying there, and part of you is grateful to still be alive. (Raphael 2004, 95)

That the men have prepared for these violent episodes is apparent from the women's stories. One woman told a researcher (Norton-Hawk 2001) in Boston that the car door handle of a customer's car had been removed so that she was unable to escape being assaulted. Lucretia described one violent episode:

> I was getting ready to give an elderly white man a blow job in his car. He stuck a knife to my throat. He took me way out to a suburb, an office complex, and in the wee hours of the morning he brutally raped me there. He handcuffed me with these flexible handcuffs. He was going to kill me. I knew I wasn't going to walk away alive. I started praying, because I didn't want to die like that. It couldn't have been nobody but God to help

me break those cuffs and help me to get up and run, and he chased me for a little while. And it was in January, below zero weather, that man stripped me from my waist down, I didn't have nothing on, but I made it to the edge of the expressway and flagged down an 18-wheeler. I stood in front of it, and when the truck stopped, I just collapsed.

Over 20 research studies, most of them in North America within the last 15 years, have documented an almost unimaginable level of violence in street prostitution (Raphael 2004). The two largest samples come from San Francisco and Chicago. Farley and Barkan (1998) reported on interviews with 130 women in prostitution on the streets of San Francisco. Eighty-two percent had experienced physical assaults in prostitution, 68 percent stated they had been rape victims since entering prostitution, and 48 percent of these reported having been raped more than five times. Posttraumatic stress disorder (PTSD) is a diagnosis describing psychological symptoms and adverse effects on mental health resulting from violence; symptoms include difficulty concentrating, hypervigilance, flashbacks or the reliving of the trauma, and disassociation—feeling emotionally numb. Sixty-eight percent of Farley and Barkan's sample met criteria for a diagnosis of PTSD. Other research confirms this result. Forty-two percent of a sample of 100 women on the streets of Washington, DC, met the criteria for PTSD in a recent survey (Valera et al. 2001), and a study of women in New York City who were involved in prostitution had higher distress scores than did samples of psychiatric in- and out-patients. (El-Bassel et al. 1997). In a large Chicago sample (Raphael and Shapiro 2002), almost 20 percent of women in the streets had been threatened with a weapon, 22 percent had sex forced on them, 24 percent had something thrown at them, and 32 percent had their clothing ripped, all more than 10 times.

Drug and alcohol use in street prostitution is also high, with percentages of 92, 95, and 100 typical in research samples (Ra-

phael 2004). Some women, like Brenda, may turn to prostitution to support a preexisting drug habit. Olivia's story elaborates a different scenario in which women and girls already in prostitution turn to or step up drug or alcohol use to help them cope or disassociate while in the sex trade. But, once addicted, they must stay in prostitution to support their habit. Olivia is adamant about the need to use alcohol and drugs to disassociate while in prostitution.

It is a myth that any woman can get up there and do that and not have something in her. It doesn't have to be hard-core drugs, but you have to take something to help you deal with it. Alcohol is probably the easiest because it is so accessible in the clubs. Before I got to work I would drink anywhere from a pint to a fifth. I found out that a couple of drinks would take off the nervousness right away. I then had the courage to get up there and take my clothes off. I was able to disassociate totally, totally. I did not have to be presently there, but I could do my job. (Raphael 2004, 54)

Lucretia's story demonstrates a scenario in which drug and alcohol use begins concurrently with prostitution involvement.

The drugs and alcohol were, at first, just to fit in, but it overcomes you in the long run, and it wears you down; it beats you up, and then you get to the point to where you got to have a drink, you have to be high just to know that some stranger is going to be doing whatever he wants to do to you. You use the drug and alcohol to take the pain away. It is not exciting and fun anymore. It's not glamorous, because now you are too deep in to get out.

Research studies have found equal numbers for these scenarios, cautioning against one single conclusion (Raphael 2004). Distinctions are difficult to discern, because entering street life as a teenager usually means participation in alcohol and drugs, and there is a need to differentiate recreational use and regular or addictive drug usage (Miller 1995). Studies that are able to make these distinctions generally find that the majority of the regular or addictive use occurred after prostitution activities had begun (Raphael 2004).

Although very little is known about customers, it seems to be a reasonable conclusion that the presence of so many needy and drug-dependent girls and women in the sex trade industry serves to attract the very men who are looking for someone to abuse; given the girls' vulnerability, drug addiction, and urgent need for money, the men feel free and can get away with violently abusing them. Due to their accessibility and visibility, women and girls selling sex on the street also become magnets and easy targets for serial rapists and murderers.

Given all the violence, is it any wonder that the industry continues to rely on agents to recruit girls and women into prostitution and to keep them participating? Persons living off the earnings of another in prostitution also serve the sex trade industry as well as themselves. Despite claims to the contrary, research studies are demonstrating that about 40 percent of women in the streets are involved with pimps, most of whom use violence to control the women (Mary Magdalene 2001; Norton-Hawk, unpublished paper; Sterk 2000). Persons serving the pimp function were an important factor in many women's lives, regardless of the prostitution venue, in a research sample in Chicago (Raphael and Shapiro 2002). Forty-one percent of women in the streets said they had a pimp, corroborating the other studies. Of these, 75 percent stated they would have been subject to physical harm if they were to stop giving money to this person. Fifty percent of the women involved in escort services said they were involved with a pimp as were 24 percent of women in exotic dancing or stripping. A significant percentage of North American prostitution may well remain pimp-controlled. Because of methodology limitations, researcher Celia Williamson (2002) believes that the involvement of pimps in the sex trade is grossly understated. Those under the control of pimps are unable to safely stop and speak with researchers, with the result

that the more independent women are more likely to be accessible for study purposes.

Because of potential violence from others who live off their earnings, girls and women seeking to exit will need a safety plan and affordable housing, as well as specialized services to recover from drug and alcohol addiction and trauma from violence. Lucretia's pimp was violent, but he met some kind of need at the time:

> I never knew my father, and when I got to know him he got killed. My pimp for me was, he took the place of my father. I thought that was protection, I thought that would protect me from anything. He had other women. It would do something for me to know that I could make more money than other women, especially if I was younger than them.

> Had I had a way to get help while I was still locked up, and had somewhere to go instead of having to go back to that pimp, knowing that there wasn't any way in the world that he was going to let me go into no treatment. If I had had a place, I would have stopped.

The Criminal Justice System

In the United States, prostitution is illegal except in rural jurisdictions of Nevada, where state law allows legal brothels to operate. Because most of North American prostitution occurs indoors, lack of undercover police resources hampers enforcement efforts, with the result that indoor prostitution has been legalized in practice. In fact, advertisements for illegal escort services in newspapers and magazines, in addition to telephone book yellow pages, often lead people to believe that these activities are now legal. The Chicago *Sun Times*, for example, runs ads for massage parlors in its sports pages. Law enforcement officials leave undisturbed free monthly magazines in news bins on downtown Chicago street corners advertising escort services, massage parlors, and stripclubs. Similar ads appear in such publications as the *Village Voice* and the *International Herald Tribune.*

Police do arrest women and girls in prostitution who seek to sell sex on the streets, but the number of customers arrested for soliciting or patronizing a woman in prostitution always lags. For example, there were 3,777 arrests of women for prostitution-related offenses in 2001 in the city of Chicago, but only 1,258 men were arrested that year for patronizing a woman in prostitution; women were arrested three times more often than their customers (O'Leary and Howard 2001). Many of the women serve small amounts of time for the offense, while the men never receive anything but fines or car impoundment fees. According to the Chicago Coalition for the Homeless' recent research study (2004), the total cost of prostitution enforcement in the city is $9 million a year.

Due to the futility of repeated arrests and ongoing complaints from residents of newly gentrifying areas of the city, the Chicago Police Department has availed itself of the discretion, under the law, to upgrade the prostitution crime to a felony on a second arrest, with increases as much as 200 percent in felony arrests in certain police districts (Chicago Coalition for the Homeless 2004). Felony records effectively foreclose employment in the regular economy, making eventual escape from prostitution even more difficult.

The criminal justice system also sweeps up many more women of color than it does whites. Although blacks represent only 36 percent of the population in Chicago, African Americans made up 75 percent of all prostitution-related arrests of women in 1999 in Chicago (O'Leary and Howard 2001). Between 2001 and 2002 in Chicago, the arrests of black women increased by 76 percent, Hispanic women increased by 17 percent, and white women decreased by 13 percent as a result of stepped-up street sweeps in neighborhoods in which residents had complained to the police (Chicago Coalition for the Homeless 2004). In Minneapolis (Hennepin County), African Americans constituted 52 percent of women arrested and convicted for prostitution in a six-month period in 1991, although blacks (men and women) represented only 13 percent of the population (Nelson 1993). Another Minneapolis study (Nelson 1993) found that the average number of days served by African-American women was almost double that for whites for sex trade offenses. And in Los Angeles County, blacks accounted for more than 50 percent of all female prostitution arrests 8 years out of 10 between 1990 and 1999 (Mary Magdalene 2001).

Although it may be likely that women of color are overrepresented within prostitution populations in the United States, because women and girls in the sex trade are drawn, as we have seen, from the ranks of the poor and needy, we certainly know that they are visible on the streets and liable to be under surveillance by police officers, a situation exacerbated by community policing and new concern about street crime in city neighborhoods. In Canada, it is Aboriginal youth who participate in prostitution in numbers well beyond their representation in the general population; in some Canadian communities, the visible sex trade is said to be 90 percent Aboriginal (Kingsley and Mark 2001).

Our current approach to the sex trade industry illustrates how issues of race, class, and gender intersect to affect these needy girls who have become enmeshed in prostitution. As participants in the sex trade industry, poor and minority girls and women, already suffering the effects of poverty and racism, become further trapped in violence, drug addiction, and poverty. Then the legal system responds by punishing these marginalized girls and women with criminal sanctions and incarceration, and by failing to protect them from violent rapists and murderers, it fully completes their journey into stigmatized deviants, who as "nonhumans" are not worthy of our protection.

For all these reasons, decriminalization of prostitution has long seemed a remedy that many could support. Given the motivations of poor and needy girls for engaging in prostitution, arrests and incarceration would appear to have no effect on preventing involvement in the sex trade, while the criminal justice system gives customers, managers, pimps, and police officers a hold over these needy women of color, stigmatizing them as "the other" or as lawless criminals, subjecting them to harassment, and preventing them from seeking help for the violence and abuse. Those who believe that the state has no legitimate business regulating private matters between consenting adults, whether they involve paid or unpaid sex, also strongly support decriminalization. Removing principles of morality from the criminal law would appear to be a reasonable next step to decriminalization of formerly illegal activities such as intimate relations between same-sex couples.

Now that brothel prostitution has been legalized in a number of locations, such as the Australian state of Victoria and the city of Sydney and the Netherlands, among others, we have some idea of the effects of this decriminalization of prostitution. Not only have the number of new legal brothels doubled, as in Victoria, but the number of illegal, or unlicensed, brothels has also exponentially increased (Sullivan and Jeffreys 2002). Since the year 2000, the sex industry has increased by 25 percent in the Netherlands (Raymond 2004). This expansion comes at a huge price. For to meet the increased demand, poor women and girls from Eastern Europe and Africa are flooding in to the Netherlands, where the sex industry reportedly accounts for 5 percent of the country's economy (Raymond 2004). One report found that 80 percent of women in the brothels of the Netherlands were trafficked from other Central and Eastern European countries (Raymond 2004). The sheer volume of foreign women and girls in the sex trade industry in these countries raises questions about the extent to which they have been trafficked by middlemen, the types of ploys used to recruit them, and the degree of violence and coercion used to hold them there. For this reason, groups in Australia have concluded that traffickers prefer to operate where there are venues to place their goods without fear of harassment, and legalization signals a lessened interest in policing the local sex trade (Sullivan and Jeffreys 2002). Janice Raymond (2003) of the Coalition Against Trafficking of Women cautions that legalization means decriminalization of the entire sex industry, not just the women, and serves to legitimize pimps as legal sex entrepreneurs.

Making the sex trade legal thus neither will automatically improve conditions for the women and girls nor prevent coercion, abuse, and violence. Involvement of the criminal justice system will continue to be necessary to prevent trafficking, violence, and coercion, approaches that have been largely missing in jurisdictions that have decriminalized prostitution. Where prostitution remains illegal, as in the United States, criminal justice approaches also need to be stepped up to prevent coercion and violence against women. Prostitution survivors such as Olivia, Lucretia, Brenda, and Sasha speak passionately about the need for comprehensive programming for girls and women in prostitution in lieu of criminal justice prosecutions. Brenda described the detrimental effects of the current approach.

> I went to jail several times during my addiction, for prostitution. I'm here to tell you that had they offered me any program or any type of counseling 15 years ago, I probably wouldn't be sitting here today. They arrested me, they locked me up for a few hours, and then they put me out there. I dropped out of school at a young age too, so I didn't know anything; all I knew was to get out there and hustle. I had no job skills, no education; the only thing I knew was to take what I wanted. And so when they released me, I did what I knew how to do best, and that is get back out there and hustle.

> Had I had the opportunity, if there were any avenues that I could have taken when I first went to jail, instead of being treated like some dirt bag, my self-esteem was already shot. So when they kicked me, I just went to the gutter, I just went deeper.

Today, Olivia, Lucretia, Brenda, and Sasha have all exited prostitution after undergoing painful rehabilitation and treatment for the drug addiction and trauma from the violence to which they were subjected since early childhood. Lucretia shall have the last word.

> The fact of something being taken from you without your wanting it to be taken from you. Being beat. Having to make love to this man who beat you, and him making you think that it is all right, or you asked to be beaten like that. To be thrown in a closet, to be locked in a closet, to be passed around, even paid for it, but to be in a room and be passed around from man to man, it does something to your self-esteem. The clean time that I do have, my worse days is better than any day that I had then. I have a 5-year-old daughter, I have a 13-year-old daughter, I would kill any one if I found out they touched either one of them. I refuse to let my kids go through what I went through.

Note

1. The author has been involved with prostitution survivors Brenda, Lucretia, and Sasha in public education programs in Chicago over the past few years and these programs were taped with their permission. All quotes from Brenda, Lucretia, and Sacha are from these presentations. Olivia Howard's quotes are taken from the author's book about Olivia's life.

Study/Discussion Questions

1. What accounts for the fact that so many poor and needy girls, and girls and women of color, become attracted to the lifestyle of prostitution?

2. Why do so many girls and women in prostitution become addicted to drugs and alcohol?

3. What, based on the facts about women and girls in prostitution, are the arguments, pro and con, for decriminalization of prostitution? What criminal justice responses would be most beneficial to women and girls in prostitution?

References

Altman, D. (2001). *Global sex.* Chicago: University of Chicago Press.

Benoit, C., and Millar, A. (2001). *Dispelling myths and understanding realities: Working conditions, health status, and exiting experiences of sex workers.* Victoria, B.C.: Prostitutes' Empowerment, Education, and Resource Society (PEERS).

Brock, D. R. (1998). *Making work, making trouble: Prostitution as a social problem.* Toronto: University of Toronto Press.

Burana, L. (2001). *Strip city: A stripper's farewell journey across America.* New York: Talk Miramax Books.

Chicago Coalition for the Homeless. (2002). *Unlocking options for women: A survey of women in Cook County Jail.* Chicago: Author.

———. (2004). *Addressing prostitution: A demonstration project for Chicago police district 14.* Chicago: Author.

Cler-Cunningham, L. (2001). *Violence against women in Vancouver's street-level sex trade and the police response.* Vancouver, B.C.: PACE Society.

Cornell, D. (1998). *At the heart of freedom.* Princeton, NJ: Princeton University Press.

Dalla, R., Xia, Y., and Kennedy, H. (2003). "You just give them what they want and pray they don't kill you": Street-level sex workers' reports of victimization, personal resources, and coping strategies. *Violence Against Women, 9,* 1367–1394.

DeGraaf, R., Vanwesenbeeck, I., Van Zessen, G., Straver, C. J., and Visser, J. H. (1995). Alcohol and drug use in heterosexual and homosexual prostitution, and its relations to protection behaviour. *AIDS Care, 7,* 35–47.

Dworkin, A. (1997). *Life and death.* New York: Free Press.

Eaves, E. (2002). *Bare: On women, dancing, sex, and power.* New York: Knopf.

El-Bassel, N., Schilling, R. F., Faruque, K. L., Faruque, S., Gilbert, L., Irwin, K. L., Von Bargen, J., Edlin, B. R., and Serrano, Y. (1997). Sex trading and psychological distress among women recruited from the streets of Harlem. *American Journal of Public Health, 87,* 66–70.

Estes, R. J., and Weiner, N. A. (2001). *The commercial sexual exploitation of children in the*

U.S., Canada, and Mexico: Executive summary. Philadelphia: University of Pennsylvania School of Social Work, Center for the Study of Youth Policy.

Farley, M., and Barkan, H. (1998). Prostitution, violence against women, and posttraumatic stress disorder. *Women & Health,* 27, 37–49.

Farley, M., and Kelly, V. (2000). Prostitution: A critical review of the medical and social sciences literature. *Women & Criminal Justice,* 11, 29–63.

Finkelhor, D. (1988). The trauma of child sexual abuse. In G. Powell and G. Wyatt (Eds.), *Lasting effects of child sexual abuse* (pp. 61–82). Newbury Park, CA: Sage.

Holsopple, K. (1996). Remarks at Moorhead State University, Moorhead, MN. Retrieved 1/7/01 at: *http//rmet.com/~wnrv/msu.htm,* accessed on 1/7/01.

——. (1999). Stripclubs according to strippers. In D. Hughes and C. Roche (Eds.), *Making the harm visible: Global sexual exploitation of women and girls: Speaking out and providing services* (pp. 252–276). Kingston, RI: Coalition Against Trafficking in Women.

Inciardi, J. A., Pottieger, A. E., Forney, M. A., Chitwood, D. O., and McBride, D. C. (1991). Prostitution, IV drug use, and sex-for-crack exchanges among serious delinquents: Risks for IV infection. *Criminology,* 29, 221–235.

Jeffreys, S. (2002). *Trafficking in women versus prostitution: A false distinction.* Address at Townsville International Women's Conference, James Cook University, Townsville, Australia. Retrieved 12/5/02 at: *http://www.austdvclearing house.unsw.edu/au.*

Kingsley, C., and Mark, M. (2001). *Sacred lives: Canadian Aboriginal children and youth speak out about sexual exploitation.* Vancouver, B.C.: Save the Children.

Kuhns, J. B., Heide, K. M., and Silverman, I. (1992). Substance use/misuse among female prostitutes and female arrestees. *International Journal of the Addictions,* 17, 1283–1292.

Lever, J., and Dolnick, D. (2000). Clients and call girls: Seeking sex and intimacy. In R. Weitzer (Ed.), *Sex for sale: Prostitution, pornography, and the sex industry* (pp. 85–100). New York: Routledge.

Mary Magdalene Project (2001). *Research report on street prostitution.* Los Angeles: Author.

Maticka-Tyndale, E., Lewis, J., Clark, J. P., Zubick, J., and Young. S. (2000). Exotic dancing and health. *Women & Health,* 31, 87–108.

McClanahan, S. F., McClelland, G. M., Abram, K. M., and Teplin, L. A. (1999). Pathways into prostitution among female jail detainees. *Psychiatric Services,* 50, 1606–1613.

McElroy, W. (1998). Prostitutes, anti-pro feminists, and the economic associates of whores. In J. Elias, V. Bullough, V. Elias, and G. Brewer (Eds.), *Prostitution: On whores, hustlers, and johns,* (pp. 333–344). Amherst, NY: Prometheus Books.

Miller, J. (1993). Your life is on the line every night you're on the streets: Victimization and the resistance among street prostitutes. *Humanity & Society,* 17, 422–446.

——. (1995). Gender and power on the streets: Street prostitution in the era of crack cocaine. *Journal of Contemporary Ethnography,* 23, 427–452.

Miller, J., and Jayasundara, D. (2001). Prostitution, the sex trade industry, and sex tourism. In C. M. Renzetti, J. L. Edleson, and R. K. Bergen (Eds.), *Sourcebook on violence against women* (pp. 459–480). Thousand Oaks, CA: Sage.

Nadon, S., Koverola, C., and Schludermann, E. (1998). Antecedents to prostitution. *Journal of Interpersonal Violence,* 13, 206–221.

Nelson, V. (1993). Prostitution: Where racism and sexism intersect. *Michigan Journal of Gender & Law,* 1, 81–89.

Nixon, K., Tutty, L., Doune, P., Gorkoff, K., and Ursel, J. (2002). The everyday occurrence: Violence in the lives of girls exploited through prostitution. *Violence Against Women,* 8, 1016–1043.

Norton-Hawk, M. (n.d.). *Prostitution is not about sex.* Unpublished paper.

——. (2001). The counter-productivity of incarcerating female street prostitutes. *Deviant Behavior,* 22, 403–417.

——. (2002). The lifecourse of prostitution. *Women, Girls & Criminal Justice,* 3: 1, 7, 8–9.

O'Leary, C., and Howard, O. (2001). *The prostitution of women and girls in metropolitan Chicago: A preliminary prevalence report.* Chicago: Center for Impact Research.

Pyett, P., and Warr, D. (1999).Women at risk in sex work: Strategies for survival. *Journal of Sociology*, 35, 183–197.

Raphael, J. (2004). *Listening to Olivia: Poverty, violence, and prostitution*. Boston: Northeastern University Press.

Raphael, J., and Shapiro, D. (2002). *Sisters speak out: The lives and needs of prostituted women in Chicago: A research study*. Chicago: Center for Impact Research.

Raymond, J. (2003). 10 reasons for not legalizing prostitution. Report from the Coalition Against Trafficking of Women. Available at: *www.catwinternational.org*.

——. (2004). *The impact of the sex industry in the European Union*. Report from the Coalition Against the Trafficking of Women. Retrieved 3/17/04 at: *http://www.catwinternational.org*.

Shenoy, R. (2003, February). Clubs promise path from poverty. *Chicago Reporter*, Retrieved at: *http://www.chicagoreporter.com*.

Silbert, M. H., and Pines, A. M. (1982). Entrance into prostitution. *Youth & Society*, 13, 471–500.

Sterk, C. (2000). *Tricking and tripping: Prostitution in the era of AIDS*. Putnam Valley, NY: Social Change Press.

Stickler, A. (2001). *Child prostitution crisis*. BBC News Report. BBC online, *www.news.bbc.co.uk*.

Sullivan, M., and Jeffreys, S. (2002). Legalization: The Australian experience. *Violence Against Women*, 8, 1140–48.

Sweet, N., and Tewksbury, R. (2000). "What's a nice girl like you doing in a place like this?" Pathways to a career in stripping. *Sociological Spectrum*, 29, 325–243.

Valera, R., Sawyer, R. G., and Schiraldi, G. R. (2001). Perceived health needs of inner-city street prostitutes: A preliminary study. *American Journal of Health Behavior*, 25(1), 50–59.

Weitzer, R. (2000). Why we need more research on sex work. In R. Weitzer (Ed.), *Sex for sale: Prostitution, pornography, and the sex industry* (pp. 1–13). New York: Routledge.

Wesely, J. K. (2002). Growing up sexualized: Issues of power and violence in the lives of female exotic dancers. *Violence Against Women*, 8, 1186–1211.

Williamson, C. (2002). Pimp controlled prostitution: Still an integral part of street life. *Violence Against Women*, 8, 1074–1092. ✦

10
Global Prostitution, Sex Tourism, and Trafficking

Jody Miller

In this chapter you will learn the following:

- To recognize the complexity of the global sex industry, including being able to make conceptual distinctions among (and understand the relationship among) sex tourism, trafficking, and international prostitution

- How "slavery-like conditions" structure much of the sex industry and the roles played by debt bondage, violence, and immigration laws in this industry

- How the global sex industry is rooted in inequalities based on gender, race, class, and nation

- The factors that have contributed to the rise of the global sex industry in recent decades

- Some of the debates surrounding policy approaches for addressing the global sex industry

At 10 you are a woman.
At 20 you are an old woman.
And at 30 you are dead

      —Saying in Bangkok's red light
        district[1]

Kevin Bales is one of the world's prominent experts on human slavery. While researching his book, *Disposable People*, Bales met Siri, a 15-year-old Thai girl sold into prostitution when she was 14. She was sore the morning Bales met her, because she had been required to have sex with 15 men the night before. Siri is from a rural village in Thailand. A woman from a neighboring village—a broker—approached her family and offered to pay them the equivalent of $2,000 to take Siri to the city for work. The family agreed, and Siri found herself in *debt bondage*. She had to work in a brothel to pay off the money given to her family, as well as additional rapidly accumulating debt. Once purchased from her family, Siri was sold by the broker to a brothel for approximately $4,000, a cost added to Siri's debt. In addition, her debt includes medicine and other living expenses, fines routinely levied against her for various "infractions," and monthly rent of more than $1,000. Three quarters of Siri's earnings from prostitution go directly to her pimp and the brothel and are not counted against the debt. With what remains, she tries to cover her expenses and reduce her debt, but the odds are against her. Siri must have sex with 300 men each month just to cover her rent; little remains to reduce her growing debt and the interest charged against it. Siri's debt bondage amounts to sexual slavery: her debt "is virtually impossible to repay" (Bales 1999, 41).

Siri escaped from the brothel shortly after she arrived, but "was quickly caught, dragged back, beaten and raped." Bales (1999) explained,

> That night she was forced to take on a chain of clients until the early morning. The beatings and the work continued night after night until her will was broken. Now she is sure that she is a bad person, very bad to have deserved what has happened to her. (pp. 36–37)

Siri's slavery is ensured by violence, by the collusion of public officials, and by the huge profits the industry generates. According to Bales (1999), "girls like Siri are sold into sex slavery by the thousands" in Thailand (p. 37).

Anna was 19 years old when she met Radhika Coomaraswamy, the United Nations Special Rapporteur on Violence Against Women. She had been arrested while working in a brothel in Zurich, Switzerland. At 17, she was lured from her home in Poland with the promise of a job as a domestic worker for a family in Berlin. Instead, after crossing the border into Germany, her passport and identity papers were confiscated by her transporters, she was raped and beaten into compliance, and was sold to a brothel owner. After over a year at this brothel, Anna managed to escape and went to Switzerland. A man she trusted in Poland told her he had a friend who could help her find a husband there. Instead, once again Anna was forced to work in a brothel. Anna confided her story to a client, and he informed the police. When the brothel was raided, Anna agreed to help the police prosecute her traffickers and was then deported back to Poland with her infant child (Coomaraswamy 1996).

Nandani was age 18 when I met her, and she was working in a brothel in Colombo, Sri Lanka. She ran away from her village home two years earlier to marry a young man her parents disapproved of. The relationship broke off. New to the city and in need of work, Nandani was thrilled when a female acquaintance came to her with the promise of a job. Instead, like Anna, she was sold to a brothel and raped into submission. She described the ordeal:

> That man dragged me to the bed and ripped open my clothes and tortured me as much as he could and stayed with me that night. I cried, I fought with him, there was a bottle I even broke that and tried to kill myself with that but nothing worked, he somehow forced himself on me. (Miller 2002, 1055)

Considering herself "ruined" in a culture that places great importance on female sexual purity, Nandani ultimately stayed in the sex trade. She told me that the man who "owned" her loved her a lot, because she now had seniority at his brothel and had remained with him while other women left (see Miller 2002).

The stories of Siri, Anna and Nandani share a number of common threads: Each was young, economically disadvantaged, and vulnerable and had limited education. All three were sold into the sex industry, and their compliance was obtained through sexual and physical violence. Their stories also represent different facets of the expansive global sex trade and highlight the complexities that we examine in detail in this chapter. Siri was sold by her family and remained in her country of origin under a system of debt bondage. Anna was trafficked across international borders: She was transported from Poland to Germany and then Switzerland without knowledge of the nature or conditions of her "work." Nandani was originally forced into prostitution but later remained of her own accord. Siri's, Anna's, and Nandani's experiences are not isolated incidents. Instead, they are representative of young women in a global sex industry estimated to generate $7 billion in profits annually around the world (Hughes 2001). According to the U.S. government, between 50,000 and 100,000 women are trafficked into the United States annually (Hughes 2001), and more than a half a million women are trafficked worldwide every year. However, given the hidden, illicit nature of the industry, many suspect the numbers are much higher (Lehti and Aromaa 2004).

This chapter examines where, how, and why the global sex industry thrives. It is a complex industry that implicates not just traffickers, brokers, and pimps but also the governments and justice systems of most countries around the world; international law and policies; the global economy, and multinational corporations and their push for profits; the tourism industry; and the continued devaluation of women worldwide. A common thread in the organization and control of the global sex industry is that it emerges from and is sustained by gender, race, and class inequalities, as well as power imbalances resulting from colonial and imperialist relations across nations (Farr 2004). According to sociologist Eleanor Miller (1991), prostitution "is work that would have no value were it not for the conditions of economic and sexual inequality under which it is performed" (p. 8; see also Raphael, this volume). While prostitution itself is anything but a new phenomenon, the current scope and nature of the global sex industry is unprecedented. Let's begin by tracing its contemporary origins, which has its roots in two important changes that occurred in the mid- to late twentieth century: (1) the development of sex tourism and (2) patterns of migration resulting from the globalization of the world economy.

Sex Tourism

The term *sex tourism* refers to the development and expansion of industries providing sexual services to tourists. These industries—which include not just the establishments that provide sex shows and prostitution but also travel agencies, hotels, and other businesses—have developed to cater primarily to Western and Japanese men who travel for business and leisure activities. Consider the growth of sex tourism in Thailand alone. In 1981, Thailand received two million international tourists a year; by 1996, this number had more than tripled to seven million. Most notably, the vast majority of tourists in Thailand—five million in 1996—were unaccompanied men, "a significant portion [of whom] were sex tourists" (Bales 1999, 75–76).

Experts link the growth of sex tourism to broader patterns of tourist growth. According to the U.N. World Tourism Organization, by the year 2000, tourism was "the single most important global economic activity" (Enloe 1989, 20). Tourism has been promoted extensively as a developmental strategy for third world countries, as a result of the imposition of Western developmental policies and the influence of multinational corporations (Enloe 1989; Mies 1986; Truong 1990). Local governments have actively promoted tourism as well, as it has become increasingly important in sustaining their economies. World-

wide, tourism is approximately a $3.5 trillion industry (Kattoulas 1995).

Sex tourism is well documented in a number of countries, including Thailand, the Philippines, China, Vietnam, Laos, Cambodia, Brazil, the Netherlands, and the Dominican Republic (Flowers 1998). It has been especially pronounced in Asia, and its roots are linked to the impact of the U.S. military presence there in the middle of the twentieth century. Though prostitution has a long history in the region, sex *tourism* is a direct outgrowth of U.S. military bases and "rest and recreation" centers established in Southeast Asia during the Vietnam War (Enloe 1989; Mies 1986; Phongpaichit 1982). These centers were created to provide sexual services to American G.I.s serving in the region and relied on the sexual labor of local women. In fact, prostitution regularly flourishes during wartime, with the tacit or explicit approval of military leaders and with little concern for harms caused to the women involved. It is often justified as a means of channeling men's presumed sexual "needs" (Enloe 1989). In Southeast Asia, the early growth in international tourism—made possible by the expansion of commercial airlines and other leisure services—occurred around the same time as the placement of American troops in the region. The infrastructures put into place to serve American military personnel were well suited to the expansion of sex tourism after military withdrawal (Truong 1990).

The structure and operation of the sex tourism industry continues to be shaped by Western imperialism, colonial legacies, and racialized notions of sexuality (Kempadoo and Doezema 1998). For instance, sex tourism is often promoted as beneficial to both Third World economies and individual sex workers and their families, thus encouraging sex tourists to see their exploits as "beneficial" (Kempadoo and Doezema 1998; Truong 1990). Moreover, the promotion of tourism and sex tourism—which includes package sex tours—advertises the sexual availability of young women and girls to tourists, highlighting the notion that Asian women are submissive, exotic, and thus sexually desirable. In these ways, sex tourism is built on the idea of male entitlement to sex, casts men's involvement in a paternalistic framework, and hinges on race-based images of the feminine characteristics and sexual availability of girls and women in the Third World. Moreover, these images are not simply based on notions of racial difference but also racial hierarchy. As illustration, consider the following travel brochures:

> Slim, sunburnt, and sweet, they love the white man in an erotic and devoted way. They are masters of the art of making love by nature, an art that we Europeans do not know. (Life Travel, Switzerland)

> [M]any girls from the sex world come from the poor north-eastern region of the country and from the slums of Bangkok. It has become a custom that one of the nice looking daughters goes into the business in order to earn money for the poor family . . . you can get the feeling that taking a girl here is as easy as buying a package of cigarettes . . . little slaves who give real Thai warmth (Kanita Kamha Travel, the Netherlands). (Bales 1999, 76–77; quoted in Truong 1990, 178).

In Siri's home country of Thailand, an estimated 500,000 to 700,000 women work in commercial sex, the vast majority of these in Bangkok. Like Siri, one-third are believed to be minors (Lim 1998). If these estimates are accurate, more than 10 percent of all young women in Thailand between the ages of 15 and 25 are involved in the sex industry (Scibella 1987). As we will see next, Thailand is a common *destination country* for trafficking in Asia. Young women and girls are trafficked into Thailand because of its well-developed sex industry, including workers from Burma, Laos, the Philippines, China, and Hong Kong (Bales 1999; Lim 1998). In addition, like Siri, young women from impoverished rural villages *within* Thailand are trafficked or migrate to Bangkok to work in the sex industry to support their families. Often these young women are the primary breadwinners in their families. As was the case with Siri,

many young women are sold—outright or into debt bondage—in exchange for money paid to their families (Lim 1998). Other young women willingly migrate to work in the sex industry, though rarely with full knowledge of the circumstances under which they will work. According to Bales (1999, 43), about 5 percent of sex workers in Thailand are fully enslaved as Siri is. However, the distinction between forced and voluntary prostitution is a complex issue to which we will return.

Both stable and changing features of local cultures help sustain the sex industry. For instance, growing consumerism in the Third World is a factor: Families in rural areas able to purchase consumer goods from the profits of their daughter's labor often receive status within their communities (Bales 1999; Kempadoo and Doezema 1998; Truong 1990). Young women's sense of obligation to their families, and in some cases the economic benefits they receive, often result in their acceptance of the circumstances of their work. Religion and the cultural devaluation of women also provide important justifications. For example, like most major religions around the world, Thai Buddhism regards women as "distinctly inferior to men" and as "impure, carnal, and corrupting" (Bales 1999, 39). Moreover, "Thai Buddhism also carries a central message of acceptance and resignation in the face of life's pain and suffering" (Bales 1999, 39). The concept of karma, a key religious principle, teaches Buddhists that the pains they endure in this lifetime are the result of their actions in previous lives; in fact, simply being born female is indicative of failures in past lives. Thus, in addition to the violence that binds her to the brothel, Siri's self-blame and ultimate submission to sexual slavery can be situated, in part, in Thailand's cultural context and the place of women in Thai society.

Gender inequality and the cultural devaluation of women help explain why prostitution itself has proliferated and why the brunt of the industry is born by young women. However, global capitalism and its push for profits are equally at the root of why these young women have become "cheap and expendable commodities" (Bales 1999, 234). As noted, the growth of the sex industry, through the development of tourism and sex tourism, has strong roots in international policies and the practices of multinational corporations. Prostitution is often recognized as a means of increasing foreign revenue to a country, despite the fact that the majority of profits generated from tourism are channeled to Western multinationals (Truong 1990). A recent study in Thailand suggests that prostitution is the country's largest underground industry, generating between 10 percent and 14 percent of the country's gross national product (Lim 1998). Bales (1999) examined the accounts of just one brothel in Thailand and found a net monthly profit of $88,000. The result is tacit acceptance and encouragement of the industry by local officials, combined with the criminalization of sex workers (Truong 1990). In fact, Thailand provides an excellent example of the contradictions of state support and sanction of the sex industry. As social researcher Thanh-Dam Truong (1990) explained,

[S]exual services are produced on the edge of legal ambiguity. Prostitution is criminalized under the Penal Code. At the same time, it is formalized under the law governing industries. Under the Penal Code it is defined as "a crime of promiscuity." It is defined as "personal services" under business law, and as "special services" by the Police Department. The law recognizes "personal services" as a business and ensures privileges to investors, and at the same time criminalizes workers in the business. Given the contradiction between the legality of "personal service" enterprises and the illegality of prostitution, the relations of power and production in prostitution are . . . complex and diverse. (p. 180)

Consequently, while women and other providers of sexual services are stigmatized and face law enforcement sanctions, the infrastructures of the industry—and those who profit from it—remain untouched. An additional benefit of this model for businesses is that when young women such as Siri become older, contract HIV, or are otherwise too sick to work, they can be easily disposed of, because the police are often in collusion with the businesses that profit from prostitution. This is not just the case in Thailand: It is a global phenomenon (Bales 1999; Kempadoo and Doezema 1998).

My research in Sri Lanka, for instance, documented widespread police collusion and participation in the sex industry (Miller 2002). Women repeatedly described officers demanding bribes, including free sexual services. One woman said the police solicit sex from women, and then "they show us their ID. . . . [They] come and ask for money. Sometimes we have to buy them drinks. . . . If we are known to them they come and ask from us." She also described police violence: "There have been times where the policeman has beaten us before [arresting] us." In fact, several police officers corroborated women's accounts. One officer described free visits to local brothels as one of the perks of his job:

After the training [to become a police officer] we gained power. One day, seven, eight of us went to [a local brothel] and had a fight. We bashed the people . . . [and] thereafter we were allowed to come to that place free of charge. . . . The owner got scared and said, "Come anytime, sir, we will serve you free." After that, we would go to that place without paying him anything. (Miller 2002, 1061)

In addition, brothel managers described paying bribes to the police to avoid being raided, or at least to be tipped off before the raids occurred in order to prepare (Miller 2002). While brothel managers and those who profit from the sex industry are typically men, it is those at the bottom of the hierarchy—women and girls—who suffer the negative consequences.

Migration, Trafficking, and Transnational Sex Work

The previous section documented the role of tourism, and the development of sex tourism specifically, in the growth of the global sex trade. In addition, broader global economic patterns in the late twentieth century have encouraged Third World women to migrate abroad in search of economic opportunities to better themselves and their families. There are currently an estimated 60 million female migrants around the globe, and they constitute fully half of the world's migrant population (Bronstein 2004). Women migrate for a range of service sector jobs, often as domestic workers, and in some cases for prostitution. While migration itself is distinct from trafficking, and trafficking from prostitution, they are interconnected in that the growth in women's migration has made trafficking, including sexual trafficking, particularly easy to achieve. This is largely because the "trafficking of girls and women often follows the same routes as legitimate migration" (Coomaraswamy 2001, paragraph 15). Women's desire to migrate enables brokers to recruit young women with false promises of other kinds of jobs, as was the case when Anna was trafficked from Poland to Germany. In addition, the movement of migrants across international borders has increased traffickers' ability to transport women without detection and control them upon arrival in foreign lands.

As with the evolution of sex tourism, trafficking has its roots in economic globalization. Discussing the work of economist Saskia Sassen, writer Zelda Bronstein (2004) explained,

> [T]he conditions that foster trafficking are at bottom the same ones that motivate less vulnerable, more resourceful third world women to choose to leave home in search of a livelihood. In both cases, women move under the press of circumstances that typify globalized third world economies: the dominance of big foreign companies and export industries; the devastation of small- and medium-sized enterprises oriented to national markets; high unemployment, particularly among men; massive and growing government debt; the imposition of draconian fiscal terms by international leaders;

severe cutbacks in social and health services; and the drastic shrinkage of the middle class accompanied by increasing extremes of wealth and poverty.

In addition, throughout the world, women are economically disadvantaged compared with men, are relegated to sex-segregated (and poorer paying) jobs, and have the added burden of child care responsibilities. Thus, the desire to seek money-generating opportunities is even more pressingly tied to economic need for females compared with males.

As I noted in the introduction to this chapter, evidence suggests that hundreds of thousands of women are trafficked and exploited within the transnational sex industry every year. Trafficking is a global activity, and nearly every country in the world serves as a source, transit, and/or receiving country. Trafficking is found in Latin America and the Caribbean, in Africa, and to and from North America, the Middle East, Europe, and Australia. However, it is believed to be highest in two regions of the world: within Asia and from Asia to other parts of the world (Coomaraswamy 2001; Dinan 2002; Lim 1998; Wijers and Lap-Chew 1997), and from Eastern Europe and the former Soviet Union to Western Europe and other destination countries (Coomaraswamy 1996; Hughes 2001; Lehti and Aromaa 2004). The intersections of race, class, and gender inequalities often dictate these routes: Ethnic minority women, and women from poorer countries, are routed to meet the desires of more privileged men.

Transnational trafficking—trafficking across international borders—has garnered the most attention and concern in recent years (Farr 2004). Anna's story is typical. International trafficking involves both legal and illegal migration. For instance, because Poland's borders were opened to Western Europe after the fall of the Eastern Bloc, Anna's entrance into Germany was legal. This makes traffickers extremely difficult to detect, particularly when the women involved do not yet realize they are being trafficked for prostitution. Once Anna was forced to work in

Germany, her status became illegal. As we will see, women's illegal status in receiving countries contributes immensely to their control and exploitation: If apprehended, they are treated as criminals, because domestic immigration laws—and concerns over "illegal immigrants"—often are prioritized over the need to assist women and bring their traffickers to justice (Chuang 1998; Hughes 2001). Traffickers and brothel owners are well aware of this and use it to their advantage.

In addition to transnational trafficking, trafficking may take place within national boundaries, as Siri's story demonstrates. Here, both trafficking and migration patterns are from rural villages to urban centers. Some countries have entrenched patterns of both internal and transnational migration. For instance, Calcutta and Mumbai (Bombay) are well-established receiving cities in India; women are trafficked from both rural areas within India and from nearby countries such as Bangladesh and Nepal (Coomaraswamy 2001). Where trafficking across borders is concerned, the same country can serve as a source, destination, or transit country. For instance, Thailand is a common destination country in Asia, and women are routinely trafficked from Burma, Laos, the Philippines, China, and Hong Kong (Bales 1999; Lim 1998). In addition, Thailand is a well-established source and transit country, trafficking its own and foreign women to Japan (Dinan 2002; Wijers and Lap-Chew 1997).

The extent and nature of trafficking are best documented in Asia. It encompasses a large spectrum of countries with diverse cultures and economies. Within the region, Japan is a major receiving country. It is estimated that 150,000 non-Japanese women, mainly from Thailand and the Philippines, are working as prostitutes in Japan. Japanese men also constitute the largest number of sex tourists in Asia (Lim 1998). Asia includes a large number of poor countries, as well as economically well-developed countries. This, along with its well-developed sex tourism industry, helps explain the high rate of trafficking within the region. High rates of illiteracy, lack of employment opportunities, cultural and religious ideologies, and patriarchal family structures make young women vulnerable to trafficking.

While trafficking from and within Asia has been most pronounced and well established, in recent decades there has been a tremendous increase in trafficking from Eastern Europe and the former Soviet Union. The increase has been so rapid and dramatic that some commentators now refer to trafficking as the "Natasha" trade (Hughes 2001). The collapse of the Soviet Union, and with it the opening of international borders combined with economic decline in the region, have resulted in highly organized Russian crime groups. Among their criminal activities is the traffic of women for prostitution. Russian and other Eastern European women and girls are found in the sex industry throughout the world, most notably in Western Europe, Japan, China, and the Middle East (Brussa 1998; Flowers 1998).

In most instances, developed or developing countries with well-established sex industries are receiving countries. These include Japan, Germany, the Netherlands, and the United States, along with Thailand, Taiwan, Korea, and India. Transnational prostitution is so pronounced that the majority of women in the sex industry in Western Europe are not natives but are migrants from Third World and Eastern European countries (Brussa 1998). Aside from exceptions like Thailand, countries most likely to send women and children abroad are those that are most impoverished and with the lowest levels of development. The historical pattern continues to be outmigration from poorer to wealthier countries, with the most vulnerable women and girls in poor countries those most likely to be trafficked. Wealth disparities between countries combine with the marginalization of women to create these patterns. As noted with regard to sex tourism, Western notions of the "exotic" sexuality of Asian, African, and Latin American women contribute to the demand (Kempadoo and Doezema 1998). Recent evidence suggests this form of racism also operates simultaneously with racial discourses favoring "white" ethnic women, creating increased demand for women from Eastern Europe and Russia (Hughes 2001).

International Legal Standards

Individual nations and international bodies have attempted to deal with the problem of trafficking off and on for the last century. The tensions and debates over international conventions illustrate both the complexities of trafficking and prostitution, and the impact of various stakeholders in their definition and implementation. The earliest international conventions distinguished between voluntary prostitution and slavery-like prostitution due to coercion and trafficking. These conventions prohibited international trafficking and regarded prostitution as a human rights violation only if it involved overt coercion (Lim 1998). This changed with the Convention for the Suppression of Traffic in Persons and the Exploitation of the Prostitution of Others, adopted by the United Nations in 1949. This convention, which has remained in effect but under heavy recent debate, takes an *abolitionist* approach. Specifically, the U.N. convention prohibits any individual who, "to gratify the passions of another . . . (1) procures, entices, or leads away, for purposes of prostitution, another person, even with the consent of that person; (2) exploits the prostitution of another person, even with the consent of that person" (1949 Convention, cited in Chuang 1998, 72). By definition, the abolitionist paradigm defines the prostitute as a victim, and third parties (e.g., brokers, pimps, traffickers, and in some cases clients) as the criminal parties. Thus, from an abolitionist approach, there is no distinction between forced and voluntary prostitution: All prostitution is deemed to be coercive (Lim 1998).

One problem, as we will see, is that international conventions are extremely difficult to enforce. Domestic laws on prostitution, particularly those that prohibit or criminalize all or some facets of prostitution, are nearly always given precedence over international conventions. Thus, women—even those coerced into prostitution—are routinely treated as lawbreakers rather than victims. The same goes for immigration laws and nations' greater concern with women's illegal immigrant status than their status as victims of trafficking. Recall that despite Anna's cooperation with the police to bust the trafficking ring that brought her to Germany and then Switzerland, she was deported back to Poland. Women who have been trafficked into prostitution and are deported back to their homelands often face both extreme economic and social hardships, stigma and ostracism, and further danger at the hands of their traffickers (Chuang 1998; Coomaraswamy 1996; Kempadoo and Doezema 1998). Sex workers' rights advocate Marjan Wijers (1998) detailed the problems women face when deported to their homelands:

> In many cases the family relies on the women's income. If [they are] deported, they return home with empty hands, with no money and with debts that will never be paid off. If it becomes known that a woman has worked as a prostitute, this can have serious social consequences. Not only has she to worry about the effect this can have for her family, she has to face the possibility that her family will not accept her anymore. (p. 75)

Wijers also noted that traffickers often find and force women back into the industry, including making "threats to inform her family about her prostitution activities, threats to harass or harm herself, her family or children if the woman does not comply with their demands" (p. 75).

In addition to the problems of enforcement and the harm caused to women by many current practices, the abolitionist definitional paradigm itself has been challenged on additional fronts in the last several decades as well. Sex workers' rights advocates object to the definition of all women in prostitution as "victims." Instead, they argue that most adult women in the sex industry choose their occupation, and that they should be free to do so. They have argued for the decriminalization of prostitution and for efforts to be targeted only at those who use coercion, deception, and exploitation. With decriminalization, these advocates believe that women can organize to improve their working conditions. However, as we will see, even their long-held distinction between free workers and victims has become more complex in recent years, as sex workers' rights advocates have found problems in the implementation of the "forced versus voluntary" definitional framework (Kempadoo and Doezema 1998).

With the growth of trafficking in the last decades, international organizations have come together to address the complexities of the contemporary problems of trafficking and global sex work. These groups have also raised serious critiques of the U.N. convention. Janie Chuang (1998), a lawyer with expertise in international law, described the problems of the U.N. convention for addressing contemporary trafficking:

> By defining trafficking as requiring both coercive recruitment and forced prostitution, women subject to one but not the other practice, as well as those subjected to non-sexual forced labor/slavery-like practices, remain ineligible for protection under international anti-trafficking law. (p. 75)

To remedy these problems, the Global Alliance Against Traffic in Women (GAATW), a coalition of agencies working to ameliorate trafficking, has fought for the adoption of a new definitional paradigm. The GAATW definition distinguishes between trafficking and forced labor/slavery-like practices. *Trafficking* is defined as

> All acts involved in the recruitment and/or transportation of a person within and across national borders for work or services by means of violence or threat of violence, abuse of authority or dominant position, debt bondage, deception and other forms of coercion. (GAATW, cited in Chuang 1998, 73)

Forced labor/slavery-like practices are defined as

> The extraction of work or services from any person or the appropriation of the legal identity and/or physical person of any person by means of violence or threat of violence, abuse of authority or dominant position, debt-bondage, deception or other forms of coercion. (GAATW, cited in Chuang 1998, 73)

This definitional paradigm addresses a number of the problems raised by Chuang. Neither trafficking nor forced labor/slavery-like practices must be tied specifically to prostitution for victims to be eligible for protection. Women who freely migrate but are then forced into involuntary labor are likewise covered under this proposed definitional paradigm.

Consider Nandani's example again. Her situation is domestic rather than international in that her sale into prostitution occurred in her home country. Nandani also was not trafficked for the purpose of prostitution, as were Siri and Anna, but instead her internal migration was voluntary; she ran away from home. However, like Siri and Anna, she was forced to submit to prostitution. The distinction GAATW makes between trafficking and forced labor/slavery-like practices thus is significant for understanding Nandani's experience of forced prostitution and doesn't preclude her from coverage because she was not trafficked. Her decision to remain in the industry once forced into it raises additional complexities about how conventions define coercion and consent. While Nandani chose to remain in prostitution, it was within the confines of extremely limited economic opportunities, exacerbated by the stigma she faced—and internalized—as a result of her initial experiences with forced prostitution (see Chuang 1998). A review of what we know about women's experiences in the international sex industry brings into greater relief the difficult challenges of ameliorating trafficking and forced labor while protecting women's human rights.

Women's Experiences With Trafficking and the Transnational Sex Industry

As I noted before, traffickers generate gross earnings of an estimated $7 billion annually (Hughes 2001). Trafficking today is well organized and is often controlled by organized crime groups. Recruiting agents can include employment agencies, brokers, "marriage" agents, acquaintances, as well as family friends or relatives. Often ads are placed in newspapers that describe well-paying job opportunities overseas in the service industries, including domestic work, dancing, and work as waitresses and hostesses. Researcher Donna Hughes (2001) estimated that about 20 percent of women are recruited for trafficking through false advertising. Recruitment methods usually involve deceit or debt bondage but can also involve violence. Women often are deceived about the nature of the work for which they are migrating, as Anna's story illustrates. When she was brought to Germany, it was with the belief that she would be working as a domestic; later, her trip to Switzerland was with the promise of marriage. Both are common deceit strategies used for trafficking (Hughes 2001). However, sometimes it is the conditions of work, rather than the nature of the work, that women are deceived about. In these cases, women may know that they will be involved in the sex industry, but they do not realize the exploitative and often violent conditions under which they will work.

Even when women know they are migrating for sex work, they are often unprepared for the working conditions they discover. For example, often trafficking generates a system of debt bondage, as was the case with Siri. With transnational prostitution, this occurs when women borrow money for the cost of travel, visas, false documents, and employment location. They are then charged exorbitant interest and required to work off the debt before accumulating their own earnings. It is not uncommon for women's debt to be sold from one employer to another, and for the new employer to then add the women's purchase price to their debt. As Siri's example illustrates, most women find it nearly impossible to pay their way out of debt bondage, and thus they remain trapped and under the control of their debtors. With transnational prostitution, women's visas and passports are routinely confiscated as security on the "loan," and this gives their debtors further control over their movement. In some instances, particularly involving the traffic in young women or children such as Siri, an advance payment is given to the family, which the trafficked youth is required to pay off with interest.

Even when migration is voluntary, women's status as illegal immigrants makes them vulnerable to exploitation and coercion in these markets; this is exacerbated when women are trafficked or migrate to foreign nations in which they do not speak the language and thus cannot communicate their experiences or easily seek assistance (Kempadoo and Doezema 1998). Evidence consistently shows that the organization of the sex industry, including the transnational sex industry, results in widespread patterns of violence, coercion, and exploitation, as well as discriminatory law enforcement. Women who are trafficked, as well as women who voluntarily migrate for sex work, often find themselves working in slavery-like conditions in which their mobility is restricted and they are not given the right to control the conditions of their work, including the choice of which or how many customers they must see.

Documenting "how slavery finds its way into the sex industry," sex workers' advocate Jo Bindman (1998) noted that:

> Most people who work in [sex] establishments lack formal contracts with the owners or managers but are subject to their control. Those who work in the sex industry are commonly excluded from mainstream society. They are thereby denied whatever international, national or customary protection from abuse is available to others as citizens,

women, or workers. The lack of international and local protection renders sex workers vulnerable to exploitation in the workplace and to violence at the hands of management, customers, law enforcement officials and the public. (p. 67)

As a consequence of conditions of illegal confinement and forced labor, women are subject to a range of abuses, including physical and sexual assault as well as exposure to HIV and other sexually transmitted diseases. Health care is minimal, and women who contract diseases are often simply discarded. For instance, Truong (1990) reported that in Thailand, brothel owners often arrange police raids and the arrest of unwanted women. Sex workers are often blamed for the spread of AIDS and other sexually transmitted diseases. Just as historian Judith Walkowitz (1980) documented with regard to the spread and control of syphilis in the nineteenth century, sex workers today "are placed under scrutiny, subject to intense campaigning and . . . define[d] as the vectors and transmitters of disease" (Kempadoo 1998, 18). In some countries, such as Sri Lanka, women found to have sexually transmitted diseases are remanded to detention facilities (Miller 1999). Most often, migrant women are deported upon discovery that they are HIV-positive and face intense stigma upon return to their homelands. In fact, "there is a fairly well-substantiated rumor that HIV-positive Burmese women returned [i.e., deported] to Burma have been executed" (Murray 1998, 56).

Advocates argue that strict migration laws, in conjunction with legal statutes governing the sex industry, allow this system to flourish and increase sex workers' dependence on outside agents (Kempadoo and Doezema 1998). Many Third World and Eastern European women who are trafficked or migrate to work in the sex industry do so as illegal immigrants. As previously noted, despite the fact that the U.N. convention has prohibited trafficking for prostitution, the countries into which women are trafficked routinely give precedence to their status as illegal aliens en-

gaged in illicit work rather than to their status as victims of trafficking or forced prostitution. This is the case even for women who knowingly work in the industry: The threat of deportation gives them little bargaining power with those for whom they work. Protests for better working conditions often result in the woman being turned over to the authorities and deported. As Kempadoo and Doezema (1998) explained,

> [T]rafficked women are first and foremost migrants—persons seeking economic, social and political opportunities away from home—yet, due to restrictive laws and policies and limited opportunities for women, are relegated to informal sector work. State policies and laws furthermore serve to position migrant women as "undesirable aliens" and criminals, yet yield benefits for traffickers. (p. 32)

Brokers, managers, traffickers, recruiters, middle men, as well as legitimate businesses such as hotels and travel agencies continue to profit from the industry, while sex workers face distinct disadvantages that undermine their ability to control their labor and that make them dependent on the individuals and organizations who exploit them (see Kempadoo and Doezema 1998; Truong 1990). In addition, police corruption, bribery schemes, and government collusion are well-documented (Miller 2002; Truong 1990).

Several particularly gruesome cases highlight the seriousness of violence against women in the international sex industry. One is a well-publicized brothel fire in Thailand, where the charred remains of women were found chained to beds. Legal analyst Margaret Healy (1995) opened her analysis of laws against child sex tourism with the horrifying case of a 12-year-old Filipino girl who was brutalized by an Australian doctor. He "forcibly inserted an electric vibrator into [her] vagina" (p. 1859), and it broke and lodged there. The girl did not receive medical treatment and died seven months later. While the doctor originally received a life sentence for the crime, the Supreme Court in the Philippines eventually reversed the decision and acquitted the doctor, who remains a free man. Donna Hughes (2001) reported two cases in which women who resisted their work in the sex industry were murdered: "In Istanbul, Turkey, two Ukrainian women were thrown off a balcony and killed while six of their Russian friends watched. In Serbia, a Ukrainian woman who resisted was beheaded in public" (p. 12).

Although it is difficult to know how typical cases such as these are, what is clear is that around the world, sex workers are "imprisoned and detained, subjected to cruel and degrading mistreatment [and] suffer violence at the hands of the state or by private individuals with the state's support" (Doezema 1998, 46). In fact, violence is an entrenched feature of the sex industry throughout the world. Jody Raphael's chapter in this volume documents the extent of violence experienced by women in the American context. This finding is mirrored in studies worldwide. Sex workers describe routine verbal, physical, and sexual abuse at the hands of clients as well as the police. Returning again to my study in Sri Lanka, here is one woman's account of her routine experiences:

> Men call us *baduwa, gona* [literally "item/thing, bull/animal"] and such. We don't say anything. By chance if we do say something they will come in the night and will drag and hit us. . . . There are people who shout at us and hit us also. (Miller 2002, 1058)

Sex workers also described being raped and gang raped in the context of prostitution (Miller 2002).

As noted earlier, though sex workers' rights advocates insist that women should have the right to engage in prostitution (Jenness 1993), they have also problematized the "voluntary versus forced" distinction because of its discriminatory effects on women who have chosen sex work. It is often the case that women who made the initial decision to engage in sex work find themselves in situations of violence as well as coercion, dependence, and debt bondage. Because their decision to migrate was voluntary, they fall outside the realm of public support and receive inadequate assistance and support. Thus, a number of activists argue that the forced/voluntary dichotomy remains a limited framework for dealing with sex work, as it often results in policies aimed only at rescuing trafficked women; women who are voluntarily involved in the sex industry continue to face exploitation and human rights violations that go unaddressed by current intervention strategies. As advocates Kempadoo and Doezema (1998) summarized, "as yet, no international conventions or anti-trafficking organizations exist that explicitly support sex workers' human rights" (p. 30; see also Coomaraswamy 2001).

Trafficking and Prostitution of Children

While most of this chapter has specifically addressed trafficking and prostitution among young women and adults, which are significant outgrowths of the global sex industry, trafficking and sex tourism has led to the rise of children's involvement in these markets. Recall that Siri was just age 14 when she was sold into prostitution. Children even younger than Siri are routinely involved. Experts suggest that sex tourism involving children has grown in recent years, as Western tourists who fear AIDS among adult prostitutes increasingly demand younger children (Boyes 1996; Kattoulas 1995). In addition, there is some evidence of organized pedophile networks in the West, exacerbated by the Internet, which provide information and organize tours abroad for the purpose of sexually abusing children (Boyes 1996; EPCAT 1997; McGirk 1996). Moreover, developmental processes within the global economy have contributed to a rise in the earning activity of Third World children in a variety of settings. Thus, the sharp increase in children's involvement in sex tourism and prostitution must be addressed "in the context of the global exploitation of child labor" more generally (Kempadoo 1998, 7).

Again, most available data focus on the Asian context, though child prostitution remains a global problem. According to a recent estimate by the U.N. International Labor Organization, more than one million children in Asia are involved in the sex trade (Kaban 1996; see also Healy 1995). Thailand, Sri Lanka, the Philippines, Cambodia, and India are believed to be among the main centers of child sex tourism (Boyes 1996; McGirk 1996). Evidence suggests that in contrast to the West, where most child prostitution involves runaways (Davis 1993), in Asia many youths work in the sex industry to support their families (Montgomery 1998; Truong 1990). Sex tourists from Western Europe as well as Australia, Japan, and the United States travel to Asia to partake in the child sex trade.

As with the sex industry more generally, the root causes of the problem appear to be a host of economic, social, and cultural factors that developing countries face. Also a factor are the demands generated by thousands of men who travel to the region annually to purchase sexual services from children, along with the multinational infrastructures that support them. Poverty is often cited as a primary cause that accounts for the increase in the number of children involved. This is the case both for parents who are induced to sell their children and for youths who see the sex industry as a viable means of earning money for their families when compared with the limited alternatives available (Montgomery 1998). Gender discrimination and the lesser value of female children also contribute to a climate in which the sexual exploitation of girls flourishes, though there is evidence of the involvement of boys in the sex industry as well.

A number of legal remedies have recently been introduced to curtail child sex tourism in particular; however, there is limited evidence of their success. There is near-uniform agreement that an abolitionist model is best, at least in theory. Children are defined as victims of the sex industry, and third parties as well as clients should be criminalized and prosecuted. Child sex tourism has become a grave international concern, resulting in both national and international efforts to ameliorate it. The U.N. Convention on the Rights of the Child has as one goal the protection of children from sexual exploitation. A number of Western nations, including the United States, have passed new laws to prosecute citizens for sex crimes against children that are committed abroad; however, evidentiary and cross-jurisdiction problems have thus far made these efforts difficult (Berkman 1996; Bureau of International Labor Affairs 1996; Healy 1995).

In addition, most of the countries where child sex tourism occurs have adopted stringent laws prohibiting the trade. In Sri Lanka, for example, new laws were passed in 1995 to curb child sex tourism by raising the minimum age of consent to 18 for boys and 16 for girls, making sexual activities with youths under those ages a crime, and providing a minimum five-year jail term for pimps and clients (Gunasekera 1996; Samarasinghe 1996, 1997). Several European tourists have been prosecuted under the new laws, though there is no evidence in the short term of a significant deterrent effect of the laws.

In addition, it is important to note that some argue the issue of children's involvement in the sex industry should be defined more broadly, to emphasize explicitly poverty and economic inequalities exacerbated by Western imperialism. As noted previously, developmental processes have contributed to a rise in the earning activities of children globally; attempts to ameliorate children's participation in the sex industry without addressing the global exploitation of children's labor more broadly provide a truncated approach, with likely harmful effects for the children involved (see Kempadoo 1998; Montgomery 1998). This call to situate children's exploitation in the sex industry within the larger problems that generate it parallels the discussions raised earlier about the need to understand trafficking within the broader context of the gender and economic inequalities that push women to migrate, making them vulnerable to trafficking.

Conclusion

This chapter has documented the tremendous proliferation of the global sex industry in the late twentieth and early twenty-first centuries, including the growth of sex tourism, trafficking, forced labor/slavery-like conditions, and child prostitution. From all of the evidence gathered over the last several decades, we know without question that this is a vast industry that generates huge profits worldwide. Very little of the money garnered from this industry, however, makes it into the hands of the young women on whose backs the sex trade is built. I have also suggested some of the difficulties of intervening in the sex industry. At its most basic level, the infrastructure of the current transnational sex industry is built on two intertwined social phenomena: (1) the global economy's push for profit without responsibility for the circumstances of its most exploited workers (Bales 1999), and (2) the continued devaluation of women, especially poor and marginalized women, worldwide (Coomaraswamy 2001, Raphael, this volume). These two overarching factors undergird the global sex trade and its current iterations around the world. Without changing these basic social facts of the contemporary era, there is little hope that the exploitative nature of the global sex industry can be eliminated.

However, reform efforts are underway. This is evidenced by the work of coalitions such as the Global Alliance Against Traffic in Women, the important accomplishments of the U.N. Special Rapporteur on Violence Against Women—and even the fact that the U.N. appointed her—as well as the efforts of scholars and activists such as Kevin Bales, who research and publicize what is happening and why, and sex workers' rights advocates around the globe. In addition, individual nations are now taking measures to investigate and ameliorate trafficking. A case in point is the U.S. Victims of Trafficking and Violence Protection Act of 2000, which was reauthorized in 2003 and is the culmination of the efforts of the government's Trafficking in Persons and Worker Exploitation Task Force (U.S. Department of Justice, n.d.).

But there remains considerable disagreement—among scholars, activists, and advocates; across nations; and within and across international bodies—about how best to define the problem, and, thus, how best to remedy it. The debates over the U.N. Convention for the Suppression of Traffic in Persons and the Exploitation of the Prostitution of Others are a good illustration of these tensions. Definitions of prostitution, trafficking, coercion, and consent all have an important influence on how the problem is addressed by organizations, nations, and international bodies. Furthermore, nations' routine practices of placing their domestic policies over international law, as well as the widespread existence of laws and policies that are discriminatory against women, have a deleterious effect on intervention and prosecutorial efforts (Coomaraswamy 2001).

At present, the best efforts have come from local nongovernment organizations (NGOs) (Coomaraswamy 2001) and sex workers' rights advocates (Kempadoo and Doezema 1998), whose efforts are dedicated to assisting, organizing, and empowering women to obtain their basic human rights. Even these groups often have competing approaches and agendas—from rescuing trafficked women, providing them with health and medical support and with occupational training, to organizing sex workers to fight for their rights as workers. Despite this diversity of approach, these various groups are doing the most important grassroots work to improve women's lives. However, by their nature, nongovernment organizations are limited in the scope of their work and in their ability to reach all of the women affected by the global sex trade. In addition to prevention and intervention for women, interventions must hold government and criminal justice officials accountable where corruption, bribery, and collusion are found (Hughes 2001). Most important, given the economic benefits derived from sex workers' exploitation and the gendered hierarchies upon which the industry is built, policies need to address these root causes. Effective efforts will target those organizations and individuals responsible for trafficking and forced labor, as well as the businesses, including multinational corporations, that ultimately profit.

Note

1. Quoted in Sachs 1994, 25.

Study/Discussion Questions

1. Comparing the experiences of Siri, Anna, and Nandani, what similarities and differences do you see? What facets of the global sex industry do each of the young women's stories illustrate, and what common threads do they share?

2. What evidence does Miller provide for how slavery finds its way into the global sex industry, and what are the consequences for women? What roles do debt bondage and violence play, and how do domestic immigration laws contribute to the problem?

3. Why does Miller argue that the global sex industry is rooted both in the oppression of women and in the global economy's push for profits? What evidence does she provide concerning who profits from the industry and how?

4. Describe the debates concerning international conventions and legal approaches to ameliorate the trafficking of women for prostitution. How do these debates illustrate the complexities of trafficking and prostitution and the positions of various stakeholders? What are the benefits and costs of making the distinction between forced and voluntary prostitution?

References

Bales, K. (1999). *Disposable people: New slavery in the global economy.* Berkeley: University of California Press.

Berkman, T. (1996). Responses to the international child sex trade. *Boston College International and Comparative Law Review, 19*, 397–416.

Bindman, J. (1998). An international perspective on slavery in the sex industry. In K. Kempadoo and J. Doezema (Eds.), *Global sex workers: Rights, resistance, and redefinition* (pp. 65–68). New York: Routledge.

Boyes, R. (1996, August 22). How the sex tourists evade justice. *Times*.

Bronstein, Z. (2004). Nowhere woman—Review of *Global women: Nannies, maids, and sex workers in the new economy. Dissent Magazine*.

Brussa, L. (1998). The TAMPEP project in Western Europe. In K. Kempadoo and J. Doezema (Eds.), *Global sex workers: Rights, resistance, and redefinition* (pp. 246–259). New York: Routledge.

Bureau of International Labor Affairs. (1996). *Forced labor: The prostitution of children.* Washington, DC: U.S. Department of Labor.

Chuang, J. (1998). Redirecting the debate over trafficking in women: Definitions, paradigms, and contexts. *Harvard Human Rights Journal, 11*, 65–107.

Coomaraswamy, R. (1996). *Report on the mission of the Special Rapporteur to Poland on the issue of trafficking and forced prostitution of women.* Geneva: United Nations Economic and Social Council.

——. (2001). *Integration of the human rights of women and the gender perspective: Addendum mission to Bangladesh, Nepal, and India on the issue of trafficking of women and girls.* Geneva: United Nations Economic and Social Council.

Davis, N. J. (Ed.). (1993). *Prostitution: An international handbook on trends, problems, and policies.* Westport, CT: Greenwood Press.

Dinan, K. A. (2002). Migrant Thai women subjected to slavery-like abuses in Japan. *Violence Against Women, 8*, 1113–1139.

Doezema, J. (1998). Forced to choose: Beyond the voluntary vs. forced prostitution dichotomy. In K. Kempadoo and J. Doezema (Eds.), *Global sex workers: Rights, resistance, and redefinition* (pp. 34–50). New York: Routledge.

Enloe, C. (1989). *Bananas, beaches, and bases: Making feminist sense of international politics.* Berkeley: University of California Press.

EPCAT (End Child Prostitution in Asian Tourism). (1997, April 20). The paedophile's club. *Sunday Leader*.

Farr, K. (2004). *Sex trafficking: The global market in women and children.* New York: Worth Publishers.

Flowers, B. R. (1998). *The prostitution of women and girls.* Jefferson, NC: Macfarland & Company.

Gunasekera, R. (1996, October 27). Sri Lanka says orphanages used in child-sex trade. *Reuters World Service.*

Healy, M. A. (1995). Prosecuting child sex tourism at home: Do laws in Sweden, Australia, and the United States safeguard the rights of children as mandated by international laws? *Fordham International Law Journal,* 18, 1852–1871.

Hughes, D. M. (2001, January). The "Natasha" trade: Transnational sex trafficking. *National Institute of Justice Journal,* pp. 8–15.

Jenness, V. (1993). *Making it work: The prostitutes' rights movement in perspective.* New York: Aldine de Gruyter.

Kaban, E. (1996, November 12). ILO says 250 million children are workers. *Reuters World Service.*

Kattoulas, V. (1995, November 30). World tourism industry dodges child sex-tour issue. *Reuters North American Wire.*

Kempadoo, K. (1998). Introduction: Globalizing sex workers' rights. In K. Kempadoo and J. Doezema (Eds.), *Global sex workers: Rights, resistance, and redefinition* (pp. 1–28). New York: Routledge.

Kempadoo, K., and Doezema, J. (Eds.). (1998). *Global sex workers: Rights, resistance, and redefinition.* New York: Routledge.

Lehti, M., and Aromaa, K. (2004). Trafficking in women and children for sexual exploitation. *ESC Criminology in Europe,* 3 (1), 16–18.

Lim, L. L. (Ed.). (1998). *The sex sector: The economic and social bases of prostitution in Southeast Asia.* Geneva: International Labor Organization.

McGirk, T. (1996, May 12). Their latest holiday destination. *The Independent.*

Mies, M. (1986). *Patriarchy and accumulation on a world scale: Women in the international division of labor.* London: Zed Books.

Miller, E. M. (1991, August). *Thinking about prostitution discourse as a way of thinking about gender as a principle of social organization.* Paper presented at the Annual Meeting of the American Sociological Association.

Miller, J. (1999). *The commercial sex industry in Sri Lanka: Some preliminary observations.* International Centre for Ethnic Studies Lecture Series, Colombo, Sri Lanka.

——. (2002). Violence and coercion in Sri Lanka's commercial sex industry: Intersections of gender, sexuality, culture and the law. *Violence Against Women,* 8, 1045–1074.

Montgomery, H. (1998). Children, prostitution, and identity: A case study from a tourist resort in Thailand. In K. Kempadoo and J. Doezema (Eds.), *Global sex workers: Rights, resistance, and redefinition* (pp. 139–150). New York: Routledge.

Murray, A. (1998). Debt-bondage and trafficking: Don't believe the hype. In K. Kempadoo and J. Doezema (Eds.), *Global sex workers: Rights, resistance, and redefinition* (pp. 51–64). New York: Routledge.

Phongpaichit, P. (1982). *From peasant girls to Bangkok masseuses.* Geneva: International Labour Office.

Sachs, A. (1994). The last commodity: Child prostitution in the developing world. *World Watch,* 9, 24–30.

Samarasinghe, M. (1996, October 30). Sri Lanka cracking down on child sex abuse. *Reuters World Service.*

——. (1997, February 11). Sri Lanka deports Swiss facing child abuse charges. *Reuters World Service.*

Scibelli, P. (1987). Empowering prostitutes: A proposal for international legal reform. *Harvard Women's Law Journal,* 10, 117–157.

Truong, T. (1990). *Sex, money, and morality: Prostitution and tourism in Southeast Asia.* London: Zed Books.

U.S. Department of Justice. Trafficking in persons information. Retrieved from: *http://www.usdoj.gov/trafficking.htm#trafficking.* See also: *http://www.usdoj.gov/ag/annualreports/tr2005/assessmentofustipactivities.pdf.*

Walkowitz, J. (1980). *Prostitution and Victorian society.* Cambridge, MA: Cambridge University Press.

Wijers, M. (1998). Women, labor, and migration: The position of trafficked women and strategies for support. In K. Kempadoo and J. Doezema (Eds.), *Global sex workers: Rights, resistance, and redefinition* (pp. 69–78). New York: Routledge.

Wijers, M., and Lap-Chew, L. (1997). *Trafficking in women, forced labour and slavery-like practices in marriage, domestic labour, and prostitution.* Netherlands: Foundation Against Trafficking in Women. ◆

11
Sexual Assault Reforms

Thirty Years and Counting

Susan Caringella

In this chapter you will learn the following:

- The history of the rape reform movement, including the impetus for it, the criticisms leveled by it (e.g., historic myths and discriminatory requirements and standards surrounding rape victimization), and the objectives and changes involved in the effort to rectify problems in rape law

- The accomplishments and failures of the rape reform movement

- The development of the backlash movement as a new hurdle for promoting greater justice in rape adjudication and in relationship to conservatives (and the liberal rape reform movement)

- Future directions to advance the protection of rape victims, women, and justice

Introduction

The topic of rape and sexual assault caught the public's attention in the late 1960s and grew like wildfire over the 1970s into the 1980s. But then national concern waned, until the backlash criticisms of the rape reform movement in the 1990s. There are a number of ways to understand this relatively recent history.

Impetus

The theme underpinning the developing rape reform movement was the critique of sexism in society, and of the legal system in particular, for the discriminatory treatment of women, especially when victimized by rape. Early feminism, as found in the Women's Liberation Movement, like the Civil Rights Movement on which it piggybacked, drew attention to the difference between the U.S. ideals of equality and justice for all and the reality of inequality for girls and women. Concern about sexist inequality naturally led to concern about the plight of females who suffered victimization by rape. The objective in bringing critical attention to rape was to increase sensitivity and fairness for rape victims in place of the unbridled victim blaming that has been corollary with the treatment of rape across the continents and centuries.

Females who are raped have been stoned, drown, banished (Brownmiller 1975), and otherwise attacked by myths written into laws that punish females for their guilt in precipitating rape, consenting to and even wanting rape, and lying about sex acts when charging rape. This has led to horrendous attrition in rape, whereby "98 percent of rape victims never see their attacker caught, tried, and imprisoned. . . . Forty eight percent of cases are dismissed before trial" (U.S. Senate Judiciary Report 1993, quoted in Hunter, Burns-Smith, and Walsh 2000, 2) in the United States. Rates in Canada and England are similar (see Du Mont and Myhr 2000, 1117–1118). For example, it was recently reported that rape resulted in only a 7 percent conviction rate (Longstaff 2002).

The growing numbers on rape also contributed to the escalating disquietude about rape victimization in the 1960s and 1970s. Researchers and government agencies began to discover the magnitude of the "dark" figure of crime that is not reported to police and how rape was the "most notoriously underreported offense in the country" (Federal Bureau of Investigation 1973, 15). Early estimates on underreporting by independent agencies and scholars ranged from a low of 25 percent to 33 percent (Ennis 1966) to highs of over 90 percent (Brownmiller 1975; Curtis 1976; Russell 1984). Government estimates from National Crime Surveys on victimization stand in the middle range, showing that between one-half to two-thirds of rape victims never come to the attention of police (U.S. Department of Justice 1973–2002). This news was terrifying enough, but add to it the huge increases in the official rates of reported rape, and the nationwide efforts to mobilize against rape become easily interpretable. The official rates of reported rape were skyrocketing. FBI figures show that forcible (*sic*)[1] rape more than quadrupled over the 1960s and 1970s (U.S. Department of Justice 1989, 427).

Critiques

The research and literature on rape abounded in parallel with the rising numbers. The work chronicled and documented how rape victims were "twice raped" (Savage 1990), first by the rapist and then by the criminal justice system. This "double victimization" (Holmstrom and Burgess 1975) was attributed to prejudicial attitudes about rape and its victims, as well as to unique legal requirements attending the criminal offense of forcible (*sic*) rape. One set of erroneous beliefs, or myths, about rape revolves around the victim-offender relationship. The stereotype of an interracial, specifically black offender-white victim, stranger attacking from the bushes or in a parking lot is a statistical rarity. The most frequent rapes are between people of the same race/ethnicity and social class, who know one another in some way, in residential settings (cf. Bureau of Justice Statistics 1973–2002). Another set of myths centers around the castigation of girls and women for becoming rape victims. Rape victims, for example, are blamed for provoking, and even deserving the victimization they suffer at the hands of men. They are damned in this light for drinking, smoking, dancing, flirting, hitchhiking, and wearing sexy cloth-

ing. Rape victims are even faulted for "wanting," not to mention "enjoying" (at least subconsciously) rape. The illogic goes, if she didn't really want "it," or didn't come around to enjoying "it," she would have resisted (more). These myths are so powerful that research has found that a majority of convicted rapists rationalize that what they did was not rape because they hold onto such beliefs (Scully 1990).

Another myth tracks around notions that prostitutes can't be raped, that promiscuous women can't be raped, and even that sexually "active" women can't be raped. The illogic here is that consent in the past to sex with a man somehow makes more probable consent in the present to another man's forced sexual violence. One further baseless belief is generated because of these groundless beliefs. This lies in the myth that females frequently falsely accuse males of rape.

Rape myths prop up legal standards that are unique to the crimes of rape and sexual assault. Glaring examples of historic inequitable principles in rape law are easily found. The corroboration requirement is unique to rape prosecution, specifying that a victim's testimony is not sufficient grounds for a conviction. This discriminates against rape victims by stipulating that additional evidence to a complaint (e.g., eyewitnesses, medical injuries, semen, all of which are regularly unavailable) is required to sustain a rape conviction. By way of contrast, victim testimony is sufficient for conviction in other criminal offenses. Resistance and consent standards are truly pugnacious, requiring only the victims of rape to resist—speaking not historically, "to the utmost" "through the entire duration of the attack." They are based on the torturous logic that victim resistance is necessary to prove the use or existence of force by offenders; that offender force is necessary to demonstrate the lack of victim consent; and that lack of victim consent must be proven to establish that the act(s) were—as traditional carnal knowledge statutes put it—"against her will."

Relatedly, rape victims' past sexual history or character, reputation, and all sex activity evidence have been discriminatorily admissible in court (even though a defendant's criminal history is generally disallowed). Again, the skeptical focus on victim behavior is unique to the legal processing of rape. Such evidence has been deemed relevant because of the myths about rape victim consent and rape victim credibility. Let one further example suffice. Cautionary instructions are exclusively given to jurors in rape trials, to inform them that rape is "an accusation easily to be made and hard to be proved and harder to be defended against by the party accused, tho never so innocent" (Hale 1971 [1680], 635).

Given the police, prosecutorial, judicial, and defense attorney interrogations (as opposed to investigations) of rape complaints, and the abysmally low conviction rates in rape (previously discussed), the two occurrences I mentioned become predictable: (1) there is a low rate of reporting, and (2) there is, in reality, a low number of false accusations. The unfounding[2] of complaints by police (which is seen as evidence of false reports) has recently been reported to be actually 1.6 percent; other estimates have frequently shown the rate to be about 2 percent (cf. Dusky 1996) as opposed to the myth that women so often falsely "cry rape." This is not surprising given how little there is to gain and how much there is to lose for a rape victim. Succinctly, then, the heightened attention to the problems of rape helped to make clear to the nation the fact that it is a horrendous myth that rape victims consent to rape. Moreover, this nature of belief has led to the persecution of rape victims in place of the prosecution of rape offenders.

Changes

The women's liberation and rape reform movements' publicity and criticisms led to alteration of rape laws in every state of the country. The changes varied greatly; in some jurisdictions the changes were not much more than semantic, in other jurisdictions the changes were vast. The most common dimensions involved changing the definition of forcible (*sic*) rape to newly entitled offenses such as deviate or criminal sexual assault. These terms often define degrees of crimes, from more to less serious according to injuries, victim age, and so forth, in order to rid historic problematic connotations associated with the treatment of rape as a strictly sexual, instead of violent, crime. New definitions of offenses such as these were expanded to incorporate male in addition to female victims, as well as a greater range of behaviors, such as oral and anal penetration, penetration by fingers and foreign objects, and criminal sexual conduct (short of penetration).

The uniquely discriminatory standards relied upon in rape prosecution were also repealed in some jurisdictions, while relaxed in others. For instance, de jure corroboration requirements have been largely abandoned; and where resistance requirements persist, they no longer require "utmost" resistance "through the entire duration" of a sexual violence episode, however long it may endure. Rape shield laws were put in place across the jurisdictions to limit, however slightly (see following "Outcomes" section), the admissibility of character, reputation, or sexual history evidence. One other significant change across the states has been the repeal of the marital exemption in rape, which said that a man cannot rape his wife because she is given unto him perpetually through marriage. In other words, laws have been altered slowly over the years as states came to recognize that marital rape is not a contradiction in terms.[3]

Rape Fades From the National Agenda

Women's groups and other victim advocates were less visible in the aftermath of the sweeping changes that were enacted in state after state. There was less grassroots, political, and legislative activity and less coverage of rape as one of the media's hot button issues. Dwindling attention to rape can also be seen to be related to mounting concern about domestic violence.[4] As intimate partner violence (IPV) swelled to preoccupy feminist and public distress about the issues confronting women,[5] and many were placated because of so much legal change, rape faded into the background.

By itself, the shift in concern from rape to domestic violence is not problematic. The issue is that one problem was obliterated by another, with only partial measures taken to rectify a minefield of issues with the first problem (i.e., rape). Moreover, domestic violence, too, was relegated to more obscure alleyways, in the relative infancy of a social movement, as IPV concerns were replaced by the war on drugs, task forces and commissions on gangs, drive-by shootings, and HIV/AIDS.

Outcomes

Missing from early perceived gains in rape legislation was any systematic assessment of rape reform law outcomes. Evaluations of reforms were few and far between, especially in comparison with the explosion of literature on the topic of rape. The dearth of research on how the modified rape laws translated into victim and case processing is a significant deficiency. This is because of the widely known difference between the law on the books and the law in action (i.e., the discrepancy between the ideal and the real in law).

The relatively sparse research that has undertaken the examination of whether or not the objectives underlying reforms have been realized has consistently yielded somewhat mixed results over the years. On the one hand, enhanced rates of arrest (Marsh, Geist, and Caplan 1982), prosecution (Polk 1985), and conviction for rape cases (Marsh, Geist , and Caplan 1982) and for rape (as opposed to nonrape) charges (Loh 181) have

been reported in a few jurisdictions under reform legislation. Moreover, similarity between sexual and other/(nonsexual) assaults have been found in charging and plea bargaining by prosecutors (Caringella-MacDonald 1985), in attrition rates (Galvin and Polk 1985) and in conviction rates (Clark and Buchner 1982) in some jurisdictions. Additionally, there is evidence to indicate that some victims have been harassed less and treated with greater sensitivity and dignity than was the case in the pre-reform era (Marsh, Geist, and Caplan 1982).

Some claim that the gains of reform laws, though, have been largely symbolic (cf. Goldberg-Ambrose 1992). This is to say that the massive reform law movement served mostly an educative function. Reform has informed the public, policy makers, and practitioners about the erroneous nature of myths about rape and the discriminatory nature of traditional rape law and rape case/victim treatment. This is positive but does not go nearly far enough.

The weight of the evidence from the limited research on implementation details how rape reforms failed. This research indicates that removing *de jure* obstacles to conviction guarantees little in actual legal practice (*de facto* law). Prejudicial standards continue to be relied upon for successful prosecution of rape cases. For instance, research has revealed the tenaciously clinging relevance of corroborative evidence, and resistance and consent, and the victim's past sexual activity (Bienen 1983; Caringella-MacDonald 1985; Chappell 1982; Clark and Buchner 1982; Hayler 1982; Marsh, Geist, and Caplan 1982; Osborne 1985). Put differently, victim testimony alone is not enough to win cases, victim consent is still questioned in the absence of resistance, and past sex acts with the same or other males as those involved in the extant complaint continue to be relied upon in criminal justice judgments in rape case processing. Conviction probability continues to revolve around biased suspicions about victim credibility.

These findings help to explain why so much of the research has failed to find increased levels of arrest (Deming 1983), prosecution (Chappell 1982; Loh 1981), and conviction (Loh 1981; Polk 1985). The research has also shown a failure to achieve comparability in the legal handling of sexual and other/nonsexual assault cases (Caringella-MacDonald 1985; Clark and Buchner 1982).

The title of Susan Estrich's now classic book, *Real Rape* (1987), epitomizes the point. Only the most heinous type of traditionally conceived rape—"carnal knowledge of a female, forcibly and against her will"—results in sustained convictions. Stated a little differently, mostly the stereotypical—which are atypical—cases continue to be viewed as real rape and result in conviction. This means that nonaggravated rapes (i.e., those not involving weapons, additional injuries, gangs, and so forth) and date and acquaintance rape, not to mention marital rape, do not get taken seriously by the legal system. It also means that discrimination on the basis of race, ethnicity, and class continue (Crenshaw 1994; Davis 1981; James 1996; LaFree 1989; Richey Mann and Zatz 1997; Wriggins 1995; Wyatt 1992). To expound, the devaluation of rape victimization in which minorities and/or lower- or working-class persons are victimized persists despite reform changes, unless minorities or the poor are the offenders who victimize white, middle- or upper-class women or girls of privilege. The ranks of illegitimate victims who are disadvantaged are populated by these groups but extend to those who violate traditional gender roles, such as single moms, allegedly promiscuous women, women who dance, drink, and so forth, as previously noted, as well as to homosexuals, bisexuals, and lesbians (James 1996).

Backlash

Were this not enough, the tacit acceptance of changed law as problem resolution that led to the failure to evaluate the consequences of changes in law, and also led to the submergence of the issues surrounding rape, was supplanted by a new kind of attention in the 1990s. This arises from the backlash. Backlash has made the issues of rape (and domestic violence) more problematic for everyone.

The backlash movement places attention *to* criticism of feminist principles, like those embedded in the rape reform movement, in place of the early attention *on* feminist critiques, like those emanating from the rape reform movement. Backlash critics denounce both the "feminist movement"[6] and the rape reform movement that led to all the changes in rape law. It began gaining momentum in the 1980s as it paralleled the swing toward political conservatism across the nation. Susan Faludi's (1991) book, entitled *Backlash*, summarizes how the movement eroded gains for women by blaming feminists for everything from too much equality and independence for females, too little value for mother and housewife roles, all the way to dissatisfaction in public as well as private life, low self-esteem, and the polarization of men and women.

A salient catalyst for the resurgent interest in rape was the publication of a slew of this new genre of backlash books and articles in the 1990s. Some of the most prominent authors are Camille Paglia (1990, 1992, 1994a, 1994b), Christina Hoff Summers (1994, 2000), Rene Denfeld (1995), Naomi Wolf (1993a, 1997), and Katie Roiphe (1993, 1995, 1997). The book that focused attacks on rape reforms and probably gained the most widespread attention across the country, was *The Morning After: Sex, Fear, and Feminism on Campus* by Katie Roiphe (1993). Roiphe's book exemplifies backlash censure of the feminist-inspired rape reform movement. She reviles feminists and rape reform advocates for turning girls and women into a bunch of victims instead of empowered females. Roiphe bemoans how women whine and whimper (and often exaggerate to the point of lying) about rape victimization at Take Back the Night (TBTN) demonstrations and rallies. She complains about how police call boxes on college campuses have become a "blue light" crisis, warning about or indeed creating an environment of imminent danger. She—along with Wolf (1993a, 1997), Hoff Sommers (1994) and Paglia (1994a)—chastises feminist reformers for telling women to imprison themselves in protections against rape. This group is joined by others such as Fox-Genovese (1994) and Matalin (1993) to ironically condemn feminist rape reforms for turning females into a bunch of prudes afraid of the hard-won right to sexual experimentation (a right hard won, not incidentally, by feminism and feminists). Roiphe (1993) and Paglia (1994a, 1994b) go yet further to claim that feminism and rape reforms are guilty of weakening women and making them seem stupid, because they excuse women of responsibility for their own behavior; behavior that allegedly contributes to being raped.

There's nothing wrong with arguing for women's independence, sexual freedom, and maturely, reasonably taken responsibility—unless the arguments are unreasonably stolen, through exaggerations and lies, on the backs of the very feminists and rape reform advocates who fought for these gains for women in the first place. The way the backlash criticisms are leveled by Roiphe and other backlashers bolsters historic myths and prejudices about females, rape, and sexual assault.[7] To declare that women are frightened or cajoled, or both, into embroidering sexual episodes into rape, or making up rape scenarios to share with others on stage (as in TBTN), reeks of myths about false accusation in rape. To pivot criticism around sexual freedom and experimentation while trivializing the problems of rape, sexually transmitted diseases (STDs), and HIV/AIDS (all characterized, once again, as exaggerated fears and caveats rather than problems by feminist reformers; see, for example, Roiphe 1993, 8–9, 12, 15) reinforces notions about loose women who desire, agree to, willingly consent to, or participate in their own sexual assaults. And to pounce on feminists and rape reforms for ridding women of responsibility for rape

smacks of myths about victim precipitation, provocation, and women who "ask for" and/or "deserve" the sexual violence of rape. This line of argument deflects attention away from, indeed it even excuses, male violence directed against females.

Liberal Feminism and Conservatives Who Call Themselves Feminist

Early feminism as manifested in the women's liberation movement of the 1960s and 1970s was that which is now known as liberal feminism. Liberal feminism, like other liberal political ideology, revolves around institutional reform, i.e., within-system change. Successfully changing the legal institution's response to rape was tacitly taken as an answer to the dilemmas in rape because this is often how liberal ideology views society, the state, and law. Many rape reform advocates who fought so hard to accomplish legislative change were appeased with the passage of transformations in one state after another.

But this early liberal view can be a short-sighted view. It overlooks deeply entrenched attitudes tied to structural arrangements, such as the gender inequality and sexism that permeate society. In this way, liberalism may treat only symptoms, such as law, while ignoring the root causes of problems, such as sexism and the approbation of violence throughout the social structural institutions of the polity, economy, criminal justice system, media, and family. Left untouched, root causes will surface, and symptomatic problems (while possibly somewhat altered) will nonetheless continue to plague women, and men. Put differently, societal-wide sexual inequality will not only taint decision making in the practice of criminal justice but also continue to lead to the rape of women in the first place. Liberal solutions tend to be "quick fix" type of solutions, doomed to be partially successful at best, as was seen in the previous "Outcomes" section. Because early liberal reforms changed policy, success was simply assumed, and the troubles surrounding rape were re-embedded. Politicians, and the public, were finished with absorption with rape, at least for a time.

Enter the reign of the conservative right, and along with it conservative women, many of whom called themselves feminist. Conservatives are typically for tradition and against change, unless it is regressive change that moves things back to earlier, more old-fashioned, arrangements. The claims from many conservative feminists reconstitute myths about what women want or should want, which is allegedly husband, home, hearth, and children. In general, conservatives scorn feminists for changing that which women should allegedly want and need (cf. Faludi 1991). The premises of the self-proclaimed "feminist" backlashers, while different from the specific premises regarding husband, home and hearth, are nonetheless aligned with the same male—or, better said, sexist—interests.

The backlash against the civil rights and feminist movements[8] and the re-production of myths about women's responsibility for rape reflect the ascendancy of male vested values. The backlash women previously noted are joined by many others—the likes of Cathy Young (1994, 1999), Sarah Crichton (1993), and Stephanie Gutmann (1993) (to name a few of prominence)—in echoing men's self-serving chorus about women, society, and rape by blaming women for everything from their own unhappiness, to their subordination, and their own victimization.

The re-entrenchment of sexism that can be seen in the backlash criticisms of feminism, feminists, and the feminist rape reform movement becomes understandable with the recognition that liberal feminism targeted symptoms of problems, including unequal criminal laws, rather than foundations such as the gendered inequality that leads to unequal education, career opportunities, jobs, and pay. Conservative backlash sentiments are indicative of men's stranglehold on the resources in society that were unchanged by the rights and reform movements. So the resurgence of sexism, the coming of the backlash, and the corollary widespread and influential condemnation of rape reform endeavors have culminated to buttress the male monopoly on power which maintains male privilege, discrimination against females, and rape victimization.

The fact that the labels of sexist or racist are neither as repugnant nor as vehemently resisted as was the case in previous eras is indicative of the forcefulness of the backlash. These labels are now even sometimes brazenly embraced by proud, non-"politically correct"-fearing men, and women. Similarly, the opposite label, of feminist, has become a "dirty word" to many who see it as only stigmatic.

Where to Go From Here

Rape reforms have been a step in the right direction. They have led to some enhancements in the rates of prosecution and conviction as well as some measure of similarity to other, nonsexual assaults in terms of attrition. And, the removal of unique requirements has led to convictions in some cases that would not have otherwise been tenable in the pre-reform era. However, the qualifying word is *some*, suggesting outcomes that are neither overwhelming nor impressive. This is what prompts the researchers who have looked at the execution of reform law to conclude that the effects have been mostly symbolic, when it comes to educating practitioners and the public that rape is about sexual violence, power, control, denigration and humiliation—not erotic desire, craving, or passion. And so, the message is out that because rape is about the violent forcing of sex, rape should be treated like other criminal violence.

There is another take on these findings, however. First, if it were your mother, daughter, sister, or you whose rape complaint was being processed, any degree of reduction in the double or secondary victimization by the criminal justice system's abusive treatment (after the first victimization by the rapist) would matter. Second, education has been *partially successful*. This should not be minimized by conclusions that only symbolic, educative functions have been accomplished, because not all goals have been fully realized yet.

The law is perhaps one of the most consequential and, therefore, powerful tools we can use to educate. And continued education is direly needed. The need is clear because the only "real rape" (Estrich 1987), in the eyes of the public and criminal justice decision makers, is still stranger—out-of-the-bushes—rape, leaving the majority of rapes by dates and acquaintances unaffected. *Unaffected* means not prosecuted or convicted; *unaffected* means the persistent insistence on corroborative evidence, resistance, additional injuries, and so on. And *unaffected* means the unsettling persistence of rape myths that attribute responsibility and blame to rape victims, dislodging fault and guilt from rape offenders.

The backlash against feminism, feminists, and rape reforms has aggravated these problems. Backlash castigation of females who "get themselves raped," or who are prudes, or who stay at home at night or otherwise "imprison themselves" with rape prevention tactics has noticeably worsened the situation. The backlash criticisms create stigmatic posturing toward females and rape victimization, which re-creates victim culpability as likely, and acceptable once again. Hence, sexist victim blaming becomes more easily engrained. We see ample evidence of the traditional conceptualizations of what constitutes rape, and the reinvigorated myths about victims, in the cases we see or read about and in the nature of discussions such coverage engenders.

The media's coverage of rape cases both reflects and reproduces these problems. Backlash influence in the media is easily observed. For instance, the stereotypical, but rare, rapes by strangers and gangs are generally featured. The media selections and emphasized coverage reifies "real rape" (Estrich 1987) as the only true rape. The result is that nonstranger, nongang rapes aren't presented or defined as real or serious rape. The representation of rape by the media also deflects from the routine, common, daily occurring rapes suffered by females. Such coverage makes the rape seem unusual. As Stanko (1990) pointed out, male violence against women happens systematically, not sporadically. In contrast, focus on the out-of-the-bushes rapes spins interest around mostly the exceptional cases.

Backlash perspectives are further evident in the disparaging focus on victims' behaviors, judgments, demeanor, and dress. Stories and commentaries, for instance, are published and aired that succeed in raising suspicions about the veracity of rape complaints, victims' ulterior motives, and victim blameworthiness.

High-profile cases show the confluence of spotlighting stereotypic cases as real rape and centering attention on victim culpability. The extensive coverage of the stranger, pool table, gang rape at Big Dan's bar in New Bedford, Massachusetts, where men cheered each other on (this case was the basis for the movie *The Accused*) and the stranger, gang, interracial jogger rape in New York Central Park, where the victim was left for dead[9] (which subsequently led to a book), and the Tawana Brawley hoax (which subsequently led to a book) establish the point. These, along with other high-profile acquaintance rape cases, such as the William Kennedy Smith, Mike Tyson, and Kobe Bryant cases, demonstrate as well how fervently victims continue to be suspected, disbelieved, and blamed. Even in one of the most unanimously acclaimed, heinous (and stereotypic) cases, involving the New York Central Park jogger, the victim was doubted and condemned—for jogging after dark (it was actually dusk), for being alone in a city park, for lying to cover up an affair, and even for falsely crying rape to cover up being in the park to "score" drugs that night. In the Kobe Bryant case, the victim's name, past sex, and private "character" evidence from personal records all became public (albeit sometimes by alleged mistakes) and circulated an alleged variety of past sexual encounters of the victim. The victim was so despised for accusing Bryant in some sectors that death threats were made against her.[10]

The fact that unexamined consequences, and indeed failures, of instituted legislative change, and dissipation of energy and effort, co-join with an extensive backlash attack on women and rape victims' rights makes crystal clear the need for a renewed, broadly-based educational campaign. The pressing need is first to redirect awareness and considerable concern to the topic of rape. Recapturing public and political attention will facilitate resource allocation to reinvest in services that have suffered from inattention, competing political agendas, and slashed budgets (e.g., crisis lines and sexual assault programs). The lack of funding has grown so problematic that rape kits (i.e., to collect evidence at hospital examinations of victims) stack up, unanalyzed and, hence, unused in court proceedings (U.S. Senate, Bill S. 149).[11] As well, there have been useful, innovative programs that need funding to survive. For example, Sexual Assault Nurse Examiners (SANE) programs that provide training for the collection of evidence and medical treatment of rape victims at hospitals, and the coordinated Sexual Assault Response Team (SART) programs that provide specialized training for police and other agency response to rape calls need resources to operate to assist victims and promote the successful prosecution of sexual assault crimes. Similarly, more attention and funding need to be allotted to sexual assault victimization in the Violence Against Women Act (VAWA), where domestic abuse enjoys the lion's share of resource allocation.

In addition to re-prioritizing rape, an educational campaign needs to engender awareness about the injustice of continued failure in legal protections for victims. Educational efforts also need to disseminate the research showing how reform laws have failed to achieve objectives, such as removing discriminatory requirements in actual practices and rendering more comparability between

the legal handling of rape and other serious crimes. Educational drives need especially to teach a variety of practitioners, as well as the lay public, that the reform goal is not about giving special protections to the weak, whining class of rape victims, as backlashers so harshly assert. Instead, the objective is simply to render more similarity to the legal processing of rape and other violence, in place of the discriminatory actions and attitudes that have so far defined rape victimization.

An educational movement additionally needs to inform about the need to re-reform laws, in jurisdictions where laws were only cosmetically changed and in all locales where prejudice and attrition endure, despite the best of reforms. Because laws on books are not laws in practice (i.e., because of the doggedness of the *de facto* differential treatment of rape), the next changes must have an eye on everyday practices. And this means legal change needs to next encompass more in-court processes as well as informal, backroom decision making, such as in-camera hearings and plea bargaining. Such overlooked processes determine experiences and outcomes in the majority of instances. Perhaps even more important, the next set of efforts simply must innovatively address the problems of acquaintance, date, and wife rape, as these are, by far, the most frequent types of sexual assault victimization.[12] Society and criminal justice continue to refuse to see these crimes for what they are—real rape, different strictly by involving people who know one another.

Finally, we also must not lose sight of long-term structural changes that are necessary to *prevent* (versus react to) male violence against women. Gender inequality and the societal-wide approbation of violence, male power, and superiority that engender beliefs and behaviors that discriminate against women in general, and rape victims in particular, must be addressed. Sexist institutional arrangements, gender role socialization (into femininity and masculinity), and deep-seated attitudes both underlie and perpetuate the sexism that infuses criminal justice processing when such prejudices are left unattended in attempts to redress violence against women.

Notes

1. I use *sic*, (i.e., as the word appears in the original, or verbatim) when quoting the term *forcible rape*, which the FBI and others have erroneously used through history. However, the term *forcible rape* is largely redundant; most all rape is *forcible*.

2. *Unfounding* means that police determine there is not enough evidence to believe a rape has occurred, and so they do not pursue arrest or bring it to the attention of prosecutors. Simply put, what happens in these instances is that the victim is told to "go home."

3. While it is beyond the scope of this chapter to detail other changes, it should be noted that there has been a host of other, allied changes that have occurred over the past couple of decades. These range, for example, from providing victim anonymity by suppressing victims' names from the press, to more recently allowing for childhood repressed memories to be introduced in later years in court, to allowing evidence of rape trauma syndrome into testimony, to permitting civil suits, to "Megan"-type laws requiring sex offender registration and notification.

4. VAWA exemplifies this, as the lion's share of projects funded stands at 93 percent for battered women while only 7 percent of such efforts are directly focused on sexual assault. And as Miller and Meloy (forthcoming, p. 261) described, 75 percent of direct victim service projects have staff working with domestic violence victims "and about 8 percent working exclusively with victims of sexual assault" (Miller and Meloy, forthcoming, p. 261).

5. Once again, research and activism heightened critical awareness about the prejudicial victim blaming that is as corollary to wife abuse and IPV as it is to rape (e.g.,

she asked for "it," the beating, she could have avoided it if she had tried to, she could have left if it was that bad). As well, the public was told about the problems surrounding the pervasiveness of spouse abuse, the temporary restraining orders that "aren't worth the paper they're written on," the lack of law enforcement from arrest through prosecution and conviction, and so on. And, once again, laws began to change.

6. Backlash writers tend to treat all feminism as one monolithic type of feminism. Moreover, backlashers tend to treat all feminism as radical feminism, ignoring variations all the way from the women's liberation movement to Marxist, postmodernist, multicultural, and socialist feminisms, for example.

7. Walter DeKeseredy, Meda Chesney-Lind, and I are in the beginning stages of editing an anthology to address dimensions such as these that emanate from the backlash against women, feminism, rape, and domestic violence.

8. The backlash against affirmative action programs designed to help disadvantaged minorities and women who have suffered discrimination should also be noted because it fits in here.

9. In the New Bedford case, six men were prosecuted (none of the bystanders who cheered them on were charged), two were acquitted, and the others received sentences of 9 to 12 years. In the New York jogger case, "seven youths were ultimately charged; three were found guilty and given the maximum 5 to 10 years on the sexual assault charges (they were acquitted on attempted murder). Two others were given lesser sentences of 1 to 4 years" (Caringella-MacDonald 1998, 66). However, an imprisoned murderer—whose DNA matched the evidence in the case—13 years later, in 2002, after all five had served time and been released, confessed to the crimes.

10. The sexist reproach of women, compared with men, can be seen in a different, but related, media event, which pertains to the "costume malfunction" during the half-time musical performance at the Superbowl. Justin Timberlake assaultively ripped off a piece of Janet Jackson's outfit, baring one of her breasts. The incident caused an outrage, and Janet was banished from the then upcoming annual music award show at which she was to perform. Justin, on the other hand, not only appeared and performed at the award ceremony, he was also crowned with several awards. So the female, not incidentally, an African-American female, was exiled for having had her breast exposed, while the Caucasian male, who had practically assaulted the female, was not only allowed to join the festivities but was honored to boot.

11. U.S. Senate, Bill S. 149 is called the Rape Kits and DNA Evidence Backlog Elimination Act. It was sponsored by Senator Mike DeWine, a Republican from Ohio. The Bill was referred to the Senate Judiciary Committee in January of 2003 for authorization of an increase in funding to deal with this and related evidence backlog problems. As of 2005, this remains the current status.

12. I have developed a model to initiate such measures. See *Addressing Rape in Law and Practice*, forthcoming from Columbia University Press.

Study/Discussion Questions

1. What was the rape reform movement about?

2. Discuss various kinds of feminism in light of rape reform.

3. Did the rape reform movement succeed? How so? Why or why not?

4. Describe the backlash movement. What is its relation to feminism? To rape?

5. What steps might we productively pursue at this juncture to improve rape (case and victim) treatment by society? The legal system? The social service professions? The media?

References

Bienen, L. (1983). Rape reform legislation in the United States: A look at some practical effects. *Victimology*, 8, 139–151.

Brownmiller, S. (1975). *Against our will: Men, women, and rape*. New York: Bantum Books.

Caringella-MacDonald, S. (1985). The comparability of sexual and non-sexual assault case treatment: Did statute change meet the objective? *Crime & Delinquency*, 31, 206–222.

——. (1998). The relative visibility of rape cases in national popular magazines. *Violence Against Women*, 4, 62–80.

——. (Forthcoming). *Addressing rape in law and practice*. New York: Columbia University Press.

Chappell, D. (1982, November). *The impact of rape reform legislation*. Paper presented at the American Society of Criminology, Toronto, Ontario, Canada.

Clark, T. F., and Buchner, D. (1982, November). *Critical issues in the prosecution of rape: A cross-jurisdictional study of 17 U.S. cities*. Paper presented at the American Society of Criminology, Toronto, Ontario, Canada.

Crenshaw, K. (1990). A black feminist critique of antidiscrimination law and politics. In D. Kairys (Ed.), *Politics of law: A progressive critique* (pp. 195–218). New York: Pantheon.

Crichton, S. (1993, October 25). Sexual correctness: Has it gone too far? *Newsweek*, pp. 52–56.

Curtis, L. A. (1976). Present and future measures of victimization in forcible rape. In M. J. Walker. and S. L. Brodsky (Eds.), *Sexual assault: The victim and the rapist* (pp. 61–68). Lexington, MA: Lexington Books.

Davis, A. Y. (1981). *Women, race, and class*. New York: Vintage.

Deming, M. B. (1983). *Rape case processing: Evaluation of legal reform*. Paper presented to the National Institute of Mental Health, Rockville, MD.

Denfeld, R. (1995). *The new victorians: A young woman's challenge to the old feminist order*. New York: Warner.

Du Mont, J., and Myhr, T. L. (2000). So few convictions. *Violence Against Women*, 6, 1109–1136.

Dusky, L. (1996). *Still unequal: The shameful truth about women and justice in America.* New York: Crown Publishers.

Ennis, P. H. (1966). *Criminal victimization in the United States: A report of a national survey.* Washington, DC: Government Printing Office.

Estrich, S. (1987). *Real rape.* Cambridge, MA: Harvard University Press.

Faludi, S. (1991). *Backlash: The undeclared war against American women.* New York: Crown Publishers.

Federal Bureau of Investigation. (1973). *Crime in the United States: Uniform crime reports.* Washington, DC: Government Printing Office.

Fox-Genovese, E. (1994). Beyond individualism. *Samangundi*, 101/102, 79–94.

——. (1996). *Feminism is not the story of my life: How today's feminist elite have lost touch with the real concerns of women.* New York: Anchor Books.

Galvin, J., and Polk, K. (1985). Attrition in case processing: Is rape unique? *Journal of Research in Crime and Delinquency*, 19–20, 126–154.

Goldberg-Ambrose, C. (1992). Unfinished business in rape law reform. *Journal of Social Issues*, 48, 173–185.

Gutmann, S. (1993, August 23). Are all men rapists? The new VAWA is sexual politics with a vengeance. *National Review*, pp. 44–47.

Hale, Sir Matthew (1971/1680). *The history of the pleas of the crown, I, Part LVIII.* London: Professional Books.

Hayler, B. (1985, August). *Rape shield legislation: How much difference does it make?* Paper presented at the Society for the Study of Social Problems, Washington, DC.

Hoff Sommers, C. (1994). *Who stole feminism? How women have betrayed women.* New York: Simon & Schuster.

——. (2000). *The war against boys: How misguided feminism is harming our young men.* New York: Simon & Schuster.

Holmstrom, L. L., and Burgess, A. W. (1975). The victim goes on trial. In I. Drapkin and E. Viano (Eds.), *Victimology: A new focus (Vol. III).* Lexington, MA: D.C. Heath.

Hunter, S., Burns-Smith, G., and Walsh, C. (2000). *Equal justice? Not yet for victims of sexual assault.* Connecticut Sexual Assault Crisis Services. Storrs: CT. Available at *http://connsacs.org/library/justice.html.*

James, J. (1996). *Resisting state violence: Radicalism, gender, and race in U.S. culture.* Minneapolis: University of Minnesota Press.

Kairys, D. (Ed.) (1990). *Politics of law: A progressive critique.* New York: Pantheon.

LaFree, G. (1989). *Rape and criminal justice: The social construction of sexual assault.* Belmont, CA: Wadsworth.

Loh, W. D. (1981). Q: What has reform of rape legislation wrought? A: Truth in criminal labeling. *Journal of Social Issues*, 37, 28–52.

Longstaff, L. (2002, November). The burden of proof. *Independent Review*, p. 11.

Marsh, J. C., Geist, A., and Caplan, N. (1982). *Rape and the limits of law reform.* Boston: Auburn House.

Matalin, M. (1993, October 5). Stop whining! The feminist fringe frets about oppression, but mainstream women want economic equality. *Newsweek*, p. 62.

Miller, S., and Meloy, M. (Forthcoming). *Vindicating victims: Exploring policies and politics of violence against women.* New York: Oxford University Press.

Osborne, J. A. (1985). Rape law reform: The new cosmetic for Canadian women. In C. Schweber and C. Feiman (Eds.), *Criminal justice politics and women: The aftermath of legally mandated change* (pp. 49–64). New York: Haworth.

Paglia, C. (1990). *Sexual personae: Art and decadence from Nefertiti to Emily Dickinson.* New York: Vintage.

——. (1992) *Sex, art, and American culture: Essays.* New York: Vintage.

——. (1994a). *Vamps and tramps: New essays.* New York: Vintage.

——. (1994b). Women's naiveté contributes to rape. In Swisher, K. L., C. Wekesser, and W. Barbour (Eds.), *Violence against women* (pp. 67–70). San Diego, CA: Greenhaven Press.

Polk, K. (1985). Rape reform and criminal justice processing. *Crime & Delinquency*, 31, 191–205.

Richey Mann, C., and Zatz, M. S., (Eds.). (1997). *Images of color, images of crime.* Los Angeles: Roxbury Publishing.

Roiphe, K. (1993). *The morning after: Sex, fear, and feminism on campus.* Boston: Little, Brown.

——. (1995). A critique of rape-crisis feminists. In B. Leone (Ed.), *Rape on campus* (pp. 74–83). San Diego, CA: Greenhaven Press.

——. (1997) *Last night in paradise: Sex and morals at the century's end.* Boston: Little, Brown.

Russell, D. E. H. (1984). *Sexual exploitation: Rape, child sexual abuse, and sexual harassment.* Beverly Hills, CA: Sage.

Savage, A. (1990). *Twice raped.* Indianapolis: Book Weaver Publishing.

Schweber, C., and Feiman, C. (Eds.) (1985). *Criminal justice politics and women: The aftermath of legally mandated change.* New York: Haworth.

Scully, D. (1990). *Understanding sexual violence: A study of convicted rapists.* Boston: Unwin Hyman.

Stanko, E. A. (1990). *Everyday violence.* London: Pandora.

U.S. Department of Justice, Office of Justice Programs, Bureau of Justice Statistics. (1989). *Sourcebook of criminal justice statistics.* Washington, DC: Government Printing Office.

——. (1973–2002). *Criminal victimization in the United States.* Washington, DC: U.S. Government Printing Office.

U.S. Senate, Bill S. 149. (2003, January 13). *Rape Kits and DNA Evidence Backlog Elimination Act.* Retrieved from: *http://www.ncvc.org/ncvc/main.aspx?dbID+DB_Legislation138.*

U.S. Senate, Senate Judiciary Committee (1993). A surprising report from the Judiciary Committee of the U.S. Senate. In T. J. Gardner and T. M. Anderson (1996). *Criminal law principles and cases* (p. 430). Minneapolis/St. Paul: West Publishing.

Walker, M. J., and Brodsky, S. L. (Eds.) (1976). *Sexual assault: The victim and the rapist.* Lexington, MA: Lexington Books.

Wolf, N. (1993a). *Fire with fire: The new female power and how it will change the 21st century.* New York: Random House.

——. (1993b). Radical heterosexuality . . . or how to love a man and save your feminist soul. In E. Buchwald, P. R. Fletcher, and M. Roth (Eds.), *Transforming a rape culture* (pp. 359–368). Minneapolis, MN: Milkweed Editions.

——. (1997). *Promiscuities: The secret struggle for womanhood.* New York: Random House.

Wriggins, J. (1995). Rape, racism, and the law. In P. Searles and R. J. Berger (Eds.), *Rape and society: Readings on the problem of sexual assault* (pp. 215–222). Boulder, CO: Westview.

Wyatt, G. E. (1992). The sociocultural context of African American and white American women's rape. *Journal of Social Issues,* 48, 77–92.

Young, C. (1994). Broad definitions of rape are harmful. In K. L. Swisher, C. Wekesser, and W. Barbour (Eds.), *Violence against women* (pp. 254–258). San Diego, CA: Greenhaven Press.

——. (1999). *Ceasefire! Why women and men must join forces to achieve true equality.* New York: Free Press. ✦

12
Intimate Partner Abuse

Joanne Belknap
Hillary Potter

In this chapter you will learn the following:

- What intimate partner abuse (IPA) is and the background of defining this issue

- The characteristics and dynamics of IPA, the experiences of victims, and the causes of IPA

- The systemic responses to intimate partner abusers and victims

- Unique issues of how race, ethnicity, gender, sexual orientation, and socio-economic status are related to IPA

Introduction

This chapter describes the research on intimate partner abuse (IPA), specifically the background of defining this issue, the characteristics and dynamics of such abuse, the experiences of the victims, the causes of this abuse, and the systemic responses to intimate partner abusers and victims. We hope the reader will complete the chapter with knowledge of the nature of IPA, how to work toward prevention of this abuse, and how to improve responses to victims, offenders, and their children, while considering unique issues related to race, ethnicity, gender, sexual orientation, and socioeconomic status.

Briefly, *intimate partner abuse* describes maltreatment directed by an individual at a current or former intimate partner. We use the term *abuse* to include not only physical vio-

lence but also verbal, psychological, and even financial abuse. We report that while violent physical behavior is a significant aspect of IPA, so are verbal threats, demeaning and abusive words, and actions directed at the property, pets, and people in victims' lives.

Throughout the chapter, we use the phrase *the criminal processing system* to refer to law enforcement and courts, specifically the key decision makers in these agencies: the police, defense and prosecuting attorneys, and judges. Consistent with Belknap (2001), we avoid the phrase "criminal justice system," as the bulk of what we report is about the overall lack of justice within the formal system that processes IPA offenders.

Defining Intimate Partner Abuse

A number of terms are used to refer to maltreatment that occurs in the context of an intimate couple, for example, domestic violence, woman battering, spousal assaults, and intimate partner abuse. We prefer the phrasing *intimate partner abuse* (IPA) because domestic violence can include child and elder abuse, woman battering focuses on physical abuse, and spousal assault ignores abuse in dating or postmarital (divorced) couples. Moreover, we prefer the term *abuse* over *violence* or *assaults* when referring generally to the issue of a current or former intimate partner's harmful behavior, because as we will discuss in detail, a significant portion of the mistreatment by persons toward their intimate partners is *not violent* per se.

Tong (1984) identified four categories of IPA: *physical* (nonsexual), *sexual, psychological*, and *destruction of pets and property*. This section describes and distinguishes these types of abuse, and it adds *economic abuse* to the list. We need to understand the many dynamics of IPA, and awareness about the numerous ways it can be practiced is necessary to comprehend and more effectively respond to it. These five forms of mistreatment exist in abusive relationships regardless of race, ethnicity, sexual orientation, or socioeconomic status (e.g., Bernard 2000; Davies, Lyon, and Monti-Catania 1998; Giorgio 2002; Hoff 1990; Renzetti 1992; Richie and Kanuha 1997). Often, in more long-term and advanced battering cases, all five types of abuse are present. However, it is necessary for only one type of abuse to be present for the relationship to qualify as abusive.

When we hear that someone is a "battered wife" or a "victim of domestic violence," we tend to restrict our definition to *nonsexual, physical* mistreatment. That is, we usually imagine such physical behaviors as slapping, hitting, punching, shoving, kicking, stabbing, shooting, and so on. While it is important to "count" these abuses, our understanding of IPA is limited when we restrict our definitions to *nonsexual, physical abuse.* It is imperative to acknowledge the four other areas of intimate abuse as well.

Sexual abuse by current and former dates, lovers, and spouses is also a significant category of IPA. This is often minimized by criminal processing officials, for example, and viewed as a case in which the couple simply disagrees about when to have sex, with no overall pressure or animosity. Research indicates that women, especially younger women, who are raped by men they know are the least likely to define these experiences as rape (Sudderth 1998). This is likely because we have ingrained in our culture the idea that rapists are strangers that jump out at us from alleys and behind bushes. So when the rape is by someone we know, including a date, somehow the victims know they were forced to have sex but do not qualify the assault as rape. In reality, marital rapes are some of the most violent rapes, given that the rapists have their victims captive and the victims are often trying not to have their resistance suspected, overheard, or witnessed by their children (see Bergen 1995; Finkelhor and Yllo 1985; Russell 1990). Date and marital rapes are often accompanied by a far greater sense of betrayal than stranger rapes, given that the date and marital rapists are individuals who often proclaimed at some point to love their partners more than anyone else.

The third type of IPA is *psychological or emotional abuse.* Such abuses can be further separated into demeaning and threatening subcategories. The *demeaning aspect* of psychological/emotional abuse is when the abuser refers to his victim in hurtful ways but does not include threats. For example, demeaning statements often used by intimate partner abusers include "you're fat," "you're ugly," "you're a bad mother," and "no one else would want you." The *threatening aspect* of psychological/emotional abuse includes statements insinuating or stating harm to the victim. Examples include threats to hurt or kill the victim, her children, her pets, her family, and her friends and harassing her at work so that she risks losing her job. The psychological/emotional abuse is often listed by victims as the worst part of the abuse. Many victims report that the damage to their emotions and self-esteem is more difficult to address and heal than the wounds of physical abuse. One aspect of intimate partner abuse that can be classified under emotional or psychological abuse is *stalking.* Stalking involves *unwanted* behaviors of checking up on someone, following, phoning, harassing, threatening, and so on (see Tjaden and Thoennes 1998). Recent research identifies stalking as a frequent behavior of many intimate partner abusers and a means by which batterers seek to control their victims (e.g., Brewster 2003; Douglas and Dutton 2001; Melton 2004). While some women and girls may initially be flattered by the attention of dates or spouses showing up at work and so on, they often find this behavior increasingly annoying and controlling. One study of 22 cities found that stalking was a risk factor for IPA cases that resulted in the victims' homicides. That is, IPA cases that include stalking are at increased risk that the abuser will kill the victim (Campbell et al. 2003).

The fourth type of abuse is *destruction of pets and property.* Again, this is often minimized by both the public and the officials who respond to IPA, but it can be especially threatening and devastating. By harming a woman's property or animals, the abuser is clearly communicating "I can do this to you, too." Moreover, the property abused or ruined may incur a significant financial impact on the victim. For example, if an abuser destroys or damages a car or a phone, and the victim cannot afford a new one or to get a broken one fixed, she is further marginalized in terms of her safety and her class. Notably, there is growing recognition that in homes where there is animal abuse, it is important for authorities to look for IPA, as well (Faver and Strand 2003; Kogan et al. 2004).

Finally, it is also important to recognize *economic abuse* in intimate partner relationships. This involves cases in which the abuser regulates all of the money (including money the victim earned or inherited) and doles it out in a controlling manner to the victim. For example, the abuser may regulate the victim's use of the telephone, electricity, car, and so on. Some abusers check their victims' bills, require receipts for all purchases, and place the victims on allowances. A study of battered black women reported how economic abuse could also include the abuser controlling government subsidies; for instance, stealing food stamps or forcing women who receive assistance with housing to allow the abuser to secretly live in the residence (Potter 2004). Residing with a person not on a lease and who receives a government rent subsidy is a violation of both the landlord's lease *and* the government housing authority. Losing these types of leases is a hardship for some women due to the already difficult task of locating this category of reduced-cost housing. In short, economic abuse keeps the victim from being equal and limits any sense of independence in the relationship.

Although nonsexual physical abuse is the type of abuse most of us think of when asked about IPA, it is essential to remember that all of the types of abuse mentioned in this section are harmful and are used to keep victims under control. When laws and/or society minimize or discount sexual, psychological/emotional, economic abuse, and the destruction of pets and property, victims are further controlled and hurt by their abusers, and abusers are empowered.

Some definitions that classify a relationship as battering or abusive require that the abuse be ongoing (or repeated). We argue that this is problematic because once there has been abuse, both members of the couple realize the potential for it to be repeated. Consider, for example, a case the first author encountered in which a husband brutally beat his wife and took photographs of her bruises and cuts shortly after their wedding. He never beat her again, but he kept the photographs and often left them for her to encounter after he had gone to work. Both members of this couple knew he did not have to beat her again to remind them who had the power in the relationship. Another example is a case reported by a judge to the first author during data collection on the court processing of domestic violence cases. This judge reported a case in which the husband/father in a family reported to his wife and children that if their puppy defecated on the floor once more, he would kill it. The next day, when the man returned from work, the excited puppy urinated and defecated on the floor. The man decapitated the puppy in the presence of his wife and children. According to the law in this judge's jurisdiction, this did not count as intimate partner or child abuse, but was "simply" *animal abuse*, although the wife and children were clearly threatened by this highly abusive behavior.

In a later section of this chapter, we discuss the gendered nature of IPA. However, it is also important to recognize that IPA can occur in same-sex intimate relationships, and examples of abuse include all of those listed so far in this section. Some of the additional abuses possible in same-sex intimate relationships include "outing" a partner (i.e., establishing the victim as lesbian, gay, bisexual, or transgendered [GLBT] to the police, family, coworkers, neighbors, etc.) and interfering with child custody (e.g., many family court judges and others view GLBT individuals as "unfit" parents) (see Allen and

Leventhal 1999; Banks 2003; Giorgio 2002; Potoczniak et al. 2003; Renzetti 1992; Russo 2003). Finally, women with disabilities also incur additional risks and types of IPA (see Banks 2003; Chang et al. 2003; Nosek et al. 2001). They are typically more reliant on their partners (because the partners are often their primary caregivers), and like GLBT victims, they face discrimination by court systems that would likely limit their parental rights should they divorce their abusers.

Historical Responses to Intimate Partner Abuse

Documentation confirms that IPA has existed for many centuries (e.g., Dobash and Dobash 1979; Gordon 1988; Martin 1976; Pleck 1989; Schecter 1982). What is unusual is that it was not until relatively recently that advocates for women abused by current and former male intimate partners surfaced in any recognizable manner. Indeed, Chapman (1990) argued that women across the globe have been victimized by men since time immemorial and refers to women's victimization by men as "ancient history" in art, literature, and women's personal accounts, such as diaries. However, she noted that intimate partner victimization has been invisible in history books until more contemporary times (Chapman 1990).

Feminist Abigail Smith Adams is credited with attempting to have her husband, President John Adams, address spousal abuse of wives in the United States in 1776. Unfortunately, he did not take her advice (Dobash and Dobash 1979). Pleck's (1983, 452) analysis of U.S. feminist responses to "crimes against women" (i.e., what we now call domestic violence or intimate partner violence) from 1868 to 1896 was flawed in some respects. However, we must acknowledge that within their historical context, these feminists were courageous and showed commitment and concern for other women "in the face of social conservatism and public indifference." The Women's Christian Temperance Union (WCTU), the largest women's organization of its day in the 1870s, began as an organization interested only in criminalizing alcohol production and consumption. By the end of that decade, however, the WCTU expanded its goals to include addressing a variety of social problems, such as their successful campaign "to pass state laws to benefit abused wives of drunkards" (Pleck 1983, 463). Pleck (1983) reported that the feminist response to "crimes against women" diminished by the 1890s, due to older women in the movement dying and "younger women and black women of all ages" viewing it as "dated" and "unappealing" and wanting "to shed more controversial and less popular issues" (p. 469).

Gordon's (1988) historical analyses of the United States from 1880 to 1960 stated that while individual women and men attempted to advocate for wives abused by their husbands, and many abused women attempted to advocate for themselves, there was no cohesive movement against spousal abuse until the second wave of the women's movement in the 1970s. One study describes the damaging silence of IPA between 1945 (post–World War II) and 1970 in England, where battered women used many resistance strategies, but few resources were available to them to escape the violence (Hague and Wilson 2000).

In the 1970s, for the first time, significant numbers of abused women started speaking out against their abuse, books were published on spousal abuse, and shelters were created to help house battered women and their children. A number of books published during and many other countries, shelters for battered women were established, often in extra the 1970s substantially increased public awareness of IPA, and many of these books were published by advocates for battered women (e.g., Martin 1976; Pizzey 1974; Walker 1979). In England, the United States, Canada, rooms in advocates' homes.

An important aspect of this increased awareness and advocacy on the part of battered women is feminists making demands on police departments to account for their lack of treating spousal abuse as a crime. Prior to the 1970s, IPA was often equated with municipal ordinance violations, such as barking dogs, and labeled a "disturbance of the peace" or as similarly minor transgressions that rarely resulted in an arrest. Given that such arrests were rare, rarer still was the likelihood that IPA cases reached the courts. By the time the few arrested cases reached the courts, many women had been lured to drop charges by a batterer (1) who promised to change and stop his abusive behavior, (2) because of the victim's financial dependency on the abuser, and/or (3) because the abuser threatened further harm toward the victim and/or her children if she did not drop charges. Similar to the police officers who failed to arrest, and perhaps even more so, prosecutors and judges have historically failed to treat intimate partner assaults and violent threats as serious offenses worthy of crime processing intervention (see Browne 1987; Cahn 1992; Rosewater 1988). The race, ethnicity, or immigrant status of some battered women may further, and more negatively, affect the extent to which police and other agents of the crime processing system respond to the victims, based on stereotypical and racist images of women of color and immigrant women (Abraham 2000; Belknap 2001; Bui and Morash 1999; Richie 1996).

Though attention to IPA has increased significantly in the past several decades, advocates assert that more work is still needed. There is needed improvement of the criminal processing system's handling of IPA victims and offenders, as well as an improvement and expansion in other social services available to victims and their children. Also, the IPA toward women of color and immigrant women requires additional examination to determine how these women may experience intimate abuse differently and, as a result, may require diverse approaches to aiding them with escaping volatile relationships.

Intimate Partner Abuse as Gendered

A recent concern and debate among both advocates for victims of IPA and scholars researching such maltreatment is the role gender plays in IPA perpetration (offending) and victimization. With the implementation of pro-arrest policies for domestic violence in the 1980s and 1990s, an unprecedented number of women were arrested for domestic violence (see Martin 1997; McMahon and Pence 2003). Women who physically protected themselves from their batterers were more frequently getting arrested, as they appeared to be the aggressors upon police arrival and assessment. Unfortunately, much of the research in this area relies on a measure of IPA called the Conflict Tactics Scales (CTS), which fails to account for who initiated the abuse, who is more afraid, who is more injured, and the general context of IPA in a manner that over-estimates women's use of force relative to men's in couples' abuse and violence toward each other. Thus, the research statistics of who reports IPA victimization and offending, as well as the IPA victimization and offending reports in official police data, over-represent women's and underrepresent men's use of force and abuse in intimate relationships (for a review, see Melton and Belknap 2003). There may also be racial, ethnic, and cultural implications in this that need to be taken into consideration, because, for instance, African American women have been found to fight back more than white women in abusive intimate relationships (Hampton, Gelles, and Harrop 1989). Obviously, the gender component of IPA is complicated when considering abuse by a lesbian/gay partner (see Giorgio 2002; Renzetti 1992).

The politics of the violence against women movement stipulate that viewing IPA as gender symmetry is a backlash to the movement: Those who decry IPA as gender-neutral are doing so more as a form of patriarchal resistance to the feminist construction of IPA than over a concern for violent women or male victims (Berns 2000). One recent study reported that male intimate partner abusers effectively rewrite reality to portray their women victims as more violent, while they minimize their own abuse and view men as victims of a police and court system that favors females (Anderson and Umberson 2001). In general, the research comparing women's and men's use of IPA indicates that

- Women and men as couples are both more likely to minimize the male's abusive behavior toward the woman (see Berns 2000; Campbell 1992; Dobash et al. 1998; Goodrum, Umberson, and Anderson 2001; Heckert and Gondolf 2000; Morse 1995; Stets and Straus 1990; Walker 1979), particularly sexual abuse (Meyer, Vivian, and O'Leary 1998).

- Men are more likely to initiate IPA, while women are more likely to use IPA in resistance or self-defense (e.g., Hamberger and Guse 2002; Hamberger et al. 1997; Molidor and Tolman 1998; Swan and Snow 2003).

- Men are more likely than women to cause serious injury and to use more serious types of violence (e.g., Archer 2000; Holtzworth-Munroe, Smutzler, and Bates 1997; Johnson and Bunge 2001; Molidor and Tolman 1998; Morse 1995; Rand 1997).

- Men are more likely than women to report using abuse to control their intimate partner (Barnett, Lee, and Thelan 1997; Brewster 2003; Hamberger et al. 1997; Hamberger and Guse 2002; Hamberger and Potente 1994).

- Men are more likely to report that their partners' abuse causes them to laugh (i.e., they find it humorous/funny) (Hamberger and Guse 2002: O'Keefe and Treister 1998), while women are more likely than men to report that their partners' abuse causes them *fear* (Hamberger and Guse 2002; Johnson

and Bunge 2001; Melton and Belknap 2003; Morse 1995; O'Keefe and Treister 1998).

Finally, it is important to stress the gendered nature of *homicide* regarding current and former spouses, dates, and lovers. When women kill, they are most likely to kill current or former boyfriends or husbands, but *women are far more likely to be killed by current and former male mates than men are to be killed by current or former female mates* (Browne and Williams 1993; Greenfeld and Snell 1999; Guathier and Bankston 1997). Stated alternatively, IPA perpetrated by men (compared with that by women) is far more likely to result in the victims' death. Moreover, research consistently reports that the most dangerous/lethal time for abused women is when they attempt to leave these abusive relationships (Campbell 1992; Pagelow 1993; Sev'er 1997), including lesbian relationships (Glass et al. 2004). It is during these escapes that women and girls are most likely to be murdered by their boyfriends and husbands.

In sum, while there is a public and scholarly debate as to the degree to which women and girls are abusive to their male partners, and while there may be some distinctions among women of different races and ethnicities, a significant amount of research contends that IPA is largely gendered: The offenders are typically male and the victims are typically female. That is the reason we refer to victims in this chapter with feminine pronouns and use masculine pronouns when referring to offenders. This does not mean that we do not recognize those cases where females are abusive to males or where the abuse occurs in same-sex couples. Moreover, Berns (2000) presented a convincing case that the conservative reaction claiming that intimate partner abuse is not gendered is driven by patriarchal resistance to the feminist framing of IPA. Berns claimed that those who frame it this way are neither interested in male victims nor female abusers in intimate couples. She reported that this focus on gender symmetry diverts "attention from men's responsibility and cultural and structural factors that foster violence" (Berns 2000, 262). At the same time, it is important to remember that IPA also occurs in lesbian relationships.

The Frequency of Intimate Partner Abuse

As previously discussed, women have been experiencing IPA for at least several hundred years. However, the rates and frequency at which they have experienced this type of victimization has only been better documented starting in the 1970s with the women's liberation movement.

According to a report published by the Bureau of Justice Statistics, 4 of every 1,000 U.S. households experienced intimate partner violence during 2002 (Klaus 2004). This rate is based on the collection of data for the National Crime Victimization Survey, which gathers information from individuals on the number of times and in what manner they have been victimized over a period of time. In an additional account of IPA as reported by victims, Tjaden and Thoennes (2000) reported the findings of a large national telephone survey that inquired about, among other topics, rapes, physical assaults, and stalking by intimate partners against survey participants. According to the survey, 22.1 percent of the women interviewed reported physical assaults by intimates and 7.7 percent of the women reported being raped by intimate partners. Tjaden and Thoennes found variations in the rate of IPA by race and ethnicity. Women of color reported significantly more incidents of sexual and physical assault than white women. Among the women of color, Alaska Natives and American Indians (classified as one group) had the highest rates of intimate partner victimization, and Asians/Asian Americans and Pacific Islanders had the lowest victimization rates when compared with both whites and nonwhites. Further, Latinas were more likely to be sexually assaulted by an intimate partner than by a nonintimate individual.

An alternative method for measuring IPA, particularly for homicides, is through police department reporting of arrests to the Federal Bureau of Investigation for the Uniform Crime Reports. Regarding homicides between intimate partners, the Uniform Crime Reports inform us that 32.1 percent of female victims were murdered by their husbands and boyfriends (in cases where the identities of both victim and offender were known), while 2.7 percent of male murder victims were killed by their wives and girlfriends during 2002 (Federal Bureau of Investigation 2003). Interestingly, between 1976 and 2000, the number of men murdered by intimate partners decreased by 68 percent, while the murders of female intimates remained relatively stable (Federal Bureau of Investigation 2001).

Causes of Intimate Partner Abuse

Often when people hear about IPA, either about a particular case or about the phenomenon as a whole, their first response is, Why does she stay? This is indicative of the victim-blaming nature that, unfortunately, still often accompanies both personal and systemic responses to IPA. It is rare to hear someone ask, Why does he abuse? But Lundy Bancroft (2003) did just that in his instructive book, *Why Does He Do That?: Inside the Minds of Angry and Controlling Men*. Bancroft spent 15 years working as a therapist with men accused and convicted of intimate partner violence. Much of this section is guided by Bancroft's important findings.

When attempting to discover what causes IPA, one of the strong predictors is a sexist culture that assumes men are the ones who make important decisions in families and have the most important careers, and women's roles primarily constitute serving their husbands and children. That is, a patriarchal society reinforces a norm that views men as the leaders and women as the followers. This unbalanced position is further exacerbated by other social ills, such as racism and classism, which enforce a hierarchical arrangement of domination. Moreover, women who fail to follow their leaders (men) are deserving of any abuse necessary to get them under control. Though stereotypes abound that African American women in particular are self-reliant, these women are subject to the same violent controls by men (Potter 2004). Although many people in U.S. culture do not agree with these sexist roles, there is still substantial support on some level for men's control of women within families, society, religions, the media, and the legal system (see Ammons 1999; Berns 2000; Bograd 1988; Haj-Yahia 1998; O'Neill 1998; Renzetti and Curran 2003; Stark and Flitcraft 1983). To that end, some say that men abuse intimate partners simply because "they can." What is meant by this statement is that there is surprisingly high tolerance by society and the legal system of men's abuse of their wives and girlfriends, particularly at the less serious levels.

It is useful in a discussion of why some men abuse intimate partners to remember that *most men do not abuse their intimate partners*. Therefore, the focus should be to examine why *some* men *choose* to do so. Researchers point out that it is not "being male," but rather, it is *being socialized as masculine* that increases the likelihood that some men will become intimate partner abusers (Boye-Beaman, Leonard, and Senchak 1993). Though this masculine socialization may be racialized, meaning that it presents differently among men of various races, it is not limited to a particular racial or ethnic group but intersects racial identities. Susan Schechter (1982) pointed out that intimate abusers often feel angry when they do not have control over their wives or girlfriends, and they feel justified in exercising abuse to gain or regain the control they believe is due them via male entitlement (via the patriarchy). In short, abuse is a highly effective means of controlling one's intimate partner (Bancroft 2003; Goolkasian 1986). In addition, some cultures advocate more than others for the control of women by their male partners even if it

means using physical force, while other cultures are more critical of such behavior (see Abraham 2000; Hamby 2000; Kantor, Jasinski, and Aldarondo 1994; Richie 1996; Yoshioka, DiNoia, and Ullah 2001).

Related to the causes of IPA perpetration, it is useful to highlight what research indicates as indicators (or "red flags") of intimate partner abusers. A key risk factor for becoming an abuser is someone with high levels of jealousy (Bancroft 2003; Barnett, Martinez, and Bluestien 1995; Molidor and Tolman 1998; O'Keefe and Treister 1998), including in lesbian intimate relationships (Glass et al. 2004). Abusers' initial jealous behaviors are often experienced as loving and romantic by some victims. They come to realize over time that the jealousy is a symptom of the abusers' highly controlling sense that "their women" *belong* to them.

Often times, drugs and alcohol are used as excuses for men who abuse their partners. However, it is important to remember that most of us are not abusive to our pets, friends, and family whether we are sober or drunk. Thus, researchers caution that alcohol and drugs should not be seen as the reason intimate partners abuse (Johnson 2000; Kantor and Straus 1987). In fact, one recent study suggests that the link between heavy drinking and IPA is *not* that the former causes the latter but, rather, that both are linked with masculinity (Johnson 2000).

Figure 12.1 is a presentation of the 15 characteristics Lundy Bancroft (2003) identified as the biggest risk factors indicating that someone an individual is dating or married to could be an abuser. Bancroft (2003) pointed out that merely one of these signs does not mean the person is necessarily abusive, "with the exception of physical intimidation. Nonabusive men may exhibit a number of these behaviors to a limited degree" (p. 122). Clearly, a major part of IPA is individuals who fail to take account of their behavior. Goodrum, Umberson, and Anderson's (2001) study reported that compared with non-batterers, "batterers minimize others' negative views of themselves [the batterers], and they dissociate themselves from their partners' [the victims'] physical and emotional injuries" (p. 221). Thus, intimate partner abusers appear to be effective in convincing themselves, their victims, and many others that their behavior is appropriate and nonabusive.

Experiencing Intimate Partner Abuse

The last section cited the most often asked question of battered women: Why does she stay? In addition to focusing on the victim's rather than the offender's troubling behavior, this question ignores questions such as, What happened when she tried to leave? and Why should she be the one to leave? as well as ignoring the many, many cases in which women *have* left (Hoff 1990). Still, it is useful to highlight the reasons women find it difficult to leave abusive relationships:

- *Danger:* Many IPA victims are afraid of what their partners will do when they leave, or they have left and the abuse escalated. As cited earlier, research repeatedly finds that leaving an abuser is the most dangerous/lethal time of relationships (Campbell 1992; Pagelow 1993; Sev'er 1997).

- *Socialization:* Girls and boys are often raised with societal expectations that women are the ones who are responsible for keeping marriages together, and women should listen to what their husbands say. Additionally, battered women's families and religious leaders often con-

---

Figure 12.1
Lundy Bancroft's (2003) 15 Warning Signs of an Intimate Partner Abuser

- He speaks disrespectfully about his former partners.

- He is disrespectful toward you.

- He does favors for you that you don't want or puts on such a show of generosity that it makes you uncomfortable.

- He is controlling.

- He is possessive.

- Nothing is ever his fault.

- He is self-centered.

- He abuses drugs or alcohol.

- He pressures you for sex.

- He gets serious too quickly about the relationship.

- He intimidates you when he's angry.

- He has double standards.

- He has negative attitudes toward women.

- He treats you differently around other people.

- He appears to be attracted to vulnerability.

Source: Lundy Bancroft (2003) *Why Does He Do That?* New York: G.P. Putnam's Sons, p. 122.

tinue to blame them for their IPA victimizations (Ammons 1999; Hoff 1990).

- *Economic:* It is often very difficult to leave an abuser without propelling one-self and one's children to poverty (see Browne, Saloman, and Bassuk 1999; Herbert, Silver, and Ellard 1991).

- *Psychological:* Oftentimes victims of IPA minimize both the abusers' mistreatment and their own injuries in efforts to deny that they are "battered women" and their husbands or boyfriends are "batterers" (see Davies, Lyon, and Monti-Catania 1998). This is hardly surprising given a society and criminal processing system that often minimizes these as well (see the next section).

It is important to stress that IPA does not affect all women equally, but rather there are unique and additional problems when the victim is of color, poor, homeless, disabled, an immigrant (particularly a nonlegal immigrant), lesbian/gay/transgendered, or otherwise disenfranchised or alienated (see Sokoloff and Dupont 2005 for an excellent overview). Some of the literature suggests that African American women may be less vulnerable to remaining in abusive relationships due to financial dependence on their abusers, given black women's history of greater participation in the paid work force than white women (Ammons 1995; Asbury 1987; West and Rose 2000). Alternatively, battered black women may be more inclined to be pressured to remain in abusive relationships because of racialized stigmas, such as fear of being the (stereo)typical single, black mother receiving government handouts (Potter 2004). Immigrant Asian American women (Yick 2001) and low-income or working-class women, who may also have significant employment histories, could be affected similarly. Lesbian victims of IPA also report pressure from their community not to "air dirty laundry" and that they are more likely than straight women to be perceived as being in "mutually combative" relationships (rather than that they are truly victims) if they fight back in any way (Giorgio 2002).

System Responses to Intimate Partner Abuse

The last section discusses some of the reactions that individuals have to IPA victimization. This section briefly reports responses by the police and courts to victims and offenders of IPA. Historically, the police have responded to IPA as a "family matter" or "disturbing the peace" of a neighborhood, but rarely as a crime (see Erez and Belknap 1998). Given this approach, it was highly unusual for batterers to be arrested and, thus, to go to court. Notably, in the 1990s many lesbian/gay organizations reported the significant problem of IPA in their communities and began outreach in these areas as well as anti-gay hate-crime victimizations (Jenness and Broad 1994).

Starting in the 1980s, following law suits won by battered women who proved the police did not take their cases seriously, and because of research and activists' pressure, some police departments, jurisdictions, and even states began adopting pro-arrest policies for IPA (see Belknap 1995 for a review). Thus, in stark contrast to minimizing or ignoring IPA calls, which are often the most frequent calls to which police respond, law enforcement officers' discretion was taken away and they were required by policy to arrest batterers. While there are varying degrees to which police departments and individual officers actually comply with pro-arrest policies and laws (Ferraro 1989; Jones and Belknap 1999), these policies significantly changed how police respond to IPA. In addition to a huge increase in arrests for domestic violence, the result of these policies was that unprecedented numbers of IPA cases progressed to the courts. Similar to the pro-arrest policies and laws, many court jurisdictions have adopted no-drop policies. These pro-arrest and no-drop policies were designed to take discretion away from police and prosecutors so that they would not ignore IPA cases. Indeed, the police were required to arrest (except in highly unusual situations), and, likewise, prosecutors and district attorneys were expected to push IPA cases through prosecution.

Despite pro-arrest policies that were established in police departments beginning in the 1980s and no-drop policies implemented in many courts starting in the 1990s designed specifically for domestic violence cases, the practice of ignoring or selectively enforcing such policies still occurs far too often (see Erez and Belknap 1998; Ferraro 1989; Jones and Belknap 1999). Feminists debate the strategy of pro-arrest and no-drop policies in terms of taking all decision making from battered women (see Ford 1983, 1991). While some argue that these policies allow the police and courts to take action against woman abusers without having to involve victims who are often fearful of their partners, others claim that these policies are a further way that IPA victims are denied agency. And as this debate continues, an entirely unanticipated result of such policies is a serious backlash by some police officers and prosecutors toward battered women who resisted their mates' abuse or whose victimizers reported (not necessarily truthfully) that their intimate female partners had abused them (see Erez and Belknap 1998; Martin 1997; McMahon and Pence, 2003). Stated alternatively, an unprecedented number of women who are *victims* of IPA have been arrested as the *offenders* of IPA. Such a response clearly further victimizes these women, empowers their abusers, and decreases the chances that they will feel safe to rely on the police and courts if they experience IPA again. Or as Miller (2001) pointed out, a paradox results for IPA victims who respond with force to their abusers and those responsible for following domestic violence laws and policies:

What is the appropriate criminal justice response to battered women who assault (as legally defined) their abuser or do other illegal acts and end up getting arrested, particularly when these acts of violence committed by victims are qualitatively different from acts of violence committed by batterers? (p. 1340)

These unintended consequences of "improved" law enforcement policies addressing IPA are further complicated when considering race relations between abused women and the police.

IPA victims who are further marginalized due to their race/ethnicity, class, disability status, or GLBTQ status frequently face additional barriers when using the legal system (e.g., racism, classism, and homophobia). Battered women of color report a lack of trust in using the formal criminal processing system to assist with their escape from abusive relationships (Bennett, Goodman, and Dutton 1999; Richie 1996; Weis 2001). A history of poor relations between criminal processing agencies (and their agents) and communities of color can account for this distrust (Brice-Baker 1994; Fishman 2002). Bourg and Stock (1994) attempted to explain the large numbers of black women arrested for "aggravated battery" compared with men and white women, suggesting that "one possible explanation for these results would be that police misperceive black females as being more angry and more threatening than white females" (p. 187). Future research must address how the documented evidence of racially discriminatory police practices (Walker, Spohn, and Deleone 2000) affect the arrests of IPA victims who are women and girls of color.

One study of systemic responses to same-sex IPA stated: "At its worst, the system can reinforce the message that the victim's batterer has conveyed all along—that no one will help a battered homosexual" (Fray-Witzer 1999, 23). This study reports that while individuals from the police to the courts often fail same-sex IPA victims, some of this is due to ignorance, thus educating and training are important (Fray-Witzer 1999). A study on lesbian IPA reported that agencies from victim advocates to the courts often discount these cases and ignore policies on same-sex IPA, and that when the police do act, they are more likely to arrest the victim than the offender if the victim is of color (and the offender is white) or the victim appears more "butch" than the offender (Giorgio 2002).

Previously in this chapter we referred to intimate partner abusers who abuse their victims' children (who are often their children, too). Sometimes they do this as part of their generally abusive manners, but often they abuse children as a means to most seriously hurt their wives or girlfriends. A heartbreaking case recently decided by the U.S. Supreme Court is *Gonzales v. Castle Rock:*

> . . . Jessica Gonzales, did exactly what she was supposed to. As soon as her estranged husband absconded with their three daughters—in violation of a court's restraining order—she called the Castle Rock, Colo., police. She called six times over an eight-hour period—including numerous calls after she had reached her husband on his cell phone and confirmed that he had the children with him. She repeatedly begged the police to enforce the restraining order and retrieve her daughters, citing the father's extremely violent and unstable history—to no avail. Over and over again, she was told to call back later. At 3:20 a.m., the father appeared at the police station, where he opened fire on officers and was shot and killed. The dead bodies of the three girls, ages 7, 9 and 10, were found in the back of his pickup (Buel 2005).

In June 2005, the U.S. Supreme Court ruled in *Gonzales v. Castle Rock* that "police are not required to enforce restraining orders, even if state law mandates that they do so" (Buel 2005). In sum, then, the U.S. Supreme Court found that Jessica Gonzales (and therefore any woman abused by a current or former intimate partner) did not have a constitutional right to police protection even in the presence of a restraining order. Sarah Buel (2005), former battered wife and current day law school faculty member and expert on IPA concluded of this ruling: "The unavoidable result of this decision is that cowardly cops will once again feel empow-

ered to ignore battered women's pleas for help," even when their children's lives are at stake.

Thus, while feminist activists and scholars have made huge inroads in systemic responses to (mostly) men who abuse their current or former intimate partners, there still exist major problems for battered women. First, too many times the laws and policies are not followed. Second, the laws and policies may take too much decision making from the victims (e.g., whether they want their abusers arrested or prosecuted). For varying reasons, some women do not want their abusers arrested, and in these cases, mandatory arrest policies may prevent these women from calling the police. Third, an alarming number of IPA *victims* across the country have been arrested as abusers.

Conclusions

This chapter is a summary of the research on intimate partner abuse (IPA). It highlighted the importance of defining IPA beyond physical violence, the history of defining IPA as a social problem, the gendered nature of IPA, what causes IPA, and victim and systemic responses to IPA, while also considering concerns of race, ethnicity, sexual orientation, culture, immigrant, and socioeconomic status among victims and perpetrators of IPA. Although a great deal has been learned about IPA in the past 25 years, there remains a significant amount of victim blaming and minimizing of this type of abuse. The second wave of the women's movement has been pivotal in bringing about awareness of IPA and changing the systemic responses to it. However, there is still a tendency to view IPA as "simply" physical violence, ignoring the devastating effects of other abusive behaviors directed at IPA victims. Implementing pro-arrest policies in law enforcement and no-drop policies in the courts has moved IPA onto the "front burner" for the first time in the history of fighting crime. However, these policies are often not enforced and judgmental views of the victims continue. Finally, it is necessary to acknowledge that IPA does not impact everyone the same. Sokoloff and Dupont (2005) provided some important recommendations regarding change in how IPA is researched and responded to by service agencies, which include giving marginalized women "voice" to report their experiences with IPA and how they were responded to, encouraging activism that places women typically at the margins in the center, calling for culturally competent services for battered women, debunking stereotypical images of battered women, and creating alternatives to addressing IPA.

Study/Discussion Questions

1. Why is it preferable to use the term *abuse* rather than *violence* when examining maltreatment between current or former intimates?

2. How is IPA gendered? What is the debate regarding the gendered nature of IPA?

3. How does IPA vary among individuals of different races and ethnicities?

4. What are some of the flaws in how IPA has been responded to by the criminal processing system?

5. Why do some people abuse their intimate partners, and what are some of the factors that make it difficult for women to leave intimate abusers?

References

Abraham, M. (2000). *Speaking the unspeakable: Marital violence among South Asian immigrants in the United States.* New Brunswick, NJ: Rutgers University Press.

Allen, C., and Leventhal, B. (1999). History, culture, and identity: What makes GLBT battering different. In B. Leventhal and S. E. Lundy (Eds.), *Same-sex domestic violence* (pp. 73–82). Thousand Oaks, CA: Sage.

Ammons, L. L. (1995). Mules, madonnas, babies, bath water, racial imagery, and stereotypes: The African American woman and the battered woman syndrome. *Wisconsin Law Review, 5,* 1003–1080.

———. (1999). What's god got to do with it? Church and state collaboration in the subordination of women and domestic violence. *Rutgers Law Review, 51,* 1207–1288.

Anderson, K. L., and Umberson, D. (2001). Gendering violence—masculinity and power in men's accounts of domestic violence. *Gender & Society, 15,* 358–380.

Archer, J. (2000). Sex differences in aggression between heterosexual partners: A meta-analytic review. *Psychological Bulletin, 126,* 651–680.

Asbury, J. (1987). African American women in violent relationships: An exploration of cultural differences. In R. L. Hampton (Ed.), *Violence in the black family: Correlates and consequences* (pp. 89–105). Lexington, MA: Lexington Books.

Bancroft, L. (2003). *Why does he do that?: Inside the minds of angry and controlling men.* New York: Putnam.

Banks, M. E. (2003). Women with visible and invisible disabilities: Multiple intersections, multiple issues, multiple therapies—Part I Preface. *Women & Therapy, 26,* xxiii–xli.

Barnett, O. W., Lee, C. Y., and Thelan, R. E. (1997). Gender differences in attribution of self-defense and control in interpartner aggression. *Violence Against Women, 3,* 462–481.

Barnett, O. W., Martinez, T. E., and Bluestein, B. W. (1995). Jealousy and romantic attachment in maritally violent and nonviolent men. *Journal of Interpersonal Violence, 10,* 473–486.

Belknap, J. (1995). Law enforcement officers' attitudes about the appropriate responses to woman battering. *International Review of Victimology, 4,* 47–62.

——— (2001). *The invisible woman: Gender, crime, and justice* (2nd Edition). Belmont, CA: Wadsworth.

Bennett, L., Goodman, L., and Dutton, M.A. (1999). Systemic obstacles to the criminal prosecution of a battering partner. *Journal of Interpersonal Violence, 14,* 761–772.

Bergen, R. K. (1995). Surviving wife rape: How women define and cope with the violence. *Violence Against Women, 1,* 117–138.

Bernhard, L. A. (2000). Physical and sexual violence experienced by lesbian and heterosexual women. *Violence Against Women, 6,* 68–79.

Berns, N. (2000). Degendering the problem and gendering the blame: Political discourse on women and violence. *Gender & Society, 15,* 262–281.

Bograd, M. (1988). Feminist perspectives on wife abuse: An introduction. In K. Yllo and M. Bograd (Eds.), *Feminist perspectives on wife abuse* (pp. 11–27). Newbury Park, CA: Sage.

Bourg, S., and Stock, H. V. (1994). A review of domestic violence arrest statistics in a police department using a pro-arrest policy: Are pro-arrest policies enough? *Journal of Family Violence, 9,* 77–89.

Boye-Beaman, J., Leonard, K. E., and Senchak, M. (1993). Male premarital aggression and gender identity among black and white newlywed couples. *Journal of Marriage and the Family, 55,* 303–313.

Brewster, M. P. (2003). Power and control dynamics in prestalking and stalking situations. *Journal of Family Violence, 18,* 207–217.

Brice-Baker, J. (1994). Domestic violence in African American and African Caribbean families. *Journal of Social Distress and Homeless, 3,* 23–38.

Browne, A. (1987). *When battered women kill.* New York: Free Press.

Browne, A., Salomon, A., and Bassuk, S. S. (1999). The impact of recent partner violence on poor women's capacity to maintain work. *Violence Against Women, 5,* 393–426.

Browne, A., and Williams, K. R. (1993). Gender, intimacy, and lethal violence: Trends from 1976 through 1987. *Gender & Society, 7,* 78–98.

Buel, S. (2005). Battered women betrayed. *Los Angeles Times,* July 4. Available at *http://www.utexas.edu/law/news/2005/070505_buel.html.*

Bui, H. N., and Morash, M. (1999). Domestic violence in the Vietnamese immigrant community. *Violence Against Women, 5,* 769–795.

Cahn, N. R. (1992). Innovative approaches to the prosecution of domestic crimes. In E. S. Buzawa and C. G. Buzawa (Eds.), *The changing criminal justice response* (pp. 161–180). Westport, CT: Auburn House.

Campbell, J. C. (1992). "If I can't have you, no one can": Power and control in homicide of female partners. In J. Radford and D. E. H. Russell (Eds.), *Femicide* (pp. 99–113). New York: Twayne Publishers.

Campbell, J. C. *Assessing dangerousness: Violence by sexual offenders, batterers, and child abusers.* Thousand Oaks, CA. Sage.

Campbell, J. C., Webster, D., Koziol-McLain, J., Block, C., Campbell, D., Curry, M. A., Gary, F., Glass, N., McFarlane, J., Sachs, C., Sharps, P., Ulrich, Y., Wilt, S. A., Manganello, J., Xu, X., Schollenberger, J., Frye, V., and Laughon, K. (2003). Risk factors for femicide in abusive relationships: Results from a multisite case control study. *American Journal of Public Health, 93,* 1089–1097.

Castle Rock v. Gonzales (04-278) *http://straylight.law.cornell.edu/supct/html/04-278.ZS.html.*

Chang J. C., Martin, S. L., Moracco, K. E., Dulli, L., Scandlin, D., Loucks-Sorrel, M. .B., Turner, T., Starsoneck, L., Dorian, P. N., and Bou-Saada, I. (2003). Helping women with disabilities and domestic violence: Strategies, limitations, and challenges of domestic violence programs and services. *Journal of Women's Health, 12,* 699–708.

Chapman, J. R. (1990). Violence against women as a violation of human rights. *Social Justice, 17,* 54–70.

Davies, J., Lyon, E., and Monti-Catania, D. (1998). *Safety planning with battered women.* Thousand Oaks, CA: Sage.

Dobash, R. E., and Dobash, R. (1979). *Violence against wives.* New York: Free Press.

Dobash, R. P., Dobash, R. E., Cavanagh, K., and Lewis, R. (1998). Separate and intersecting realities: A comparison of men's and women's accounts of violence against women. *Violence Against Women, 4,* 382–414.

Douglas, K. S., and Dutton, D. G., (2001). Assessing the link between stalking and domestic violence. *Aggression and Violent Behavior, 6,* 519–546.

Erez, E., and Belknap, J. (1998). Battered women and the criminal justice system: The service providers' perceptions. *European Journal on Criminal Policy and Research, 6,* 37–57.

Favor, C. A., and Strand, E. B. (2003). To leave or to stay?: Battered women's concern for vulnerable pets. *Journal of Interpersonal Violence, 18,* 1367–1377.

Federal Bureau of Investigation. (2001). *Supplementary homicide reports, 1976–2000*. Washington, DC: U.S. Department of Justice.

——. (2003). *Crime in the United States, 2002: Uniform Crime Reports*. Washington, DC: U.S. Department of Justice.

Ferraro, K. J. (1989). Policing woman battering. *Social Problems, 36*, 61–74.

Finkelhor, D., and Yllo, K. (1985). *License to rape: Sexual abuse of wives*. New York: Free Press.

Fishman, L. T. (2002). The black bogeyman and white self-righteousness. In C. R. Mann and M. S. Zatz (Eds.), *Images of color, images of crime: Readings*, (2nd Edition, 77–191). Los Angeles: Roxbury Publishing.

Ford, D. A. (1983). Wife battery and criminal justice: A study of victim decision making. *Family Relations, 32*, 463–475.

——. (1991). Prosecution as a victim power resource: A note on empowering women in violent conjugal relationships. *Law and Society Review, 25*, 313–334.

Fray-Witzer, E. (1999). Twice abused: Same-sex domestic violence and the law. In B. Leventhal and S. E. Lundy (Eds.), *Same-sex domestic violence* (pp. 19–42). Thousand Oaks, CA: Sage.

Gauthier, D. K., and Bankston, W. B. (1997). Gender equality and the sex ratio of intimate killing. *Criminology, 35*, 577–600.

Glass, N., Koziol-McLain, J., Campbell, J., and Block, C. R. (2004). Female-perpetrated femicide and attempted femicide. *Violence Against Women, 10*, 606–625.

Giorgio, G. (2002). Speaking silence: Definitional dialogues in abusive lesbian relationships. *Violence Against Women, 8*, 1233–1259.

Goodrum, S., Umberson, D., and Anderson, K. L. (2001). The batterer's view of the self and others in domestic violence. *Sociological Inquiry, 71*, 21–240.

Goolkasian, G. A. (1986). *Confronting domestic violence: The role of criminal court judges*. Washington, DC: U.S. Department of Justice.

Gordon, L. (1988). *Heroes of their own lives: The politics and history of family violence: Boston, 1880–1960*. New York: Viking.

Greenfeld, L. A., and Snell, T. L. (1999). *Women offenders*. Washington, DC: U.S. Department of Justice.

Hague, G., and Wilson, C. (2000). The silenced pain: Domestic violence 1945–1970. *Journal of Gender Studies, 9*, 157–169.

Haj-Yahia, M. M. (1998). Beliefs about wife beating among Palestinian women. *Violence Against Women, 4*, 533–558.

Hamberger, L. K., and Guse, C. E. (2002). Men's and women's use of intimate partner violence in clinical samples. *Violence Against Women, 8*, 1301–1331.

Hamberger, L. K., Lohr, J. M., Bonge, D., and Tolin, D. F. (1997). An empirical classification of motivations for domestic violence. *Violence Against Women, 3*, 401–423.

Hamberger, L. K., and Potente, T. (1994). Counseling heterosexual women arrested for domestic violence: Implications for theory and practice. *Violence and Victims, 9*, 125–137.

Hamby, S. L. (2000). The importance of community in a feminist analysis of domestic violence among American Indians. *American Journal of Community Psychology, 28*, 649–669.

Hampton, R. L., Gelles, R. J., and Harrop, J. W. (1989). Is violence in black families increasing?: A comparison of 1975 and 1985 national survey rates. *Journal of Marriage and the Family, 51*, 969–980.

Heckert, D. A., and Gondolf, E. W. (2000). Predictors of underreporting of male violence by batterer program participants and their partners. *Journal of Family Violence, 15*, 423–443.

Herbert, T. B., Silver, R. C., and Ellard, J. H. (1991). Coping with an abusive relationship: How and why do women stay? *Journal of Marriage and the Family, 53*, 311–325.

Hoff, L. A. (1990). *Battered women as survivors*. London: Routledge & Kegan Paul.

Holtzworth-Munroe, A., Smutzler, N., and Bates, L. (1997). A brief review of the research on husband violence. *Aggression and Violent Behavior, 2*, 285–307.

Jenness, V., and Broad, K. (1994). Antiviolence activism and the (in)visibility of gender in the gay/lesbian and women's movements. *Gender & Society, 8*, 402–423.

Johnson, H. (2000). The role of alcohol in male partners' assaults on wives. *Journal of Drug Issues, 30*, 725–740.

Johnson, H., and Bunge, V. P. (2001, January). Prevalence and consequences of spousal assault in Canada. *Canadian Journal of Criminology,* pp. 27–45.

Jones, D. A., and Belknap, J. (1999). Police responses to battering in a pro-arrest jurisdiction. *Justice Quarterly,* 16, 249–273.

Kantor, G. K., Jasinski, J. L., and Aldarondo, E. (1994). Social cultural status and incidence of marital violence in Hispanic families. *Violence and Victims,* 9, 207–222.

Kantor, G. K., and Straus, M. A. (1987). The "drunken bum" theory of wife beating. *Social Problems,* 3, 213–230.

Klaus, P. A. (2004). *Crime in the nation's households, 2002.* Washington, DC: Bureau of Justice Statistics, U.S. Department of Justice.

Kogan, L. R., McConnell, S., Schoenfeld-Tacher, R., and Jansen-Lock, P. (2004). Crosstrails: A unique foster program to provide safety for pets of women in safehouses. *Violence Against Women,* 10, 418–434.

Martin, D. (1976). *Battered wives.* San Francisco: Glide.

Martin, M. (1997). Double your trouble: Dual arrest in family violence. *Journal of Family Violence,* 12, 139–157.

McMahon, M., and Pence, E. (2003). Making social change: Reflections on individual and institutional advocacy with women arrested for domestic violence. *Violence Against Women,* 9, 47–74.

Melton, H. C. (2004). Stalking in the context of domestic violence. *Women & Criminal Justice,* 15, 33–58.

Melton, H. C., and Belknap, J. (2003). He hits, she hits: Assessing gender differences and similarities in officially reported intimate partner violence. *Criminal Justice & Behavior,* 30, 328–348.

Meyer, S., Vivian, D., and O'Leary, D. K. (1998). Men's sexual aggression in marriage. *Violence Against Women,* 4, 415–435.

Miller, S. L. (2001). The paradox of women arrested for domestic violence: Criminal justice professionals and service providers respond. *Violence Against Women,* 7, 1139–1376.

Molidor, C., and Tolman, R. (1998). Gender and contextual factors in adolescent dating violence. *Violence Against Women,* 4, 180–194.

Morse, B. J. (1995). Beyond the Conflict Tactics Scale: Assessing gender differences in partner violence. *Violence and Victims,* 10, 251–272.

Nosek M. A., Howland, C. A., and Hughes, R. B. (2001). The investigation of abuse and women with disabilities: Going beyond assumptions. *Violence Against Women,* 7, 477–499.

O'Keefe, M., and Treister, L. (1998). Victims of dating violence among high school students: Are predictors different for males and females? *Violence Against Women,* 4, 195–223.

O'Neill, D. (1998). A post-structuralist review of the theoretical literature surrounding wife abuse. *Violence Against Women,* 4, 457–490.

Pagelow, M. D. (1993). Justice for victims of spouse abuse in divorce and child custody cases. *Violence and Victims,* 8, 69–83.

Pizzey, E. (1974). *Scream quietly or the neighbors will hear.* Middlesex, England: Penguin.

Pleck, E. (1983). Feminist responses to "crimes against women, 1868–1896. *Signs,* 8, 451–470.

——. (1989). Criminal approaches to family violence, 1640–1980. In Ohlin, L. and Tonry, K. (Eds.), *Family violence,* (pp. 19–58). Chicago: University of Chicago Press.

Potoczniak, M. J., Mourot, J. E., Crosbie-Burnett, M., and Potoczniak, D. J. (2003). Legal and psychological perspectives on same-sex domestic violence: A multisystemic approach. *Journal of Family Psychology,* 17, 252–259.

Potter, H. A. (2004). *Intimate partner violence against African American women: The effects of social structure and black culture on patterns of abuse.* Unpublished doctoral dissertation, University of Colorado, Boulder, CO.

Rand, M. R. (1997). *Violence-related injuries treated in hospital emergency departments.* Washington, DC: U.S. Department of Justice.

Renzetti, C. M. (1992). *Violent betrayal: Partner abuse in lesbian relationships.* Newbury Park, CA: Sage.

Renzetti, C. M., and Curran, D. J. (2003). *Women, men, and society* (5th Edition). Boston: Allyn and Bacon.

Richie, B. E. (1996). *Compelled to crime: The gender entrapment of battered black women.* New York: Routledge.

Richie, B. E., and Kanuha, V. (1997). Battered women of color in public health care systems.

In M. Baca Zinn, P. Hondagneu-Sotelo, and M. A. Messner (Eds.), *Through the prism of difference: Readings on sex and gender.* Boston: Allyn & Bacon.

Rosewater, L. B. (1988). Battered or schizophrenic? Psychological tests can't tell. In K. Yllo and M. Bograd (Eds.), *Feminist perspectives on wife abuse* (pp. 200–216). Newbury Park, CA: Sage.

Russell, D. E. H. (1990). *Rape in marriage.* Bloomington: Indiana University Press.

Russo, A. (2003). Intimate betrayal: Domestic violence in lesbian relationships. *Psychology of Women Quarterly, 27,* 86–88.

Schechter, S. (1982). *Women and male violence: The visions and struggles of the battered women's movement.* Boston: South End Press.

Sev'er, A. (1997). Recent or imminent separation and intimate violence against women. *Violence Against Women, 3,* 566–589.

Sokoloff, N., and Dupont, I. (2005). Domestic violence at the intersections of race, class, and gender. *Violence Against Women, 11,* 38–64.

Stark, E., and Flitcraft, A. (1983). Social knowledge, social policy, and the abuse of women: The case against patriarchal benevolence. In D. Finkelhor, R. J. Gelles, G. T. Hotaling, and M. A. Straus (Eds.), *The dark side of families: Current family violence research* (pp. 330–348). Beverly Hills, CA: Sage.

Stets, J. E., and Straus, M. A. (1990). Gender differences in reporting marital violence and its medical and psychological consequences. In M. A. Straus and R. J. Gelles (Eds.), *Physical violence in American families: Risk factors and adaptations to violence in 8,145 families* (pp. 151–165). New Brunswick, NJ: Transaction.

Sudderth, L. K. (1998). "It'll come right back at me": The interactional context of discussing rape with others. *Violence Against Women, 4,* 559–571.

Swan, S. C., and Snow, D. L. (2003). Behavioral and psychological differences among abused women who use violence in intimate relationships. *Violence Against Women, 9,* 75–109.

Tjaden, P., and Thoennes, N. (1998). *Stalking in America.* Washington, DC: U.S. Department of Justice.

——. (2000). *Extent, nature, and consequences of intimate partner violence: Findings from the National Violence Against Women Survey.* Washington, DC: U.S. Department of Justice.

Tong, R. (1984). *Women, Sex, and the law.* Totowa, NJ: Rowman and Allenheld.

Walker, L. E. (1979). *The battered woman.* New York: Harper & Row.

Walker, S., Spohn, C., and Deleone, M. (2000). *The color of justice: Race, ethnicity, and crime in America* (2nd Edition). Belmont, CA: Wadsworth.

Weis, L. (2001). Race, gender, and critique: African American women, white women, and domestic violence in the 1980s and 1990s. *Signs, 27,* 139–169.

West, C. M., and Rose, S. (2000). Dating aggression among low income African American youth: An examination of gender differences and antagonistic beliefs. *Violence against Women, 6,* 470–494.

Yick, A. G. (2001). Feminist theory and status inconsistency theory: Application to domestic violence in Chinese immigrant families. *Violence Against Women, 7,* 545–562.

Yoshioka, M. R., DiNoia, J., and Ullah, K. (2001). Attitudes toward marital violence: An examination of four Asian communities. *Violence Against Women, 7,* 900–926. ✦

13
Women, Race/Ethnicity, and Criminal Justice Processing

Vernetta D. Young
Terri Adams-Fuller

In this chapter you will learn the following:

- How race and ethnicity intersect with gender at various stages of the crime processing system, often producing unjust outcomes

- The role of police discretion in producing different crime-processing system outcomes by race/ethnicity and gender

- How racial/ethnic variations in in-group dynamics may contribute to differences in offending patterns

- Racial disparities in incarceration in the United States

- How drug offenses have contributed to increases in arrest, conviction, and incarceration rates for females across racial/ethnic groups

Introduction

Law enforcement agencies, courts, and correctional facilities are the integral parts of our criminal justice system. In this criminal justice system there are numerous decision-making points, including arrest, charging, preliminary hearing/grand jury, trial, sentencing, and ending with release from jail/prison. At each of these points an alleged offender can either be released or processed further into the system. While gender plays a role in how individuals are treated at the various stages of the crime-processing system, race and ethnicity have been cited as major contributing factors as well. Sometimes the intersection of race and gender confounds justice by lifting the veil of what is purported to be a blind justice system.

This lifting of the veil is a result of a long history of racial prejudices that has permeated all aspects of social life, including the crime-processing system. Although the system hinges on the ideals of justice and equality, the implementation of these ideals is influenced by the values and beliefs of the custodians of the system. As Higginbotham (1978) stated, "The legal process has never been devoid of values, preferences, or policy positions" (p. 13).

Much of the dialogue around issues related to race, gender, and crime focuses on the overrepresentation of African American and Hispanic women in the crime processing system. While many scholars highlight the disproportionality issue, few provide context for this topic. The overrepresentation of women of color in the crime processing system is a result of a number of political, social, and economic factors. Some of the most compelling factors include high rates of poverty among these populations, reduction of public benefits, and differential treatment within the crime processing system.

Although we acknowledge the disproportionate involvement of women of color in crime relative to their contribution to the population, we have chosen not to focus on the concept of disproportionality because it has been used primarily to identify blacks as "typical" criminals (Young 1994, 79). Careful review of the breadth of data and critical issues associated with the crime processing system reveals nothing typical about the "typical" criminal. This chapter synthesizes existing information about women and crime at the various decision-making points in the crime processing system across racial and ethnic categories. It assesses the nature of the criminal justice research enterprise as it relates to women as a heterogeneous group and reexamines Gilbert's (2001) assertion that the "evidence on disparate processing of women of color [is] not clear" (p. 223). Through this process, the chapter assesses the degree to which racial and ethnic disparities among women exist in the crime-processing system.

Extent and Nature of Female Offending

Although traditional sources of offender data are generally used to provide offender demographics, these sources rely on the entry of individuals into the crime processing system at arrest. The National Crime Victimization Surveys (NCVS) and self-report studies were initially developed to allow a more inclusive collection of crime data that includes both reported crimes and unreported crimes that may not have otherwise been documented. These alternative sources of crime data were also intended to provide information on the extent and nature of crime without the imposition of discretionary influence of law enforcement. However, it became apparent, early on, that these sources of data had their own flaws. Still, the NCVS are administered annually and provide another source of information/data that assesses the magnitude of crime in the United States from the victims' perspective.

According to the 2002 NCVS (Rennison and Rand 2003), an estimated 23,036,030 personal and property crimes were perpetrated against victims in the United States. Property crimes accounted for over three-fourths of all crimes, while personal crimes accounted for approximately 24 percent. For those victimizations in which an offender's sex was known, females accounted for about 21 percent of all offenders. When the victimization involved a single female offender, white females were identified as offenders in 63 percent of the victimizations; black females in 23 percent; and other females, in 12 percent.[1] When the victimization involved multiple female offenders, white females were identified as offend-

ers in 55 percent of the victimizations, black females in 23 percent, and other females in 21 percent. Although these estimates are crude, they indicate that for both single and multiple victimizations, white females were reported to be the offenders in the majority of cases. And while white females still outnumbered black females in victimizations involving multiple offenders, there was an almost equal representation of victimizations in which the female offenders were identified as other or black. "Other" offenders seem to be twice as likely to commit crimes as part of a group (21 percent) than as individuals (12 percent). The data reveal that a larger percentage of white and other female offenders commit crimes in groups than do their black counterparts. These statistics lead to several questions. Are there differences in socialization patterns among black, white, and other racial/ethnic females that lead some to participate more in group deviance versus acting as lone agents in the commission of a crime? Are there differences in in-group dynamics among black, white, and other racial/ethnic females that may lead some to participate in in-group criminal behavior? Answers to these questions may pose some interesting insights into the nature of the differences in female offending by race.

While the NCVS data provide some insight into the magnitude of female offending patterns, these surveys fail to provide detailed data on the race and ethnicity of the specific race/ethnic groups that constitute the "other" category, thereby limiting not only the analysis but also the types and extent of discourse that can take place around these data. The "other" category (at over 10 percent and 20 percent of the total figure) makes a significant contribution to the total number of female offenders; therefore, it would seem relevant to consider, where possible, the nature and character of those in this category who are involved in crime.

The criminal justice system has been characterized as a filtering process in which some defendants are processed through to the next level and others are released. The introduction of the estimates from the NCVS provides a foundation for discussions about this filtering process. A review of the perceived race and gender of perpetrators of crime via the NCVS in comparison with other reported data suggests that white females are more likely to be filtered out of the system, whereas others, more specifically women of color, are more likely to be caught in the crime processing system. This observation is important when we consider that a large percentage of crimes go unreported and that official statistics rest solely on the number of crimes reported or detected by the police and their use of discretion.

On-going debates among criminologists regarding police discretion and the influence of race and gender are common. It has been argued that, in part, the differences in arrest patterns among racial/ethnic groups can be attributed to police discretion. It is important to highlight the power of discretion that law enforcement officers have, as arrest marks the entryway into the crime processing system. The influence of age, sex, race, class, mannerism, and attractiveness might influence an officer either to make an arrest or simply issue a warning. This discretion is manifested at various points in the policing process, including stops and arrest.

The literature points to racial differences in police use of discretion with respect to men; this is particularly true for black and Latino men. However, mixed findings exist with regard to the treatment of women by police (Belknap 2002). Belknap (2002) reported that the findings from studies of police decision making were contradictory: two studies concluded that women were discriminated against; three found that women were treated chivalrously; and one reported that women were treated equally (p. 140). Part of the explanation for the differences in findings might be related to the specific type of offense under investigation. Another part of the explanation might be related to the tendency to examine women as a homogeneous group.

Gilbert (2001), in a review of police studies, concluded that legal and situational fac-tors, community standards, and agency policies rather than gender accounted for the racial differentials in processing. Beyond the literature review by Gilbert (2001), there is scant literature examining police discretion as it relates to the intersection of race and gender. While a recent review of literature offers no conclusive evidence concerning differential treatment of women of color by law enforcement officers, the earlier work of Young (1984) suggests that black women are treated differently based on differences of gender role expectations. There is no reason to believe that there have been significant improvements in law enforcement's response to women of color.

Arrest

Although the Uniform Crime Report (UCR) data do not represent the totality of criminal offenses, they do provide a baseline measure of the number of individuals being filtered through the crime processing system. Decision making in the criminal justice system begins with the police, their use of discretion, and their response to crimes that are reported to them and those that they discover. According to the UCR, 2,225,730 women were arrested in 2003 (Federal Bureau of Investigation 2004). They accounted for close to one-fourth of all arrests. This is more than double their contribution to total arrests in 1960. This pattern is consistent across geographic areas, with arrests for women in urban and suburban areas accounting for close to 25 percent of all arrests, whereas those in rural areas were right behind, accounting for just over 21 percent of all arrests.

The UCR also allows us to look at differences among women by age. According to the 2003 reported data (FBI 2004), the majority of the females arrested were adults over the ages of 18. In fact, over one-third of all females arrested were between the age of 25 and 39 in 2003 (see Table 13.1). Women between the ages of 25 and 39 have consistently accounted for the majority of female arrests over time.

Table 13.1
UCR-Reported Female Arrests by Age, 2003

Age of Arrest	Percentage of Female Arrests
Under 18	20.4
18–24	22.3
25–29	11.7
30–34	11.1
35–39	10.9
40–44	9.3
45–49	5.3
50–54	2.4
Over 55	1.9

Editors note: Because of rounding, the percentages may not add up to 100.

Source: FBI, *Crime in the United States*, 2003. *www.fbi.gov/ucr/ucr.htm*.

Table 13.2
UCR-Reported Female Arrests by Type of Crime, 2003

Part 1 Index Crimes	Percentage of All Female Arrests
Violent Crime Index	**17.8**
Murder	10.3
Forcible Rape	1.3
Aggravated Assault	20.7
Robbery	10.4
Property Crime Index	**30.8**
Larceny-theft	37.1
Burglary	13.7
Motor Vehicle Theft	16.6
Arson	15.6
Part 2 Crimes	
Prostitution	64.2
Runaway	58.7
Embezzlement	49.8
Fraud	44.6
Forgery-Counterfeiting	40.3

Source: FBI, *Crime in the United States*, 2003. *www.fbi.gov/ucr/ucr.htm*.

The UCR program classifies crimes as Index or Part I offenses and non-index or Part II offenses. Index or Part I offenses include a *violent crime index*, which comprises murder, forcible rape, aggravated assault, and robbery, and a *property crime index*, which comprises larceny-theft, burglary, motor vehicle theft, and arson. These crimes are considered the most serious and most commonly reported. Non-index or Part II offenses include all other crimes. The UCR for 2003 (FBI 2004) indicates that females were arrested for 27 percent of total index offenses, 18 percent of all violent index offenses, and 31 percent of all property index offenses. Among arrests for index offenses, aggravated assault and larceny-theft were the largest contributors to total female arrests (see Table 13.2). Females made more sizable contributions to arrests for Part II offenses, accounting for a sizable proportion of all arrests for prostitution, runaways, embezzlement, fraud, and forgery and counterfeiting (see Table 13.2).

A review of UCR data from 1965 to 2000 indicates that these patterns of arrest have not changed over time (Steffensmeier and Schwartz 2004). Nevertheless, over the last 10 years the number of female arrests has increased by 14 percent (FBI 2003). The of-

fenses showing the greatest percentage of change are embezzlement, offenses against family and children, drug abuse violations, and liquor law violations. Although there is continuing interest in violence by women, the only index offense that increased between 1993 and 2002 was aggravated assault (see Renzetti, this volume). The only other violent crime that increased was the more general category of other assaults.

There is little additional information that we can garner from these published reports. Unfortunately, they provide no information on arrests by race for women or men. However, the Supplemental Homicide Reports (Espy and Smykla 1987), which are also presented to the FBI by local law enforcement, do allow us to examine differences across race/ethnicity among female arrests. These data, which have been collected since the

1960s, consist of age, sex, race of victims and offenders, the type of weapons used, the victim-offender relationship, and the circumstances of the crime. They allow researchers to study the contextual nature of homicide.

There were 429,729 cases of homicide reported from 1976 to 1999. Females were identified as the offender in a little less than one-third of the cases in which the sex of the offender was indicated. Black females accounted for over one-half of female homicide offenders; white females accounted for a little over 40 percent; Native Americans accounted for 1 percent; and Asian and Pacific Islanders accounted for less than 1 percent. These data show similarities and differences among female homicide offenders by race/ethnicity. First, women in all of the categories of female offenders were more likely to kill male victims than female victims. Still, almost one-third of the victims of Asian/Pacific Islander females were female.

Second, the largest percentage of all homicide cases was intra-racial, with 94 percent of the victims of both white and black female offenders being members of their respective races. However, for American Indian (37 percent), Asian/Pacific Islander (24 percent) and "other" females (22 percent), a significant number of the victims were white. Another interesting finding is that although most of the incidents involved one victim and one offender, white (22 percent) and American Indian (24 percent) females were more likely than those in other race/ethnic groups to be involved in incidents involving one victim and multiple offenders. This finding mirrors the data reported by the NCVS, that white females are more likely to participate in incidents involving multiple offenders than their black counterparts. However, other racial/ethnic females (nonblacks and nonwhites in the NCVS data) were more like black females with respect to their proportionate involvement in incidents involving multiple offenders. These data provide some interesting insights into the need to examine race/ethnic variations because differences in in-group dynamics may play a key role in the differences in offending patterns.

To get a more inclusive picture of the differences in female offending in crimes other than homicide; we have to refer to studies and reports conducted at the local level. Two recent reports give more specific data on two areas: New York City and Oklahoma. These reports provide information on a much broader range of offenders. The Women of Color Policy Network (2003)[2] testified before the New York City Council about arrests of women in New York City from 1995 to 2001. The data indicated that black females evidenced the highest arrest rates among females from 1995–2001. Their rate of 3,106 per 100,000 was almost twice that of Hispanic females and just over six times the arrest rates for white females.

Controlled substances, assault, larceny, miscellaneous other causes, and prostitution were the leading causes of arrest among women by race/Hispanic origin. There were some differences by race/ethnicity. The leading cause of arrest across all three racial groups was controlled substances. This offense accounted for over 20 percent of arrests of black, Hispanic, and white women. The groups differed with respect to the other leading offenses. Assault was the second most frequent cause of arrests for black and Hispanic women; however, for white women, larceny was the second most frequent cause of arrests. The Women of Color Policy Network (2003) also examined the leading causes of arrest of other women whose pattern of arrest differed from the specific race/ethnic groups. The miscellaneous other causes category accounted for almost one-third of all arrests of other women, followed by larceny and prostitution.

Simpson and Wright (2000) analyzed arrest rates in Oklahoma for 1998. White females accounted for the largest percent of female felony arrests (71 percent), followed by black females (18 percent), American Indian females (8 percent), and Hispanic females (2 percent). Simpson and Wright (2000) reported that drug offenses, larceny, and fraud accounted for almost 60 percent of all arrests of women in Oklahoma in 1998, with drug offenses representing the largest arrest category. From 1985 to 1998, drug arrest rates for women in Oklahoma increased almost 187 percent. Hispanic females evidenced the largest increase, 860 percent, followed by American Indians at 231 percent, whites at 193 percent, and blacks at 152 percent.

The FBI Uniform Crime Reports provide data on the distribution of arrests of females relative to males, the pattern of female arrests, and the percentage change in female arrests, all over time; but as previously noted, this information is not published by gender across race/ethnic groups. Fortunately, there are some jurisdictional studies of arrests across race/ethnic groups, but not a sufficient number. The caveat to the review of these studies is that it is difficult to make comparisons across the studies, as the base of analysis is different. However, reviews of the patterns of arrest and the local reports indicate that arrest rates are increasing for women, and these rates are increasing most in the category of drug offenses. This was found at the local level in New York and Oklahoma, and it also contributed to a sizable proportion at the national level, signaling that drugs may be a major contributing factor to the increase in female incarceration (Simpson and Wright 2000; Women of Color Policy Network 2003).

These findings reflect the sentiment of other scholars who assert that the war on drugs[3] has played a major role in the increase in arrest rates of both men and women. Tougher drug policies have required more people to be processed through the crime processing system. According to findings reported for the Arrested Drug Abuse Monitoring (ADAM) Program, close to 68 percent of adult females arrested tested positive for marijuana, cocaine, methamphetamine, opiates, or PCP in 2000 (Bureau of Justice Statistics 2003). In addition, women accounted for 17 percent of arrests by the Drug Enforcement Administration (DEA) in 2001 (Office of National Drug Control Policy 2003). In sum, drugs have accounted for a major increase in female arrest rates in general, and this is true across racial/ethnic lines.

Pretrial

The injustices associated with pretrial detention and who was detained led to the founding of the Vera Institute more than four decades ago. A number of research studies found that whether or not the accused was released on bail pending trial affected the outcome of the accused's case. The early focus was on the effect of income on release. Albonetti and colleagues (1989) examined the impact of race and stratification on pretrial release. They found that legal and extralegal factors (e.g., education, income, length of residence, marital status, employment status, history of bail jumping, dangerousness to the community, type of crime, prior felony convictions, race, stratification resources, community ties, and statutory seriousness of the crime) influenced the decision. In addition, two of these factors (i.e., statutory severity of the offense and dangerousness of the offense) "worked to the relative disadvantage of whites." However, overall white defendants fared better than black defendants, because they "received better returns on their resources" (p. 80).

Katz and Spohn (1995) looked at the effect of both race and gender on the amount of bail imposed and on pretrial status. They found that with respect to the amount of bail, gender, but not race, was the determining factor. However, in the case of pretrial status, both gender and race influenced the judge's decision. White defendants were more likely to be released prior to trial than black defendants, and female defendants were more likely than male defendants to be released. When the interaction effects were examined, white females were more favored, followed by white males, black females, and black males.

Gottfredson and Jarjoura (1996) also looked at the impact of gender and race on pretrial decision making. More specifically, they wanted to determine if the risk prediction devices used to make decisions about presumptive bail recommendations were correlated with race and gender. Gottfredson and

Jarjoura (1996) used the risk component of the Marion County Indiana bail guidelines system to test this hypothesis. This risk-prediction device comprises a number of items, including those used to ascertain the defendants' living arrangements, the "maintenance" of a personal telephone, the consistency of employment, the nature of the charged offense, prior arrest history, and prior failures to appear in court. They found that this device was in fact correlated with gender and race but concluded that unbiased models could be employed with little loss of predictive utility.

Walker, Spohn, and DeLone (2000), in a more recent review of the research literature on bail, concluded that

> . . . racial minorities are no longer routinely jailed prior to trial because of judicial stereotypes of dangerousness or because they are too poor to obtain release. Nevertheless, there is evidence that judges in some jurisdictions continue to take race into account in deciding on the type and amount of bail. (p. 39)

Regrettably, most of the recent studies did not address the differential impact of race and gender on bail decision making.

If bail is denied, then the alleged offender must remain in custody. Quereshi and King (1998) reported that the processing time between the date a case is filed and the date of disposition varies according to race, gender, and psychopathology. In the case of race and gender differences, Quereshi and King (1998) found that blacks have significantly longer processing time. In regard to gender differences, they found that white women had shorter processing time than white or black men, whereas black women had longer processing time than either white men or women, but shorter processing time than black men.

Bail decision making is but one of the decision-making points prior to trial. Gilbert (2001) also reviewed the literature on prosecutorial charging, noting that as a result of changes in sentencing policies, the judge's role had been neutralized. Gilbert (2001) argued that although race was the most studied

characteristic influencing charging and sentencing, other factors (e.g., urban residence, unemployment, and receipt of public assistance) were also important. She contended that African American women experience different life chances from white women as a result of poverty, abuse, and limited economic opportunities and that these differences impact negatively the treatment of black and other nonwhite women.

Farnsworth and Teske (1995) reported differences by race among females with respect to charge reductions. White females were more than twice as likely as minority females to have assault charges reduced to nonassault charges. As with many of the other points in the system, only a limited number of studies examine differences among women by race/ethnicity, and most of these were published prior to the late 1990s. Although the empirical work examining race/ethnicity, gender, and pretrial decisions is scant, the preponderance of research supports the *chivalry hypothesis*, which assumes that females—more specifically, white females—receive preferential treatment in the criminal justice system. Unfortunately, very little research has looked beyond the black/white dyad.

Probation[4]

There are a number of alternatives to incarceration. Unfortunately, although a majority of women who are convicted of crimes are sentenced to probation, very little research exists on female probationers (Olson, Lurigio, and Seng 2000). In 1985, women accounted for 16 percent of total probationers (Beck, Brown, and Gilliard 1999). By year-end 2002, women made up 23 percent of all adults on probation, an increase of over 40 percent in a 17-year period (Glaze 2003). Over one-half of the probationers were white and a third were black. In addition, half of these probationers were convicted of a felony, 25 percent of which were drug law violations. We have no indication of how this breaks down by race and gender.

McGee and Baker (2003), examining the differences in treatment among women on probation, found that fewer behavior conditions were imposed on black women than on their white counterparts, the implication being that fewer resources were being directed at black women's treatment. In addition, among those who received treatment for substance abuse, a larger percentage of black women than white were unsuccessful in their treatment. McGee and Baker (2003) asserted that these findings highlight differences in risk factors (e.g., drug abuse history, employment status, and number of felony convictions) and treatment measures among black and white women on parole. Moreover, treatment measures were more likely to prevent recidivism among white women at risk than for black women.

Sims and Jones (1997) examined success and failure among felony probationers in North Carolina. Of the total sample, 7 percent were white females, 9 percent were black females, and 1 percent were other females. Regarding the differences in success among the female probationers, a greater percentage of white (81 percent) and other females (77 percent) had successful probation outcomes than black females (59 percent). Sims and Jones (1997) found that unstable employment, marital status, and the number of past convictions were significant predictors of success or failure on probation.

Though scant, the research examining race and gender differences in parole outcomes provides evidence that white females are more likely than their black or Hispanic counterparts to be successful on parole. However, this statement is made with caution, as the absence of disaggregated data at the national level and the limited number of studies at the local level make it difficult to make sweeping observations about differences in treatment at the parole stage of the crime processing system. It should also be noted that there is a dearth of literature (except for research conducted in Great Britain) around the issue of the differences in who is granted probation instead of jail or prison time.

Incarceration

Although males account for the largest percentage of the nation's jail and prison population, the rate of female incarceration has skyrocketed over the past 10 years, increasing by 84 percent compared with a 64 percent increase for men. By the late 1990s, women made up 12 percent of the total jail population, a 50 percent increase since 1985 when they made up 8 percent of the jail population (Gilliard 1999). Even more astounding has been the actual increase in the female jail population. In 1983, 15,682 women resided in local jails. By 1990, the female population had increased over 130 percent to 37,198. The female jail population has continued to increase over the years. By 2002, there were 76,817 women in local jails, a 529 percent increase in just under two decades.

Finally, even though official reports provide information on jail inmates by race and ethnicity, with nearly equal proportions of whites and blacks housed in local jails, it is difficult to determine how this breaks down by race/ethnicity and gender (Gilliard 1999). Surprisingly, although there is very little information on American Indian females, Minton (2003) reports that American Indian women account for 18 percent of the total population in jails in Indian country.

Corresponding increases in the federal and state female prison populations are also indicated. It must be emphasized that these increases have been attributed not to changes in behavior but to the introduction of a number of mandatory sentencing policies that include increases in sentences for drug-related offenders, truth in sentencing statutes, and mandatory sentencing. In 1980, 503,586 people were in federal and state custody. At year-end 2002, 2,166,260 persons were incarcerated in the United States (Harrison and Beck 2003). Almost two-thirds (63 percent) were held in federal and state prisons. This is an increase of 270 percent in 22 years.

Women account for almost 7 percent of all state and federal prison inmates. This represents a steady increase in the female contribution to the total prison population over the years from just over 4 percent in 1985, to 5 percent in 1990, to close to 6 percent in 1995. Moreover, the total female prison population increased 42 percent from 1995 (68,468) to 2002 (97,491). Harrison and Beck (2003) reported that Texas, the federal system, and California accounted for more than one-third of all female inmates. What's more, Oklahoma, Mississippi, Louisiana, and Texas had the highest female incarceration rates in 2002. These rankings have been consistent for at least the last decade.

At year-end 2002, black females (36,000) and white females (35,400) accounted for about equal proportions of the female incarcerated population, with Hispanic females adding an additional 15,000 inmates. However, of these three groups, black females have experienced the largest increases. In 1980, there were 6,300 black female prisoners. This increased to 20,100 by 1990. The total for 2002 represented a 571 percent increase over 1980 and a 179 percent increase over 1990 (Harrison and Beck 2003).

Hispanics and whites also experienced increases in the number of females from their respective populations who have been incarcerated over the last decade. There were 6,500 Hispanic females and 20,200 white females incarcerated in state and federal institutions in 1990. The numbers indicate that from 1990 to 2002, the Hispanic female incarcerated population evidenced a 131 percent increase, while the white female incarcerated population increased by 75 percent. So, although the number of female incarcerates from all three groups increased significantly over time, the increases were much larger for black women (Harrison and Beck 2003).

Looking at the comparative contribution of race/ethnic specific groups to the prison population tells but one part of the story. Another important consideration is the impact of the incarceration of specific race/ethnic groups on their respective populations. A look at the rates of incarceration will give us insight into this concern. Data are available for whites, blacks, and Hispanics. The rates

for 2002 differed significantly by race, with black females incarcerated at a rate of 191 per 100,000 population compared with the Hispanic female incarceration rate of 80 per 100,000 and a white female incarceration rate of 35 per 100,000. This means that black females were almost five and one-half times as likely as white females to be in prison, whereas Hispanic females were over twice as likely as white females to be in prison. The racial disparity is obvious. Moreover, this same pattern of racial disparity in incarceration has been evident at least since 1980 (Harrison and Beck 2003).

What is very interesting here is that blacks and Hispanics make up a minority proportion of the general population, but an increasingly larger proportion of the incarcerated population. The statistics indicate that the women who account for the largest proportion of the female incarcerated population are women in the childbearing and childrearing age groups. Black and white females between the ages of 30 and 34 accounted for the largest percentage of their respective incarcerated populations, followed by those between the ages of 35 and 39 and those between 25 and 29. Among Hispanic females, those between the ages of 30 and 34 accounted for the largest proportion of the incarcerated population, but those between the ages of 25 and 29 (3,000) and 35 and 39 (2,900) contributed almost equally to the prison population (Harrison and Beck 2003; Simpson and Wright 2000). The removal of these women from their respective populations at this increasing rate has far-reaching consequences that we will subsequently discuss in more detail.

The Women of Color Policy Network (2003) testified before the New York City Council about the incarceration rates of women in New York City from 1995 to 2001. The data indicated that black females evidenced the highest incarceration rate among females from 1995 to 2001. Their rate of 731 per 100,000 was almost twice that of Hispanic females (342 per 100,000) and just over six times the incarceration rate for white females 115 per 100,000).

According to the Women of Color Policy Network (2003), controlled substances, burglary, larceny, miscellaneous other causes, and prostitution were the leading causes of incarceration among women by race/Hispanic origin. There were some differences by race/ethnicity. The leading cause of incarceration across all three racial groups was controlled substances. This offense accounted for almost 32 percent of causes of incarceration of black females, 34 percent for Hispanic women, and 32 percent for white women. The groups differed with respect to the other leading offenses. The miscellaneous other causes category was the second most frequent cause of incarceration for black and Hispanic women (21 percent each); whereas for white women, prostitution was the second most frequent cause of incarceration (24 percent). The Women of Color Policy Network (2003) also examined the leading causes of arrest of other women whose pattern of arrest differed from the specific race/ethnic groups. The miscellaneous other causes category accounted for 70 percent of all incarcerations of other women, followed by prostitution (13 percent) and larceny (8 percent).

Simpson and Wright (2000) analyzed female incarceration rates in Oklahoma, the state with the highest female incarceration rates in the nation. Overall, females accounted for 24 percent of all convictions in the state in 1999. White females accounted for the largest percentage of total female felony convictions (67 percent) followed by black females (24 percent), American Indian females (6 percent), and Hispanic females (3 percent). Among females in 1999, almost 35 percent of felony convictions were for drug offenses, followed by 26 percent for fraud and 18 percent for larceny. But when we look at incarceration, drug offenses accounted 45 percent of all females incarcerated from 1997 to 1999. This is a great deal larger than the percentage convicted. Fraud (17 percent) and larceny (14 percent) followed in the same order as conviction, but the differences were not as dramatic (Simpson and Wright 2000).

Drug offenses accounted for 58 percent of felony convictions of Hispanic females, 48 percent for white females, 43 percent for black females, and 35 percent for American Indian females. For Hispanics, blacks, and American Indians, larceny and then fraud completed the pattern in order of prevalence of convictions. The pattern for white females was the reverse, and fraud (17 percent) accounted for a larger percentage of convictions than larceny (11 percent) (Simpson and Wright 2000).

These authors looked more closely at the nature of drug convictions and reported that over one-half (53 percent) of all drug convictions of females were for possession. One-third of the female drug convictions in Oklahoma were for distribution. The specific types of drugs for possession were amphetamine-methamphetamine and cocaine, 41 percent each. There were no breakdowns by race/ethnicity for female incarceration by specific type of crime.

Finally, Simpson and Wright (2000) compared felony arrest rates and felony convictions by race and gender. They reported that the largest differences were evident for black females with 18 percent felony arrests in 1998 compared with 24 percent felony convictions in 1999. The difference in the felony arrest rates of white females (71 percent) and the felony convictions (67 percent) was small, but there was a clear decrease as white females moved from arrest to conviction. The differences for Hispanic and American Indian females were slight.

Perhaps the most striking finding is that the increase in the percentage of women in prison has been fueled by incarceration for drug offenses (Greenfield and Snell 1999). Some have argued that the war on drugs has translated into a war on women and a war on blacks (Bush-Baskette 1998; Chesney-Lind 2003; Covington 2000). Chesney-Lind (2003) reported that as a result of tough sentencing policies, such as mandatory sentences and the 100 to 1 crack-cocaine differential, introduced in the war on drugs, the number of women arrested for drug offenses increased from 1 in 10 in 1970 to 1 in 3 in 1998.

Bush-Baskette (1998) emphasized "the need to investigate the possible interactive effects of race and gender on the treatment of the black female within the criminal justice system in general and the war on drugs specifically" (p. 193).

Parole

The next phase in the crime-processing system is postincarceration, which includes parole. *Parole*, which is generally defined as early release from the crime-processing system, holds the potential for continued oversight. This oversight generally involves a set of requirements, which if not successfully met could lead to reincarceration. Women accounted for 7 percent of the total adult parole population in 1985, 8 percent in 1990, 10 percent in 1995, 12 percent in 2000, and 14 percent at year end 2002 (Beck, Brown, and Gilliard 1999; Glaze 2003). According to Greenfield and Snell (1999), the number of women under parole grew by 80 percent between 1990 and 1998.

Mann (1993) found that black women convicted of property crimes and drug offenses had less successful parole outcomes than white women. According to Hall, Baldwin, and Prendergast (2001), a number of women are not successful on parole. Barriers, which include the lack of services, both vocational and treatment, and the refusal on the part of treatment programs to accept children on site, often impede success of parole requirements. The lack of sufficient data by race and gender prohibits a comprehensive discussion of the differences among various racial/ethnic groups of women.

The Death Penalty

The United States holds the dubious distinction of housing more women condemned to death than any other country in the world, although this population remains virtually invisible unless a woman is scheduled for imminent execution. (Schulberg 2003, 284)

Women account for less than 2 percent of all people condemned to death in the United States. Aside from reports that provide data on the number of women who have been condemned to death and those who have been executed, there is little additional information on women and the death penalty. Probably the most interesting finding is that from 1632 to 1861, black women accounted for close to 60 percent of all executions of women. However, since the turn of the century, there has been a drastic change. From 1900 to 2003, 49 women were executed in the United States. Over two-thirds (67 percent) were white, almost 30 percent were black, and females from other race/ethnic groups accounted for about 4 percent (Beck, Karberg, and Harrison 2002; Harrison and Beck 2003; Stana 2000).

Recent data provide more detailed information on the race/ethnicity of females condemned to death. Since 1973, 148 women have been sentenced to death. This is a racially and ethnically diverse group: 94 white women, 40 black women, 10 Latino women, and 4 Native American women (Death Penalty Information Center 2004). White women accounted for 63 percent of all women sentenced to death since 1973 and 90 percent of women executed since 1976. This is just the reverse of earlier reports.

Conclusion

A number of scholars have argued that women exist on the fringes of criminal justice discourse. When women are included in the analysis, they are often treated as a homogeneous group. This segmentation process has left a void in understanding women as a heterogeneous group and the impact of these differences on their experiences in the crime processing system. This is particularly problematic given that women represent a growing portion of the offender population.

When racial differences are considered, the focus is primarily on how different black women are relative to whites, almost to the exclusion of research on other racial and ethnic groups. This singular approach to understanding female offending is a missed opportunity for understanding the complexities of these women across racial, ethnic, and class categories in relation to the crime processing system. This dearth of information leads to categorizations of female offenders as a homogeneous group. The absence of analysis of the differences across racial/ethnic and class lines also fosters cultural misunderstandings, generalizations, and use of stereotypes as white women are generally placed at the center of the analysis and others exist on the fringes. Mann and Zatz (1998) noted that "millions of people are stigmatized, stereotyped, and victimized by our social institutions—in particular, the juvenile and criminal justice systems and the police" (p. 1).

One of the impediments in the way of garnering a more comprehensive approach to understanding female offending patterns is the limitations that are associated with official data sources. However, existing data and research support the assertion that disparities do exist in the crime processing of women by race and ethnicity. Subsequently, it is argued that research literature and data collection and recording methodologies that utilize a binary, black versus white, approach severely limit the extent of the examination and the depth of the analysis about these disparities. While there have been a number of gains in factoring women into criminal justice discourse, this continued representation of race as a dichotomous variable is problematic given the diverse ethnic composition of American society.

Women in all racial and ethnic categories have experienced an increase in contact with aspects of the crime-processing system. However, black and Hispanic females are overrepresented at each stage of criminal justice processing. And the data show that these differences become more substantial the further into the system a woman is processed. Prior research suggests that these differences are, at the least, in part attributable to differential treatment based on race, and recent research, though scant, tends to support this view.

Perhaps, the age-old argument of the chivalry factor—based on patriarchal notions of womanhood that traditionally have not been bestowed upon women of color in America—may be a factor in the differential treatment experienced by white women, who fare better than others in the crime-processing system. The history of exclusion and discrimination poses a barrier for those who are not white in the crime-processing system. Or perhaps, differences in social and economic support networks contribute to the disparities that exist within the crime processing of women. Whatever the case, it is difficult for concrete assertions to be made when criminal processing data that delineate race and ethnic differences are simply not available. This assessment shows that a research agenda that considers the heterogeneity and multiple intersections of womanhood is essential to the analysis of gender and crime.

Although major limitations are associated with the available data on women and the crime-processing system, it can be reported that there has been a significant increase in the number of women processed through the crime-processing system over the past 10 years. And, while women, like men, tend to commit crime for economic reasons, their patterns of crime differ from their male counterparts. Women are more likely to commit less violent offenses and are better known for committing what are commonly referred to as female offenses, such as prostitution, embezzlement, forgery, and counterfeiting. However, over the last decade, a growing number of women of all racial and ethnic backgrounds have been arrested, tried, and incarcerated for drug-related offenses, which much of the research attributes to the effects of the war on drugs campaign.

Examining the effects of the war on drugs on incarcerated women, Bush-Baskette (2000) reveals that the increase in the rate of female incarceration is largely due to the anti-drug legislation. And, while the increase, for some, may indicate success, the greater rate of female incarceration has had the unintended consequence of separating the custodial parent from her children, as family situations are no longer considered during the sentencing process (Bush-Baskette 2000). This creates other social, familial, and economic strains on the families who are left behind.

According to statistics, slightly more than 64 percent of incarcerated women are mothers to an estimated 1.3 million young children (Mumola 2000), and unlike their male counterparts, a large percentage of these women were the primary caretakers of their children prior to incarceration (Snell and Morton 1994). Consequently, as research has shown, a considerable number of children are displaced as a result of their mothers' incarceration (Phillips and Harm 2000). In essence, when their mothers are placed behind bars, the children are forced either to live with other family members, who take on the social and economic responsibility for them, or to be placed in the foster care system, where they become the social responsibility of the state and the financial responsibility of the tax payers.

Separation of children from their parents has long been a major concern to both welfare and mental health professionals. Despite interest in this general area, the children of incarcerated parents are overlooked by the crime-processing system. Punishment in the crime-processing system has traditionally been, and remains, focused on the individual offender with little regard to its wider effects on offenders' children, their families, and society at large.

The irony of this situation becomes apparent when we consider the correlation between parole success and the maintenance of family ties while in prison. Although the reported consequences associated with female incarceration hold true across race and ethnic lines, the fact that a disproportionate number of black and Hispanic women are incarcerated means that these communities are more heavily affected by the incarceration of women.

Notes

1. Respondents to the National Crime Victimization Survey who report victimization are asked if the offender was white, black, or other. If they respond "other," the respondents are asked to specify the perceived race of the offender.

2. The Women of Color Policy Network conducts research on policies related to poverty, welfare, employment, health, and incarceration of Asian, Black, Hispanic, and Native American women.

3. *The war on drugs* is a term used to describe the policies and practices used by the government to increase efforts by the Drug Enforcement Agency and the accompanying criminal justice policies. These efforts began during the Reagan era and continue with increased punishments against drug users and drug dealers.

4. In this chapter, the term *probation* designates the sentence a person is given in lieu of a jail or prison sentence.

Study/Discussion Questions

1. How does police discretion affect arrest rates of women? Is there evidence of differential treatment based on race/ethnicity?

2. What is the chivalry hypothesis, and what impact has it had on the differences of women of color in the crime-processing system?

3. What role have drugs played in the increase in incarceration for women?

4. What are the limitations associated with discussing differences of offending patterns by race and gender?

References

Albonetti, C., Hauser, R., Hagan, J., and Nagel, I. (1989). Criminal justice decision-making as a stratification process: The role of race and stratification resources in pretrial release. *Journal of Quantitative Criminology*, 5, 57–82.

Beck, A., Brown, J., and Gilliard, D. (1999). *Correctional Populations in the United States 1996.* USDOJ BJS NCJ 170013. Washington, DC: Government Printing Office.

Beck, A, Karberg, J., and Harrison, P. (2002). *Prison and jail inmates at midyear 2001,* (NCJ191702). Washington, DC: Bureau of Justice Statistics.

Belknap, J (2002). *The invisible woman: Gender, crime, and justice.* Belmont, CA: Wadsworth.

Bureau of Justice Statistics. (2003). *Compendium of federal justice statistics, 2001.* Washington, DC: Government Printing Office.

Bush-Baskette, S. (1998). The war on drugs as a war against black women. In S. L. Miller (Ed.), *Crime control and women: Feminist implications of criminal justice policy* (pp. 113–129). Thousand Oaks, CA: Sage.

——. (2000). The war on drugs and the incarceration of mothers. *Journal of Drug Issues,* 30, 919–924.

Chesney-Lind, M. (2003). Reinventing women's corrections: Challenges for contemporary feminist criminologists and practitioners. In S. F. Sharp (Ed.), *The incarcerated women: Rehabilitative programming in women's prisons* (pp. 3–14). Englewood Cliffs, NJ: Prentice Hall.

Covington, J. (2000, November). *African Americans, drugs, and incapacitation.* Paper presented at the Annual Meeting of the American Society of Criminology, San Francisco, CA.

Death Penalty Information Center. (2004). Women and the death penalty. *http://www.deathpenaltyinfo.org/article.php?did=230&scid=24#executed.*

Espy, M. W., and Smykla, J. (1987). *Executions in the United States, 1608–1991: The Espy file* (machine-readable data file). Ann Arbor, MI: Inter-University Consortium for Political and Social Research.

Farnsworth, M., and Teske, R. (1995). Gender differences in felony court processing: Three hypotheses of disparity. *Crime and Delinquency,* 35, 136–168.

Federal Bureau of Investigation (FBI) (2003). *Crime in the United States, 2002.* Washington, DC: Government Printing Office.

——. (2004). *Crime in the United States. 2003.* Washington, DC: Government Printing Office.

Glaze, L. (2003). *Probation and parole in the United States, 2002.* Washington, DC: U.S. Department of Justice.

Gilbert, E. (2001). Women, race, and criminal justice processing. In C. M. Renzetti and L. Goodstein (Eds.), *Women, crime, and criminal justice: Original feminist readings* (pp. 222–231). Los Angeles: Roxbury Publishing.

Gilliard, D. (1999). *Prison and jail inmates at midyear 1998.* Washington, DC: U.S. Department of Justice.

Gottfredson, S. D., and Jarjoura, G. R. (1996). Race, gender, and guidelines-based decision making. *Journal of Research in Crime and Delinquency,* 33, 49–69.

Greenfield, L., and Snell, T. (1999). *Women offenders.* Washington, DC: U.S. Department of Justice.

Hall, E., Baldwin, D., and Prendergast, M. (2001). Women on parole: Barriers to success after substance abuse treatment. *Human Organization,* 60, 225–233.

Harrison, P., and Beck, A. (2003). *Prisoners in 2002.* Washington, DC: U.S. Department of Justice.

Higginbotham, A. L. (1978). *In the matter of color: Race and the American legal process, the Colonial period.* New York: Oxford University Press.

Jordan, B. K. (1996). Women in prison: Prevalence of psychiatric disorders among incarcerated women convicted felons entering prison. *Archives of General Psychology,* 53, 513–519.

Katz, C., and Spohn, C. (1995). The effect of race and gender on bail outcomes: A test of an interactive model. *American Journal of Criminal Justice,* 19, 161–184.

Mann, C. (1993). *Unequal justice: A question of color.* Bloomington: Indiana University Press.

Mann, R., and Zatz, M. S. (1998). *Images of color, images of crime..* Los Angeles: Roxbury Publishing.

McGee, Z., and Baker, S. (2003). Crime control policy and inequality among female offenders. In R. Muraskin (Ed.), *It's a crime: Women and justice* (3rd edition) (pp. 196–208). Englewood Cliffs, NJ: Prentice Hall.

Minton, T. (2003). *Jails in Indian Country, 2002,* Washington, DC: U.S. Department of Justice.

Mumola C. (2000). *Special report: Incarcerated parents and their children.* Washington, DC:

U.S. Department of Justice, Office of Justice Programs.

Office of National Drug Control Policy. (2003). Drug facts: Women and drugs. *http://www. whitehousedrugpolicy.gov/drugfact/women/index.html*.

Olson, D., Lurigio, A., and Seng, M. (2000). A comparison of female and male probationers: Characteristics and case outcomes. *Women and Criminal Justice*, 11, 65–79.

Phillips, S., and Harm, N. (1998). Women prisoners: A contextual framework. *Women & Therapy* 20 (4): 1–9.

Quereshi, M. Y., and King, M. S. (1998). Processing time as a function of ethnicity, gender, and psychopathology. *Journal of Offender Rehabilitation*, 27, 15–22.

Rennison, C. M., and Rand M. (2003). *Criminal victimization 2002*. NCJ 199994.

Renzetti, C. M. (2006). Gender and violent crime. In C. M. Renzetti, L. Goodstein, and S. L. Miller (Eds.), *Rethinking gender, crime, and criminal justice: Feminist readings* (pp. 93–106). Los Angeles: Roxbury Publishing.

Schulberg, D. (2003) Dying to get out: The execution of females in the post-Furman era of the death penalty in the United States. In R. Muraskin (Ed.), *It's a crime: Women and justice* (pp. 273–288). Englewood Cliffs, NJ: Prentice Hall.

Sims, B., and Jones, M. (1997). Predicting success or failure on probation: Factors associated with felony probation outcomes. *Crime and Delinquency*, 43, 314–327.

Simpson, D., and Wright, D. (2000). *Gender, crime, and incarceration in Oklahoma*. Oklahoma City: Oklahoma Sentencing Commission.

Snell, T., and Morton, D. (1994). *Women in prison*. Special report. Washington, DC: Bureau of Justice Statistics.

Stana, R. (2000). *State and federal prisoners: Profile of inmate characteristics in 1991 and 1997*. US GAO. Report to the Honorable Charles B. Rangel, House of Representatives.

Steffensmeier, D., and Schwartz, J. (2004). Trends in female criminality: Is crime still a man's world? In B. R. Price and N. J. Sokoloff (Eds.), *The criminal justice system and women: Offenders, prisoners, victims and workers* (3rd Edition) (pp. 95–112). Boston: McGraw-Hill.

Walker, S., Spohn, C., and DeLone, M. (2000). *The color of justice: Race, ethnicity, and crime in America* (2nd Edition). Belmont, CA: Wadsworth.

Women of Color Policy Network. (2003, February 27). *Criminalization of black and Hispanic women*. Testimony for the Women's Issues Committee of the New York City Council.

Young, V. D. (1984). Gender expectations and their impact on black female offenders and victims. *Justice Quarterly*, 3, 305–327.

——. (1994). *The politics of disproportionality: African-American perspectives on crime causation, criminal justice administration, and crime prevention*. Boston: Butterworth-Heinemann. ✦

14

Issues Facing Women Prisoners in the Early Twenty-First Century

Tammy L. Anderson

In this chapter you will learn the following:

- The unique problems facing women prisoners and how well the criminal justice system has responded to them

- That criminal justice policy regarding women prisoners has historically been characterized by inequality, resulting in serious consequences for women prisoners in terms of health and access to health care as well as parenting

- The consequences of women's incarceration not only for inmates themselves but also for their families, their communities, and the larger society

Introduction

Presently, America's prisons are crowded with low-income drug offenders, who are increasingly lower-class females and disproportionately racial and ethnic minorities. Studies funded by the Bureau of Justice Statistics (Beck, Karberg, and Harrison 2002) show that the female prisoner population has more than doubled between 1990 and 2001, from 44,065 to 94,336, respectively. Data from 2001 show that females accounted for 6.7 percent of all prisoners nationwide, up from 4.1 per-

cent in 1980 and 5.7 percent in 1990 (Beck et al. 2002). As is the case with men, African-American and other minority women are disproportionately represented among the prison population (Beck, Karberg, and Harrison 2002).

Unfortunately, the population growth of female offenders is not confined to prisons but has also been witnessed in each component of the correctional system. For example, the number of women per capita involved in the correctional system has grown 48 percent since 1990, while the proportion of men incarcerated has risen 27 percent. Between 1990 and 1998, the proportion of women under probation supervision climbed 40 percent, the jail rate 60 percent, and the imprisonment rate 88 percent (Greenfield and Snell 1999). The correctional presence of women does not reflect the general population. Lower-income, minority women dominate, which raises considerable problems for their families and communities.

What types of crime drive these imprisonment rates? The majority of women in prison today are serving time for a drug offense or a drug-related property offense. In addition, about half reported using alcohol, drugs, or both at the time of offense (Greenfield and Snell 1999), providing further indication that the current predicament of women in prison revolves heavily around the use and abuse of illicit substances.

The significant increase in women's incarceration since the 1980s is an outcome of the war on drugs and other punitive criminal justice policies (e.g., mandatory minimum sentencing). Such policies have fundamentally altered the criminal justice system, social institutions (including families, communities, and public and private agencies), and—some would argue—the very fabric of society. This predicament has caused feminists to issue a call for alternative sentencing, raising an interesting equity of justice debate. This debate is important to consider here because many of the arguments for alternative sentencing policies are rooted in the past and present experiences of women in prison.

Equity and the Call for Alternative Sentencing

Briefly, a central premise of feminists' call for a diversion of women from the prison is that women and girls enter the criminal justice system as a result of circumstances distinctly different from those of men and are further disadvantaged by correctional policy engineered to fit men's lives, which cannot respond to their unique needs (Richie 2000). Moreover, the incarceration of female offenders often wreaks considerably more damage not only to the offenders themselves but also to their families, communities, and the larger society (WPA 2003). This is especially the case for racial and ethnic minority women as well as for the poor.

Criticism of the criminal justice system's inability to effectively deal with female offenders is longstanding. Earlier work noted the chivalrous treatment of women, stemming from patriarchal ideas about how they should behave rather than about equitable principals of justice. In other words, women offenders have been historically sanctioned via their fit to gender norms in addition to de facto policies regarding certain offenses. In some cases, this resulted in more serious penalties for females (e.g., girls were detained for truancy while boys were not). In other instances, less serious sanctioning followed. The "chivalry" debate remains relatively unsettled today (Edwards 1989; Farnsworth and Teske 1995; Spohn 1999).

Daly's (1994) seminal work in New Haven, Connecticut, addressed the gender and sentencing disparity issue head on. She found that women received shorter sentences than their male counterparts, which was largely due to their greater obligation to the family (e.g., child care). Debate has persisted about the fairness of policies like these. Some believe that sentences more often fit the offender rather than the crime. Responding to these concerns, Daly raised a critical question about what to do with the disparity. Should women's sentences be increased to match those of men's or should men's be decreased to parallel women's?

This question has been answered, inadvertently, by war on drugs policies, not by scholars or policymakers who have taken up the issue. Female incarceration rates have risen dramatically since the 1980s, due largely to war on drugs policies favoring mandatory sentences (Mauer, Potler, and Wolf 1999). The criminal justice system's shift to mandatory sentencing or sentencing guidelines has removed much of the discretion judges had to practice chivalrous treatment of female offenders. Sentencing guidelines today disallow gender-based decision making that influenced sentencing in the past. Today, the gap in men's and women's imprisonment is the smallest it has ever been (Mauer, Potler, and Wolf 1999; WPA 2003).

Critics of female incarceration argue that war on drugs policies had a tragic impact on women and that mandatory minimums and other punitive policies are unfair and unwise. Chesney-Lind (1998, 68) calls this "vengeful justice," a cynical mode of justice that emphasizes treating women offenders punitively, as though they were men, in the name of justice.

The debate about female offenders takes place simultaneously with one about the fairness of mandatory minimums, sentencing guidelines, three-strikes policies, and other punitive responses of the war on drugs for all offenders. For example, scholars (e.g., Mauer 1999) writing about male offenders also point to the unfairness of harsh war on drugs policies that have cluttered the prison system with low-income, minority males. The argument against punitive war on drugs policies is also compelling, if not more so, for ethnic and racial minority group members of both genders. Thus, how do we make sense of the call for lighter or diversionary sentencing for female offenders?

The purpose of this chapter is to review the current situation of women in prison and discuss the consequences of their increased incarceration. It will help inform this correctional policy debate while educating students about women's prison experience. It begins with a historical review of how the prison system has responded to women in order to situate present-day concerns.

History of Women's Incarceration

Historically, women offenders have received little attention from scholars of crime and justice. For example, the history of the U.S. correctional system is largely a story about men's imprisonment. Only recently have criminologists begun documenting the history of women's confinement. Most accounts, however, are constrained to the United States in the second half of the twentieth century. Two major exceptions exist. The first is Rafter's (1985) comprehensive chronicle of women's incarceration in the states from the late nineteenth century throughout the twentieth century. A second significant work is Bosworth's (2000) recent piece on women's seventeenth- and eighteenth-century confinement in France. It is an important precursor to the U.S. experience. I carefully review both accounts to educate the student about the origins, nature, and continuity of female correctional policy.

Perhaps the most consistent theme to characterize women's experience throughout time is their confinement for violating sexuality and gender role expectations and morals. For example, promiscuity and the failure to marry or "act like a woman" could lead to institutionalization. They were also confined for legal violations, but even more often for "gender indiscretions." Women's deviation from gender norms was considered a matter for the correctional system. Thus, prisons were in the business of controlling gender as much as they were to control crime (Bosworth 2000; Rafter 1985). Men were not held accountable in the same fashion. Thus, women have historically experienced disparate justice due to the influence of sexuality and gender-based moral expectations about their behavior.

For example, the first account of women being confined for criminal offenses was at the Salpetriere hospital in Paris around 1684 (Bosworth 2000). The Maison de Force, a women's unit, was part of the Paris hospital and was opened in 1656 by Louis XIV. It was a forerunner to the nineteenth century penitentiary system. The Maison de Force housed sick, healthy, pregnant, infertile, mad, and foolish women. Many of the women at Maison de Force were prostitutes, who served fairly short sentences. Another group of women was placed there by their families, often for gender deviance, and could remain confined indefinitely. Still others were sent to countries such as the United States to find a husband (Bosworth 2000).

Approximately 1,200 women were housed at the Maison de Force in the mid-1800s. Both extreme isolation and overcrowding characterized their confinement (Bosworth 2000). The women were sentenced for variable lengths of time, more often based on their families' wishes than on legal provisions. The correctional model employed at the time focused on reformation. Officials ordered women offenders to reform themselves through "feminized" labor (e.g., sewing and cooking). Reformers believed such work would ultimately restore female offenders to their proper roles as wives and mothers (Rafter 1985; Bosworth 2000).

Over time, female reformers took notice of the deplorable and inhumane conditions of institutions like the Maison de Force and began campaigns for change. They attempted to rectify problems such as inadequate food and lodging, corrupt staff, and sexual assault by prison personnel. Unfortunately, they were minimally successful. Moreover, they did not address the tendency of officials to incarcerate women for "inappropriate" gender-related behavior. This practice continued well into the nineteenth century.

Enter L'Ecole de Reform, that is, a new institution—school—utilizing a medical approach to reform wayward women. A modern scientific revolution, called the Enlightenment, ushered in a shift toward the medicalization of treatment. It promised a new approach to criminality, one combining medicine, treatment, and work instead of punishment and work (Bosworth 2000). Despite this major social change, however, the idea persisted that certain types of women needed to be confined. Phrased differently, the double standard of sanctioning women for moral deviation continued.

First Women's Prisons in the United States

Rafter (1985) observed that the Mt. Pleasant prison in New York, which opened in 1839, was the first all-female prison in the United States. It remained the only prison for women until the 1870s. It was remarkably similar to its European counterparts (i.e., women were severely punished for offenses against morality in addition to violations of the law). Harsh treatment continued. For example, women were often straitjacketed, placed in solitary confinement, put on extended bread and water diets, and given "shower baths" (i.e., bombarded with water until they nearly drowned). The situation improved gradually as more and more women's prisons were established. However, degradation and inequities continued.

By 1940, 23 states had separate women's prisons (Kurshan 2000). Two kinds of facilities existed. Custodial institutions, much like those for men, simply warehoused women. They offered no pretense of rehabilitation. Reformatories, however, were intended to improve the moral character of women. Reformatories did not exist for men. Nearly every state had a custodial woman's prison, but most women, especially white women, in the Northeast and Midwest were placed in reformatories.

There were far fewer reformatories in the South, and those that did exist housed white women exclusively. However, distribution of women in reformatories and custodial institutions was along racial lines primarily, as the women in the custodial institutions were black whether in the North or the South. They had to undergo the most degrading conditions. Typically, the higher the proportion of women of color, the worse the institutional conditions. Thus, the physical conditions of incarceration for women in the custodial prisons were abysmal compared with the reformatories (Kurshan 2000).

Soon, custodial prisons and reformatories merged. The onslaught of radicalism, demise of progressive and feminist movements, and emergence of the Great Depression helped extinguish the reformatory model of correctional policy and usher in a "just deserts" or crime control model featuring punitive policies. However, one victory was realized for the prison reform movement: It successfully established separate prisons for women.

In these women-only facilities, matrons were hired to work with women inmates. They were supposed to instill middle-class virtues, but many came from the same backgrounds as the inmates. Thus, they did not know how to do what the reformers wanted them to do, and they soon came to be perceived as an unnecessary expense (Rafter 1985).

Consequently, states eliminated matrons and left women inmates to fend for themselves. This policy change made them highly vulnerable to abuse and attack by male guards, a problem that persists, somewhat, today (see following discussion). Women were often not given much attention (Grana 2002). They had little contact with others and received few resources or privileges from prison staff. Women had less access to the physician and chaplain and could not go to workshops, mess halls, or exercise yards with the same frequency as men. They were given menial tasks to do, such as fixing men's clothes. Food and needlework were brought to their quarters. They often remained in that area for the full term of their sentence because they were thought to have less need for recreation and less capacity for industrial labor.

In the first half of the twentieth century, women in the United States were still subjected to a double standard in correctional policy. Characteristically, they were sent to reformatories for public order offenses or "moral failure," lewd and lascivious conduct, stubbornness, idle and disorderly behavior, drunkenness, vagrancy, fornication, serial premarital pregnancies, keeping bad company, adultery, venereal disease, and vagrancy. They could be incarcerated if a relative disapproved of their behavior or if they had been sexually abused (they were, unfortunately, considered at fault for this). Most were rebels of some sort (Rafter 1985). Thus, correctional policy regarding women in the United States in the first half of the 1900s mirrored that in Europe during the eighteenth century.

With separate women's prisons now a staple of twentieth century U.S. correctional policy, the focus in the second half of the century was on prisoner rights due to the abuses long documented in history and the cultural shift toward civil rights in the 1960s. While much of this legislation centered on men's experiences, some important advances were made for women. The famous *Todaro v. Ward* (1977) case was the first to challenge women's access to health care in correctional institutions via the Eighth Amendment. It began to force improvements in women prisonsers' health care.

Today, with minor exception, programs at women's prisons are the same as those at men's facilities. This is a recurrent criticism feminists raise about correctional policy and is a major reason to challenge punitive sentencing policies. Consider, for example, policies on visitation and telephone use. The National Institute on Corrections (NIC) (1998) report indicates they are overwhelmingly the same for male and female inmates, yet women inmates have greater responsibilities to children than males and, consequently, greater needs. This is one area that desperately needs reconsideration due to the unique parent-child concerns of female inmates, as I will discuss. Furthermore, only some of the institutions in the NIC (1998) study reported having specific policies or procedures for pregnant inmates (e.g., prenatal examinations and hospital transportation

for childbirth). In summary, women-specific programs found in state institutions today typically include such things as workshops on low self-esteem, life or "survival" skills development, victimization (i.e., domestic violence or physical and sexual abuse) coping, and parenting. While 49 state departments of corrections reported providing programs such as these for women, availability within facilities remains low. Thus, prison programming is not keeping pace with the changing demographics of its population and, more important, is less likely to meet women's needs than men's. Owen's (1998) major study is one of many to show that women's imprisonment is still fraught with inequities and harsh conditions that make prison life difficult and adjustment after release complicated.

Today's Female Offender

Demographics and Criminal Involvement

Today, the profile of women in prison has not changed much from what was in the past. The majority of female inmates are nonwhite, in their 30s (median age of 34), uneducated, poor, and unemployed. While women's demographic profile is similar to that of men's, important differences exist in their backgrounds that have caused scholars to question the increasing punitive trend that has narrowed the gap between women and men in prison.

One such challenge is based on the victimization histories of women offenders. For example, the majority of women in state prisons report a history of physical and sexual abuse at levels four to five times higher than their male counterparts (WPA 2003). Early physical and sexual trauma fosters complications well into adulthood, and this in turn can motivate criminal offending (Richie 2000). Thus, some argue that women are unfairly placed at greater risk for offending due to their victimization by others early in life.

The criminal justice system, therefore, should take this into consideration (i.e., as a mitigating factor) and sanction them differently.

Second, women in prison have much higher illness rates than their male counterparts or females in the general population. For example, women inmates are more likely to be HIV positive and have Hepatitis C, high rates of substance abuse, and mental illness (Anderson 2002; Marquart et al. 1997; Maruschak 1997; Maruschak and Beck 1997). The following section on health care further describes women's health problems and the prison system's inability to respond effectively to them. Inequities in health care utilization between men and women inmates exacerbate this problem. Thus, the health problems of women offenders also challenge the incarceration response to female offending.

Third, research has noted that women and men are differentially motivated to commit crime (Richie 2001). These differences also call into question the appropriateness of punitive policies for female offending. For example, the typical female prisoner has been convicted of a drug or property crime, with some criminal involvement in the same in the past (i.e., prior convictions) (WPA 2003). A primary motivator of women's illegal activities is to support themselves and their families. This is much less often the case for male offenders (see Anderson 2005). Many argue that since such a large portion of women offenders are nonviolent offenders who have participated in illegal activities to support their families, their motivation is less threatening to society and should, therefore, be responded to differently. While a considerable portion (29 percent) of women in prison are also there for violent crimes, many of these situations were precipitated by domestic violence. In fact, male significant others more often influence female offending than vice versa.

Issues Facing Female Inmates

Diminished health and inequitable health care. Research on the physical and mental health of offenders and prisoners reveals important differences between men and women, with women presenting a greater prevalence of more serious conditions than their male counterparts. The extent and severity of women offenders' health problems are further reasons that scholars and activists have called for the diversion of women from the prison system.

To begin, the prison system is ill equipped to address women-specific health care needs due to its reliance on a generic model of healthcare that was created for men. Today, correctional institutions continue to offer inadequate health care to women inmates and far less than what they offer male offenders (Acoca 1998; Marquart et al. 1997).

Justification for this disparity rings a familiar bell: Women comprise a much smaller portion of the prison population and, consequently, warrant less attention and investment by the state. Given the current rise in female incarceration rates, this explanation may no longer be valid if, in fact, it ever was. The historical neglect of women prisoners, coupled with rising incarceration rates, makes the health care problem increasingly salient today.

Other matters add to the urgency for the prison system to accommodate women inmates' health care needs. These include the health issues chemically dependent inmates pose to the system and the special reproductive problems women face that men do not. For example, the prison system remains largely unable to provide adequate care for women's reproductive issues. Continued inattention to the unique health care needs of women offenders may have considerable economic and social consequences not only for the women themselves but also for their families and the larger communities in which they live. Moreover, such costs could cripple society and future generations. According to Acoca (1999), "health care issues are a tsunami and will engulf social justice, and many other issues, within the next decade if we don't make them a priority" (p. 35). This is yet another reason that incarcerating women at the rate of males is problematic.

Physical health problems. In general, women have higher illness rates for such physical health conditions such as infectious disease, respiratory and digestive system conditions, injuries, ear diseases, headaches, genitourinary disorders, and skin and musculoskeletal diseases. Nonfatal, chronic conditions for things such as varicose veins, constipation, gallbladder and thyroid conditions, chronic enteritis and colitis, anemia, migranes, and chronic urinary disease are also more prevalent among women (Anderson 2002; Marquart et al. 1997; Maruschak 1997; Maruschak and Beck 1997). Add to this a plethora of female-specific conditions related to reproduction and the physical health problems women inmates face set them apart from male inmates and may justify a separate approach.

Mental health. Similar to research findings on physical health problems, women inmates' mental health problems are both more frequent and more serious than their male counterparts (Harlow 1999). The leading mental illness problems among female prisoners include physical and sexual trauma, victimization, depression, and substance abuse (Young 1998). Women in prison have higher rates of substance abuse, antisocial personality disorder, borderline personality disorder, post-traumatic stress disorder, and histories of sexual and physical abuse compared with their male counterparts. Women more frequently engage in self-mutilating behaviors, are verbally abused, and report numerous suicide attempts (Henderson, Schaeffer, and Brown 1998).

Higher rates of mental illness among female inmates must be interpreted cautiously for at least three reasons. First, research has documented mental health reporting differences among male and female inmates (i.e., women are more likely to seek counseling and to utilize mental health services than males) (Anderson 2002). Second, deinstitutionalization of mental health facilities in the 1980s hit women especially hard (Marquart et al. 1997), leading to proportionate increases in prison. A third explanation of this disparity is that women suffer higher rates of childhood trauma and victimization (Harlow 1999) that drive mental illness in adulthood.

Many women have histories of physical and sexual abuse that translate into long-standing depression and resultant somatic sequelae in adulthood. In addition, women offenders tend to carry tremendous guilt and shame not only about their illegal activities but also from childhood scars. These negative self-images make them believe that they do not deserve being treated well by anyone. Thus, as Maeve (1999) stated, "Women in prison could not simply have changed their lives though sheer acts of personal will. The lack of mutually responsive and enhancing relationships in their lives directly led to an unrelenting sense of vulnerability and, over time, concretized their roles as victims of the world" (p. 61).

Inequities and services challenges. Throughout time, correctional institutions have struggled to provide adequate health care and other types of health services to women prisoners. Early reform efforts were more concerned with restoring women offenders to their proper roles as wives and mothers than with their health problems. Rafter (1985, 1989) has noted that early custodial institutions often warehoused women along with men and exposed them to horrible conditions. Sexual abuse was rampant, and babies born in prison often died.

Prison conditions remained like this until *Todaro v. Ward* (1977) began to force improvements. Afterward, a movement was launched by professional organizations to reform health care standards in prisons (Resnick and Shaw 1981). Today, health care for inmates has improved and so have the avenues to secure more equitable treatment. However, women still receive fewer resources than their male counterparts and have less opportunity to initiate legal action when faced with deficiencies or inequities.

The prison healthcare crisis. Economically, prison costs have exploded due to punitive crime control policies that have increasingly led to the incarceration of men and women who are more and more unhealthy (Anderson 2002). The American Correctional

Association noted that in the late 1990s, prison spent at least 10 percent of their operating budgets on health care. These costs are expected to increase as long as the country retains its current anti-drug and crime policies (ACA 2000).

A review of existing studies reveals at least three main problems in accessibility to health care services for female prisoners. First, access to treatment for both general and drug-related health problems is seriously limited. Moreover, women have far less access to health care in prison than do their male counterparts (Pollock-Byrne 1990). Second, the health care provided to women is often mediocre. Third, medical professionals working in women's facilities are underskilled and have been known to withhold care or show little concern for women's needs (Fletcher, Shaver, and Moon 1993). In fact, most lawsuits filed by women in prison are for complications in receiving medical services (Belnap 2000).

To sum up, health care for women in prison is largely an effort to "catch up," in that considerable effort is most often necessary to raise women's health to legally minimal standards (Maeve 1999). Resources for women thus remain unequal with those afforded males and inadequate to meet women's needs. Sentencing alternatives may provide an improved way to address the healthcare needs of women offenders while also keeping check on the costs to society.

Separation From Children and Isolation From Family and Friends

A second challenge to the increased incarceration of women pertains to the interpersonal and familial complications that result from the separation of mothers and their children, which are complicated by the geographical isolation of women in prisons. To begin, nearly two-thirds of women inmates have minor children at home compared with less than one-half of men.

Research shows (see Anderson 2005 for a discussion) that today's female offender, espe-cially the lower-class, drug-involved minority female who predominates in correctional facilities, ran the household and provided sustenance needs for dependents even while engaging in illegal activities prior to incarceration. She gets help from female relatives, such as her mother, sisters, aunts, or cousins. Male partners and the fathers of these children are largely absent, especially in inner-city families, and often fail to perform their parenting responsibilities. For example, when mothers are incarcerated, other family members take care of their children 80 percent of the time. When fathers are incarcerated, mothers most often take care of the children (WPA 2003). Thus, incarcerated mothers are most often primary caregivers who have developed strong emotional bonds with their children. They are, in many cases, the only parent many children will ever know. Separation of mothers and children is, consequently, a much more problematic issue.

Moreover, scholars estimate that 5 percent to 10 percent of women entering prison are pregnant, further complicating the parent-child separation and geographical isolation aspects of women's correctional policy. Next, I describe some of the complications to mothers, children, families, communities, and society due to the separation phenomenon. A case can be made that the social consequences of incarcerating women, taken together, are enormous (i.e., greater than men's on this dimension) not only in the present but also, potentially, in the future.

Today, most states have just one women's prison, despite the massive prison boom that commenced in the 1980s and continues today (Grana 2002). One-half of women in prison are incarcerated more than 100 miles from home. As many as 38 percent will not see their children once during incarceration, which is the number one concern about the prison experience among women (WPA 2003).

In contrast, male inmates are much more likely to serve time in their own communities or somewhere close by. Moreover, male inmates are visited more often by intimate partners, friends, and family, but women inmates are most often visited by female family members, if they are visited at all. The men in their lives seldom show up. Because there are so few women's prisons, doing time is much harder for women than men. This translates into another instance of unequal justice.

As of 2001, only 10 states allowed overnight visits for mothers and children. States have been very slow to provide child visitation benefits to incarcerated mothers. While mother-child visitation programs do exist, they are too few in number and are overshadowed by justice policy in nearly all states that automatically separate mother and child, even when the mother is serving a short sentence for a nonviolent crime and her child is a newborn. All states have laws for the termination of parental rights, and this hangs over the heads of female inmates.

What happens to the children of incarcerated women? About 50 percent live with maternal grandparents, 25 percent live with their other parent, and 20 percent live with another relative. Five percent end up in foster care (WPA 2003). The negative effects on children are wide ranging, including social, educational, and emotional (e.g., bonding with the mother) consequences. Research shows that children of incarcerated parents are far more likely to be incarcerated themselves as adults. Other problems include deterioration of the mother-child bond. In fact, many kids end up hating their mothers. Mothers, on the other hand, develop a deep sense of guilt and shame that cripples them in future, more conventional pursuits.

Prison Staff Mismanagement of Women Inmates

A third critical issue warranting attention is the mismanagement of women at the hands of correctional staff. As I have noted, female prisons contain staff, especially security staff, who are both male and female. The placement of male correctional officers in female institutions and on all female cellblocks has resulted in instances of sexual manipulation and abuse. Reports of verbal harassment and outright sexual assault by male officers have been recorded in numerous institutions and constitute a major problem today (Calhoun and Coleman 2002; Van Wormer and Bartollas 2000).

Problems with prison staff's abuse or harassment of inmates is not unique to female facilities or to women offenders. It has been reported in men's institutions as well (Human Rights Watch 2001). However, the abuse and harassment of female offenders by male staff is decidedly sexual in nature (i.e., sexually exploitative). Given the profile of women's abuse histories previously mentioned, such victimization by male staff is unquestionably problematic and may be counterproductive to promoting the kinds of motivations and characteristics necessary for successful reintegration. Thus, it comprises yet another reason that feminists have called for alternative sentencing of female offenders.

Resources for Re-entry: Prison Programming

Given the massive number of men and women incarcerated in prison today, a central concern for criminal justice policy centers on inmates' effective reintegration into the community. Today, there is an increased policy move toward providing needed services, in addition to punishment, in order to achieve the reintegration goal. What this means is the relatively smooth transition back into the community, absent unnecessary complication, and with offenders equipped to better adopt conventional and productive lifestyles. Reintegration promises to help circumvent both future safety and economic threats posed by crime and imprisonment. Thus, resultant programs are increasingly being viewed as fiscally sound and more beneficial to offenders, his or her victims, and the society at large.

The topic of prisoner reentry is fairly new, and not much attention has been paid to how the experience and resources allocated to promote it might differ by race and gender. A few scholars (Belknap 2000; Bloom and Covington 2000; Richie 2001), however, have addressed women inmates' reentry issues. Much of what they have found is consistent with the themes running through this chapter. For example, Belknap (2000) noted that most prison programs are geared toward making women good wives and mothers, instead of making them financially independent. As previously discussed, parenting classes typically abound in women's prisons. However, women's prisons lack educational and skills training programs. Most offer only the General Education Degree (GED) and do not require all women to obtain one before release. Consequently, few women do so. In addition, few prisons offer programs beyond the GED, and those that do usually provide vocational programs that teach traditionally feminine skills in low-paying jobs, such as cosmetology and cooking. Still, only a modest number of women inmates participate in such training. Thus, most remain significantly underskilled to enter the labor force (Belknap 2000).

This strikes a familiar theme from the past, suggesting that institutions are still geared toward controlling women's femininity or perpetuating a gender-based morality. Moreover, such efforts may worsen matters by fostering dependency rather than economic self-sufficiency among a group of women whose pool for intimate relationships (e.g., black males) is also disproportionately incarcerated or economically marginalized.

Elsewhere, I (Anderson 2005) argued that female offenders have much more power in high-crime communities (i.e., due to responsibilities in running households and supporting themselves and families), than policy makers and researchers acknowledge. For example, women's experience in raising revenues for family support is an important experience that will help them with more reintegration undertakings, including providing for themselves and others (i.e., economic independence and money management) and securing positive and fulfilling relationships. Such experience should be incorporated into correctional programming. However, it should not be the only focus of reentry programming, as it may deny them a more complete self-fulfillment or existence outside of the family. Thus, prison programs that simply teach women how to be good wives and mothers are not only inadequate for their reintegration needs, but they also are not based in the realities of women's lives. This point substantiates the argument about the prison system's inability to effectively address women's issues and experiences and calls for alternative sentencing or massive reform in prison programming.

How could the prison system better address women's needs and promote more successful reintegration if the punitive sentencing trend continues to incarcerate them at current levels? Successful reintegration of women offenders might begin with an ideology or orientation that fosters a more empowered female able to operate independently in society. Covington (2002) has identified five goals for such a strategy. They are (1) nurturing vitality, (2) an empowerment to act, (3) a thorough knowledge of self and others, (4) increased self-worth, and (5) a desire for more connection to law-abiding others. These goals are likely best achieved by offering gender-responsive programming fitted to the realities of women offenders' lives.

Bloom and Covington (2000) have outlined some guiding principles for gender-responsive programming in prison. First, institutions need to make available opportunities that are relevant to each gender rather than generic programs that profess to fit all. It was previously noted that prisons offer mostly generic programs for both sexes and that female-specific programs are far less available. For Bloom and Covington (2000), equity in programming means the availability of programs fitted to men's and women's lives, not equitable enrollment in generic, one-size-fits-all programs.

Second, since positive self-concepts are critical to reintegration and are best promoted in gender-specific groups, Bloom and Covington (2000) advised against co-ed self-concept or mentoring groups that many institutions currently offer. The unique needs of women would be better served in a woman-focused environment that is safe, trusting, and supportive. Cultural sensitivity should also be a vital component of any such programs. Other programs should provide comprehensive treatment for drug abuse and recovery from trauma (e.g., victimization and domestic violence) and increased educational opportunity, job training, and parenting skills.

Once women are released from prison, the reintegration effort must continue, since the female offender will likely have to comply with conditions of probation or parole, achieve financial stability, access health care, locate housing, and attempt to reunite with her family (Bloom and Covington 2000). Accomplishing these goals requires developing a system of support within the community. Recently, feminists (Acoca 1998, 1999; Jacobs 2001) have called this system a continuum of care, which includes wrap-around services that holistically address the re-integration goal.

If women are to be successfully reintegrated into the community, a continuum of care can connect them to the community following their release. This means locating and providing resources that can empower them toward self-sufficiency and reconnect them with their families. Wrap-around services feature a holistic, culturally sensitive plan for each individual that draws on a coordinated continuum of services located within the community (Jacobs 2001). These can be very effective because they address multiple goals and needs in a coordinated way and facilitate access to services. Specific programs include public assistance, child support and regaining custody of children, housing assistance, health care and drug treatment, and various other human services (e.g., domestic violence programs and educational opportunity).

Conclusions

This chapter began with a discussion of a gender-oriented sentencing debate fueled by incarceration trends and shortcomings for female offenders. In short, the massive increase in female imprisonment raises critical issues not only for an overwhelmed prison system unable to deal effectively with women's needs but also for communities and the larger society, who will witness consequences for generations to come. This chapter has attempted both to educate the reader about the past and present situation of women in prison and to show that the call for alternative sentencing of female offenders can be justified by their diverse backgrounds and experiences and by shortcomings in prison administration and programming.

The seemingly unilateral focus in the United States on punishing wrongdoers via incarceration is bringing us closer to crisis every day. It has exploded the prison population, narrowed the gap between male and female inmates, and levied an unbearable economic crisis on the states. Due to the overwhelming number of individuals incarcerated, and the type and length of their offenses and sentences, reintegration into the community is now a fundamental component of the crime control agenda. Alternative sentencing—especially community corrections programs, drug courts and treatment, and restorative justice initiatives—may also become just as vital to future justice endeavors.

Women offenders, I have argued here, are good candidates for alternative sentencing not only because of their modest and nonviolent criminal histories overall but also because the prison system continues to fail them in numerous and significant ways. If, however, the punitive crime control model continues to incarcerate women at present rates, it is hoped that future criminal justice practitioners will embrace the guidelines offered here for a more just and safe future.

Study/Discussion Questions

1. In what ways has the imprisonment of women paralleled the social control of gender in the United States?

2. Do the issues women inmates face warrant alternative sentencing? Explain.

3. How could the prison system better address the needs of women while meting out equitable justice in the current era of punitive policies?

References

Acoca, L. (1998). Diffusing the time bomb: Understanding and meeting the growing health care needs of incarcerated women in America. *Crime and Delinquency, 44,* 49–70.

Acoca, L. (1999). Getting healthy and staying healthy: Physical and mental health/substance abuse. In *National Symposium on Women Offenders* (pp. 33–360). Washington, DC: U.S. Department of Justice.

Anderson, T. L. (2002). Issues in the availability of healthcare for women in prison. In S. Sharp (Ed.), *Female prisoners in the United States: Programming needs, availability, and efficacy* (pp. 49–60). Englewood Cliffs, NJ: Prentice Hall.

——. (2005). Dimensions of women's power in the illicit drug economy. *Theoretical Criminology, 9*(4), 371–400.

Beck, A., Karberg, J., and Harrison, P. (2002). *Prison and jail inmates at midyear 2001.* Washington DC: U.S. Department of Justice, Bureau of Justice Statistics.

Belknap, J. (2000). *The invisible woman: Gender, crime and justice* (2nd edition), Belmont, CA: Wadsworth.

Bloom, B., and Covington, S. (2000, November). *Gender-specific programming for female offenders: What is it and why is it important?* Paper presented at the Annual Meeting of the American Society of Criminology, Washington, DC.

Bosworth, M. (2000). Confining femininity: A history of gender, power, and imprisonment. *Theoretical Criminology, 4,* 265–284.

Calhoun, A. J., and Coleman, H. D. (2002). Female inmates' perspectives on sexual abuse by correctional personnel: An exploratory study. *Women & Criminal Justice, 13,* 101–124.

Chesney-Lind, M. (1998, December). The forgotten offender. *Corrections Today,* pp. 66–72.

Covington, S. (2002, January). *A woman's journey home: Challenges for female offenders and their children.* Paper presented at the From Prison to Home Conference, National Institutes of Health, Bethesda, MD.

Daly, K. (1994). *Gender, crime, and punishment.* New Haven, CT: Yale University Press.

Edwards, A. R. (1989). Sex/gender, sexism, and criminal justice: Some theoretical considerations. *International Journal of the Sociology of Law, 17,* 165–184.

Farnsworth, M., and Teske, R. (1995). Gender differences in felony court processing: Three hypotheses of disparity. *Women and Criminal Justice, 6,* 23–44.

Fletcher, B. R., Shaver, L. D., and Moon, D. (1993). *Women prisoners: A forgotten population.* Westport, CT: Praeger.

Grana, S. (2002). *Women and (in)justice.* Boston: Allyn and Bacon.

Greenfield, L. A., and Snell, T. L. (1999). *Women offenders.* Washington, DC: U.S. Department of Justice, Bureau of Justice Statistics.

Harlow, C. W. (1999). *Prior abuse reported by inmates and probationers.* Washington, DC: U.S. Department of Justice, Bureau of Justice Statistics.

Henderson, D., Schaeffer, J., and Brown, L. (1998). Gender-appropriate mental health services for incarcerated women: Issues and challenges. *Family Community Health, 21* (3), 42–53.

Human Rights Watch. (2001). *No escape: Male rape in U.S. prisons.* New York: Author.

Jacobs, A. (2001, Spring). Give em a fighting chance: Women offenders re-enter society. *Criminal Justice Magazine, 45, http://www.abanet.org/crimjust/cjmag/16-1/toc.html.*

Kurshan, N. (2000). *Women and imprisonment in the U.S.: History and current reality.* Retrieved April 15, 2004 from *http://prisonactivist.org/women/women-and-imprisonment.html.*

Maeve, M.. K. (1999). Adjudicated health: Incarcerated women and the social construction of health. *Crime, Law, and Social Change, 31,* 49–71.

Marquart, J. W., Merianos, D. E., Hebert, J. L., and Carroll, L. (1997). Health condition and prisoners: A review of research and emerging areas of inquiry. *Prison Journal, 7,* 184–208.

Maruschak, L. (1997). *HIV in prisons.* Washington, DC: U.S. Department of Justice, Bureau of Justice Statistics.

Maruschak, L., and Beck, A. (1997). *Medical problems of inmates.* Washington, DC: U.S. Department of Justice, Bureau of Justice Statistics.

Mauer, M. (1999). *Race to incarcerate.* New York: New Press.

Mauer, M., Potler, C., and Wolf, R. (1999). *Gender and justice: Women, drugs, and sentencing policy.* Washington, DC: Sentencing Project.

National Institute on Corrections (NIC). (1998). *Current issues in the operation of women's prisons.* Longview, CO: Author.

Owen, B. (1998). *In the mix: Struggle and survival in women's prison.* Albany: State University of New York Press.

Pollock-Byrne, J. M. (1990). *Women, prison, and crime.* Pacific Grove, CA: Brooks/Cole.

Rafter, N. H. (1985). *Partial justice: Women in state prisons 1800–1935.* Boston: University Press of New England.

——. (1989). Gender and justice: Three equal protection issues. In L. Goodstein and D. MacKenzie (Eds.), *The American prison* (pp. 89–109). New York: Plenum Press.

Resnick, J., and Shaw, N. (1981). *Prison Law Monitor,* 3 (3/4), 57, 68, 83, 89, 104, 115.

Richie, B. E. (2000). Exploring the link between violence against women and women's involvement in illegal activity. *Research on Women and Girls in the Criminal Justice System,* 3, 1–14.

——. (2001). Issues incarcerated women face as they return to their communities: Findings from life history interviews. *Crime and Delinquency,* 47, 368–389.

Spohn, C. (1999). Gender and sentencing drug offenders: Is chivalry dead? *Criminal Justice Policy Review,* 9, 365–399.

Todaro v. Ward (1977).

Van Wormer, K. S., and Bartollas, C. (2000). *Women and the criminal justice system.* Boston: Allyn and Bacon.

Women's Prison Association (WPA). (2003). *WPA focus on women and justice.* Retrieved April 14, 2004 from Women's Prison Association, New York: *www.wpaonline.com.*

Young, D. (1998). Health status and service use among incarcerated women. *Family Community Health,* 21, 16–31. ◆

15

Workplace Problems in Police Departments and Methods of Coping

Women at the Intersection

Merry Morash
Robin N. Haarr
Dian P. Gonyea

In this chapter you will learn the following:

- The history of women in policing and how legislation passed since the 1970s has made female officers eligible to hold the same types of positions and do the same types of work as men

- Police departments in the United States have not been successful in recruiting anything close to 50 percent of female officers, and women who do work in policing may face difficulties with stereotyping, harassment, and exclusion based on gender in combination with ethnicity, race, and other attributes

- Hiring practices, especially in departments with few or no women or minorities, often reproduce a low female-to-male ratio among employees

- The environment of police departments has improved for most groups of police officers over time, but African-American and Hispanic women continue to experience high levels of negative reaction, and police departments are still not as supportive for women in all groups as they are for male employees

- European-American males still are the most likely to feel that police organizations are welcoming and supportive places for them to work, and until more profound changes occur in the workplace for other groups, recruiting and retention cannot succeed in producing a more diverse police force

This chapter focuses on the experiences of women who work as police officers in contemporary U.S. police organizations. Information on the history of women's work in police departments provides the backdrop against which to assess their contemporary experiences. The section on history is followed by a description of the results of an original analysis of data from two sources: (1) a longitudinal survey of gender-related changes between 1990 and 2003 in problems that officers experience in police agencies, in stress, and in approaches that police officers use to address their workplace problems, and (2) in-depth interviews with police women to explore the way that European-American, African-American, Hispanic, and Asian-American women in the police organization perceive and manage workplace problems and stressors. Because women's and men's race and ethnicity affect gender differences, both pieces of original research paid close attention to the intersection of race, ethnicity, and gender as they influence working in a police department. In other words, care was taken not to assume that all women had the same experiences at work. Instead, these sources explored whether women's workplace experiences and activities depended on whether or not they were members of a racial or ethnic minority group. The chapter ends with a consideration of the current status of women in policing and their potential contributions to policing.

History of Women in Policing

Women's role in policing has changed dramatically since the 1880s, when they served as police matrons caring for women and children. At the time, many people believed that women possessed a moral superiority to men and an inherent feminine ability to be sensitive and nurturing. This view of women allowed some of them to act as citywide mothers, disciplining females and children with immoral lifestyles. Lacking the right to vote and having little work experience outside of the home, in the period of 1880 to 1910, primarily socially prominent and politically connected upper-middle-class women born in the United States created the position of police matrons for themselves (Schulz 2004). Their primary purpose was to focus on the sexual purity and morality of girls and women and to eradicate prostitution and to control venereal diseases. The earliest female police officers served as both social controllers and social workers who intervened in the lives of uneducated, poor, and immigrant women and children with the goal of saving them from a life of immorality, crime, and delinquency (Schulz 1995, 2004).

In 1910, Alice Stebbin Wells became the first person in the United States to be called a *policewoman*. Between 1910 and 1917, about 125 policewomen were employed in about 30 U.S. cities (Schulz 2004). Policewomen were typically college educated, native born, and upper middle class. They did not view themselves as female versions of policemen, and they did not consider men who worked in policing, who were usually of a lower class and less educated, as their equals. In fact, they tried to physically separate themselves from policemen and what they considered to be masculine aspects of policing, for example, by not wearing uniforms and by not carrying firearms. The policeman role was incongruous with the women's self-identification as agents of crime and delinquency prevention among women and children. Even though policewomen willingly worked on assignments that policemen did not want, policemen were re-luctant to accept them as coworkers (Schulz 2004).

African-American policewomen were present in the early twentieth century, but were clearly a racial minority within a gender minority. They were often teachers, social workers, or ministers' wives with status in their communities, and they sought out the role of policewoman to work specifically with African-American children and women (Schulz 2004). Minority racial status and gender together had powerful effects on limiting both the nature of police work and the target population for women's efforts at policing.

By 1919, at the end of World War I, the number of policewomen had doubled to about 300 individuals working in more than 200 U.S. cities (Schulz 2004). Although the women did not demand greater integration into the police environment, they did actively seek to more fully define their specialized roles. They established women's bureaus that were responsible for processing all matters pertaining to women and children. Policewomen also attempted to create a mechanism that would allow women to rise through the ranks of the women's bureaus.

By 1929, the number of policewomen had grown to about 600, and women worked in at least 150 cities (Schulz 2004). In the 1930s, however, many of the numerical and bureaucratic gains that policewomen made were eradicated as a result of the Depression, which limited funds to hire policewomen, and the emergence of the FBI, which strengthened the ideology that police are masculine crime fighters. The crime-fighter image was inconsistent with the social work role that policewomen had created for themselves. By 1940, there were no more than 500 policewomen, most of whom did very specialized work in the largest U.S. cities (Schulz 2004).

During World War II, there was a renewed focus on morality and delinquency, and policewomen were hired in increasing numbers to perform the traditional policewoman's job. Women began to have expanded assignments and responsibilities (Schulz 1995, 2004). They were teamed with male officers on undercover assignments and began investigating crimes that were not morality-based. They were also issued special uniforms and expected to carry a gun, usually in their handbags. In 1950, there were more than 2,500 policewomen, slightly more than 1 percent of all police officers (Schulz 2004). The post-World War II period and the decade of the 1950s were very important to policewomen's history, in part because unlike their predecessors, the women attracted to the work were middle-class careerists with goals of upward mobility through civil service.

In 1968, the Indianapolis Police Department assigned two policewomen, Betty Blankenship and Elizabeth Coffal, to patrol. They were the first policewomen to wear a patrol officer's uniform, strap a gun belt to their waists, drive a marked patrol car, and answer general police calls for service on an equal basis with policemen (Schulz 2004). In 1972, The U.S. Congress enacted the Equal Employment Opportunity Act (EEOA), which extended the provisions of the Civil Rights Act to state and local governments, including police departments. Aided by federal legislation and the courts, female police officers demanded greater equality and promotional opportunities in U.S. police departments. Women who entered policing throughout the 1970s were no longer similar to social workers. In contrast, they were female police officers who entered the profession self-identified as crime fighters focused on enforcing laws, maintaining order, and providing public safety as did their male coworkers (Schulz 1995, 2004).

Number of Women Employed as Police Officers

Despite the EEOA and departments' special initiatives to increase the recruitment and hiring of females and racial and ethnic minorities, the number of female and racial/ethnic minority full-time sworn personnel in police departments has remained low. In 1986, women constituted only 8.8 percent

of police officers in cities greater than 50,000 (Martin 1990). In 2000, females were only 16.3 percent of full-time sworn personnel serving populations of 250,000; blacks made up 20.1 percent of all police officers, Hispanics were 14.1 percent, 2.8 percent were Asian/Pacific Islander, and 0.4 percent were Native American (Reaves and Hickman 2002). It is difficult to determine the number of women in specialized units and ranks above police officer because the few surveys of upward mobility use the term *command ranks*, a phrase that in police departments of 25 or fewer officers might mean sergeants or lieutenants, whereas in departments of 1,000 or more officers it might mean assistants or deputy chiefs. In 2000, there were 175 women police chiefs, a high proportion of whom were on forces that served colleges, universities, or small communities (Schulz 2004). Policewomen, particularly those who are racial and ethnic minorities, remain a very small proportion of all officers, and women are poorly represented in the highest levels of leadership in large departments. The segregation of policewomen into leadership positions primarily within small and college communities and the low proportion of women who work as police in any setting is reflective of a broader trend in the United States, which is a long-standing and continuing mix of employees characterized by a majority of each sex working in an occupation in which the other sex is underrepresented or absent (Reskin 1993, 247).

Gender and Workplace Problems

Women's acceptance into police work by male peers has historically been marginal. Policing, like other male sex-typed occupations, provides a social context that is typically uncomfortable for women. Women in this arena are often viewed as deviants and tokens (Morash and Haarr 1995, 113; see also, Feinman 1986; Remmington 1983). At the extreme, women's involvement in policing and patrol work has been met with organized and hostile resistance. In some departments, men who believe that women are inferior and less capable of performing their duties have ostracized their female counterparts and formed brotherly alliances. For example, Men Against Women, a Los Angeles Police Department clandestine subculture that has existed since the mid-1980s has the goal of driving women from the police force (Spillar and Harrington 1997).

Different theories attempt to explain the resentment toward women and minorities in the workplace. The theory of gendered organizations (Acker 1990, 1992) contradicts a common assumption that organizations are gender-neutral and jobs are an abstract concept, waiting to be filled by disembodied workers who are there only for the job. In contrast, gendered organizations are characterized by distinctions between masculine and feminine, males and females, and these distinctions are connected to patterns of disadvantage and advantage, control and exploitation, and the wage differential for men and women in the workplace. The gendered organization is typically characterized by male dominance and female submission, both of which are reflected in language, ideology, and workplace subcultures.

Tokenism is the focus of the alternative explanation that a woman in a male-dominated field, or a minority in an otherwise homogeneous occupation, has unique problems in interactions with peers and superiors (Kanter 1977). For example, tokens are more visible than other workers, and thus are open to more observation and potential criticism, and it is more difficult for them to be assimilated into work groups and work subcultures. However, a recent study of female officers in Texas found tokenism theory to be unsupported (Greene and del Carmen 2002). The researchers compared females who worked in one of 16 departments, in which females were less than 13 percent of the officers with female who worked in one of 13 police agencies where their female population was at least 13 percent. The two groups of

women did not report a difference in their perceptions of acceptance or treatment, and the officers' perceptions of male and female colleagues were not different. Greene and del Carmen (2002) suggested that the type of occupation, rather than gender, explained the perception of stress-related issues among female officers. However, these findings can also be criticized, since "13 percent and over" may not reflect a departure from tokenism. The authors' conclusions would be more compelling if they compared departments having closer to 50 percent female representation with those having much smaller percentages of females.

Stereotypes of females also create difficult if not hostile working conditions. For example, women who display stereotypically female attributes may not be respected and may be criticized for being unsuitable for the job. Likewise, women who act in a way that is viewed as "too masculine" are criticized for not acting like a woman (Garcia 2003). It also should be noted that in some police settings, men who focus on areas such as community-oriented policing or the investigation of crimes against children may be viewed as carrying out work that is inconsistent with idealized versions of masculinity that emphasize the use of force and the overt exercise of authority. For women (and for men), trying to define oneself according to other people's gender ideologies, which are their beliefs about gender differences, can result in occupational stress and frustration. That is, high stress is associated with job burnout (Gaines and Jermier 1983; Maslach and Jackson 1984; Territo and Vetter 1981), job dissatisfaction and absenteeism (Kearns 1986; Wright and Saylor 1991).

Much research has indicated that policewomen do experience unique workplace stressors, including sex discrimination, language harassment, lack of role models and mentors, and the demands of emotional work to respond to these difficulties (Haarr and Morash 1999; Martin 1980; Martin and Jurik 1996). At the point of recruitment, historically women have been disproportionately screened out by the physical requirements (Morash and Greene 1986). Strategies such as relying on ex-military personnel and concentrating recruitment efforts at male-oriented sporting events and military bases further reduced the chance of attracting females to the police force, at the same time that they perpetuated the male stereotype (Gold 2000). Tests to screen for qualified applicants, including throwing medicine balls and bench pressing one's own weight, disproportionately disqualified women (Horne 1999). For instance, an employer's arrangement of potential employees into "gender queues" (i.e., with one gender group preferred and another gender group seen as less than ideal,) has been documented for a large number of occupations that hire disproportionately large numbers of males (Reskin and Roos 1990).

Police hiring policies are greatly influenced by the current gender composition of a department (Sass and Troyer 1999). Male-dominated departments are more likely to employ physical fitness tests that impede women's entry into the force. This practice reinforces a cycle of populating male-dominated departments with new male recruits. Departments vary greatly in their recruiting approaches, and some approaches are more successful at bringing women into police work, but overall, little progress has been made in recruiting women in a proportion even close to their representation in the population.

Once a woman is employed as a police officer, it is more the exception than the norm that she is accepted as an equal. In many settings, there is a so-called macho work culture that is dominated by crude jokes, personal attitudes, and a demand that women assume male characteristics to be accepted (Martin and Jurik 1996). It is not uncommon for male police officers to describe their female counterparts as "bitchy" or as lesbians (Gold 2000). Women are seen as having interpersonal skills but as mentally weaker, disadvantaged because of their femininity, and unable to command public respect. Covert and overt male resistance is related to the nature of policing and its occupational culture, and it impedes

women's progress in policing by limiting their advancement opportunities.

Further problems encountered by women in policing include sexual harassment and discrimination, which have resulted in numerous court cases that have cost police departments across the nation millions of dollars (Appier 1998; Horne 1999). In five large urban police departments, 63 percent of the 72 female officers reported they were sexually harassed on the job (Martin 1990). Sexual harassment encompasses more than the overt "hitting on" or unwelcome touching. It also includes language harassment in the form of offensive comments or jokes as well as viewing pornographic material and items that offend the women who are present. One woman officer said,

> I can't believe the atmosphere is still like this—I'm talking to a coworker in Homicide and he pulls out a centerfold. Right in front of me. Doesn't bat an eye. In our station house, there are pictures pasted up all over. One is a poster of a frog with a hard-on. These are your coworkers. (Fletcher 1995, 103)

Sexual harassment also includes female officers finding dildos, vibrators, and sex magazines in their lockers, or encountering betting pools on which male officer will be the first to have sex with the new female officer (Martin 1980). Though behavior such as this is less overtly tolerated now than in the past, women officers continue to describe sexual pranks, jokes, and comments that make it clear that women are outsiders. When men sexualize the workplace, they communicate their gender superiority and undermine the practice of equality (Martin and Jurik 1996).

Gender and Strategies for Coping With Workplace Problems

Early research on police focused on men's maladaptive coping strategies, such as alcohol use and emotional dissonance (Haarr and Morash 2005), but in the 1990s, there was a shift toward understanding new strategies for coping with stress and the relationship of these strategies to gender, race, and ethnicity. In addition, because of their earlier exclusion and oppression in police work, women and minorities are now likely to be more critical of dominant norms and practices in the occupational world (Haarr and Morash 2005). As a result, their coping strategies are likely to differ from those of the dominant male European-American group.

Some women cope with adverse working conditions by leaving police work altogether. A 1990 Police Foundation study indicated that women's turnover rate in state police agencies (8.9 percent) compared with men's (2.9 percent) is nearly three times greater (Martin 1990). Women's responding to stress and other problems in the workplace by leaving police work exacerbates the problem of underrepresentation of females in policing.

Women also cope by fitting in and adopting a male attitude. However, trying to be "one of the boys" can lead to negative stereotype labels, such as *dyke* or *bitch*, that imply that women police officers are not real women (Martin and Jurik 1996). Conforming to the male world of police work can support discrimination by implying it is acceptable. Some female officers have described a code that forbids filing grievances or mourning for others, and violating the code can result in a slow "death" through ostracism (Fletcher 1995).

> There's a code. Some will tell you there isn't a code anymore. Bullshit. There is a code. It's more subtle now and it's harder to deal with when it's subtle. The code is: You don't complain and you put up with their bullshit. (Fletcher 1995, 235)

As an alternative to adapting to a negative environment, some women emphasize a team approach to police work, project a professional image, and use humor to deflect sexism; these approaches lead to acceptance by male coworkers and provide future female officers with a new role model (Martin and Jurik 1996). However, to integrate into work groups, when women cannot change sexism in the department through friendly discussion, they usually avoid challenging current practices that perpetuate the sexism (Chaiyavej 2002). For policewomen, having positive work groups may require living with negative workplace practices and interactions.

Major shortcomings of much of the policing research are evident. In general, studies have reflected the experiences of mostly Caucasian male police officers, not involved women in framing the important research question, and neglected the perceptions and experiences of female officers (e.g., Hillgren et al. 1976; Spielberger et al. 1981). Many of the early police stress studies actually excluded women, as well as racial and ethnic minority police officers, and assumed that the causes of stress are the same for all officers. This approach failed to consider distinctive types of workplace problems linked to gender, race, and ethnic minority status. Also, lesbian and bisexual police women must cope with hostility related to their sexual orientation (Miller, Forest, and Jurik 2003). Some research, however, has provided insight into the experiences of policewomen at the beginning of the twenty-first century.

Feminist theory and research focus on the oppression and inequality of people because of their gender, and feminist theorists design research that can produce results that are useful in reducing gender-related disadvantage. For example, the theories we have described—about gendered organizations, tokenism, and gender stereotypes—are feminist. Also, the amount of influence that gender can have on one's personhood and on one's location in a police agency, depends on race, social class, and other status markers. *Intersections*, an important concept in feminist theory, refers to the notion that people are not just women or men, but that they are women or men of a certain race, ethnicity, age, and so on. It is always difficult to take all relevant statuses into account in a particular research project, but it is critical to differentiate among several subgroups of people. Research on lesbian and bisexual women who work in policing, for example, suggests that they cope with hostility in the workplace through creative approaches, including reshaping their roles as police to attend to the needs of citizens who are most disenfranchised from society (Miller, Forest, and Jurik 2003). The research described in the remainder of this chapter was designed to examine the intersections of gender with race and ethnicity as they pertain to police.

Police Workplace Problems, Stress, and Coping Survey: Changes From 1990 to 2003

A survey was done in 1990 and again in 2003 to gather information on police workplace problems. Questions were based on earlier observation of policewomen in settings where they talked openly about their problems and how they coped with them. Because the survey questions for workplace problem and coping scales were developed from the observations of women, they captured the range of issues that the policewomen talked about, sought training to address, and experienced. (See Table 15.1 and Table 15.2.)

In 1990, 526 officers from 11 police departments across the United States participated in the survey on workplace problems, coping strategies, and stress (Haarr and Morash 1999; Morash and Haarr 1995). In 2003, 849 officers from the same 11 departments completed the same survey. Males were just over 72 percent of the sample in 1990 and 2003, and females were 27 percent of the sample. In addition, 69 percent of the officers were Caucasian, and racial minority officers made up at least 30 percent of the sample in both years. The samples did not represent the actual proportions of women and men, or racial minority and racial majority officers in the departments. Instead, they were designed to allow for comparison among gender and race/ethnic groups.

Between 1990 and 2003, the International Association for Women in Policing, state groups for women police officers, and the National Center for Women in Policing have worked to improve the workplace for police-

women. Members of these groups have filed lawsuits, undertaken union activities, and made other efforts at the local level (Martin and Jurik 1996). Do women now experience fewer problems? In our study, we identified significant changes in workplace problems and stress from 1990 to 2003 in just some of the gender-race/ethnic groups of officers.

Minority females did not experience a statistically significant change (i.e., a change that in all probability was not due to chance) in any of the workplace problems from 1990 to 2003. In comparison, European-American females reported lower levels of racial bias and language harassment in 2003 than they reported in 1990. Minority males reported decreases in the greatest number of workplace problems; people less often underestimated their physical abilities, officers less often thought they lacked advancement opportunities, and there was less bias, language harassment, racial/ethnic harassment, and stigma due to one's race or appearance. European-American males also reported improvements in several workplace problems, particularly problems with overestimation of their physical abilities, being treated like they were "invisible," opportunities for advancement, and bias.

To see whether changes since 1990 had left some groups more or less disadvantaged in the workplace by 2003, we compared the average levels of workplace problems and stress for four different gender-race/ethnic groups in 2003. Except for stress, minority females stood out as experiencing these workplace problems more often than did officers from the other groups. In 2003, European-American females reported the highest levels of stress, had had more problems with language harassment than did minority males, and had more problems with bias and language harassment than did European-American males. Minority females had the highest levels of sexual harassment, and European-American females reported the next highest levels of sexual harassment. As expected, European-American males reported the lowest levels of sexual harassment. Thus, minority

Table 15.1
Examples of Questions Used to Measure Different Types of Workplace Problems Experienced by Police Officers

Workplace Problems	Examples
Other people overestimate the officer's physical abilities.	It is common for people on the job to think I can do more than my physical abilities permit. I find my superiors overestimate my physical capabilities at work.
Other people underestimate the officer's physical abilities.	People at work do not realize how good my physical abilities are. My superiors underestimate my physical abilities.
Equipment and uniforms do not fit or are unavailable.	Little effort has been made to provide me with equipment suited to my body. I've had to wear uniforms or use equipment that didn't fit well.
The officer feels that advancement opportunities are more limited than for other coworkers.	I've had less chance to advance in my job than others. I haven't had as much opportunity for promotion as my coworkers.
The officer feels that she has no influence at work.	I do not have a say in how things get done in my department. I do not have the power to change how things get done.
The officer feels that she is "invisible" at work.	Coworkers and superiors forget I'm here, forget to invite me to things, or forget to introduce me. My coworkers/superiors don't look me in the eye when we talk.
Other officers ridicule and set up the officer.	Coworkers/superiors have tried to get me to take unnecessary or dangerous risks on the job. My superiors/coworkers have set me up to make mistakes on the job.
Bias and prejudice are experienced by the officer.	There is bias against people of my sex, race, age, or ethnic group. I spent time and energy dealing with prejudice and bias directed at me.
The officer reports that others use offensive language at work.	My superiors/coworkers use profane language that offends me. My superiors joke about sex to the point it bothers me.
Other officers stigmatize the officer because of her race or appearance.	My superiors/coworkers make jokes about my physical size to the point it offends me. My superiors/coworkers make unwelcome jokes or comments about how unattractive I am.
Supervisors and coworkers sexually harass the officer.	A superior/coworker has tried to force me to hug, kiss, or be physically intimate. A superior/coworker has tried to force me to have sexual intercourse physically or with threats.
Supervisors and coworkers harass the officer because of race or ethnicity.	My coworkers/superiors make offensive comments about my race of ethnic background. My superiors/coworkers make jokes about my race or ethnic background.

Table 15.2
Examples of Questions Used to Measure Different Approaches That Police Officers Use to Cope With Workplace Problems

Coping Approaches and Support	Examples
The officer seeks an escape.	During the year, I suffered in silence. During the year, I avoided superiors or coworkers.
The officer expresses his or her feelings.	I let people know how angry I was. I made it very clear how the situation affected my feelings.
The officer takes formal action.	I have taken part in a class action. I have taken legal action on my own or with a small number of other individuals.
The officer makes attempts to get others to like him or her.	In the past year, I have put forth a lot of effort to try to get my coworkers or superiors to like me.
The officer seeks camaraderie from his or her coworkers.	During the last year, I sought understanding from another woman/man or mentor. During the year, I got together with others to joke and blow off steam.
The officer keeps written records.	During the year, I kept a written record of my own actions to protect myself. I kept a written record of things that I consider offensive.
The officer changes job assignments.	I changed my job but still satisfied my career goals. I changed my job but had to sacrifice my career goals.
The officer forms racial bonds with others of similar race.	During the year, I sought understanding or help from people at my work who have a racial or ethnic bond with me.
The officer has family support.	When my job gets me down, I know I can turn to my family for support to make me feel better. My spouse or mate really understands me and makes me feel better when things at work aren't going well.
The officer has superiors' support.	I find that my superiors often encourage me to do the best job in a way that we really would be proud of. My superiors often encourage me to to think of better ways of getting the work done that may never have been thought of before.
The officer has coworkers' support.	In my most recent year, coworkers backed me up when I made mistakes that were unavoidable on the job. I find that my fellow officers often complimented me for doing a job well.

females reported the highest levels of workplace problems, and European-American females were the next most disadvantaged group. Minority females, most of whom were African American, did not enjoy the desirable reduction of workplace problems that other gender-race/ethnic groups experienced in our research.

From 1990 to 2003, there were significant changes in almost all of the gender-race/ethnic groups in their use of coping strategies. Each of the gender-race/ethnic groups more often used informal coping strategies, including escape, expressing feelings, getting others to like them, relying on coworker camaraderie, and forming bonds with other officers of the same race/ethnicity. By 2003, each group also had significantly increased its use of formal coping strategies, including taking formal action (e.g., filing a complaint), keeping written records, and changing job assignments.

Although all of the groups increased their use of both informal and formal methods of coping with workplace problems, in 2003 there were significant group differences. European-American females stood out from most other groups in their greater use of some of the informal coping strategies, such as escape, expressing feelings, getting others to like them, and reliance on coworker camaraderie. Both minority females and minority males tended to rely less on informal coping strategies and more on the formal coping strategies, such as keeping written records and taking formal action. Regardless of gender, minority officers also relied on forming bonds with coworkers along racial or ethnic group lines as a way of coping with workplace problems.

Doing Gender, Doing Race/Ethnicity, Doing Police Work

Qualitative research provided an in-depth look at how European-American, African-American, Hispanic, and Asian-American female police officers experience the intersections of gender and race/ethnicity in the police organization. In-depth interviews were conducted over a three-year period (2001 to 2003) with 25 female police officers working in two Southwest police departments. The 25 female officers included 9 European-American females, 7 African-American females, 6 Hispanic females, and 3 Asian-American females. The women had varying levels of seniority (i.e., 6 to 30 years of service) and rank (i.e., patrol officer, detective, supervisor, and administrator) and were assigned to different units and bureaus.

The interviews confirmed that policing is still heavily influenced by European-American males, and thus, female officers must confront issues of gender and race/ethnicity throughout their careers. In the training academy, female officers quickly became aware of their status as women and racial/ethnic minorities. All recalled a range of unique workplace problems and stressors connected to their status as women of different races and ethnicity. The following quotes reveal some of common problems of female officers in the training academy.

I know a lot of the women really struggled with the training academy. It seemed like they [academy staff] really pushed the women on the physical fitness portion, more than anything, because when it came to classroom work, the women do just as well as the men. But when it came to the physical part of the academy, we're not as strong, so they really put a lot of pressure on us. I was lucky, I was athletic, so I could pretty much keep up on the runs, and if they put us in a sprint, I would even beat the guys. I could also get over the wall, so I didn't get hassled as much. (Hispanic female)

There were no men in my class that made us feel that women shouldn't be cops. . . . I always did feel though, even in the academy, that sometimes male officers will do something wrong and it really doesn't get noticed. . . . But if a female would do the same, you'd hear: "Do you know what she did?" So I was always striving to not have that type of reputation; I tried to always do good and not be one of those females that everybody talked about for doing something that would cause others to say, "She's such an idiot, I can't believe she did that." (Hispanic female)

I think what's important is that you just need to know that you're female and that you're different. You're definitely not the majority. Most of our instructors were male. Our recruit-training officers were male. We did have one female recruit-training officer. Most of the training sergeants were male, and the lieutenants were male. So it was very male dominated, and it still is, but you just realize that you were watched even more. (European-American female)

Consistent with theories regarding gendered organizations and tokenism, it is clear that the interviewed women felt that their actions were scrutinized because of their gender. They realized they were in a male-dominated organization that assumed they needed to be pushed to achieve physically on the job. At least some women, however, felt camaraderie with their peers. As one woman put it, "[T]here were no men in my class that made us feel that women shouldn't be cops." This indicates that women can also feel support from their male colleagues in policing. Despite the experience of being a token, as the quantitative data showed, it is not unrealistic for women to rely on camaraderie with their peers.

Once female recruits complete basic training, they begin field training, an important stage in the process of socialization into the organization and occupation. The field-training phase presents the first real opportunity for a police recruit to experience the police officer role, engage in actual police work, and experience the environment and culture of the organization. During this phase, the majority of female officers were assigned to male field-training officers and to predominantly European-American male squads.

> I remember putting on my vest and thinking I can't breathe, I'm like oh my God I have to spend 10 hours with this thing on. I thought, I'm not gonna make it. You're just not used to all the weight, and my FTO is like putting crap in my pockets, you need to carry this, you need to carry this, you have to have this around here, and this is stuffed in your pockets. I'm thinking system overload, wait a minute, oh my God this is terrible. I really struggled with that, I mean I remember him telling me when you put your uniform on your blood pressure should go up; it's just part of the job. I'm like okay, whatever. That's what he always told me: "Yeah your blood pressure will go up because of the anxiety of going out on the street and you should always be alert." I'm like okay, whatever you say; maybe your blood pressure goes up, but not mine. I'm thinking women and men are so different. (European-American female)

Since women are typically smaller than men, and given the potential for a tight fit of a vest

around women's breasts, seemingly ordinary experiences in policing can be unique for women. Predominantly male peers and superiors will not usually be able to offer understanding to women trainees in the same way that men can offer these aids to each other.

During field training and in the patrol bureau, the majority of female officers reported experiencing a variety of sexist and racist attitudes, overt and covert hostility, and various degrees of sexual and racial discrimination and harassment from their male coworkers and supervisors. Not all female officers experienced the same degree of "status connected" workplace problems and stressors. Like the survey, the interviews showed that African-American female officers experienced the most problems:

> I went to a patrol squad of men, all men, and I was the only African-American—period. So there I was faced with both my race and gender. I'm not really sure what my coworkers perceptions were, in my early 20s, I'm not sure how much I was really perceptive in terms of my environment. There wasn't anything that was outwardly notable. With the exception of one person who seemed to have a problem with me. He was on my squad and would not communicate with me, and I had to ride with him when both of my primary trainers were off. I dreaded those days, and I didn't have enough time in service to take off. The reason I dreaded those days is because he wouldn't communicate with me and I had to ask all the questions. Like where are we going to have lunch? And he would say things like "Didn't you bring your lunch?" And I would say, "No, I didn't bring my lunch." Then, he would not even make provisions to stop for me, so that I could get lunch. There was no talk in the car and I was really uncomfortable. (African-American female)

The quote provides an illustration of what it is like to be treated as if one were "invisible." It further indicates a problem beyond being not noticed—having one's most basic needs noted and then not met.

Early in their careers, most policewomen quickly recognized that there is an unspoken norm. They repeatedly needed to prove to their male coworkers and supervisors that they were competent and capable police officers.

> You have to work twice as hard, to get half the credit as a female on the police department. You do, and it doesn't matter what rank you are, it doesn't matter what position you are, you will always be judged as a female on the department. You will be measured up to men and you better perform twice as good, to get half the credit. (Hispanic female)

> When I was pregnant, I worked on patrol for 5 months because I was trying to prove a point. I didn't have to do that, but I was like, I'm gonna show you guys I can work this way. I did things that now I look back and say, "Why did I do that? Nobody cares." But you do that stuff to prove you're capable. (Hispanic female)

The usual increases in power that come with promotion were not felt by women in policing, because they were being judged as questionably competent women, and not assessed based on just their experience.

Female officers used a variety of coping strategies to deal with and manage unique "status connected" workplace problems and stressors, including escapism and avoidance, confronting the individual, taking formal action or filing a formal complaint, reporting the situation to a supervisor, exercise, changing job assignments, and seeking support and mentorship from other female officers and/or officers of the same race or ethnicity.

> It definitely angers men. You go, "[T]his isn't fair, I'm a good officer, I can do just as much if not more than some of the men in this department." I know a lot of females in this department and in other departments that can do the job a lot better than some of the men, and will stay in there toe-to-toe in a fight. Does anybody give a guy a hard time

if he doesn't go toe-to-toe in a fight? No, because it's a male. But if it was a female, they would. So it can make you angry, it's tough sometimes. I learn how to bite my tongue. I manage my anger by just sitting there. I don't have a choice. I could sit there and get into an argument with another officer, but half the time it's just because they're naive or close-minded. Some of the younger officers don't have that perception, which is a good thing. When I started 15 years ago it was different. When I talk to a couple of my friends that have 20 years on, they say "I was the only female in the academy. I was the only female in my squad or working this particular shift, and the guys were making all the gender comments, they picked on you on purpose, and they put you in a position to see you fail. They actually hoped you would fail." (Hispanic female)

Female officers' strategies of coping tended to change over time. One officer described the change:

> I know that in my 20s I wasn't as forthright as I am now. I was very young and naïve, and much more cautious and more quiet. I think that the closer you get to 40, the more vocal you become and the more you just don't care too much when it comes to what other people think, so you pretty much speak your piece. (African-American female)

The interview data showed that women often shifted from more passive, escape and avoidance strategies to more direct strategies of taking formal action, reporting the situation to a supervisor, and seeking support from other female officers and/or officers of the same race or ethnicity.

Having mentors in the workplace was very important to helping some female police officers cope effectively with workplace problems. Most women were able to identify one or more mentors; however, several maintained they did not have any mentors. European-American, Hispanic, and Asian females had European-American males as their mentors, while African-American females had other African-American females as their mentors. Mentors encouraged women to advance in their careers via pursuing higher education, specialized assignments, and promotions. On many occasions, particularly among African-American female officers, mentors would assist women in preparing for promotional exams and interviews. Women who were promoted up the ranks to administration often talked about the important role that their mentors played.

While it is often difficult for female officers to "fit in" to police work because of their inability to identify with the dominant gender of the police organization, and doubly difficult for female officers of color to "fit in" because of their inability to identify with either the dominant gender and race/ethnicity of the police organization, female officers do not regret their decision to enter into police work. All of the women took pride in their policing career and accomplishments and advancement within the organization.

Conclusions

Contemporary police departments have broken with the past by providing the same job descriptions for women and for men. However, a number of common practices persist that ensure continued gender disadvantage, particularly for minority women. These practices are reflected in recruiting and training policies and programs. Less obvious and unofficial patterns of action also reproduce gender and minority group disadvantage when police are trained and when they are working in departments. Although workplace problems seem to be reduced for officers as a whole, this is not the case for African-American women. European-American males still are the most likely to feel that police organizations are welcoming and supportive places for them to work. Until there are more profound changes in the workplace for other groups, recruiting and retention cannot succeed in producing a more diverse police force.

Several of the workplace problems that we have identified as high for women predict stress, and certainly having to deal with harassment and myriad other difficulties at work takes away time from other valuable activities. Departments would increase their capabilities by reducing these problems. Police officers who use informal methods of coping face a dilemma. Do they risk more rejection by superiors or peers by taking formal actions, or should they use informal methods to try to "fit in"? Minority males most often use formal methods, and they did achieve reduced levels of workplace problems. Our data cannot show whether the harassment and other negative reactions that minority policewomen face have not been overcome simply because prejudices and sexism are intractable, or whether either more or less formal coping approaches would improve the situation. The data do show that the gendered organization is very much a reality in policing, and women and racial/ethnic minorities are very much tokens in some departments. Police departments need to attend to workplace problems of women, and women need to consider using a variety of strategies to better their situations.

Study/Discussion Questions

1. In what way has the job of policing and the status of women in policing changed over the years for women?

2. What are some alternative explanations of African-American women's continuing high levels of workplace problems, while for other groups these problems seem to have lessened?

3. Discuss the pros and cons for policewomen who try to fit in with a sexist organizational environment.

4. What recommendations would you give to police in different racial and gender groups about how to minimize problems at work and how to maximize the contributions of all police officers at work?

References

Acker, J. (1990) Hierarchies, jobs, babies: A theory of gendered organizations. *Gender & Society*, 4, 139–158.

Acker, J. (1992). Gendering organizational theory. In A. J. Mills and P. Tancred (Eds.), *Gendering organizational analysis* (pp. 248–260). Newbury Park, CA: Sage.

Appier, J. (1998). *Policing women: The sexual politics of policing in the LAPD*. Philadelphia: Temple University Press.

Chaiyavej, S. (2002). *Responses to sexual harassment by Thai and U.S. women police officers*. Unpublished doctoral dissertation, Michigan State University, East Lansing, MI.

Fletcher, C. (1995). *Breaking & entering: women cops talk about life in the ultimate men's club*. New York, NY: HarperCollins.

Gaines, J., and Jermier, J. M. (1983). Emotional exhaustion in a high stress organization. *Academy of Management Journal*, 26, 567–586.

Garcia, V. (2003, August). Difference in the police department: Women, policing, and "doing gender." *Journal of Contemporary Criminal Justice*, 19(3), 330–344.

Gold, M. (2000). The progress of women in policing. *Law & Order*, 48(6), 159–161.

Greene, H. T., and del Carmen, A. (2002). Female police officers in Texas: Perceptions of colleagues and stress. *Policing*, 25, 385–398.

Haarr, R. N., and M. Morash (1999). Gender, race, and strategies of coping with occupational stress in policing. *Justice Quarterly*, 16, 304–336.

——. (2005). Police coping with stress: The importance of emotions, gender, and minority status. In K. Copes (Ed.), *Policing and Stress* (pp. 158–177). New Jersey: Pearson.

Hillgren, J. S., Bond, R., and Jones, S. (1976). Primary stressors in police administration and law enforcement. *Journal of Police Sciences and Administration*, 4(4), 445–449.

Horne, P. (1999). Equality in policing. *Law & Order*, 47 (11), 52–61.

Jones, L. (2003). Matrons to chiefs in one short century: The transition of women in U.S. law enforcement. *Women Police*, 37 (2).

Kanter, R. M. (1977). *Men and women in the corporation*. New York: Basic Books.

Kearns, J. (1986). *Stress at work: The challenge of change*. Englewood Cliffs, NJ: Prentice Hall.

Martin, S. (1980). *Breaking and entering: Policewoman on patrol*. Berkeley: University of California Press.

——. (1990). *On the move: The status of women in policing*. Washington, DC: Police Foundation.

Martin, S., and Jurik, N. (1996). *Doing justice, doing gender*. Thousand Oaks, CA: Sage.

Maslach, C., and Jackson, S. (1984). Burnout in organizational settings. *Applied Social Psychology Annual* 5, 99–113.

Miller, S. L., Forest, K. B., and Jurik, N. C. (2003). Diversity in blue: Lesbian and gay police officers in a masculine occupation. *Men and Masculinities*, 5, 355–385.

Morash, M., and Greene, J. R. (1986). Women on patrol: A critique of conventional wisdom. *Evaluation Review*, 10, 230–255.

Morash, M., and Haarr, R. N. (1995). Gender, workplace problems, and stress in policing. *Justice Quarterly*, 12(1), 113–140.

Prussel, D. (2001). Women where? *Law & Order*, 49 (3), 87.

Reaves, B. A., and Hickman, M. J. (2002). *Police Departments in Large Cities, 1990–2000*. Washington, DC: Bureau of Justice Statistics.

Reskin, B. (1993). Sex segregation in the workplace. *Annual Review of Sociology*, 19, 241–270.

Reskin, B., and Roos, P. (1990). *Job queues, gender queues: Explaining women's inroads into male occupations*. Philadelphia: Temple University Press.

Sass, T., and Troyer, J. (1999). Affirmative Action, political representation, unions, and female police employment. *Journal of Labor Research*, 20, 571–587.

Schulz, D. M. (1995). *From social worker to crimefighter: Women in U.S. policing*. Wesport, CT: Praeger.

——. (2004). Invisible no more: A social history of women in U.S. policing. In B. R. Price and N. J. Sokolof (Eds.), The criminal justice system and women: Offenders, prisoners, victims, and workers (3rd edition), (pp. 483–492). New York: McGraw-Hill.

Spillar, K., and Harrington, P. (1997) National Center for Women and Policing. The verdict on male bias: Guilty. *Los Angeles Times*. Retrieved October 9, 2003 at: *http://www.womenandpolicing. org/oped051697.asp*.

Territo, L. (June, 1981). Stress and police personnel. *Journal of Police Science and Administration*, 9(2), 195–208.

U.S. Department of Commerce, Bureau of the Census. (2004). Retrieved December 7, 2005 at: *http://factfinder.census.gov*.

Wright, K. N., and Saylor, W. G. (1991). Male and female employees' perceptions of prison work: Is there a difference? *Justice Quarterly*, 8(4), 505–524. ✦

16
Women Criminal Lawyers

Cynthia Siemsen

In this chapter you will learn the following:

- Women lawyers' historical connections to the feminist movements of the 1860s and 1960s

- What Kanter's redistributive hypothesis is as well as several gendered choice theories—human capital theory, cultural feminism, and gender socialization—and how they relate to types of legal practice

- The hierarchical organization of law: How law is segregated by gender and race, ghettoization in the least desirable areas of law, and structural barriers and status inequalities embedded in law's organizational practices.

- The masculine milieu of law and the nature of gender displays in the courtroom

- Women's roles as criminal lawyers within the larger goals of feminism

Introduction

More than 20 years have passed since Cynthia Fuchs Epstein first published her landmark book, *Women in Law*, a work that began in the early 1960s as a study in social deviance (Epstein 1993). Epstein made it clear that women lawyers were not deviant in the pejorative sense of the word; rather, as a sociological category, they deviated from the career norm for women. For example, Epstein told readers that Harvard Law School admitted its first women law students only in 1950.

Despite the vast work dedicated to the study of women lawyers since Epstein published *Women in Law*, there still remains a hole in the literature: The coherent story has yet to be written of the women who practice law in the criminal justice system as private attorneys, public prosecutors, legal aid lawyers, and public defenders. My purpose in this chapter is to bring together what we know about these women within the larger context of the hierarchical and gendered organization of law. I begin with a discussion of women's historical inroads into the legal profession—those intricately linked to the women's movements of the 1860s and 1960s. Then I examine the gendered segregation of law, structural barriers and status inequalities embedded in law's organizational practices, and the women who practice in the masculine milieu of law. Finally, I situate women's roles as criminal lawyers within the larger goals of feminism.

Women's Historical Inroads Into Law

No doubt women have made vast advances into the legal profession. Much has been written about the early tribulations (and trials) of women that challenged American courts in the latter part of the nineteenth century for admission of women to practice law. The 1870s and 1880s were the same historical moment that members of the women's suffrage movement demanded their right to full citizenship and political participation under the Fourteenth Amendment of 1868. Congress, that exclusively white male body, indeed decided that would-be women attorneys had rights, but that they were different than men's, and certainly different than those of the 40,000 plus male lawyers of the day (Drachman 1998). For women, in general, this meant decades of court battles for inclusion into the American polity through the vote; for women wishing to practice law this meant decades of court challenges for admission to the bar.

Thus, the stories of women lawyers who often referred to themselves as "sisters-in-law" (Drachman 1998) cannot be separated from larger historical social fights for equality and justice. The first American woman was admitted to practice law in 1869. Arabella A. Mansfield convinced a local Iowan judge that under the state constitution's gender pronoun statute, women were subsumed under the word "he" in attorney licenses. Within 11 years, 75 women were practicing law in a field of 64,137 (Drachman 1998). These included the first African-American woman admitted to the bar in 1872, Charlotte E. Ray, daughter of leaders in New York's underground railroad. She applied and was accepted to Howard University Law School under the name C. E. Ray to disguise her gender. The last court challenge on the basis of gender in 1923 came roughly three years after the passage of the Nineteenth Amendment granting women the right to vote, in the same year that the National Women's Party first advocated the enactment of an Equal Rights Amendment. By the 1920s, the number of women lawyers had grown to 1,738 compared with 120,781 men lawyers, or 1.4 percent; even the male-dominated field of medicine had 5 percent women practitioners at that time (Drachman 1998). In Canada, where a good amount of work about women lawyers has been done, women made up only 1 percent of all lawyers in 1931 (Brockman 2001; Hagan and Kay 1995).

Fast forward 40 years to feminists' next historical push for equality—the 1960s. The percentage of U.S. women practicing law in the '60s had slightly increased to somewhere between 3.5 and 4 percent of the profession (Epstein 1993), still less than the 5 percent of women medical doctors in the United States in 1920. These percentages mirror roughly the 3.8 percent of women in law school in 1963. According to Epstein (1993), the law itself with the passage of the Civil Rights Act, which restricted discrimination on the basis of sex in education, "became a mechanism

for change as it was implemented by the concerted action of women's movement activists, by feminist lawyers, and by the acceptance of legal methods as effective tools for winning women's entry into the male-dominated establishment" (p. 5). Legal practice "as an instrument of social change" began to attract growing numbers of college students (Abel 1988). By 1970, approximately 4.8 percent of practicing U.S. attorneys were women; a year later, 5 percent of Canada's practicing attorneys were women. The percentage of women law students in the United States in the '70s grew to 8.5 percent, and in another 10 years over one-third of all law students were women.

The growing movement of women into legal practice in the 1960s and 1970s corresponds closely to a striking increase in legal aid societies and governmental public defender offices. U.S. Supreme Court Justice Earl Warren ruled in 1963 that poor defendants facing felony charges were entitled to defense counsel at the government's expense. In 1971, the Supreme Court expanded the right to legal representation to all poor persons facing prison. Public defender offices, which had numbered only five in 1917, grew to 163 in 1973 (Abel 1988).

Women's Lack of Advancement in the Legal Profession

The Gendered and Raced Segregation of Law

Sociological theory has it that women working in traditionally masculine professions will be concentrated in the lower-ranking areas of specialization (Epstein 1993; McBrier 2003). The prestige hierarchy of law runs on two axes (see Table 16.1): type of firm and type of practice. Regarding the first axis, lawyers in the large elite law firms have the greatest status, small government and legal aid lawyers have the least. Partners and associates in large corporate law firms occupy the top position in this hierarchy; while corporate counsel, small-firm lawyers, and solo practitioners rest near the middle; and government, legal aid, and public-interest lawyers are relegated to the bottom of the heap (Abel 1988; Hagan and Kay 1995; Hull and Nelson 2000; McBrier, 2003).

The second axis corresponds to the moral division of labor—that is, the type of practice the attorney performs. Hughes' (1971) concept of "dirty work" is instructive here. Within occupational hierarchies, those at the bottom perform "the dirty work of society . . . acting as agents for the rest of us" (p. 93). Work tasks vary not only along lines of "knowledge and skill required, but [also] in the social relations and social roles involved" (Hughes 1971, 402). The closer one works with society's downtrodden, the more one is contaminated. In the legal world, there are those lawyers directly tainted by their close proximity to social problems associated with the criminal defendant (Abel 1988). The profession ranks criminal courtroom law as the lowest form of litigation (Epstein 1993). Lawyers who perform legal office work are ranked higher than trial attorneys in general (Abel 1988).

All indicators place the majority of women lawyers in the negative, lower left quadrant of Table 16.1. Litigators are predominantly male (Epstein 1993; Pierce 1995), although the trend of women into criminal litigation was recognized as early as 1967. That year, a U.S. national sample of women lawyers found that 45.6 percent were trial attorneys, and 27.7 percent handled criminal cases. By the 1970s and early 1980s, "women were more likely than men to work in legal aid, public defender jobs, or other government positions, while men were more likely than women to be in private practice, including positions as associates and partners in large law firms and solo practices" (McBrier 2003, 1214). Generally, the trend holds that one-quarter of the men entering legal practice in the United States will secure first positions in government or public service, compared with one-third of the women. Women remain significantly more likely than men to begin their legal careers in government, legal aid, and legal education, even "when controlling for years out of law school, prestige of law school, class rank in law school, a later start in law, race/ethnicity, and father's occupation" (Hull and Nelson 2000, 241). Likewise, minorities are more apt to take jobs in government and public interest than are nonminorities, especially in prosecution positions (National Association for Law Placement [NALP] 2002). While some might argue that first jobs in government are the individual woman's or person of color's "choice" (as is subsequently discussed in this chapter), the intersection of gender and race is instructive. In a study of African-American women lawyers practicing in New York state, Simpson (1996) found that only 27 percent of the 42 percent recent black women law-school graduates who wished to begin their careers in law firms actually landed those first jobs; in contrast, 44 percent of the same pool of black women law-school graduates accepted their first legal jobs in government, despite the fact that only 21 percent desired those positions. As Simpson found, the career choices of African-American women lawyers were affected negatively by the interaction of gender and race.

By the year 2002, 25.4 percent of men entering the U.S. legal profession found employment in government and public interest law and in judicial clerkships; the corresponding percentage for women was 30.1 (NALP 2002). That same year, women made up 49 percent of all first year enrollments in law schools, and in 2003 they comprised 29.1 percent of all lawyers practicing in the United States (American Bar Association [ABA] 2004). Sheer numbers tell us that women lawyers in the United States are making great headway into the profession.

Redistributive hypothesis. Rosabeth Moss Kanter (1977) predicted more than 25 years ago that the increase in relative numbers of women and persons of color in predominantly white male professions would challenge the workplace and reorganize its distribution of awards. Sure, Kanter argued,

Figure 16.1
Prestige Hierarchy of Law

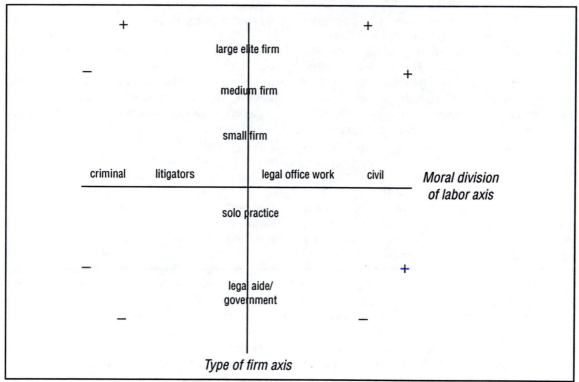

there would be "tokens" at the top of the organizational hierarchy, but apart from those highly visible few, women and other minorities would be structurally placed in crowded, low-end, dead-end jobs. However, the disadvantages that the outsiders to the white masculine organization experienced due to their comparative rarity—such as segregation, increased performance pressures, and barriers to advancement—would somehow be alleviated, especially for the visible few at the top, as their relative numbers increased. This argument has been termed the *redistributive hypothesis* (Chambliss and Uggen 2000, 43).

In their study of elite law firms, Chambliss and Uggen (2000) found that increases in the numbers of women and minorities at the top of the legal hierarchy (i.e., as partners of large law firms) did indeed increase their representation as associates. However, for as accurate as the redistributive hypothesis is

in predicting the enhanced opportunities for women and minorities who make it to the top echelons of the profession, the fact remains that the majority of women in the legal profession are occupationally segregated in legal aid, public defender, and government positions. This is also the case for minorities, especially minority women. The 1993 "class" of new lawyers entering government and public interest law was as follows: 27.1 percent multicultural women; 23.2 percent multicultural men; 15.2 percent white women; 12.6 percent white men (ABA 1994). A case in point is prosecutorial positions. Census data from 1990 reveal that 7.5 percent of all attorneys were minorities; 2.9 percent were women of color. However, in 1991, 15 percent of all new prosecutors were minorities and 8.2 percent of those were women of color (NALP 2001). And, as Miller, Maier, and Meloy show in the following chapter in this volume, many women lawyers and judges are likewise segregated in family courts, dealing with issues of divorce, alimony, child custody and support, and domestic violence. The question remains, Why? Researchers have set forth a wide range of explanations from choice theories to theories of constraint. They, however, have yet to ask how the redistributive hypothesis might be inverted to examine the change potential emerging from the many women working in legal aid, public defender and government positions.

Gendered choice. The underlying assumption for gender choice theories when applied to the legal profession is that women lawyers make conscious choices to enter government work or public interest law. Law placement officers in the 1960s directed new graduates to government practice for ideological and practical reasons (Epstein 1993). For the individual woman, civil service would be a terrain committed "to merit as the criteria for job selection rather than the irrelevant characteristics of national origin, race, or sex" (Epstein 1993, 113). For women as a category, the supposed meritocracy of government resonates with feminist ideals, professing the grander notions of equality. Government work was also said to be more secure and demanded fewer hours (Hull and Nelson 2000), although more than a normal work week was required in the more intriguing government work (Epstein 1993). (Imagination suggests Epstein was referring to the long hours associated with criminal law in the public setting.) Women would also choose government work because of the gendered expectation of performing "good works." "One reason offered by lawyers of both sexes is that if women are to be in a male occupation, they should do something womanly within it: namely, help people" (Epstein 1993, 120).

Three theories fall under the larger umbrella of gendered choice: human-capital theory, cultural feminism, and gender socialization.

Human capital refers to the literal skills and qualities individuals acquire through invest-

ments into themselves, such as acquiring a legal education, which can then be translated into earnings in the marketplace. Human-capital theorists imply that women's professional inequality begins with the women themselves, as would its solution (Hagan and Kay 1995). In other words, if women lawyers were willing to put in the same effort as men lawyers, they might reap similar rewards.

Recent studies of women professionals have linked human-capital theory with Bourdieu's (1977) theory of cultural capital, which exposes the class and gendered discriminatory processes of social reproduction (Acker 1990; Hagan and Kay 1995; Kay and Hagan 1998; Sommerlad 1998). Implicit to both theories is the notion that acquired knowledge and skill may be translated into real monetary advantage. Bourdieu made the case that successful participants in high-status professions acquire across their lifetimes a cultural awareness that will help advance their careers in the dominant white male culture. Especially in elite law firms, lawyers must have knowledge of upper-class skills of impression management and the ability to create social networks. Kay and Hagan (1998) argued that "women . . . may be under greater pressure than men to communicate their assets and abilities more explicitly so as to compensate for their 'foreigness' to law firms" (p. 731). Bluntly put, women's capital, in general, and women-of-color's capital, in particular, is less desirable because of the lack of connections in white male social networks that value masculine socializing processes, such as sports talk and power dining and drinking (Sommerlad 1998).

Clara Shortridge Foltz acknowledged the difference between human and cultural capital approximately 125 years ago. Foltz was the first woman admitted to California's bar. Despite the fact that Foltz had passed the bar exam in 1878, she recognized that her lack of a formal legal education put her at a disadvantage with men who had access to law school. In 1879, Foltz argued and won her case before the California Supreme Court for admittance to Hastings Law School; there she garnered further human capital. When commenting upon entering the practice of law, Foltz said, "I had many secret misgivings as to my ability to cope with men who had a thousand years advantage over me" (Foltz, quoted in Schwartz, Brandt, and Milrod 1985, 8); that was the men's cultural capital, something acquired across lifetimes and through millennia of advantage, not in three years of legal training.

Cultural feminist theory has been used to explain why women's choices entering the legal field are different than men's, and why they approach legal practice using "a different voice" (Gilligan 1982; DuBois et al. 1985). This brand of thinking does not attribute choice to women's conscious decisions "to invest in careers that allow for greater balance between domestic and career goals" (Hull and Nelson 2000, 232), as would human-capital theory. Rather, women's socially acquired voices emphasize values of connectedness, care, and responsibility (Gilligan 1982; Hull and Nelson 2000). Women choosing a male-dominated profession gravitate toward specialties that are conducive to their different moral voice, which puts the priorities of others before their own. Perhaps the most-used metaphor for legal life has been the game. Gilligan found when interviewing lawyers about the game of law a man would respond, "[Y]ou play by the rules because society hangs together by the rules . . . if you cheat on them, even for a laudatory purpose, eventually you break down the rules." In contrast, a woman lawyer would say, "I have to preside over these decisions and I try to make them as non-disastrous as possible for the people who are most vulnerable. The fewer games you play, the better" (Gilligan, quoted in DuBois et al. 1985, 60).

Theories that emphasize early *gender socialization* concentrate on the social production of gendered differences in nurturing, interests, and cognitive processes (Chodorow 1978). In this reading, women in legal aid and public defense careers become nurturers to their clients and the maternal support of their offices. By combining cultural feminist and gendered socialization theories, we would predict that women entering law would choose specialties that allow fulfillment of their nurturing role in the home, and that their legal approach would be "concerned with maintaining relationships so that no one will be hurt" (Pierce 1995, 103).

None of these three theories explains the structural barriers women and minorities experience during their legal careers, nor their moral dilemmas. In their large study of Chicago lawyers, Hull and Nelson (2000) concluded that human capital theory is weak in explaining career trajectories of lawyers when gender is a variable. The researchers found that the human capital that lawyers acquire in law school and practice does indeed affect career trajectory; however, human capital cannot explain gender differences in later career positions. Cultural feminist theories lead us to conclude that women are inculcated with an ethic of care at an early age; hence, occupational segregation is the consequence of conscious decision making on the part of women lawyers rather than a consequence of structural discrimination. Gender socialization theory suggests that women are instilled with an ethic of care that runs deep; "women [lawyers] are perceived as 'opting-out' without any examination of whether the work structure has within it impediments or obstacles that preordain the outcome" (Menkel-Meadow, quoted in Sommerlad 1998, 5–6).

Hull and Nelson (2000) found that the human capital that lawyers acquire in law school and practice affects later career development, but human capital theory does not account for the gender differences in men's and women's legal career trajectories. Women "opting out" of high-prestige positions and instead choosing government and legal aid positions appears reasonable as an explanation, at least superficially. However, women's preferences cannot completely explain their ghettoization in the least desirable areas of law. In familial life, men also make choices; in career life, male coworkers make choices as well. Rhode (2003) argued that not only do male spouses fail to carry their equal weight in household responsibilities, thus constraining women's professional choices, but male colleagues also fail to support equitable working arrangements for their female counterparts. Logically, it follows that the significant representation of women in high-prestige legal positions will not occur until there is a major reorganization of the domestic sphere (Epstein et al. 1999; Rhode 2003). Until that time, the constraints women experience in their professional choices will continue to appear freely made, as will their apparent gendered preferences for working in the highly charged fields of criminal and family law.

Structural Barriers and Status Inequalities

Employers make choices as well. However, those choices may be discriminatory and reinforce the organizational barriers women face in law, reproducing gender inequality (Hull and Nelson 2000). Obviously, employers may, and do, deliberately discriminate. But recent research points to the more subtle social psychological qualities of gender discrimination in the work environment (Hull and Nelson 2000; Ridgeway 1997). Perhaps the best example of the less obvious version of employers' discrimination comes from the literature on women lawyers' commitment.

Lawyers describe the legal milieu as a work world in perpetual crisis, with "long bursts of work activity extending through nights and often weekends . . . to meet deadlines and to coordinate with the competing schedules of other participants" (Epstein et al. 1999, 20). The institution's greedy demands on lawyers' lives are reflected in employers' hiring choices. In her study of British women solicitors, Sommerlad (1998) found that commitment to career was the decisive factor in employment and partnership decisions. Despite the tremendous strides women have made into lawyering, employers still perceive that women lack commitment to the profession due to competing domestic de-

mands, such as maternity leaves. However, employer perceptions have been proven wrong.

Hull and Nelson (2000) found that "male and female lawyers who practiced full-time averaged identical numbers of hours within practice settings" (p. 252). In fact, domestic priorities may prove to be their opposites for women lawyers; the need to demonstrate professional commitment often turns into the demotion of familial demands (Sommerlad 1998). Rather than women lawyers' maternity leaves contributing to professional disinterest, women return to lawyering highly committed (Kay and Hagan 1998). The ironies of these findings should not be ignored.

First, although men and women lawyers invest roughly the same hours in their careers, men are more concerned with money and status, while women's concerns reflect their "value of work to the community" (Sommerlad 1998, 9). Men's commitment is more instrumental while women's represents an altruistic orientation, one that supports cultural feminism's tenet of different moral voices for men and women (Gilligan 1982). Second, although fatherhood significantly increases a man's odds of being made a partner, the same positive impact for motherhood does not hold true for women, who often demonstrate high levels of commitment after childbirth, even to the detriment of their children (Sommerlad 1998). Third, women, who are not often credited with commitment, still end up in less prestigious areas of practice, including criminal law, that arguably require the greatest emotional commitment for the least economic gain (Siemsen 2004). Ultimately, Hagan and Kay (1995) argued "women lawyers are more committed to the legal profession than men" (p. 185).

There is little doubt that the gendered hierarchy of law holds men's instrumental variety of commitment superior over women's. Unfortunately, each instance corresponds to the male/female dichotomy of rational/emotional that continues to divide the legal world on gendered lines. This particular interpretation of women's subordinate position easily masks the coercive nature of the masculine legal arena. Historically, Anglo-American law has been the province of privileged white men. As Baer (1999) so eloquently put it, "law's 'heavenly chorus' has sung not only 'with a strong upper-class accent' but also in a low pitch" (p. 71). We must not forget that only in 2003 did women become one-third of practicing lawyers in the United States, and the practice remains male. The primary tenet of feminist jurisprudence might be summed up as this: Law is male; law's traditions are male; and law's practice is male.

Continuing in that vein, the only change in the past 30 years is that both women and men now engage in law's male activities. Evelyn Fox Keller's reflection on the masculine nature of medicine has been applied to law: "Women, or any 'outsiders' for that matter, come to internalize the values of a world to which they aspire to belong" (quoted in Baer 1999, 71). The argument follows, women who accept the male model of law "consent to their social position in a legal order dominated by men" (Siemsen 2004, 31). Of course, the majority of women practicing criminal law would disagree. Still, there is little doubt that the social practices of law within courtroom dramas work as "masculinizing agencies" (Collier 1998, 22).

Women Practicing in the Masculine Milieu of Law

A great deal of criminal lawyering takes place within the courtroom. Utilizing, once again, the metaphor of the game, the lawyer's role is often adversarial, antagonistic, and "stereotypically hypermasculine in nature" (McBrier 2003, 1243; Pierce 1995; Siemsen 2004). It could be argued that legal maneuverings for control and domination represent the ideal type of masculine gender displays. Thus, "doing gender" in court for women lawyers can be complicated (West and Zimmerman 1987). Confrontation might be a good tactic for a man attorney, but the same behavior by a woman might be inter-

preted as overly brash. However, perceived feminine behavior in the field of law would likely be seen as incompetence (Martin and Jurik 1996).

In her ethnography of the world of women paralegals and litigators, Pierce (1995) found gendered behaviors, as well as identities, must be analyzed in relation to the legal structure. Gender becomes "a principle of organization and an aspect of identity" that situates one within the organization (Pierce 1995, 180). A woman lawyer is not only bound by her gendered identity and behaviors, but also by her gendered-specific location in law. While some gendered and racial disparities in law are subtle, others are outright prejudicial responses to women's and minorities' very presence in the courtroom that call into question the white masculine nature of the field. Pervasive accounts of the ill treatment of women and minority lawyers in the courtroom abound from their earliest days of practice to the present.

For example, "She is a WOMAN, she cannot be expected to reason; God Almighty decreed her limitations . . . this young woman will lead you by her sympathetic presentation of the case to violate your oaths and let a guilty man go free" were the nineteenth-century words of a San Francisco district attorney in response to criminal defense attorney Clara Shortridge Foltz (quoted in Schwartz, Brandt, and Milrod 1985, 7). (Foltz went on to win her case. She also went on to found the legal aid and public defender movement.)

When contemplating his position in the criminal justice system, a federal prosecutor said, "When you're fighting a war against crime, you don't send a girl to the front lines" (Baer, quoted in McBrier 2003, 1243).

According to the American Bar Association, "the white female client of an African-American female attorney was addressed as 'counsel' by a white female judge even though the client wore jeans and the lawyer wore a suit and briefcase" (ABA 1994, 27).

I am convinced, based on a decade of work in a public defender's office and nearly two years of field research on women defense attorneys and minority prosecutors, women's and minorities' lack of advancement in law is more complex than women achieving a critical mass at the top of the organization, gendered choices, or structural constraints. We began with the redistributive hypothesis—that is, once women achieved membership in law's upper echelons, they would work for change and others would join them. However, those women who make it to the top are also more apt to internalize the male values of law. Gendered choice theories appeal to our preconceived cultural perceptions of men and women. But, "women's choices are constrained by men's view of their appropriateness, as well as a structure which makes only certain choices possible" (Sommerlad 1998, 16). In addition, the idea that women might somehow demonstrate an ethic of care in male-dominated organizations has been severely discredited by the participation of women military police in the Iraqi prisoner scandal. What we have seen instead is a mass of women and minority lawyers, but their representation is only significant in the least desirable areas of lawyering. Unfortunately, criminal lawyering might well be the least explored of these.

By their presence in the lower echelons of law, women and minorities stand a greater chance of being recipients of verbal cruelty in the courtroom and being assigned emotionally difficult cases, cases that call into question their conflicting identities. The public defender and the legal aid lawyer will find themselves appointed to represent defendants charged with child abuse, rape, and murder, especially if they are women. Accompanying the influx of women into public defense work was the strategy of women being assigned cases in which a defendant had committed a violent crime against another woman, or a child, the goal being to gain juror sympathy. Just by sitting at the defense table next to an alleged rapist or child molestor, the woman defense attorney was thought to convey the defendant's innocence (Siemsen 2004).

Conclusion

Women's Roles as Criminal Lawyers and Feminism's Goals

Despite law's organizational barriers that keep all but a few women and minorities out of its high-status positions, those who end up as criminal lawyers are repeatedly asked by acquaintances to justify their positions in the criminal justice system. The question posed to them is "How can [you] defend a man who has raped another woman, especially if [you have] feminist sensibilities?" (Siemsen 2004, 4). Likewise, minority deputy district attorneys are criticized by their communities for prosecuting their "own" (Cose 1997; Siemsen 2004). Their answers are most instructive in this exploration of women and minority criminal lawyers as agents of social change. An Asian-American woman who had practiced criminal law for over 25 years noted that there is a movement to take away individual rights away.

> My job . . . is to make sure that the government does not get out of hand. That is, the police, the prosecutors, the courts, probation . . . or they're going to have to contend with people like myself. We're here to keep the balance. . . . And that's important for women, too. Because women are also in the groups that have been discriminated against throughout history. . . . And as long as you have the defense bar out there maintaining an equilibrium, then everybody has a better chance—feminists, foreigners, immigrants, the criminal defendant, people of color. (Siemsen 2004, 138)

An African-American prosecutor of 26 years said,

> When I was in the '60s there were a lot of issues, the Black Panthers, racist whites coming in and occupying the black community. It's still happening today. . . . I say, "Well, if you want white cops to stop kicking your butts, maybe you ought to be prosecutors." The joke around here is that justice is just that: just us. (Siemsen 2004, 174)

The larger "feminist project . . . to make large-scale organizations more democratic and more supportive of humane goals" (Acker 1990, 140) is represented in these lawyers' justifications of their roles. Their rationales for working in criminal law have much more to do with the sexism and racism that they experience on a daily basis, and the class biases that pervade the criminal justice system. We would do better by viewing women and minority lawyers' career choices as continuations of earlier feminist and civil rights struggles that recognize legal practice as a mechanism for change. The rapid increase of women criminal attorneys in recent years represents feminism's third wave of hope into law. Despite a Canadian study that found law schools to be a "poisoned environment" for women, especially women of color (Krakauer and Chen 2003, 69), Lani Guiner and her colleagues found some hope for institutional change in their study of women students at the University of Pennsylvania Law School, a markedly gendered and classed elite law school. They found that the university, as a "formerly all-male educational [institution] cannot . . . take advantage of difference without changing from within" (Guinere, Fine, and Balin 1997, 75). However, they also found an institution that reproduced social stratification by gender and race, rather than challenged it.

For the majority of women criminal defense attorneys I studied (Siemsen 2004), criminal defense work was consistent with their views of feminism. *Feminism*'s basic definition, for most of them, was equal treatment for all under the Constitution, including equal treatment for the rapist and the child molester. This stance does not mean women defense attorneys easily escape emotional conflict through ideological justifications, especially if they self-identify as lesbian. For example, one attorney did find rape trials to compete with her identity as a woman and as a lesbian; she is now a law school professor. Despite the fact that most of the women defenders described emotionally difficult cases involving violence against women and chil-

dren, the women lawyers who experienced the greatest conflict in these cases were two of the three women who self-identified as lesbian. For the most part, the women defense attorneys' stories painted the picture of a career pathway marked by similar phases and hurdles, as they adjusted their attitudes toward clients and victims to minimize their own emotional conflicts. Women defense attorneys new to the profession, who had practiced law less than 10 years, inhibited any identification with the victim. Midcareer women defense attorneys, those who had been in their profession about 15 years, grew to empathize with their clients. Several saw defendants as the true victims of their terrible life histories; one said, "They've been kicked around and hurt" (Siemsen 2004, 167). The most seasoned of the women defense attorneys distanced themselves from both victims and defendants. But even more, they took on the mantel of their profession's highest ideals, consistent with feminism's goal of equal treatment under the law. I found the longer that women defense attorneys stayed in their line of work, the better they became at reconciling the emotional dilemmas of their profession through constitutional ideals. In the words of one,

> And I say to you, and I say loud and clear, everybody has a right to a fair trial, and everybody gets the same rules. Whether you're black or white. Whether you're a Hell's Angel, or an Earth Angel, rules are not adjusted for defendants. Nothing excuses any kind of violation of the oath up there on that stand. That is our system. It is the light that never fails. (Siemsen 2004, 168)

The women and minority criminal lawyers discussed throughout this chapter are well-situated to produce change within the legal institution by rejecting its male biases. However, we await the further exploration of the positive impact that women lawyers who practice daily in the criminal and family law courts might have on the criminal justice system. These criminal lawyers might be termed *tempered radicals* (Meyerson and Scully 1995), those who identify with the profession, recognize "that the criminal justice system reproduces gender and racial inequalities," and advocate for social change all at the same time (Siemsen 2004, 36). Their presence and influence cannot be ignored, especially when projections tell us that in the 2010s women will be 40 percent of the practicing lawyers in the United States (American Bar Association 1994). The part to be played by an inversion of the redistributive hypothesis in the change awaits further explanation.

References

Abel, R. L. (1988). The United States: The contradictions of professionalism. In R. L. Abel and P. C. Lewis (Eds.), *Lawyers in society: The common law world* (pp. 186–243). Berkeley: University of California Press.

Acker, J. (1990). Hierarchies, jobs, bodies: A theory of gendered organizations. *Gender & Society*, 4, 139–158.

American Bar Association (ABA). (1994). *The burdens of both, the privileges of neither.* Chicago: Author.

———. (2004). *A current glance of women in the law.* Chicago: Author.

Baer, J. A. (1999). *Our lives before the law: Constructing a feminist jurisprudence.* Princeton, NJ: Princeton University Press.

Bourdieu, P. (1977). *Outline of a theory of practice.* Cambridge: Cambridge University Press.

Brockman, J. (2001). *Gender in the legal profession: Fitting or breaking the mould.* Vancouver, BC: University of British Columbia Press.

Chambliss, E., and Uggen, C. (2000). Men and women of elite law firms: Reevaluating Kanter's legacy. *Law and Social Inquiry*, 25, 41–68.

Chodorow, N. (1978). *The reproduction of mothering: Psychoanalysis and the sociology of gender.* Berkeley: University of California Press.

Collier, R. (1998). (Un)sexy bodies: The making of professional legal masculinities. In C. McGlynn, (Ed.), *Legal feminisms: Theory and practice* (pp. 21–48). Brookfield, VT: Ashgate.

Cose, E. (Ed.). (1997). *The Darden dilemma: Twelve black writers on justice, race, and conflicting loyalties.* New York: Harper Perennial.

Drachman, V. G. (1998). *Sisters in law: Women lawyers in modern American history.* Cambridge, MA: Harvard University Press.

DuBois, E. C., Dunlap, M. C., Gilligan, C. J., MacKinnon, C. A., and Menkel-Meadow, C. J. (1985). Feminist discourse, moral values, and the law: A conversation. *Buffalo Law Review*, 34, 11–87.

Epstein, C. F. (1993). *Women in law.* Chicago: University of Illinois Press.

Epstein, C. F., Seron, C., Oglensky, B., and Saute, R. (1999). *The part-time paradox: Time norms, professional lives, family, and gender.* New York: Routledge.

Gilligan, C. (1982). *In a different voice: Psychological theory and women's development.* Cambridge, MA: Harvard University Press.

Guinier, L., Fine, M., and Balin, J. (1997). *Becoming gentlemen: Women, law school, and institutional change.* Boston: Beacon Press.

Hagan, J., and Kay, F. (1995). *Gender in practice: A study of lawyers' lives.* New York: Oxford University Press.

Hughes, E. (1971). *The sociological eye: Selected papers.* New Brunswick, NJ: Transaction.

Hull, K. E., and Nelson, R. L. (2000). Assimilation, choice, or constraint? Testing theories of gender differences in the careers of lawyers. *Social Forces*, 79, 229–264.

Kanter, R. M. (1977). *Men and women of the corporation.* New York: Basic Books.

Kay, F., and Hagan, J. (1998). Raising the bar: The gender stratification of law firm capital. *American Sociological Review*, 63, 728–743.

Krakauer, L., and Chen, C. P. (2003). Gender barriers in the legal profession: Implications for career development of female law students. *Journal of Employment Counseling*, 40, 65–79.

Martin, S. E., and Jurik, N. C. (1996). *Doing justice, doing gender: Women in law and criminal justice occupations.* Thousand Oaks, CA: Sage.

McBrier, D. B. (2003). Gender and career dynamics within a segmented professional labor market: The case of law academia. *Social Forces*, 81, 1201–1266.

Menkel-Meadow, C. (2002). A different voice in the lawyering process? In K. T. Bartlett, A. P. Harris, and D. L. Rhode (Eds.), *Gender and law: Theory, doctrine, commentary* (pp. 858–860). New York: Aspen.

Meyerson, D. E., and Scully, M. A. (1995). Tempered radicalism and the politics of ambivalence and change. *Organization Science*, 6, 585–600.

National Association for Law Placement (NALP). (2001). *Jobs for new law graduates*. Washington, DC: Author.

——. (2002). *Employment comparisons and trends for men and women, minorities and non-minorities*. Washington, DC: Author.

——. (2004). *Women and attorneys of color at law firms*. Washington, DC: Author.

Pierce, J. (1995). *Gender trials: Emotional lives in contemporary law firms*. Berkeley: University of California Press.

Rhode, D. L. (2003). Gender and the profession: An American perspective. In U. Schultz and G. Shaw (Eds.), *Women in the world's legal professions* (pp. 3–30). Portland, OR: Hart Publishing.

Ridgeway, C. (1997). Interaction and the conservation of gender inequality: Considering employment. *American Sociological Review*, 62, 218–235.

Schwartz, M. D., Brandt, S. L., and Milrod, P. (1985, Spring). The battles of Clara Shortridge Foltz. *California Defender*, pp. 7–11.

Siemsen, C. (2004). *Emotional trials: The moral dilemmas of women criminal defense attorneys*. Boston: Northeastern University Press.

Simpson, G. (1996). The plexiglass ceiling: The careers of black women lawyers. *Career Development Quarterly*, 45, 173–188.

Sommerlad, H. (1998). The gendering of the professional subject: Commitment, choice, and social closure in the legal profession. In C. McGlynn, (Ed.), *Legal feminisms: Theory and practice* (pp. 3–32). Brookfield, VT: Ashgate.

West, C., and Zimmerman, D. (1987). Doing gender. *Gender & Society*, 1, 125–151. ✦

17
Women on the Bench

The Voices and Experiences of Female Judges

Michelle L. Meloy
Shana L. Maier
Susan L. Miller

In this chapter you will learn the following:

- How paths to becoming lawyers and judges differ for men and women

- How women's experience on the bench differs from men's experience

- The challenges that female judges experience balancing their professionals and personal lives

- Whether changing the gender representation of judges improves the quality of justice due to women's different contributions

- How gender plays a role in the way judges interpret or react to a case

- The differences between the maximalist and minimalist approaches, the two approaches that address the different values and behaviors of men and women

Introduction

Despite inroads gained by women in employment outside of the home, the public labor market remains stratified and creates and reproduces gender inequality (Reskin and Roos 1990; Williams 1995). The repro-duction of gender inequality is true also in the legal system, specifically the judiciary: Women's presence in the judiciary is "smaller than the overall percentage of women in the profession and is minuscule relative to the number of men on the bench" (Coontz 2000, 70). And although, in 2001, women were one-third of all attorneys, only one in five judges was a woman (Vogel-Short 2001). Women are well-represented in law schools and as practicing attorneys but are not reaching the bench at an equal pace to men. This chapter raises questions about women and the law. For example, are the paths to becoming lawyers and judges different for men and women? Once women are on the bench, what is the courtroom climate like? Will changing the gender representation of judges improve the quality of justice due to women's different contributions? How do women's different experiences, attitudes, and values affect decision making? In other words, do female judges use a "different voice" in approaching justice? We begin by providing a brief history of women's entrance into the legal field.

History of Exclusion of Women in the Legal Field

Lawyers cannot practice law without first attending law school and passing the bar. This posed a challenge for women because the first law school did not admit women until 1869 (Martin and Jurik 1996). By 1920, women were allowed to practice law in every state (Coontz 2000), but they often found it difficult to find employment practicing law, and most found themselves working as volunteers for social service agencies. As time progressed, however, women increased their representation as lawyers: In 1999, there were 17,468 female attorneys, and by 2001, one-third of all attorneys were women (Girth 2000; Vogel-Short 2001).

Women's judicial appointments proceeded even more slowly. For most states, there was a lapse of about 50 years between when the first woman was admitted to the bar in the state and the first woman was appointed to the bench (Cook 1987, 165). Moreover, although the first woman was elected to a general jurisdiction court in 1921, and the first woman was appointed to the federal bench in 1934, it wasn't until 1979 that a woman had served at some level of the judicial system in all fifty states (Coontz 2000; Martin and Jurik 1996). Although the exact number of women on the bench at the state level is not available, the most recent estimates indicate that 10 to 15 percent of state judges are female (Neubauer 2002).[1] With state courts of last resort, at this level women comprise 28 percent of justices, but at the intermediate appellate court level, 23 percent of justices are female (National Center for State Courts 2002). On the federal level, women comprised 7 percent of all federal judgeships in 1987, which grew to 19 percent a decade later (American Bar Association 1997) and approximately 22 percent by 2004, according to the U.S. Federal Courts.

Despite the apparent increase in female judicial officers, at both the state and federal level, women continue to be grossly underrepresented on the bench. It wasn't until 1981 that the first female, Justice Sandra Day O'Connor, was appointed to the Supreme Court, and the second one, Justice Ruth Bader Ginsberg, followed in 1993. However, in the past two decades, greater diversification on the bench has been achieved, with background characteristics such as age, localism, career patterns, and method of judicial selection being most pronounced among women and African American judges (see Martin and Pyle 2002). While their numbers still do not reflect their increased presence in the legal profession, African Americans represented 7 percent of state high court justices in 1998, (Esterling and Anderson 1999), and in 1999, 9.7 percent of federal trial and appellate court judges (Goldman and Slotnick 1999). The method of judicial selection—relying on "eligible pool" criteria—seems to account for some underrepresentation by women and people of color. However, greatly influ-

encing the selection process is resistance to access by those who control traditional gatekeeping avenues (Cook 1987; Martin and Pyle 2002).

Debate remains whether the gender composition of the judiciary has truly shifted to become more gender neutral. Some scholars argue that although women have progressed in the legal field, the shift in the judiciary is only symbolic; women's token status in the courts perseveres (Cook 1987; Coontz 2000). However, others argue that because of the sharp increase in the number of women judges, women have overcome tokenism and are no longer as highly visible as sole representatives of their group (Steffensmeier and Hebert 1999). Regardless of which argument holds more weight, women in any field that is male-dominated face barriers. In occupations traditionally held by men, interactions between men and women are gendered and sexualized (Martin and Jurik 1996, 40). Beginning in 1983, under the urging of the National Organization for Women's Judicial Educational Program, a publication of the nation's first gender task force was released (New Jersey Task Force on Women and the Courts). To date, more than 40 statutes and nine of the 13 federal circuits have established task forces to study the degree to which gender bias exists within the court system and to propose ways of eliminating it. What used to be invisible is now grounds for reversal and sanction (Schafran 2000). We review these findings in the next section.

Gender Bias

Gender bias involves actions or attitudes that negatively impact an individual or group primarily because of gender (Hemmens, Strom, and Schlegal 1998, 23). Women in the legal field experience gender bias throughout their careers: as students in law school, as attorneys, and as judicial officers. In law school, women are degraded and often feel isolated, which could negatively affect their performance. A study that examined law classes at the University of Pennsylvania between 1987 and 1992 found that even when men and women entered law school with identical credentials, due to alienation experienced by female law students and male law students' greater comfort with the competitive environment in law classes, the men were three times more likely to be in the top 10 percent of the class at the conclusion of the first year (Guinier, Fine, and Balin 1997). Moreover, female law students tend to be mentored less and called on less often by professors, unless it is a topic pertaining to women's issues (Girth 2000; Martin and Jurik 1996). For women lawyers who join law school faculty, the gender bias continues. Equally credentialed women are routinely hired at a lower rank (assistant professor) than their similarly situated male counterparts (who are hired as associate professors), and women are overrepresented at lower tiered schools and are less successful at securing tenure than men (Jones-Merrit and Reskin 1997). This pattern has resulted in what Levit (2001) refers to as the "pink-collar ghetto of legal academia where women are congregated in lower-ranking, lower-paying, lower-prestige legal positions" (p. 775).

Gender bias persists once women enter legal occupations. Female attorneys are more likely than male attorneys to be addressed by their first names, by infantalizing or endearing terms, or by alternative names that emphasize their status as a woman; they are also more likely to be asked if they are "real" attorneys (Martin and Jurik 1996; National Association of Women Judges 1991a; Schafran 1987b). In addition, females receive inappropriate comments or sexist remarks made about their appearance or style of dress by male colleagues or male judges (Schafran 1987a, 1987b). The boundaries between male and female attorneys are maintained through disrespect, through exclusion from events where social networking takes place or shutting women out of the old-boy network (discussed in the next section), and through sexual harassment (Miller and Meloy 2000). Moreover, gender bias exerts a powerful effect on jurys' and clients' perceptions of case

outcomes: If cases are lost, clients may blame their lawyer's gender for the reason, especially if she was accorded less respect by other court professionals (Schafran 1987b).

Research documents that women feel that gender plays a significant role in judicial nominations and hiring practices (see Hemmens, Strom, and Schlegal 1998, 37). Gatekeepers to the bench are disproportionately white men, and an unwritten qualification for the bench is that the applicant needs to be male, preferably with political clout (Cook 1987; Coontz 2000; Martin and Jurik 1996). Older, wealthy, corporate attorneys are awarded high judicial selection ratings at the expense of women who are less likely to share similar background characteristics, career patterns, and political activism (Beiner 1999; Githens 1995).

> No doubt the key to judicial selection lies in the political system. Since federal and state bar associations exert substantial influence over judicial appointments, it is significant that women are largely excluded from the boards of governors of bar associations and from executive positions within these organizations. Rather, political party leaders who slate judicial candidates tend to follow value systems that invariably favor the selection of male candidates. (Flynn 1982, 319)

These gatekeeping activities work against judicial diversification by race and gender.

Another way that such attitudes emerge is through development of the "all-male clubhouse," where "[i]n such work environments, participants often value the exclusivity of totally male companionship as a desirable goal in itself" (Wilson 1982, 366). The process is informal, with old-boy networks established through which favors are exchanged, barriers to inclusion are constructed, and bonding among the dominant male players is facilitated (Farr 1988). Socializing and other informal interactions with colleagues contribute to a more satisfying working environment. Women are typically more isolated than men in the criminal justice profession, given the scarcity of female colleagues (Miller and Meloy 2000). This isolation is exacerbated for women occupying high positions in their professions, such as judgeships (Merlo and Pollock 1995). Apart from the job morale/ satisfaction issue, informal exchanges with colleagues also offer opportunities to learn important job-related information. Women become disadvantaged if they are excluded from these:

> [I]f you don't sit down and talk with your colleagues, you miss an awful lot of information: What's going on? What bills are pending in the legislature? Who's going to be the next director of something or other? If you just go about your business, you'll be the only one who doesn't know that something critical is about to happen and you'll look foolish because you ask stupid questions. It's a big dilemma. (Baunach and Rafter 1982, 351–352)

Some women face an additional barrier in their route to the bench: balancing the demands they experience as both professionals and mothers. Meshing work and family is a tremendous hurdle for women in the legal field, as working a second shift at home often prevents their success or curtails promotions. They are unable to dedicate the extra hours at work because of the additional eight hours that they may need to dedicate to their daily family responsibilities. For example, when Ruth Bader Ginsburg applied for a clerkship after graduating law school at the top of her class, she was not offered the position until a teacher convinced the district judge that she could handle the dual responsibilities of motherhood and a law career (Thomas 1993, 1876). Females often report difficulty in "weaving" the demands of their legal career with parenthood or personal responsibilities, noting how such demands affect their professional choices (Garey 1999; Girth 2000; Martin and Jurik 1996; Miller and Meloy 2000). Although women's second shift at home may prevent them from being appointed to the judiciary, once women take the bench, they continue to struggle with balancing between their personal and professional responsibilities. Women judges may

face barriers in competing for higher-level positions because of their burden at home (Martin 1990, 205). For instance, one female judge was often told: "You ought to be at home with your kids, their diapers are dirty" (Huber 2003). Overall, they experience much more conflict and tension negotiating between these two worlds than do most of their male colleagues.

When women do overcome various obstacles and are appointed to the bench, they experience much of the gender bias indicated by female attorneys. Female judges report being treated with less respect than their male counterparts and being addressed by their first names, endearing terms, or inappropriate titles such as "ma'am" by attorneys, male judges, and other courtroom players (Bogoch 1999; Hemmens et al. 1998; Schafran 1987b). This illustrates the assertion made by Martin and Jurik (1996), "In occupations traditionally held by men, interactions between men and women are gendered and sexualized" (p. 40). In addition, female judges, like female attorneys, experience a double bind—they are dismissed as lacking the force required for a judge if they act passive or feminine but are also faulted for acting with too much aggression. As stated by one female judge in the Delaware Gender Fairness Task Force, *Final Report* (1995), "Female judges are referred to as 'bitch' where for the same behavior a male judge is considered 'tough' " (p. 26).

In conclusion, past task force reports show that male attorneys and judges are less likely to recognize or report gender bias, and judges deny that any bias exists in their jurisdiction, even if it does exist elsewhere (National Association of Women Judges 1991a; Schafran 2000). Many courtroom players and others who have the ability to create a more level playing field are ignorant of, or ignore the prevalence of, gender bias. As stated by Schafran (1987a), "Gender bias is one of the most troublesome aspects of our entire legal system, and the reason it is so troublesome and so insidious is because there is a failure to recognize its existence" (p. 282). It is likely that males in the legal system find it easy to ignore gender bias, and females find their standpoint and experiences marginalized, given larger cultural patterns and social practices that advantage men and disadvantage women. Gender bias does not exist in a vacuum; the experiences of female attorneys and judges reflect attitudes and actions that are tolerated in our society.

Women in the Judiciary: Different Experiences, but Different Voices?

Most of the empirical research on women judges follows two directions: (1) case outcome, i.e., Are female judges more sympathetic to cases or policy issues of interest to women?; or, (2) jurisprudence, i.e., Do female judges use different legal reasoning than do men, given their unique experiences? (Palmer 2001). If ideally, as some argue, nonlegal factors (e.g., judges' gender) should play no role in case outcome, knowing whether or not women make different decisions from men may introduce profound implications for equal treatment under law (Coontz 2000, 59).[2] We examine both lines of inquiry here, beginning with research germane to both questions.

When women enter fields traditionally held by men, job segregation within the field persists. Women are given different responsibilities or assignments, and they are steered toward specialization in areas that reflect their "feminine" qualifications. Female attorneys and judges dominate family law and family court (Steffensmeier and Hebert 1999; Toutant 2001). Men and women have different values that not only may not be shared by members of the opposite gender but also may not be perceived by members of the opposite gender (Scales 1986). Men may not recognize the ways they are different from women; women may not recognize the ways they are different from men. There are two different perspectives that address the different values and behaviors of men and women: the maximalist approach and the minimalist

approach. The *maximalist approach* asserts that men and women are fundamentally different as a result of their experiences and socialization and therefore exhibit real differences in the way they make decisions (see Martin, Reynolds, and Keith 2002). However, the *minimalist approach* asserts that there exist few gender differences between men and women and decision making is governed more by one's legal training than by his or her personal experiences (Steffensmeier and Hebert 1999). Moreover, it could be that through the process of being socialized into the legal profession, men, and women's differences diminish as they learn to conform to existing norms and institutional cultures (Guinier, Fine, and Balin 1997; Palmer 2001).

Empirical research findings are somewhat equivocal on these issues. Research conducted using sentencing data from Pennsylvania courts between 1991 and 1993 found that women judges sentence more harshly than male judges do (Steffensmeier and Hebert 1999). On average, women are about 10 percent more likely to incarcerate, and they impose prison terms that are about five months longer (Steffensmeier and Hebert 1999, 1183). The same study found that female judges are more likely to be influenced by the demographic characteristics, prior record, and current circumstances of the offender. Other research findings demonstrate that the gender of the judge matters because personal experiences and values have an impact on judicial decisions and interpretations, and one's experiences and values are influenced by gender (Coontz 2000; National Association of Women Judges 1991b). Using scenarios of hypothetical cases that manipulated characteristics of plaintiffs/defendants, Coontz (2000) examined state trial judges in Pennsylvania, finding that gender of judge had an effect on case outcome, although litigant characteristics did not. Although the study did not ask what legal reasoning has been used, gender differences between male and female judges emerged that may indicate a difference in how judges' lived experiences shape legal interpretations. In particular, some of her findings included the following: female judges were more likely than male judges to find a male defendant, rather than a female defendant, guilty of assault; female judges were twice as likely to find a female defendant claiming self-defense guilty of homicide than were male judges; male judges were not unanimous, as were women judges, in awarding alimony; male judges imposed shorter sentences for simple assault than female judges; male judges were more likely to award civil damages for simple assault and awarded one-third the damages awarded by female judges (Coontz 2000, 68). In research regarding sex discrimination cases, female judges serving on state supreme courts, U.S. courts of appeals, and the U.S. Supreme Court tend to be the strongest supporters of women's rights, regardless of their ideology (see Palmer 2001 for review). The research suggests that even the addition of one single woman to a court noticeably affects case outcomes (Martin 1990; O'Connor and Segal 1990), leading researchers to conclude that the "presence of a woman on the bench was one of the best predictors in favor of women filing sex-discrimination claims" (Palmer 2001, 93; see also Gryski, Main, and Dixon 1986). Songer, Davis, and Haire's (1994) study examined votes of male and female judges on appeals court decisions in three areas. They found no difference in obscenity or criminal search and seizure cases, but in employment discrimination cases, female judges were significantly more liberal. Thus, they found limited support for gender differences in case outcome, but they did not look at the judges' legal reasoning behind their votes.

In contrast, the minimalist approach finds some support in the empirical research. Although Steffensmeier and Hebert's (1999) research highlighted the differences between women and men, the overall findings supported more of a minimalist approach. Steffensmeier and Hebert (1999) concluded, "We find that in many respects women and men judges have similar sentencing practices, which suggests that both are governed more by their legal training and legal social-

ization than by their socially structured personal experiences" (p. 1187). Other research has supported that the gender of the judge does not make a great deal of difference on their judicial interpretation or decision making (Gruhl, Spohn, and Welch 1981; McCormick and Job 1993; Songer and Crews-Meyer 2000). For instance, in Gruhl and colleagues' (1981) research on sentencing behavior in rape cases, there was no difference between male and female decisions. In fact, when the same data were examined with a variety of types of crimes, female judges were twice as likely to send female defendants to jail as were male judges. While female judges treated male and female defendants similarly overall, male judges behaved with greater paternalism toward female defendants (Gruhl, Spohn, and Welch 1981, 320).

The limitations of prior research on gender and case outcomes may reveal more about the weaknesses of the data and methodology employed in these studies than resolving the debate about whether or not a judge's gender might affect decision making. Coontz (2000, 62–63) suggested several explanations for the contradictory nature of the findings. For example, most of the research exploring gender differences looks at judges on high courts, which may not be representative, especially since most female judges are concentrated on lower (state trial) courts; most studies have analyzed criminal courts while it may be that family court is most relevant for examining gender differences since more women are affected by cases heard there (e.g., divorce, alimony, custody, child support); and, access to judges is limited and most of the studies examine public record data rather than sampling judges directly about their decision-making process. In addition, Coontz (2000) suggested there is no adequate theoretical framework to use to interpret judicial behavior. We concur and argue that the studies conducted so far, many of which we have summarized, provide an incomplete understanding of the issue, since the conclusions rest on survey data or case votes, which are decisions that reflect self-reported behavior or discrete case outcomes (Palmer 2001). If one were to examine the context of judges' written explanations for their decisions, subtle gendered differences could emerge (Palmer 2001). Quantitative data may mask subtle distinctions between how male and female judges operate. Thus, work that examines the contextual reasoning behind judicial decision making, often called the "different voice perspective," is very appealing.

Developmental psychologist Carol Gilligan is credited with creating the theory of different voices, a perspective that has shaped the debate on whether or not the integration of women into the judiciary would impact legal jurisprudence. Gilligan (1982) asserted that women use what she referred to as an *ethic of care* and men use an *ethic of justice* when they solve problems, resulting from their unique socialization experiences as male or female (See also Martin and Jurik 1996; Pierce 1995; Pruitt 1994; Scales 1986). The ethic of care shows concern with communication, mediation, conflict diffusion and the preservation of relationships, reflecting women's "outsider" status that brings with it greater empathy and understanding of others' plights because of women's own membership in a subordinated group (Martin, Reynolds, and Keith 2002). This understanding lends less allegiance to a male legal model that stresses competition, winning, adversarial interactions, and objectivity. As Fox and Van Sickel (2000, 262) summarize, "[t]hrough the ethic of care, according to Gilligan, women place greater value on such phenomenon as concrete relationships, attention to context, a concern for the welfare of others. . . . In contrast, the ethic of rights places greater values on hierarchy, abstract rules and principles [and] individual autonomy." Since American law has been developed, interpreted, and dominated by men, the male "voice" is the one that shapes jurisprudence (Palmer 2001). If a female "voice" played a bigger role, we might see a greater focus on what is best for all involved parties, rather than a (male) concern with maintaining control through following formal procedures or laws. Gilligan (1982) argued that

these voices are simply different, not that one voice is superior to the other.

Some studies have found support for "different voices," while others insist that the different voices in the legal system are not equal and that the ethic of justice is the only voice that can be heard in the criminal justice system (Daly 1989). Yet, female and male judges may "attach different weights to the factual aspects of identical situations" (Coontz 2000, 71). Other research has concluded that both men and women on the bench exhibit both the ethic of care and the ethic of justice at different times (Fox and Van Sickel 2000). As the empirical evidence is inconclusive at best, the debate regarding "different voices" continues, to the chagrin of some. For example, Sandra Day O'Connor, the first female Supreme Court Justice, resents such stereotypes assigned to men and women on the bench by the different voices perspective. In a speech in 1991 at New York University, O'Connor expressed that she thought this way of thinking resembled the notion of "true womanhood" that kept women out of law (Rosen 2001, 36). She is quoted as saying, "Asking whether women . . . speak with a 'different voice' than men do is a question that is both dangerous and unanswerable" (in Rosen 2001, 36).[3] Some scholars echo O'Connor's concern that a "feminine" type of legal reasoning encourages a conservative understanding of women's roles (Baer 1991, 1999; MacKinnon 1987, 1989). Moreover, some scholars fear that "different voice" research in judicial circles is dangerous because it ignores the differences within gender categories and the diversity among the experiences, attitudes, and performance of men and women (Martin and Jurik 1996). Because the duty of law is to enhance the diversity of life, scholars need to recognize not only diversity between men and women but also the diversity within both gender categories (Scales 1986).

Work that has examined the jurisprudence that guided decisions made on the U.S. Courts of Appeals Ninth Circuit found that men were just as likely to use a "different" voice perspective (Davis 1992–1993) and that

Texas Supreme Court justices demonstrated no discernable "different" voice among the four female justices who served from 1997 to 1999 (Abbate 2000). Why might this be the case? Palmer (2001, 95) contended that "to be successful in the field of law, women must suppress this alternative approach to legal reasoning, or that the structure of law school education subverts this different voice, or that Gilligan's theory is simply wrong" (see also Davis 1992–1993; Solimine and Wheatley 1995). Coontz's (2000) work in the state courts, where the greatest concentration of female judges is located, lends support to the different voice perspective with its finding that judges interpret the same facts in the same cases differently. Despite the equivocal findings of evidence of a different voice perspective, the idea continues to generate interest in women's ability to transform traditional legal jurisprudence.

Since the research findings are inconclusive, further research should be pursued. What seems to be needed is a *deeper*, more qualitative examination of the social context of the judiciary through an exploration of individual attitudes of female judges and their role orientations, as well as of the organizational and social factors that affect them (e.g., see Miller and Meloy 2000). Using a sample of female judges collected from two contiguous states, we explore their perceptions and experiences. We highlight the major findings from this research project since they reflect issues salient to judges nationwide.

Data and Methods

The sample reflects a merger of two data sets: In 1990, a total of 20 active female judges were identified in state A, and in 1998, a total of 32 active female judges were identified in state B, using state bar association information.[4] All 52 female judicial officers were invited to participate in in-depth interviews designed to explore their judicial experiences, attitudes about gender and career issues, and the role that gender plays within their decision making and legal reasoning. Five judges from state A and 18 judges from state B agreed to be interviewed, with in-depth interviews occurring about 10 years apart. Additional judges who declined to be interviewed did answer written questionnaires; we report here only the analysis of the in-depth interviews. The judges from state A are all Caucasian, range in age from 41 to 68, and all have children. State B's judges reflect greater diversity, as 14 are Caucasian, two are African American, one is Hispanic, and one is Asian American; they range in age from 30 to 55 (with one retired judge over 75), and the majority (89 percent) have children or stepchildren. In addition, judges from both states come from families steeped in the legal professions, which may play a role in facilitating the women's interest in law. This type of familial influence may be typical of the women who headed for higher education before the great changes of the 1970s.

While overall the judges from states A and B converged on many of the issues asked in the interviews, despite the 10 years in-between the data collection, there were some striking differences. The biggest differences had more to do with identity issues and the political nature of the profession (to be discussed in a subsequent section). For instance, in terms of identity, the judges from state A adamantly self-identified as feminists and offered no apologies for their positions. In contrast, the judicial officers from state B waffled in their answers to this question, displaying concern about the negative connotations associated with the word *feminist* and discomfort with drawing attention to gendered notions of what a feminist is. As one judge from state B clarified:

> That term is so misused. If the definition of feminism is that everyone should have the same opportunity, then yes, I am a feminist, and even my husband would be a feminist. But other definitions go too far and create negative images of feminists in society.

Several judges prefered the term *humanist* or *equalist*, and four judges emphatically rejected the feminist label, as illustrated by one judge's explanation:

> I guess I see a feminist as someone who is going to go forward and say, "Women can do it all. Women have been discriminated [against] for so long, hear our voices and hear it now" kind of philosophy. I don't believe that. I personally don't feel I've been discriminated [against] because I'm a woman. I think we are pretty much equal now, so I don't go out and advocate for women's rights. I don't think we are being denied anything.

It is possible these differences between judges interviewed in 1990 and judges interviewed almost a decade later may stem from the movement toward the conservative right and the corresponding backlash against liberals that has helped to shape the national discourse on social issues, particularly about crime, in the past decade. There was greater convergence when judges were asked about the political or social causes in which they were most interested, such as the following: women's rights, domestic violence, gender bias in the courts, women in the law, financial problems experienced by economically dependent spouses, parents' responsibility to children, child abuse, issues relating to juveniles, gender equality in education, availability of nursing homes for senior citizens, environmental issues, diversity in the American Bar Association, and gender bias in the courts.

The women in this combined sample attended law school for various reasons and their decision to do so was influenced by a variety of people. However, male family members who were attorneys were noted to be most influential. Once in laws schools, participants from both states experienced moderate to little support from male professors. Although some families were supportive of their daughters' decisions to attend law school, many parents, particularly mothers, were unsupportive of the decisions because they thought law school was "too much" for their daughters, would prevent them from marrying, or prevent them from adequately caring for children. One judge from state B reflected that her mother was unsupportive of her decision to attend law school after having two children and thought it was "child abuse" to leave her children to attend school. Gender stereotypes concerning appropriate careers and roles for women were factors that the female judicial officers were forced to contend with on professional and personal levels at various junctures in their careers.

The following sections will explore women's entrance process to the judiciary and their impressions of the gatekeeping process, the intricacies involved with balancing their professional and private lives, the isolating effects of the bench, and judges' own perceptions of how being female might affect their decision making, opinions on criminal justice and legal issues, and relationships with colleagues.

Impressions of the Gatekeeping Process

Gatekeeping practices continue to impede female judicial officers seeking to advance within the field; while some report experiences of blatant sexism, others suggest that a female's blocked access to the political culture or political insiders creates barriers to advancement. Most of the participants experienced gender bias in the legal field prior to their judicial appointment, although it was more pronounced in the stories told by judges from state A. For instance, all judges from state A indicated that although they faced discrimination, they did not challenge these instances because of the possibility of jeopardizing their futures. State B judges shared fewer stories about overt discrimination but nonetheless provided many examples of more covert discriminatory treatment. For instance, judges recalled being called inappropriate names such as *honey, sweetie, tough cookie* or *bitch* by male attorneys, being asked irrelevant questions about personal lives during job interviews, being ignored by male colleagues or judges, or being excluded from social events. One judge from state B recalled receiving a bonus and 25 percent salary increase at a firm where she had worked for 14 years. The partner of the firm told her she was the lowest paid attorney in the firm, but the position should be a second job since her husband was also an attorney:

> And I said, "If this is a second job, then I'll start working a thirty-five hour work week." Last time when I went in to have a discussion with him about an increase in my salary, he said, "I was thinking about giving you X." And I said, "X isn't going to make it, this time I want Y."

After giving reasons why she thought she deserved the higher salary, he replied,

> "Fine, I'll agree to increase your salary by Y, but I want the agreement also that if we run into some financial tightness, you'll be willing to go back to the salary with the increase I suggested." And I said, "That's fine, as long as you ask every man in this firm to do the same thing. That's the deal." And at that time I was the only female in the office.

Another judge from state B reflected on the old-boy network—she was excluded from golf games or fishing trips by the male attorneys in her firm. Judges from state A also discussed the double standards used in forms of address and social opportunities for men and women on the bench. These exclusions create difficult barriers for female attorneys seeking a judicial appointment or for judges seeking advancement within the court system, as networking is key to entry into areas of power in the profession. Unlike in state A, many judicial officers from state B specifically reflected on the need to be "political" in order to be appointed to a judicial position. The judges stated that they were at a disadvantage because they were not political, and that their future opportunity to be appointed to a higher judicial position would be blocked because they lacked political ties. A judge from state B explained that:

> Prior to now I don't feel I have been blocked at all. However, I am blocked at this point.

> The next step [will be] . . . tough to obtain because it involves political involvement.

The judges from state B emphasized that advancement opportunities are limited, not because of gender but because of their inability to be political in current positions:

> Not because I am a female. The main reason is political. You have to be very political to get a position as a judge. As [judges], we're prohibited from doing anything political. But judges [especially appointments to higher courts] are going to get picked, usually, from private practice where they are able to be political and have big political affiliations.

These statements demonstrate that the women are savvy to the political networking process even if their access to this network is more restricted than that of members of the (male) political in-group. Judges also discussed specific factors that helped them to get to the bench. One judge from state A explained her strategy:

> First, [I developed] a plan. The plan was to cultivate the Judicial Nominating Committee, place myself in a position of prominence, in continuing legal education and in [the] Bar Association, and cultivate the person best known to have the Governor's ear.

Another judge from state B reflected on the importance of exposure:

> I had established a reputation. I had exposure within my area of expertise, was on the board of bar examiners, my exposure by working on various committees within the bar association....that gave me the exposure I needed to be considered for a position like this.

Another judge from state B reflected on the importance of political ties:

> I think that the advantage that I had was that the Governor knew my work first hand. I had been politically active and my husband had been politically active, and I don't think that hurts.

Unlike in state A where three judges (60 percent of sample) indicated that it is easier for women to become judges because "those in power" were deliberately searching for qualified female candidates, only one judge from state B indicated that it is easier for women than men to become judges due to the governor's interest in promoting diversity on the bench. Others indicated that gender is not influential because political ties, timing, the governor, and the composition of the court are more significant. Seven judicial officers indicated that it is easier for men to receive judgeship positions because men are more political and have more political ties. One judge from state B explained why she thinks it is easier for men to get appointed to the bench:

> In the sense that men have had the networking available to them a lot longer than women, have had the social, political, and business contacts developed usually before women, in the sense that in the past probably more mentoring was done of men than it was done of women . . . in that sense yes, I definitely feel that men have an advantage.

In sum, women's advancement to judicial positions may be hindered by exclusion from the old-boys network throughout their legal careers, exclusion from political involvement, and lack of opportunity to develop political ties. These barriers were particularly salient for judges in state B, perhaps reflecting a different political culture than what is in state A.

Reconciliation of Personal and Public Lives

Balancing career concerns and family needs is a continuing difficulty for the vast majority of judges. However, without prompting, many judges indicated that their experience as mothers has been advantageous to their judicial work. All judges from state A and the majority (83 percent) from state B discussed difficulties in balancing their career and family responsibilities.[5] Some reported that their chances for promotion were constrained due to their family responsibilities, which prevented them from being available for their career 24 hours a day. However, unlike judicial officers from state B, who stressed the importance of prior work experience, judges from state A repeatedly stressed that motherhood prepared them best for the bench.

> I think that being a mother has got to be a good background for being a judge. You do a lot of decision making when you are raising a family—all the time. You learn skills that are very, very useful on the bench. (Judge, state A)

Similarly, being a "working mother" helped the following judge to appreciate the dilemmas that many women face when balancing family and professional responsibilities:

> I am very sympathetic to childcare problems. And I've had women write to me, thanking me for understanding that they have to go, for example, at 5:00 pm because they have to have their kids picked up by 5:30 pm, and they've gone in front of other judges who don't understand. I would never make a lawyer who couldn't stay for those reasons stay. . . . Not everyone can afford care in the house and they don't choose that method and kids need to be dealt with and it's a societal issue. So in that respect, I certainly think my gender and experience as a working mother have played a big role. (Judge, state A)

Although the judges from state B agreed with state A judges that the balance between their personal and private lives was harder for them to negotiate than for their male colleagues, their interviews highlighted more about the accommodations made and changes that occurred once they left private practice for the bench and once their children grew older:

> Frankly, that's the reason I am where I am, is because, like I said before, I don't know whether I'd be able to balance private practice with the other areas of my life. I'm able to leave Court usually and not think about anything else but my home life when I get home. In fact, coming to work is like a vaca-

tion for me after the weekend. Oooh, it's Monday! I get to go to work! (Judge, state B)

What I found was I was getting so stressed out from my employment that it was impacting on my relationship with my daughter. But in terms of balancing the things that I did, my family, my child, is my number one priority. . . . I don't care what's going on and everything else gets rescheduled around her things. I haven't [found a way to balance the two.] I still struggle. Sometimes I can't meet my expectations, and I just have to accept that. Managing work and family is the hard part, [and] having the energy and the time to go home. (Judge, state B)

Yes, it's difficult. It's just that when it doesn't work, it's usually horrendous. Like a jury trial example where it ended at 7:30 pm. Male judges—I have never seen a male judge have a problem with late days in court. Simply finishing the trial because they felt like finishing it. I always have to recess and make calls. (Judge, state B)

The difficulties I've encountered because I'm a woman are related to motherhood. The men here who have small children, to a large extent, have wives and their wives perform certain functions. . . . I don't have a wife like they do to make the doctors' appointments and the other arrangements and pick-ups and all that traditionally [a] mom does. . . . There is a lack of appreciation for what a male colleague will assume is perfectly acceptable for his own wife to do but not appropriate for another wife who happens to be working there. (Judge, state B)

Most of the judges from both states found their jobs socially isolating, though it is unclear whether isolation results from judicial position, gender, or other factors; their relationships with friends and colleagues changed because they were no longer able to discuss work issues and their positions demanded they avoid the appearance of impropriety.

Isolated? Yes. Appearance of impropriety rules mandate isolation; Only lawyers, you know, have no chance of appearing before you, that you can see socially on a court day. (Judge, state A)

The isolation factor, which I think is common to all judges, is that we have a different code of ethics than attorneys do. The appearance of impropriety is probably one requirement that is the hardest for attorneys and judges to deal with because there's just no firm set rule as to what's the appearance of impropriety. I had friends in the bar, still have friends in the bar, who felt uncomfortable going out to lunch with me because I am now on the bench. (Judge, state B)

Female judicial officers continue to struggle to balance their professional careers with their personal lives. Their motherhood role may be a double-edged sword: Although their experiences as mothers (i.e., time management, informal conflict resolution, decision making under pressure) may better prepare them for their experiences on the bench, the duties of motherhood may slow their advancement and create additional challenges once awarded a judicial appointment.

Gender-Related Attitudes and Justice-Based Philosophies

All judges were queried on a variety of topics related to gender, such as: Does being a woman play a role in decision making? Do female judges impose harsher sentences to overcompensate for any stereotype that women are more lenient than male judges? Do their experiences as women shape their legal reasoning? In state A, judges explicitly acknowledged that being a woman did play a positive role in how they responded to some cases. The judges generally felt that they behaved more patiently, and more humanely and possessed the ability to admit when they don't always have all the answers. The judges did not perceive these traits as weaknesses, however, but as positive skills and strengths that women judges bring to the bench to complement their legal knowledge and professional experiences.

We're all a product of who we are, and I think there's a difference somehow in the way we do our jobs as judges. . . . I don't feel hung up on not being able to admit [when I don't know the answer]. I don't feel I have to pretend that I know everything. (Judge, state A)

I think any woman has empathy for a woman [who] comes before her [and] has been beaten. I think we can relate to what this woman is going through, how embarrassed she is to stand up in front of the world and talk about being beaten by her husband. . . . (Judge, state A)

Respondents in state B spoke of advantages and disadvantages of being a judge in ways that were revealing about their gender. For instance, when asked what they liked most about their jobs, judges referred to traditionally feminine roles, such as educating people, helping people solve their problems, interacting with the litigants and attorneys, and "making a difference." Among their comments were these:

I just enjoy trying to get the best information there is about a case so that I can make an educated decision. And I also enjoy trying to explain to people what's going on, making sure they understand the process. (Judge, state B)

I feel really good when I get off the bench and I think I've made somebody understand, what happened in there [court room], what they are expected to do, and what's going to happen if they don't do what they're supposed to do. (Judge, state B)

When asked what they enjoyed least about the job, judges referred to the "emotionally draining" aspect of their position, including seeing how difficult people's lives are and knowing that their decisions impact families.

The vast majority of judges acknowledged that their gender did play a role in how they interpreted a case or reacted to a case. Specifically, the judicial officers generally felt that they behaved more compassionately, more patiently, more sensitively, and generally were better mediators than men.

Do I think in general women make better mediators than men? I would have to answer yes to that. Men I think are less inclined, whether it has to do with how they were raised or societal influences, to listen to other sides. I don't think they are as astute in understanding what is being said. (Judge, state B)

Judges referred specifically to the influence of skills traditionally associated with women, such as caregiving roles and interpersonal communication skills, on their judicial perspective:

I feel like my gender helps me a lot in criminal cases: You have these young people who come before you, you know, first time offenders. I look at them, I see my children, or their friends. I'm sure men have their skills and I think women look at things—we make just as good decisions, but many times we're not as objective as the men because we have that emotional quotient that come[s] in there just naturally. You know I think we all come up with the same decisions in the end, but we come to it from a different way. (Judge, state A)

I think that gender brings, the female gender brings a little bit of the human side and the understanding side for women who have families. . . . I think it is impressed more upon females—the whole sense of family thing—than upon the males. (Judge, state B)

You're a product of everything you are, and if you're a female, you have a different viewpoint, a different perspective than you would if you were a man. I like being a female, I like the female perspective, I just think it's different. I mean when I'm dealing with kids and I look them in the eyes, I'm a mom, and I'm looking at them as though I'm their mom, and a mom [has] compassionate feelings that no one else has. (Judge, state B)

A few judges minimized the effect of gender and referred to general differences in personality or experience.

I'm not sure that gender is as important. I think it was important when we only had one gender making all the decisions, but I think that is less and less the case. Gender becomes less significant because then you can see the differences in the judicial personalities and the temperaments in decision making. (Judge, state B)

Although women may bring a different perspective to the bench, based on their unique experiences as women or personal characteristics, many judges believed that these factors *should not* have any bearing on the outcome of the case. Nonetheless, most acknowledged that personal characteristics might exert an effect. For example, judges in both samples expressed the belief that one's gender may make a difference when presiding over rape cases. Because female judges are better able to empathize with female victims, they may treat them in a more sensitive manner than a male judicial officer.

> Whether it [gender of judge presiding over rape case] does [make a difference] or not, I don't know. I suppose on some level, it's probably even on a subconscious level more frightening for a female because you can imagine it happening to yourself. (Judge, state A)

However, female judicial officers may be more likely to blame rape victims in order to deny their own vulnerability to victimization. This would be consistent with what Lerner (1965) has termed the "just world" hypothesis, which asserts that events that happen to other people may introduce negative associations with the event in one's own life. Therefore, to make ourselves feel safer and different, we direct attention away from our own vulnerability and toward the victim and her "bad" choices. As one judge said,

> If . . . the person is similar to you but you only believe they are similar to you on what I call a surface level—we are the same sex—and something bad happens to you, it's almost imperative for me to push you away from me to protect myself from what happened to you. Because I have to find something different

about you, dissimilar about you, so that I can justify what happened to you, on a psychological basis. (Judge, state B)

Furthermore, although female judicial officers may hold a different perspective than male judicial officers do when presiding over rape case, the judges expressed "hope" that it would not affect the actual outcomes of the cases. As one judge, said,

> . . . I think our new breed of males may be a little different, but so many [older] men I've heard them say 'oh, she asked for it,' or 'what's the big deal' and things like that. I don't know that the men have caught on yet that rape is such a violent act. It's not really a sexy act; it's an act of violence against women . . . with domestic violence cases that we hear all the time and some of my own colleagues, and the comments they make, make me realize how insensitive they are. You know, I've even heard them say [she pretends to sound like a man while saying this], 'well, you know, women like to be roughed up,' and 'you don't understand—a lot of women *like* that.' Until they get away from that attitude, until they realize, then, we have a problem. (Judge, state A).

All of the judges expressed strong interest in the topic of domestic violence. The judges from state A focused on the enforcement aspect, reflecting the trend to arrest batterers rather than relying on alternatives to law enforcement, such as separation and mediation. However, judges from state B were more likely to mention that counseling, treatment, and anger management are essential for the batterer. This belief reflects the more recent trend that suggests that arrest alone is insufficient; but, these answers do not take into account the push for more coordinated community and criminal justice responses, as encouraged in recent research findings.

> Well, it depends on the circumstances. I think that the arrest option must be available to the victim. In other words, we have fought for many years now to finally get a law on the books that requires an officer to make the arrest and that permits such cases

to be brought into criminal court in a manner that's workable and effective. That's not to say that there aren't other alternatives, or that other alternatives aren't appropriate in many cases. But sometimes, nothing short of arrest is going to work. (Judge, state A)

Counseling is definitely a requirement. I know I have ordered many people to attend domestic violence counseling, and the feedback that I'm getting is always positive. (Judge, state B)

Overall, the interview data reveal a marked difference in judges' philosophies about gender-crime issues that may be atypical of those held by traditional male judges. For years, advocates of women's rights, lawyers, and others have opposed and challenged the manner in which the criminal justice and legal systems treat female victims of violent crimes committed by male offenders. The extant literature demonstrates that the enforcers (police), interpreters (lawyers and judges), and punishers (corrections) are primarily male and have been socialized and trained to believe assumptions and expectations about appropriate gender roles in society (Price and Sokoloff 1995, 2004; Stanko 1985). The judges in this sample seem to recognize the results of this institutionalized and systemic sexism: victim blaming and differential treatment of women. Part of this heightened understanding is shaped by their own experiences.

In summary, the judges' responses indicate the salience of the role that gender plays not only in the dynamics of specific crimes but also in the understandings of these crimes by members of our social and legal institutions. These beliefs are consistent with findings revealed in research on state supreme court justices that suggest that female judges tend to have a "pro-woman" stance on a large range of issues that directly affect women and often vote against the male majority on matters related to sex discrimination, sexual conduct and abuse, medical malpractice, and property settlements (Allen and Wall 1987, 1993). Although judges from state A and state B generally felt that they behaved more

compassionately, more patiently, more sensitively, and generally were better mediators than men, they believed that theses factors *should not* have any bearing on the outcome of cases. Most judges expressed pro-women attitudes by supporting such issues as rape shield laws, the introduction of a history of abuse for battered women who kill their abusive partners, stronger victim restitution programs, and a range of enhanced criminal justice and treatment responses to domestic violence.

Discussion and Conclusion

In this chapter we have explored the experiences and perceptions of 23 female judicial officers as well as offered insight into the way in which women judges view themselves within social and judicial contexts. The depth and richness of the interviews provide more detailed information than is typically collected by close-ended survey instruments or data gleaned from voting records or sentencing outcomes. The judges describe their own experiences and perceptions, prompting refined questions about gender and its influence on jurisprudence. It does not appear that these factors have transformed over time; although data were collected in state A in the early 1990s and data were collected in state B almost a decade later, the themes that emerged from the interviews remained similar. Both groups of judges reported the experience of gender bias and felt the effects of being token players in the masculine world of the judiciary.

The key difference between the judges from the two states was their views on the importance of political ties in judicial ascension. Judges from state B stressed that timing, the composition of the court, the governor, and political ties were more influential in being promoted to a judicial position, or advanced to higher judgeships, than gender. It may be that once a court is "integrated" with the addition of only one woman, that is seen as enough (see Bratton and Spill 2000). But to achieve the initial appointment or to move up the judicial hierarchy, the personal becomes more political, and men are better positioned to use their networks. As Martin and Pyle (2002) suggested in their research on gender and racial diversity on state supreme courts,

> [A]nother major impediment to women and minorities attaining judgeships may be an emphasis on traditional white male career patterns as a standard for judging eligibility. Historically, the white male lawyers tapped for judgeships have followed a relatively narrow political-legal career path. There is substantial evidence that non-traditional lawyers do not follow the career patterns that white men lawyers do. This may be, as many have suggested, because women and African American lawyers do not have the same range of opportunities as white men lawyers do. (p. 37)

Connecting back to Gilligan's different voice perspective and the role that gender may play in legal reasoning, the majority of the judges from both states believed that being a woman played a part in the "voice" they brought to the bench. Most prior research that has identified gender-related difference among judges has focused exclusively on the types of sentences they impose. This kind of research hides the importance of background factors and experiences that shape one's world views and also ignores differences in the social construction of gender roles and expectations in our society. Gender alone may not exert significant influences on sentencing decisions per se, but the different experiences and philosophies that men and women have create a contextualized construct that may supercede formal legal training in judicial decision making (Coontz 2000; Davis 1992–1993; Rush 1993; Sherry 1986; West 1991). Indeed, recent research suggests that the "new generation" of female and African American judges brings different backgrounds to the bench than their counterparts of 20 years ago: younger ages, fewer educational ties to the states in which they hold office, and a greater likelihood of having had prior

legal careers in government (Martin and Pyle 2002). The differences that men and women may bring to the bench typically remain unacknowledged because they contradict the model of the impartial arbiter. The information gleaned from the judges' voices here lend support to hopes that women's "emphasis on connection and contextuality might similarly transform law" (Sherry 1986, 165), as well as to hopes of interrupting gender bias operating against women in the courts. Moreover, a study conducted with New Zealand judges determined that 70 percent of female judges (compared with 39 percent of male judges) believed that judicial officers "judge by what they think is right and proper and that necessarily involves a particular set of values and standards which are influenced by gender" (Barwick, Burns, and Gray 1996, 32).

Moreover, one's motherhood status is both an asset and a liability to female judicial officers. While some judges believed that their parenting skills better prepared them for the bench, many stated that parenting commitments prevented them from advancing in their career and from making various choices because of these responsibilities on the home front. Despite rhetorical changes that suggest respect and value for dual commitments to home and work in the corporate world with "family friendly" policies and such, most of the judges reported much difficulty in balancing their family needs with work responsibilities. However, many judges reported success in reconciling these diverse role-strain pressures. The judges have reconceptualized the traditional caretaking role of motherhood to be one that offers excellent preparation for the bench. This interpretation differs greatly from "male" attributes of detachment and autonomy because it explicitly recognizes the benefits of familial and intimate experiences (Anleu 1995).[6] This kind of characterization permits women judges to use their conventional sex roles to claim legitimacy in their nontraditional career choices. In fact, as Miller and Meloy (2000) suggested in an earlier examination of judges from state A, the judges have been successful at negotiating and balancing their personal and professional obligations. In fact, by imbuing women's traditional female roles with honor, and insisting that these attributes are the reason for their greater clarity of judicial vision, the women judges present themselves as innovative mavericks who are more sensitive to situations of personal, familial, and/or economic injustice. (p. 424)

Although the judges emphasized that their decisions were fair, equal, strict, and just, they recognized that being female may bring a uniquely feminine understanding to the situation. The judges interviewed in this study stressed that they believe that both male and female judges ultimately reach the same legal conclusion but that they follow different paths to get there—paths that are indeed related to gender. This raises a puzzling contradiction: At the same time that the judges admit that they may have greater insight and empathy related to women's legal issues, they maintain that these strengths do *not* influence their final case outcomes. The judges describe their judicial style as patient, empathic, reasonable, with a willingness and openness to hear all sides, and they recognize that these characteristics may be misperceived or misunderstood by others as indicating that they are lenient or coddle criminals (i.e., "soft" on crime). The judges, however, insisted that this was not the case. Their rulings were simply shaped by different understandings of the situations and were enhanced by these understandings, not harmed or weakened. It is likely that defendants and victims felt that they were treated with more respect because of the judges' demeanor and style, regardless of case outcome. In fact, other research suggests that offenders treated with more respect perceive greater levels of procedural justice and satisfaction (Paternoster et al. 1997).

Similar to gender bias task force findings, the judges believed that the sexist comments and actions they experienced did contribute to an inhospitable working environment throughout their legal and judicial careers.

They also described feeling isolated and alienated from males in the field as well as from other lawyers and judges. These working conditions may reflect the consequences of being treated as tokens due to their scarcity in numbers and heightened visibility, so that their "non-achievement characteristics . . . eclipse performance" (MacCorquodale and Jensen 1993, 583). As such, these findings echo those of Rosenberg, Perlstadt, and Phillips (1993) in their research on sexist work experiences of women lawyers: Gender disparagement and sexual harassment are manifestations of "gendered systems that maintain and reinforce inequalities between men and women on the job" (p. 415).

By bringing their personal and professional experiences into the courtroom, the women revealed that they were able to dispense justice with gentleness as well as a firmness that belied their own imaginings and expectations of a more humane courtroom setting. In fact, these views are consistent with findings reported in other studies that demonstrate that women judges opt for more participatory management styles, in contrast to men's preference for more hierarchical courtroom styles, and that women judges are more likely to acknowledge others' emotions and fears than are male judges ("Different Voices" 1990). A promising avenue for future research is to follow the standpoint theory analysis used by Martin, Reynolds, and Keith (2002) in Florida, which found that female judges have more of a feminist consciousness than male judges. Whether this awareness translates into practice remains an open question. Knowing more about judges' gendered and raced experiences will provide further insight into how people in multiple subordinated positions shape the legal institution (Martin, Reynolds, and Keith 2002). Although quantitative studies may demonstrate that female judges' sentencing outcomes could be comparable or dissimilar to male judges' outcomes, the gendered paths that they follow—paths that are strikingly apparent in qualitative research, yet masked in statistical analyses—are distinctly different. Furthermore, an analysis of the task force findings provides insight into the "gendered machinery" of the court system and complements the interviews of the female judges. Hearing the voices of women and the nature of their thinking and experiences offers a much richer context in which to explore the judicial process (Miller and Meloy 2000, 424–425). However, even if women judges do nothing differently from their male counterparts, their presence on the bench is necessary for its own sake because it helps give legitimacy to the judicial process by ensuring that judges better reflect the population they serve (Malleson 2003).

Although this research does not provide conclusive evidence that gender influences case outcomes, it does highlight the persistence of the gender bias in the legal field. Based on what is learned here and elsewhere, it is reasonable to assume that the cumulative life experiences and socialization of women will impact their approach to justice and their interactions with those they serve in a way that is distinct from men. Still, it may be time to move beyond searching for measurable differences in judicial decision making among female judges and focus more simply on what their judicial presence can mean for society: equality for women and legitimacy in the process. In the final analysis, we argue that promoting gender equality on the bench, irrespective of difference in case outcomes, is a laudable goal in itself, one that should be aggressively pursued at both the state and federal levels of government.

Notes

1. These percentages reflect only a rough estimate of the actual representation of women serving as judicial officers in courts of general jurisdiction (usually referred to as trial courts) and lower level appellate courts. Our attempts to secure accurate and updated statistics on women judges at the state level included contacting the following sources: National Center for State Courts, National Association of Women Judges, National Organization for Women, Women and Law committee of the American Bar Association, the U.S. Federal Courts, the Bureau of Justice Statistics and several librarians at law schools. Unfortunately, the data obtained from these sources were either incomplete, more than a decade old, or simply unavailable or nonexistent.

2. The rationale behind promoting gender equality on the bench suggests that women bring unique contributions as a result of different life experiences, values, and attitudes. As Malleson, (2003, 1) argued, while it is appealing to "give legitimacy to the undervalued attributes traditionally associated as feminine while also promoting the merit principle by claiming to improve the quality of justice," difference theory arguments are problematic because of their theoretically weak and empirically questionable and dangerous strategies (see her article for a through discussion of these criticisms).

3. A number of studies have examined the jurisprudence in Justice O'Connor's decision making on the U.S. Supreme Court. Some of these studies suggest that although she tends to vote with the conservative bloc, her writing shows nuances and a "preference for contextual determinations" (Sherry 1986, 159; see also Behuniak-Long 1992; Sullivan and Goldzwig 1996). Other scholars, however, portray O'Connor's voting record and perspectives as more mixed and not likely shaped by her uniquely female experiences, but rather they are due to her prior experience as a majority leader in the Arizona senate (Maveety 1996; Miller 1985; Roberts 1991; Taub 1991). Less work has focused on Justice Ginsberg's decisions, but scholars suggest that her legal writings do not seem to project a "different" voice based on gender (Bonneau and Baker 1998; Varnan 2000).

4. To ensure confidentiality of participants, the states under investigation are not revealed. Respondents held attorney-judgeships in any capacity (e.g., civil, criminal,

appellate) in the states under investigation. The larger number of judges from State B reflects the structure of that state's judicial system in that, at the time of data collection, it differentiated between lower-level judicial officials presiding in family courts and other judges serving in higher-ranking positions. However, we include all judicial officers since they make decisions regarding determination of guilt/innocence, impose sentences, and so forth. In fact, given Coontz's (2000) discussion of the limitations of prior studies regarding "different voices," it is appropriate and even advantageous to include all judicial officers from family courts in empirical studies exploring gender differences because more women are affected by cases heard there. For ease of presentation and to protect respondents' confidentiality, we refer to all judicial officers as judges rather than identifying ranks or court assignments.

5. Of the three judicial officers from state B who reported that they did not struggle with this balance, one had a supportive husband, one did not have children, and one exhibited what Garey (1999) referred to as "sequencing," in that she waited until her children were grown before entering the legal profession.

6. Feminist scholars no doubt recognize that just as essentialist positions about women are problematic, there are also potential problems when introducing essentialist characteristics of men.

Study/Discussion Questions

1. What are the major findings of studies examining gender bias in legal occupations?

2. What obstacles do female judges face in their career paths?

3. Do women and men have unique styles of legal reasoning? If so, why might they exist? (contrast the maximalist and minimalist approaches)

4. According to the female judges highlighted in this chapter, how might their different socialization experiences and attitudes affect their decision making?

References

Abbate, L. (2000, March). *Approaching the bench: Women justices of the Supreme Court of Texas.* Paper presented at the Annual Meeting of the Southwestern Political Science Association.

Allen, D., and Wall, D. (1987). The behavior of women state supreme court justices: Are they tokens or outsiders? *Justice System Journal*, 12, 232–244.

——. (1993). Role orientations and women state supreme court justices. *Judicature*, 77, 156–165.

American Bar Association. (1997). *American Bar Association Commission on Women in the Profession: 1997 goal IX report card.* Federal Judicial Center, National Center for State Courts.

Anleu, S. L. R. (1995). Women in the law: Theory, research, and practice. *Australian & New Zealand Journal of Sociology*, 24(2), 329–375.

Baer, J. (1991). Nasty law or nice ladies? Jurisprudence, feminism, and gender difference. *Women & Politics*, 11, 1–31.

——. (1999). *Our lives before the law: Constructing a feminist jurisprudence.* Princeton, NJ: Princeton University Press.

Barwick, H., Burns, J., and Gray, A. (1996). *Gender equality in the New Zealand judicial system: Judges' perception of gender issues.* Wellington, N.Z.: Joint Working Group on Gender Equity.

Baunach, P. J., and Rafter, N. H. (1982). Sex-role operations: Strategies for women working in the criminal justice system. In N. H. Rafter and E.A. Stanko (Eds.), *Judge, lawyer, victim, thief* (pp. 341–358). Boston: Northeastern University Press.

Behuniak-Long, S. (1992). Justice Sandra Day O'Connor and the power of maternal legal thinking. *Review of Politics*, 54, 417–444.

Beiner, T. (1999). What will diversity on the bench mean for justice? *Michigan Journal of Gender and Law*, 6 (113), 1–36.

Bogach, B. (1999). *Courtroom discourse and the gendered construction of professional identity. Law and Society Inguiry*, 24(2), 329–375.

Bratton, K., and Spill, R. (2000, April). *Moving beyond tokenism: The effect of existing diversity on the selection of women to state supreme courts.* Paper presented at the Annual Meeting of the Midwest Political Science Association.

Cook, B. (1987). Women judges in the opportunity structure. In L. Crities and W. Hepperle (Eds.), *Women in the courts and equality* (pp. 143–174). Newbury Park, CA: Sage.

Coontz, P. (2000). Gender and judicial decisions: Do female judges decide cases differently than male judges? *Gender Issues*, 18 (4), 59–73.

Daly, K. (1989). Criminal justice ideologies and practices in different voices: Some feminist questions about justice. *International Journal of the Sociology of Law*, 17, 1–18.

Davis, S. (1992–1993). Do women judges speak 'in a different voice'?: Carol Gilligan, feminist legal theory, and the Ninth Circuit. *Wisconsin Women's Law Journal*, 7–8, 143–173.

Delaware Gender Fairness Task Force. (1995). *Final report.* Dover, DE: Author.

Different voices, different choices? The impact of more women lawyers and judges on the judicial system. (1990). *Judicature*, 74 (3), 138–146.

Esterling, K., and Anderson, S. (1999). *Diversity and the judicial merit selection process: A statistical report.* Chicago, IL: American Judicature Society.

Farr, K. A. (1988). Dominance bonding through the good-old-boys sociability groups. *Sex Roles*, 18, 259–277.

Flynn, E. E. (1982). Women as criminal justice professionals: A challenge to tradition. In N. H. Rafter and E. A. Stanko (Eds.), *Judge, lawyer, victim, thief* (pp. 305–340). Boston: Northeastern University Press.

Fox, R., and Van Sickel, R. (2000). Gender dynamics and judicial behavior in criminal trial courts: An exploratory study. *Justice System Journal*, 21 (3), 261–277.

Garey, A. (1999). *Weaving work and motherhood.* Philadelphia: Temple University Press.

Gilligan, C. (1982). *In a different voice.* Cambridge, MA. Harvard University Press.

Girth, M. L. (2000). UB's women in law: Overcoming barriers during their first hundred years. *Buffalo Women's Law Journal*, 51, 51–96.

Githens, M. (1995). Getting appointed to the state court: The gender dimension. *Women and Politics*, 15 (4), 1–24.

Goldman, S., and Slotnick, E. (1999). Clinton's second-term judiciary: Picking judges under fire. *Judicature*, 82, 264–285.

Gruhl, J., Spohn, C., and Welch, S. (1981). Women as policymakers: The case of trial judges. *American Journal of Political Science*, 25, 308–322.

Gryski, G,. Main, E., and Dixon, W. (1986). Models of state high court decision making in sex discrimination cases. *Journal of Politics*, 48, 143–155.

Guinier, L., Fine, M., and Balin, J. (1997). *Becoming gentlemen: Women, law school, and institutional change.* Boston, MA: Beacon Press.

Hemmens, C., Strom K., and Schlegel E. (1998). Gender bias in the courts: A review of the literature. *Sociological Imagination*, 35 (1), 22–42.

Huber, S. W. (2003, December 17). Female judges find acceptance. *Daily Oakland Press*, Accessed December 12, 2003 from: *http://www.zwire.com/site/news.cfm?newsid=106744115&BRD=982&PAG=461&.*

Jones-Merrit, D., and Reskin, B. F. (1997). Sex, race, and credentials: The truth about Affirmative Action in law faculty hiring. *Columbia Law Review*, 97, 199–300.

Lerner, M. (1965). Evaluation of performance as a function of performer's reward and attractiveness. *Journal of Personality and Social Psychology*, 1, 355–360.

Levit, N. (2001). Keeping feminism in its place: Sex segregation and the domestification of female academics. *Kansas Law Review*, 49, 775, Feminist Theory Symposium.

MacCorquodale, P., and Jensen, G. (1993). Women in the law: Partners or tokens? *Gender & Society*, 7, 583–593.

MacKinnon, K. (1987). *Feminism unmodified.* Cambridge, MA: Harvard University Press.

——. (1989). *Toward a feminist theory of the state.* Cambridge, MA: Harvard University Press.

Malleson, K. (2003). Justifying gender equality on the bench: Why difference won't do. *Feminist Legal Studies*, 1, 1–24.

Martin, E. (1990). Men and women on the bench: Vive la difference? *Judicature, 73,* 204–208.

Martin, E., and Pyle, B. (2002). Gender and racial diversification of state supreme courts. *Women & Politics, 24,* 35–52.

Martin, P. Y., Reynolds, J. R., and Keith, S. (2002). Gender bias and feminist consciousness among judges and attorneys: A standpoint theory analysis. *Signs, 27,* 665–705.

Martin, S. E., and Jurik, N. (1996). *Doing justice, doing gender: Women in law and criminal justice occupations.* Thousand Oaks, CA: Sage.

Maveety, N. (1996). *Justice Sandra Day O'Connor: Strategist on the Supreme Court.* New York: Rowman and Littlefield.

McCormick, P., and Job, T. (1993). Do women judges make a difference? An analysis by appeal court data. *CJLS/RCDS,* 8 (1), 135–148.

Merlo, A. V., and Pollock, J. M. (1995). *Women, law, and social control.* Boston: Allyn and Bacon.

Miller, M. (1985). Justice Sandra Day O'Connor: Token or triumph from a feminist perspective. *Golden Gate University Law Review,* 15, 493–525.

Miller, S. L., and Meloy, M. L. (2000). Women on the bench: Mavericks, peacemakers, or something else? Research questions, issues, and suggestions. In R. Muraskin (Ed.), *It's a crime: Women and justice* (pp. 413–428). Upper Saddle Ridge, NJ: Prentice Hall.

National Association of Women Judges. (1991a). Gender bias in the courts: The judge's role. *Women's Rights Law Reporter,* 12, 239–253.

——. (1991b). Making a difference: Women on the bench. *Women's Rights Law Reporter,* 12, 255.

National Center for State Courts. (2002). Women justices serving on state courts of last resort and intermediate appellate courts. Retrieved April 30, 2004 from *http://www.ncsonline.org.*

Neubauer, D. (2002). *America's courts and the criminal justice system.* Belmont, CA: Wadsworth.

O'Connor, K., and Segal, J. (1990). Justice Sandra Day O'Connor and the Supreme Court's reaction to its first female member. *Women and Politics,* 10 (2), 95–103.

Palmer, B. (2001). Women in the American judiciary: Their influence and impact. *Women and Politics,* 23 (3), 91–101.

Paternoster, R., Brame, R., Bachman, R., and Sherman, L. (1997). Do fair procedures matter? The effect of procedural justice on spouse assault. *Law and Society Review,* 3, 163–204.

Pierce, J. (1995). *Gender trials.* Berkeley: University of California Press.

Price, B. R., and Sokoloff, N. J. (Eds.) (1995). *The criminal justice system and women: Offenders, victims, and workers.* New York: McGraw-Hill.

Price, B. R., and Sokoloff, N. J. (Eds.) (2004). *The criminal justice system and women: Women offenders, victims, and workers* (2nd edition). New York: McGraw-Hill.

Pruitt, L. (1994). A survey of feminist jurisprudence. *University of Arkansas at Little Rock Law Journal,* 16, 183–210.

Reskin, B., and Roos, P. (1990). *Job queues, gender queues: Explaining women's inroads into male occupations.* Philadelphia: Temple University Press.

Roberts, D. (1991). Sandra Day O'Connor, conservative discourse, and reproductive freedom. *Women's Rights Law Reporter,* 13, 95–104.

Rosen, J. (2001, June 3). A majority of one. *New York Times Magazine,* p. 32.

Rosenberg, J., Perlstadt, H., and Phillips, W. R. F. (1993). Now that we are here: Discrimination, disparagement, and harassment at work and the experience of women lawyers. *Gender & Society,* 7, 415–433.

Rush, S. E. (1993). Feminist judging: An introductory essay. *California Review of Legal and Women's Studies,* 609, 627–632.

Scales, A (1986). The emergence of feminist jurisprudence: An essay. *Yale Law Journal,* 95, 1373–1403.

Schafran, L. (1987a). Documenting gender bias in the courts: The task force approach. *Judicature,* 70 (3), 280–290.

——. (1987b). Practicing law in sexist. In L. Crites and W. Hepperle (Eds.), *Women, the courts, and equality* (pp. 191–207). Newbury Park, CA: Sage.

Schafran, L. (2000). Two anniversaries of challenge and change. *Columbia Journal of Gender and Law,* 10 (1), 51–55.

Sherry, S. (1986). The gender of judges. *Law and Inequality,* 4, 159.

Solimine, M., and Wheatley, S. (1995). Rethinking feminist judging. *Indiana Law Journal,* 70, 891–920.

Songer, D., and Crews-Meyer, K. (2000). Does judge gender matter? Decision making in state supreme courts. *Social Science Quarterly,* 81, 752–764.

Songer, D., Davis, S., and Haire, S. (1994). A reappraisal of diversification in the federal courts: Gender effects in the court of appeals. *Journal of Politics,* 56, 425–439.

Stanko, E. (1985). *Intimate intrusions: Women's experience of male violence.* London: Routledge & Kegan Paul.

Steffensmeier, D., and Hebert, C. (1999). Women and men policymakers: Does the judge's gender affect the sentencing of criminal defendants? *Social Forces,* 77, 1163–1196.

Sullivan, P., and Goldzwig, S. (1996). Abortion and undue burdens: Justice Sandra Day O'Connor and judicial decision-making. *Women and Politics,* 16 (3), 27–54.

Taub, N. (1991). Sandra Day O'Connor and women's rights. *Women's Rights Law Reporter,* 13, 113–116.

Thomas, J. S. (1993). Ruth Ginsberg: Carving a career path . . . through a male-dominated legal world. *Congressional Quarterly Weekly Report,* 51 (29), 1876–1877.

Toutant, C. (2001). Latest judge rotations make clear family courts are still the trenches. *New Jersey Law Journal,* 165, 7.

Varnan, B. (2000). Sisterhood on the U.S. Supreme Court: The opinions and decision-making behavior of Sandra Day O'Connor and Ruth Bader Ginsburg. Paper presented at the Annual Meeting of the Southwestern Political Science Association (March 2000).

Vogel-Short, M. (2001). Women who refuse to be 'type'-cast. *New Jersey Lawyer,* 3.

West, R. L. (1991). The difference in women's hedonistic lives: A phenomenological critique of feminist legal theory. In M. A. Fineman and N. .S. Thomadsen (Eds.), *At the boundaries of law: Feminism and legal theory* (pp. 115–134). New York: Routledge.

Williams, C. (1995). Still a man's world: Men who do 'women's work.' Berkeley: University of California Press.

Wilson, N. K. (1982). Women in the criminal justice professions: An analysis of status conflict. In N. H. Rafter and E. A. Stanko (Eds.), *Judge, lawyer, victim, thief* (pp. 359–374). Boston: Northeastern University Press. ✦

18

'Yes, I've Paid the Price, but Look How Much I Gained'[1]

The Struggle and Status of Women Correctional Officers

Mary K. Stohr

In this chapter you will learn the following:

- About "pioneering" women correctional officers and women's history as officers in correctional environments

- How legal cases and legislation have opened employment opportunities in corrections to women

- The obstacles women correctional officers continue to face on the job, including sexual and gender harassment

- The similarities and differences in female and male correctional officers' perceptions and beliefs

Introduction: An Officer and a Woman

It wasn't until the last few decades of the twentieth century that corrections work became "women's work." This is true because women, for the most part and with the exception of some limited ability to work with accused and convicted/adjudicated women and girls, were proactively excluded by law and practice from paid employment in most correctional environments and with most of-fenders. They were hired only after the Civil Rights Act of 1964 (and its Amendment in 1972) was passed and presidential pressure was applied to "affirmatively" hire them. Even then they had to sue. Even then it took decades. Even now the number of women as correctional employees does not begin to equal the number of men so employed.

Women in correctional work have paid a price, as all women have (as per the subject of the 1970s Helen Reddy anthem, "I Am Woman"), but they have also gained. The story of women correctional officers, then, is mostly a tale of triumph, peppered with instances of political battles, discrimination, and harassment. Women overcame enormous political and social barriers to achieve their equal employment opportunities in corrections, and in the end, they won that battle. Moreover, now that they are established employees in virtually every correctional environment, the evidence is that most men do support their presence and accept them as colleagues (Hemmens et al. 2002; Lawrence and Mahan, 1998; Simon and Simon 1993). There are, however, still instances when women are discriminated against in employment and advancement in corrections, and sexual and gender harassment by a few men still occurs in these workplaces.

According to the *Sourcebook of Criminal Justice Statistics*, 2002, women occupied 40 percent of the correctional officer positions in American jails, but their employment in prisons can no longer be determined from national statistics—as these statistics are not available in publications by the federal government—though it is thought to be much less than in jails (Maguire and Pastore 2002). About 22 percent of correctional officers in Canadian minimum- and medium-security federal prisons are women (Correctional Service of Canada 2003), which is probably close to the American employment level. Though these numbers are not particularly impressive, they do represent an increase since 1988 when Zupan (1992) reported that women constituted only 15 percent of correctional officers nationally and 10 percent in Canadian federal prisons in 1984 (Correctional Service of Canada 2003). Clearly, women have made huge strides in obtaining employment in corrections, but these figures indicate that they have hardly achieved parity.

How women in corrections reached this point and who got them there is a fascinating tale of bravery and perseverance by some women and by supportive men. What issues and challenges those women faced and continue to wrestle with, once hired, are integral parts of the story of their ultimate success.

Pioneer Women and Breaking Frames

A Brief History

As Carrie Chapman Catt, one of the most prominent freedom fighters for women in this country, once said, it took the concentrated efforts, along with outrageous sacrifices, of thousands of women and men over a period of many decades to get women the vote in this and other western countries (See Carrie Chapman Catt, quoted in Dworkin 1993). Most of those women and men never saw victory or witnessed the passage of the Nineteenth Amendment in 1920; they just labored in the belief that justice would someday be theirs. They believed, despite the prejudice and sexism they confronted on a daily basis, that women would someday gain suffrage in this country. A similar effort and struggle has been made to gain equal employment for minority group women and men and white women.

Historically, women have constituted a relatively small number of jail and prison inhabitants, both as security staff and as inmates. It really wasn't until after the enactment of equal employment opportunity statutes (Title VII of the Civil Rights Act of 1964) and the subsequent development of affirmative action plans and programs for public agencies (1972 amendment to Title VII) and numerous lawsuits over a period of 30 years that women have been accorded a general correctional

role. The rampart for these laws and lawsuits and the belief that women could succeed as correctional staff were established over at least two centuries by women pioneers in corrections who weren't afraid to break away from the established expectations for women's behavior.

This breaking away was necessary for pioneer women in this field as the history of women's corrections is one of incarceration in predominately male prisons and jails and being watched over by male guards and wardens. It wasn't until the mid-1800s that women and girls were even routinely separated from the men and boys in male prisons (Belknap 1996; Pollock 2002; Smykla and Williams 1996; Young 2004; Zupan 1992). Sometimes this separation did occur by race and usually this meant that African-American women were given lesser facilities (Young 2004). It wasn't until women reformers demanded change, to prevent the continued sexual and physical abuse of women, as well as neglect of female needs, that women and girls were removed to separate parts of male and/or their own correctional facilities. As Pollock (2002) wrote, "[W]omen were isolated in a separate wing in Auburn Prison in 1825, but no matrons were hired until 1832. Even then, the managers and administrators were men until the women were moved to Bedford Hills and other separate facilities for women in New York" (p. 176). It is still true today that women and girls are held in small sections of predominantely male jails.

Matrons were essentially female correctional staff hired to work exclusively with women and girls. Some of these women were educated, middle-class, white reformers intent on helping female inmates. Typically, they were paid less than men and, particularly if they worked in a female section of a male facility, they had fewer opportunities for promotion (Pollock 2002; Zupan 1992). Women also performed nonsecurity work in support service capacities in correctional facilities (e.g., clerical, nursing) in early prisons and jails—as they do today (Chapman et al. 1983).

The reformatory movement for juveniles and women in the late 1800s and early 1900s in this country opened up a number of employment opportunities for females (Pollock 2002; Rafter 1985; Zupan 1992). New facilities were built and women were hired to work in them and even run them. Some state legislators required that only women be hired in women's and girl's facilities (Zupan 1992). Later in the 1900s, sexism prevailed at the same time that it became more difficult to recruit enough qualified women, and so those female-gender-only requirements for work in women's facilities were dropped by the states. Today, in part because of the same equal employment laws that forced male correctional facilities to hire female officers, in a few female institutions more men work as correctional officers than women do (National Institute of Corrections 1998). Unfortunately, because some of these facilities are not well managed, history is repeating itself as a few unsupervised male staff with easy access to women in living units, sexually abuse female inmates (Henriques and Gilbert 2003; Morash and Schram 2002).

Two Women Pioneers in Corrections

In separate 1998 and 2002 articles appearing in *Women & Criminal Justice*, two women pioneers in corrections—Edna Mahan (1900–1968) and Margaret Moore (1948)—were featured (Hawkes 1998; Yates 2002). They are pioneers in the sense that they had many "firsts" in correctional employment. Mahan was the youngest superintendent in the country when hired as the superintendent of the New Jersey Reformatory for Women (Clinton Farms) in 1928 at age 28 (Hawkes 1998). She served in that capacity for 40 years. Likewise, Margaret Moore, who began her career as a corrections counselor in 1974, was hired as the first woman deputy commissioner of corrections in Pennsylvania in 1993. Later, in 1994, she was the first woman and African American to be hired as the director of the

District of Columbia Department of Corrections (Yates 2002).

Despite the fact that these two women's careers differed in that they bookended both the beginning and the end of the twentieth century, over the course of their work lives, they encountered the same type of resistance to their ideas and efforts, and to their very presence as females in a traditionally male workplace. They broke the "frame" or set of expectations that determined what was the appropriate place and work for women, and they did this despite the hardships they faced when growing up.

Mahan. Edna Mahan's father, a miner, abandoned his family during her childhood. Yet she managed to enter and graduate from the University of California, Berkeley (Hawkes 1998). She launched her corrections career with the Los Angeles County Probation Department. Mahan's career was guided in part by her mentor in the probation department Miriam Van Waters (Hawkes 1998).

Her career was marked by a number of successes, along with a constant struggle to meet the needs of the women she supervised for adequate housing, programming, and medical care. She had to convince the board of managers that "colored" babies of inmates deserved the same care as white babies. She also had to convince them of the need for a full-time female physician and a part-time psychologist to attend to the inmates. Initiatives early in her career, which continued throughout her administration, included the removal of all bars on the windows of the cottages. She also argued for the housing of all female felons at Clinton. She maintained an open-door management style for staff and inmates, advocating student government for inmates. She fought to increase the pay of staff so that it matched what men made in men's institutions.

Notably, on the pay issue, Mahan was less successful. She did not make much headway in pay increases during the 1930s but even in 1940 men working in male facilities still made three times what the women made working at Clinton ($150 per month versus

$50 per month) and they worked much less per day than the women (8 hours versus 12 hours) (Hawkes 1998). In 1951 the shifts were standardized to 8-hour days, but it wasn't until 1965 that female "cottage officers" were paid the same as male "correctional officers."

Moore. Margaret Moore was the youngest of four children, the only girl born into a relatively poor family in Mississippi (Yates 2002). Her mother and the competition with her older brothers were motivating forces in her life. She was a single mom at 16, but with her mother's assistance, she earned a degree from the University of Pittsburgh in 1973.

Much like Mahan, Moore was greatly assisted in her early career by a female mentor, in her case Barbara Neely, who identified her talents early, guided her, and pointed her to opportunities. After starting as a counselor in a women's prerelease program in Pittsburgh, Moore decided that correctional work was for her. She saw that she had much in common with these women, albeit without the criminal involvement. The difference, as Moore saw it, was that she had managed to get her needs (e.g., for housing, food, medical care, and affordable daycare) met by successfully negotiating the system.

After earning a master's degree in social work, Moore advanced quickly up the ranks in Pennsylvania. In her career, she directed community centers, treatment programs, women's prisons, men's prisons, and the building, opening, and operation of several prisons. She finished her correctional career as the director (appointed in 1994) of the Washington, DC, Department of Corrections. As a woman who accomplished many firsts for her gender and race in corrections, Moore experienced instances of sexism and racism from her male colleagues on several occasions. Her reaction was to refuse to allow others to discriminate against her. She also ignored the male staff who told her she had no chance, as both an African American and a woman, of ever running an agency.

A key achievement during her time as director of transition of some institutions was to move them from a traditional hierarchical management style to a more participatory management style. *Traditional management* styles value top-down communication, a rigid hierarchy, and little input by lower level staff. *Participatory management* styles emphasize greater communication and input from the lower levels of staff and greater control by lower-level staff of decisions that affect their workplace. Much like Mahan's efforts to democratize the living unit for women inmates in the New Jersey Clinton prison, Moore was trying to do the same for all staff in the Pennsylvania prisons. Yates (2002) quoted Moore as wanting to be remembered in the corrections industry as "unashamedly African American and unapologetically feminist" (p. 24).

What Can We Learn From These Life Stories?

The stories of Mahan's and Moore's experiences in corrections work are instructive for several reasons. Though faced with poverty and discrimination based on gender and race, the latter only in Moore's case, in their early lives and careers, these women persevered. Both women faced terrible odds in their efforts to make something of themselves and to be a force for good in corrections. On both fronts they were, by any measure, spectacularly successful. What was their secret?

Their biographers mention a determination to succeed that typified both women. They also mention an unwillingness to consider defeat. Both women experienced setbacks and opposition in their careers, and both just mowed right past those and carried on.

Penny Harrington, a pioneer herself in the policing field—she was the first woman chief of a large city (Portland, Oregon) in the 1980s[2]—gave some sage advice for young women and men entering the policing field, much of which is relevant for work in corrections (Harrington 2002). All of Harrington's advice is made more relevant because she faced incredible barriers to her own hiring and promotion in policing. Almost from the onset, she had to sue and struggle to be hired and then to be promoted through the ranks, until finally a progressive male mayor appointed her chief.

Harrington (2002) warned women entering the profession that they are likely to get special scrutiny on the job as either a "first" female hire in a position or as one of a few females, a "token," on the job. She also warned that a woman's behavior on the job, how she performs the role, might be different from her male colleagues and thus less appreciated or understood. Specifically, given women's cultural training, she indicated that they may be less aggressive and more willing to listen than their male colleagues (we will discuss gender-based styles later in this chapter).

She advised women entering the profession to avoid adopting a "one of the boys" attitude, which can lead to personal and professional traps. Instead, she said that women and men should try to keep a sense of perspective about their work that is balanced by outside interests, family, and friends. This sense of perspective, she commented, will also allow those who work in policing (corrections too) to avoid the "us vs. them" (p. 7) attitude toward community members that in corrections can lead to abusive behavior by staff toward inmates.

She provided descriptors of "types" of men and women in the profession to avoid or be careful of, but promoted the search for a mentor. Should a new recruit find one, or several of these, as both Moore and Mahan did, they should latch onto them and learn all they can, according to Harrington. She also discussed the benefits (e.g., the chance to learn about the profession) and pitfalls (e.g., hazing and sexual harassment) that new women on the job might encounter at the academy, during the field training experience, or during their probationary period.

Finally, Harrington (2002) offered advice on how to set one's personal code in the police workplace, advice that would be appropriate for any job in the human service field, including corrections. She noted that whenever she made a decision in policing, she weighed the consequences for all involved, including the specific person affected, the community, the police department, and herself.

On the career front, her code is to "always tell the truth," (p. 10) to not complain about the job to coworkers, and to not do something unless it feels right and unless she would feel okay if her family saw it on the nightly news. She urged public servants to stay current on the news and research in the field and females to join a women's professional organization, in which they are likely to be informed about issues facing women and supported in their careers (Harrington 2002). Her code also included the recommendation that people in the profession maintain their physical and mental health through fitness, and by stress reduction techniques and practices. Professional people need to approach their jobs with a positive attitude. Her final advice was to know one's community by participating in it and reading about it. In Harrington's (2002) opinion, these activities are likely to make a woman or man in human service work a better prepared and informed officer, as well as a better citizen.

Affirmative Action and Corrections Work, or How Women Became Officers

Both Harrington in policing and Moore in corrections noted that they would not have been hired, or promoted, without the weapon that equal employment and affirmative action laws provided them. For example, Mahan was hired before these laws were passed and initiatives were adopted, but remember she worked exclusively with women. It is worth noting that Mahan still struggled with equal pay issues for women in corrections. As mentioned, these pay issues were not resolved until 1965, which, not coincidentally, was the same year that the Equal Pay Act was passed by Congress. In other words, our history tells us—and much of this is relatively recent history—that without the force of law behind them, women would still be excluded from corrections work. Zimmer (1989) made the additional point that the law alone, however, is not a perfect remedy for increasing women's employment opportunities. She argued that administrators have a responsibility to be proactive in these areas as well.

In any case, the law on equal employment and how it is implemented (e.g., affirmative action) is controversial (Stohr 2005). The discussion of equal opportunity (EO) or affirmative action (AA) in the classroom or the workplace tends to stir debate, sometimes heated debate, between those on both sides of this issue. This is understandable as EO and AA initiatives in government and the private sector have had a real effect on the ability of many female and minority male workers to secure jobs. Some people are threatened and frightened by the existence of formal AA plans and their promotion.

Affirmative action simply means that an organization takes positive steps to ensure that their hiring practices are fair and that they do not disparately affect a targeted, underrepresented group. AA is a more proactive remedy than EO for employment discrimination (Camp et al. 1997). AA as law has been used to promote the hiring of minority group members and white women.

But before we discuss the most current form of affirmative action, we need to recognize that it has always existed in correctional employment. In the past, an informal qualification for correctional work with adult males (i.e., where most of the jobs were) was that the applicant be white and male. Thus, there was a plan, albeit informal in recent years, but out in the open before that, that only white males would be hired to work with adult males in corrections. For example, the State of California didn't start hiring any female correctional officers to work in male prisons until the early 1970s, or after the Civil Rights Act of 1964 was amended in 1972 to apply to gender discrimination in hiring (*Pulido v. State of California et al.* 1994). In other words, they didn't start hiring women until they were forced to. But then, many correc-

tional institutions didn't hire women until many years later.

At the prison in Washington State where I began work in 1983, I was the second woman hired, and the first, a woman who was a niece of a sergeant, had been hired only a month before. It is worth noting that this was more than 10 years after the applicable statute had passed and almost 20 years after the Civil Rights Act of 1964 (Stohr 2003). The warden told me in private once that he had fought central office for five years before he gave in and hired a woman. Another time, he told me that he had no intention of hiring African Americans. Appropriately enough, he informed me of this just as he told me that I was to serve on the Affirmative Action committee and do nothing to recruit minorities. He also proactively worked to prevent the promotion of the one Hispanic male officer. Not surprisingly, as of fall 1986, when I left prison work for graduate school, no African Americans had been hired at that prison, and other than this one Hispanic officer—who left for a promotion to sergeant at another prison within the year—no other persons of color were hired either.

In another instance of this kind of discrimination, and at the same time I had applied for the prison job, I had been in the selection process for a jail correctional officer job in a large urban center in the Northwest. Out of the hundreds of applicants for these correctional officer positions, I scored in the top three after oral, written, physical, psychological, and comprehension tests. But I was not hired for one of the 15 jobs that were open, while everyone above me and several people below me on the list were hired. When I asked the personnel specialist for this county, whom I had come to know and who was a white male, why this was, he told me in confidence that they were not hiring any women; I was the only woman who had scored so high (some of the men at the top of the ranking were given extra veteran's points) and they were hiring around me.

This kind of informal, and sometimes formal, discrimination in hiring was common in American and Canadian corrections until a few decades ago (Belknap 1995; Correctional Service of Canada 2003; Zupan 1992). To establish this fact, all one need do is examine the employment rolls for correctional agencies before the 1970s and 1980s. We will also examine some evidence in the following section that indicates such intentional discrimination still exists.

Civil Rights Legislation

Civil rights legislation first appeared in 1866 and 1871 and was concerned with employment discrimination that might be faced by ex-slaves (Stohr 2005). Several presidents issued executive orders barring employment discrimination in federal employment and in organizations having federal contracts, starting with Franklin Roosevelt in 1941. Correctional entities were not affected, for the most part, by this legislation or the executive orders until 1961, when President Kennedy's executive order imposed the first requirement for affirmative action. He required that federal agencies and those with federal contracts institute a "plan" and implement a program to ensure that the methods used for employment practices be nondiscriminatory. Affirmative action plans were also intended to address the methods used to make up for past discriminatory practices in employment. In other words, affirmative action plans were premised on fair employment in the present and the provision of remedies for past employment discrimination. Both Presidents Johnson and Nixon reaffirmed the importance of AA with their own executive orders.

In 1964, however, the Civil Rights Act was passed and included several titles. This act made it illegal to discriminate in voter registration requirements, public accommodation and facilities, and employment (for a brief social and political history of the CRA of 1964, and the movement that birthed it, see *www.congresslink.org*). The act also created the Equal Employment Opportunities Commission to review complaints, though the EEOC's ability to enforce change was weak.

The most important title of the CRA of 1964, for our purposes here, was Title VII that came as an amendment to the act in 1972. Title VII essentially made it unlawful to discriminate in the hiring, maintaining, or discharging of people because of their race, color, religion, sex, or national origin.

The Civil Rights Act of 1964 originally only covered employers of more than 25 persons but was eventually extended to cover both private and public employment agencies, including those on the state and local level that employed 15 or more people. Correctional agencies of any size were now required to reform their hiring practices and to institute affirmative action plans. As my experience in 1983 in Washington State and with an urban jail in a Northwest city demonstrates, compliance with this law came only gradually and incrementally from facility to facility; and it took several years and countless lawsuits to compel compliance.

Intentional Discrimination Continues

Some people argue that women and minority group men no longer need affirmative action plans to ensure equal employment. Yet there is recent evidence that indicates this is far from true. For instance, from a 1997 agreement between the United States Justice Department (DOJ) and the Arkansas Corrections System, we gain some insight into employment discrimination in corrections, more than 30 years after passage of the CRA of 1964 (U.S. Department of Justice 1997). In the agreement, the details of which were released by the DOJ before it was approved by the court, it is noted that similar practices of employment discrimination against women in corrections were litigated and settled with the DOJ in Indiana, Massachusetts, Florida, Delaware, New Jersey, and North Carolina. The agreement with Arkansas stipulated that "[t]he state will take steps to ensure that female corrections officers assigned to male prisons are given an equal chance to be hired for a job, obtain assignments and seek promotions" (U.S. Department of Justice 1997, 1). The DOJ (1997) noted that before its investigation, women correctional officers in male prisons in Arkansas were "[l]imited to posts such as guard towers or switchboards. These assignment restrictions severely limited the opportunity of women to gain advancement" (p. 2). Under the agreement, the state was to open all assignments to women in male facilities, except in some limited instances where the privacy interests of males prevailed. Moreover, the state was to give back pay to the women who had been discriminated against and engage in the priority hiring of 400 women and priority promotion of about 40 women—"with retroactive seniority and benefits"—as a remedy for the victims of this discrimination (U.S. Department of Justice 1997, 2).

Furthermore, in a relatively recent analysis of employment data provided to the Equal Employment Opportunity Commission by employers of over 50 employed in 1999, and supported by the Ford Foundation, two Rutgers University law professors, Blumrosen and Blumrosen (2002), found a continuing pattern of widespread intentional discrimination in employment that impacts both minorities (African Americans, Hispanics, Asian and Pacific Islanders, American Indians) and white women (Stohr 2005). They did not have data for correctional organizations. Nevertheless, what they found illustrates that discrimination in employment did not end with the institution of affirmative action plans, though they did note some serious improvement in the employment of minorities and women since 1979. For this study, Blumrosen and Blumrosen (2002) defined the existence of *intentional discrimination* as the rate of employment of minorities and women that fell two standard deviations below the average rate for all those employed in that industry, job category, and metropolitan area.

As one might expect, they found that intentional discrimination differed by group and state. For instance, in New Jersey, Arkansas, and Iowa, there was a 30 percent, 32

percent and 34 percent chance, respectively, that a minority group member would face intentional discrimination in employment. For white women, the chance was 29 percent in Iowa, 31 percent in Arkansas, and 34 percent in New Jersey. In these three states, and among the largest racial/ethnic groupings of African Americans, Hispanics, and Asian and Pacific Islanders—which they did not separate by gender—Asian and Pacific Islanders were believed to face the greatest chance of discrimination at 64 percent in Iowa and Arkansas and 41 percent in New Jersey. For African Americans, the chance of discrimination was 39 percent in Iowa and Arkansas and 40 percent in New Jersey. For Hispanics, the chance was 50 percent in Arkansas, 38 percent in Iowa, and 36 percent in New Jersey (Blumrosen and Blumrosen 2002; see the full report at *www.eeol.com*). Notably, when comparing just these three states, one sees that the risk of being intentionally discriminated against in employment is still high for some groups in our society, but that it can vary widely.

Reverse Discrimination

When affirmative action plans are employed, many have argued, reverse discrimination against dominant groups, usually white males and sometimes white females, can occur (Stohr 2005). This argument was used in a recent Supreme Court case, *Grutter v. Bollinger et al.* (2003), in which Grutter, a white female applicant to the University of Michigan's Law School, maintained that she was denied admission because of her race, again while applicants with lesser academic credentials were admitted. Because women, particularly white women, now make up about 50 percent of law school entrants, they are rarely accorded protected status requiring affirmative action any more. The Court held, as per Justice Sandra Day O'Connor writing for the majority, that the University of Michigan Law School had a "compelling interest in attaining a diverse student body." This meant that the law school could discriminate against a white female applicant because she did not add to that diversity. Interestingly enough, and as noted by Justice O'Connor, major American businesses supported the affirmative action efforts by the school as they thought a diverse workforce was key to staying competitive in the world marketplace. Justice O'Connor noted that the consideration of race as one factor in admissions policies was lawful.[3] She also noted that the law school's admission policy that places a value on diversity does not define that term only in relation to racial and ethnic origin. She argued that the majority opinion in this case was in keeping with the *Bakke* (1978) decision (which allowed reverse discrimination against a white male in medical school admission) as it accorded some consideration of race and ethnicity in admissions policies.[4]

What the *Grutter* case indicates is that affirmative action for law school admissions for white women is no longer necessary. The courts will, however, allow it for minority women and men, as they are still underrepresented in law school classes. For corrections, this ruling likely means that affirmative action as an employment practice is allowed when the goal is to achieve a diverse work force that is representative of the larger population. However, should a given group achieve proportional representation in the workplace (as white women did for law school admissions), they would no longer need affirmative action as an equal employment device.

Although discrimination in any form, whether directed at minority or majority groups, is blatantly unfair, there is reason to believe that reverse discrimination does not occur as frequently as one might expect in corrections. For instance, Camp and his colleagues (1997) found that equal employment and affirmative action initiatives did not appear to help minority group men and women or white women employees disproportionately in federal prisons; rather, it tended to level the playing field for all groups in terms of employment and promotions. In the four years on which Camp et al. (1997) focused (1991–1994), black officers and white women were sometimes overrepresented among those promoted, but in other years they were not.

Equal Employment Versus Privacy Interests of Inmates

One of the arguments that has been used to exclude females from equal employment in male prisons and male sections of jails, where numerically most of the jobs in corrections are, has been the privacy interests of the men. Correctional officers need to be able to pat down inmates, including in the genital area, do visual body cavity searches, and enter cells and shower rooms, where inmates may be only partially clothed or nude. Male inmates who otherwise might not object to the presence of female officers have complained bitterly about this matter in the courts. Female correctional officers have countered in suits that they are effectively excluded from most correctional work if they are not allowed to work in male facilities. After many years of litigation, the female correctional officers' right to equal employment has generally prevailed over the male inmates' right to privacy. Notably, though, this matter remains somewhat unsettled in practice, especially as it relates to cross-gender supervision of male officers and female inmates (Bennett 1995; Maschke 1996) but also when involving male inmates and female officers (recall the Arkansas settlement mentioned previously).

As Maschke (1996) wrote, after analyzing the case law regarding the privacy/equal employment arguments: "For the most part, the judicial response has been to elevate the employment rights of employees above the privacy rights of prisoners" (p. 24). In a series of cases, the Supreme Court has indicated that inmates have few if any privacy rights or expectations. Although some of the lower courts have recognized the abuse history of women inmates and moved to restrict some supervision by men, at the same time, the courts have gradually recognized the equal employment claims of women.

The only real exception to the dominance of the equal employment argument for correctional officers over the privacy argument by inmates occurs when a prison excludes cross gender supervision because of a *bona fide occupational qualification* or *BFOQ* (Bennett 1995). In other words, a female officer could be excluded from employment in a male maximum security prison in Alabama if gender (being a man) was a BFOQ for working in such a violent and potentially dangerous environment (Supreme Court decision in *Dothard v. Rawlinson* 1977). Or male officers could be excluded from employment in the living units of a women's prison if gender (being a woman) was a BFOQ for providing a rehabilitative atmosphere for women inmates. This exclusion of male officers from some search practices was successfully argued in only a few courts and was allowed, as a high percentage of the female inmates had experienced sexual or physical abuse by males in the past (Seventh Circuit Court of Appeals decision in *Torres v. Wisconsin* 1988; Ninth Circuit Court of Appeals decision in *Jordan v. Gardner* 1993; see Bennett 1995; Maschke 1996). In the *Jordan* case, the likely outcome was that administrators would need to restrict male officer pat downs of female inmates to emergency situations only (Bennett 1995).

The end result of this debate has generally been that female and male correctional officers' equal employment argument prevails over inmates' privacy argument in corrections, but this is not always true. As Maschke (1996) concluded, "Although judges tended to rule that equal employment rights outweighed the privacy interests of male and female prisoners, they also upheld some job restrictions for both male and female correctional officers. In doing so, they revealed the complexities of gender in the prison setting" (p. 38)

Another of Those Complexities: Sexual and Gender Harassment

Sexual and gender harassment are a problem in many employment environments for women (and men), but particularly in the correctional workplace. This is true because correctional agencies are historically and predominately male work environments. As mentioned previously, most of the employees and most of the inmates/supervisees in corrections are male, and this has always been so. Therefore, women are regarded by some as interlopers, and one method of making that point clear is to harass them. The unfortunate truth is that if you are a woman working in corrections, particularly in male institutions with mostly male staff, you are a "token" and are going to experience some harassment (Belknap 1995; Lawrence and Mahan 1998; Pogrebin and Poole 1997; Stohr et al. 1998; Zupan 1992). The good news is that much of this harassment will be minor (e.g., jokes and comments), may be short lived (especially once you complain), and will mostly originate from only a few staff.

Male staff may believe that women are incapable of being physical enough to adequately do the job of a correctional officer in a male prison (Belknap 1995; Jurik 1985; Zimmer 1986; Zupan 1992). They might feel that women just aren't tough enough emotionally for the work. They might continue to regard them as sex objects rather than as proper work partners (Pogrebin and Poole 1997). As Pogrebin and Poole (1997) put it, "Harassment sustains both male workplace power and male power to treat women as sexual objects" (p. 43).

Sexual harassment is of two varieties: quid pro quo (something for something) and hostile environment. *Quid pro quo* sexual harassment occurs when an unwelcome demand for sexual intimacy is made in exchange for keeping or advancing in one's job. This could include requests for dates, touching (sexual assault and battery), or threats. *Hostile environment* sexual harassment occurs when the workplace is sexualized with jokes, pictures, or in other ways such that it is offensive to one gender. Although male officers might be offended equally by a sexualized environment, even when the harassment isn't directed at them, usually, but not always, these behaviors are directed at female officers by male colleagues.

Gender harassment includes behaviors that are aimed at demeaning, deprecating, and diminishing the abilities, skills, and existence of one gender. Though usually aimed at women by men, this is not always so. The behaviors associated with gender harassment can overlap with sexual harassment and at times they can be indistinguishable. The main difference may lie partially in intent. Someone engaged in gender harassment probably wants the victim to feel unwelcome in the workplace and may want them to leave, whereas a person engaged in sexual harassment may be intent on sexual gratification at the expense of their victim, and so will want them to stay on the job.

But the effects of both types of harassment are remarkably similar for the victim and the organization. Such harassment can lead to stress, physical and mental health problems, decreased morale, turnover, discord in the work environment, and lawsuits. The organization that doesn't properly train staff on sexual and gender harassment prevention nor adequately monitor staff behavior in this regard is liable, but that is little solace for the victims who rarely bring lawsuits, let alone complain (Zimmer 1989).

In their study of four county jail facilities, Pogrebin and Poole (1997) found numerous instances of gender and sexual harassment reported by female deputies (correctional officers). The gender harassment they reported included putdowns, jokes, being called "honey, babe, dear" when in a professional context and in front of inmates or colleagues, being told they have PMS, and just general "gutter mouth." For example, one female officer reported, "[Male deputies] go out of their way to make you feel inferior. Constant putdowns, smart-ass remarks, smirks . . . things that make you feel uncomfortable . . . [t]hey enjoy it" (quoted in Pogrebin and Poole 1997, 48–49). The sexual harassment that was reported to Pogrebin and Poole (1997) was even more disturbing: "I've been touched, poked,

brushed against—I've had a guy come up from behind me and lick the back of my neck and say, 'Real nice, sweetheart. You smell good enough to eat'" (pp. 50–51).

This research by Pogrebin and Poole (1997), viewed in tandem with all the other research on sexual and gender harassment in corrections, indicates that it is not uncommon, varies in severity, is rarely formally complained about, and has deleterious effects on the victim and the organization. The remedies lie, of course, in complaints and lawsuits, but since these are imperfect devices in that they are rarely employed, are not always successful, are costly on several levels, and take too long, perhaps the best remedy is just to manage well. Correctional administrators have it in their power to create a respectful environment for all employees and inmates/supervisees. Whether they choose to do so marks the difference between a professional and an unprofessional workplace for women and men.

Differences in Supervision Styles, Attitudes, and Preferences by Women and Men in Corrections

As women have moved increasingly into the corrections field, their performance and perceptions of their work have been the subject of much study (Belknap 1995; Carlson, Anson, and Thomas 2003; Cullen et al. 1985; Farkas 1999; Jenne and Kersting 1996; Jurik 1985, 1988; Jurik and Halemba 1984; Kim et al. 2003; Lawrence and Mahan 1998; Leiber 2000; Lovrich and Stohr 1993; Lutze and Murphy 1999; Martin and Jurik 1996; Pollock 2002; Simon and Simon 1993; Stohr, Lovrich, and Mays 1997; Walters 1992; Wright and Saylor 1991; Zimmer 1986; Zupan 1986). In most respects, the research indicates that men and women in correctional work are more similar than dissimilar in their attitudes and perceptions. For instance, men and women correctional officers have been found to have remarkably similar levels of job satisfaction and perceptions of job enrichment and job characteristics.

The major differences in how the work environment is perceived and experienced by gender has to do with sexual/gender harassment (which we just discussed), stress, and work role perceptions. The research on stress indicates that, in some studies, female officers have been found to report or exhibit more stress than male officers (Cullen et al. 1985; Lovrich and Stohr 1993; Wright and Saylor 1991). In other studies, researchers haven't found a difference in level of stress by gender (Carlson et al. 2003). When a difference has been found, the source of this stress is indeterminate (Gross et al. 1994). That is, the women may be more stressed by the characteristics of the job or its environment (e.g., gender or sexual harassment), or the source of stress could be variables outside the work (e.g., child care).

Some of the researchers in this area have noted that women themselves have more of a "service" or "caring" or "rehabilitation" orientation toward the correctional role than men have. Jurik (1985) was one of the first to note that women and men differed in how they viewed and performed their correctional work. She noted that the female staff in her prison research tended to value a service orientation over pay and benefits, which were more of a concern for the male staff in her study. Jurik (1985) found that 55 percent of the female officers took the correctional job to work in rehabilitation, whereas only 23 percent of the male respondents indicated the same motivation. Several other researchers have found that women correctional staff tend to be, or are perceived by males and females as being, more supportive of a human services role (Farkas 1999; Fry and Glaser 1987; Kim et al. 2003; Leiber 2000; Stohr 1997; Zimmer 1986; Zupan 1986). Moreover, some researchers established in the 1980s, based on performance evaluations and inmate surveys (or the perceptions of male supervisors and male inmates), that women's work styles had a calming effect on the be-

havior of male inmates (Jurik 1988; Zimmer 1986).

On the other hand, Jenne and Kersting (1996) found in their study of Northeastern male and female correctional officers that the women were just as aggressive as the men when reacting to hypothetical situations. Since the response rate in this study was rather low (37 percent), the authors also conducted in-depth interviews of their female subjects to try to determine why they found few differences between the men and the women. They found that the women officers were socialized on the job to react like men in situations involving violence. At the same time, they found that both men and women tended to prefer a more human services orientation when violence was not involved.

In two separate studies I conducted with colleagues of several mixed gender and exclusively women's jails (e.g., Stohr, Lovrich, and Wood 1996; Stohr, Lovrich, and Mays 1997), we also found that both male and female officers tended to prefer and value service training over security training. Similarly, Farkas (1999) found that both male and female correctional officers believed that women were more service-oriented and men were more security-oriented in their work roles, but when they were asked to respond to hypothetical situations, their styles were more alike than not. In fact, both Farkas (1999) and Jenne and Kersting (1996) found that, if anything, the female officers were more aggressive in their responses to hypothetical situations. We, of course, should keep in mind that these are hypothetical situations, not real-life incidents.

Finally, and relatedly, a number of studies have found that male officers may not have as positive an assessment of female officers' job performance as females have, though these differences may hinge on the age, military service, or other characteristics of the males and the institutions in which they work (Belknap 1996; Farkas 1999; Hemmens et al. 2002; Lawrence and Mahan 1998; Lutze and Murphy 1999). This lack of support by some male officers, and the masculinized environment that prefers the use of violence in some institutions, particularly male medium- and maximum-security prisons, may lead to a devaluing of the abilities of officers of both genders who adopt a style that befits a more service or rehabilitative role (Hemmens et al. 2002; Lutze and Murphy 1999). When one considers the fact that women correctional staff in jails and prisons has been regarded as tokens, or sex objects, and as inferior to their male colleagues (Pogrebin and Poole 1997; Zimmer 1986) and that the workplace has been sexualized by some male colleagues (Pogrebin and Poole 1997), it is not difficult to believe that the staff's ability to do the job is often unfairly in question (Hemmens et al. 2002; Lawrence and Mahan 1998).

Notably, some recent research on three jail and three prison environments in the west by Hemmens and his colleagues (2002) indicates that most male officers tend to positively assess the abilities of their female colleagues. However, the female officers are more positive than the male officers regarding the abilities of women in the correctional role. Moreover, these researchers found—as had Lawrence and Mahan (1998) and Lutz and Murphy (1999), in part—that those males who were less positive regarding female abilities were distinguished by a military background and worked in a higher-security male prison (composed of more male staff).

As a fitting denouement to our story, I would like to mention the findings from some research on female wardens conducted by Kim and colleagues (2003). They found, after surveying 641 wardens from state-run prisons in the United States, that the 90 female wardens in their sample were more interested in programming and amenities in their prisons that promoted the health, education, and programming for inmates than were the male wardens. Having said this, the authors of this study really found more similarities than differences between the male and female wardens, and thus they conclude: "Though the differences between male and female wardens [were] somewhat noticeable, the similarities were more apparent and sup- port the notion that correctional employees' roles, particularly in the administrative realm, are becoming more gender neutral" (Kim et al. 2003, 423–424).

Conclusions

Women in corrections have indeed made great strides. They currently represent about 25 percent of most correctional environments, though there are far fewer in high-security male institutions and in administrative positions and more in jails than prisons. Though the tale of their progress is fraught with obstacles and challenges, many of these have been overcome when the force of law was behind the effort. Such progress and laws were made possible only because of the individual struggles of pioneers in this field and the collective efforts of feminist men and women backing them up. Women and men entering the field need to recognize, appreciate, and further the work done on their behalf to make the corrections workplace more decent and just for all.

Notes

1. The first part of this title comes from the song, "I Am Woman." Music and lyrics by Helen Reddy and Ray Burton. Capitol Records (1972).

2. In the early 1980s, I followed the Harrington story of promotion to chief in the Portland newspaper, the *Oregonian*. At the time, I was a correctional officer and then a counselor (almost a "first") in an adult male prison located about 30 miles away in Washington State, so her story had particular relevance for me.

3. According to the opinion written by Justice O'Connor, the University of Michigan Law School receives about 3500 applications for admission each year and admits only 350 of these students. Admission is based on whether the applicant is likely to be successful in school and the practice of law and whether he or she is likely to contribute in diverse ways to others and their community.

The law school was also interested in admitting a mix of students from different backgrounds and experiences who will be able to learn from their colleagues. GPA and LSAT scores are important but do not guarantee admission as these other considerations are taken into account. Many different types of "diversity" might be considered, of which one's race/ethnic background is but one consideration.

4. These cases are available in law libraries or you might easily access them over the Web by going to the Supreme Court Collection of the Legal Information Institute of Cornell Law School *http://www.straylight.law.cornell.edu.*

Study/Discussion Questions

1. What kinds of obstacles did Mahan and Moore, our two featured "pioneers," face in their correctional careers? How did they work to overcome those obstacles?

2. What is the importance of the Civil Rights Act of 1964 for the employment of women in corrections?

3. How did mentors help Mahan and Moore in their careers? What does Harrington have to say about their worth?

4. What are sexual harrassment and gender harrassment? What is it about correctional environments that make the existence and prevalence of harrassment more likely?

5. What are the best remedies for harrassment? What did Moore do when she found it in the Washington, DC, correctional facilities?

6. How are male and female correctional officers similar and dissimilar in their attitudes, preferences, work styles, and experiences in corrections?

References

Belknap, J. (1995). Women in conflict: An analysis of women correctional officers. In B. R. Price and N. J. Sokoloff (Eds.), *The criminal justice system and women: Offenders, victims, and workers* (2nd edition), (pp. 404–420). New York: McGraw-Hill.

——. (1996). *The invisible woman: Gender, crime, and justice.* Belmont, CA: Wadsworth.

Bennett, K. (1995). Constitutional issues in cross-gender searches and visual observation of nude inmates by opposite-sex officers: A battle between and within the sexes. *The Prison Journal, 75,* 90–112.

Blumrosen, A., and Blumrosen, R. (2002). The reality of intentional job discrimination in metropolitan America—1999. Accessed from: *http://www.EEO1.com.*

Camp, S. D., Steiger, T. L., Wright, K. N., Saylor, W. G., and Gilman, E. (1997). Affirmative action and the 'level playing field': Comparing perceptions of own and minority job advancement opportunities. *Prison Journal, 77,* 313–334.

Carlson, J. R., Anson, R. H., and Thomas, G. (2003). Correctional officer burnout and stress: Does gender matter? *Prison Journal, 83,* 277–288.

Chapman, J. R., Minor, E. K., Rieker, P., Mills, T. L. and Bottum, M. (1983). *Women employed in corrections.* Washington, DC: Government Printing Office.

Civil Rights Act of 1866. (1866). 14 Stat. 27.

Civil Rights Act of 1871. (1871). 17 Stat. 13.

Correctional Service of Canada. (2003). Women correctional officers in male institutions, 1978. Accessed April 29, 2004 from: *http://www.csc.scc.gc.ca.*

Cullen, F. T., Link, B. G., Wolfe, N. T., and Frank, J. (1985). The social dimensions of correctional officer stress. *Justice Quarterly, 2,* 505–533.

Dworkin, A. (1993). Against the male flood: Censorship, pornography, and equality. In P. Smith (Ed.), *Feminist jurisprudence* (pp. 449–466). New York: Oxford University Press.

Farkas, M. A. (1999). Inmate supervisory style: Does gender make a difference? *Women & Criminal Justice, 10,* 25–45.

Fry, L. J., and Glaser, D. (1987). Gender differences in work adjustment of prison employees. *Journal of Offender Counseling, Services, and Rehabilitation, 12,* 39–52.

Gross, G. R., Larson, S. J., Urban, G. D., and Zupan, L. L. (1994). Gender differences in occupational stress among correctional officers. *American Journal of Criminal Justice, 18,* 219–234.

Harrington, P. E. (2002). Advice to women beginning a career in policing. *Women & Criminal Justice*, 14, 1–14.

Hawkes, M. Q. (1998). Edna Mahan: Sustaining the reformatory tradition. *Women & Criminal Justice*, 9, 1–21.

Hemmens, C., Stohr, M. K., Schoeler, M., and Miller, B. (2002). One step up, two steps back: The progression of perceptions of women's work in prisons and jails. *Journal of Criminal Justice*, 30, 473–489.

Henriques, Z. W., and Gilbert, E. (2003). Sexual abuse and sexual assault of women in prison. In R. Muraskin (Ed.), *It's a crime: Women and justice* (pp. 258–272). Upper Saddle River, NJ: Prentice Hall.

Jenne, D. L., and Kersting, R. C. (1996). Aggression and women correctional officers in male prisons. *Prison Journal*, 76, 442–460.

Jurik, N. C. (1985). An officer and a lady: Organizational barriers to women working as correctional officers in men's prisons. *Social Problems*, 33, 375–388.

——. (1988). Striking a balance: Female correctional officers, gender role stereotypes, and male prisons. *Sociological Inquiry*, 58, 291–305.

Jurik, N. C., and Halemba, G. J. (1984). Gender, working conditions, and the job satisfaction of women in a non-traditional occupation: Female correctional officers in a men's prison. *Sociological Quarterly*, 25, 551–566.

Kim, A-S., DeValve, M., DeValve, E. Q., and Johnson, W. W. (2003). Female wardens: Results from a national survey of state correctional executives. *Prison Journal*, 83, 406–425.

Lawrence, R., and Mahan, S. (1998). Women corrections officers in men's prisons: Acceptance and perceived job performance. *Women & Criminal Justice*, 9, 63–86.

Leiber, M. (2000). Gender, religion, and correctional orientations among a sample of juvenile justice personnel. *Women & Criminal Justice*, 11, 15–41.

Lovrich, N. P., and Stohr, M. K. (1993). Gender and jail work: Correctional policy implications of perceptual diversity in the work force. *Policy Studies Review*, 12, 66–84.

Lutze, F. E., and Murphy, D. W. (1999). Ultramasculine prison environments and inmates' adjustment: It's time to move beyond the 'boys will be boys' paradigm. *Justice Quarterly*, 16, 709–734.

Maguire, K., and Pastore, A. L. (Eds.) (2002). *Sourcebook of criminal justice statistics*. Accessed May 9, 2004 from: *http://www.albany. edu/sourcebook*.

Martin, S. E., and Jurik, N. C. (1996). *Doing justice, doing gender: Women in law and criminal justice occupations*. Thousand Oaks, CA: Sage.

Maschke, K. J. (1996). Gender in the prison setting: The privacy-equal employment dilemma. *Women & Criminal Justice*, 7, 23–42.

Morash, M., and Schram, P. J. (2002). *The prison experience: Special issues of women in prison*. Prospect Heights, IL: Waveland Press.

National Institute of Corrections. (1998). *Current issues in the operation of women's prisons*. Longmont, CO: Author.

Pogrebin, M. R., and Poole, E. D. (1997). The sexualized work environment: A look at women jail officers. *Prison Journal*, 77, 41–57.

Pollock, J. M. (2002). *Women, prison & crime* (2nd edition). Belmont, CA: Wadsworth.

Rafter, N. (1985). *Partial justice: State prisons and their inmates, 1800–1935*. Boston: Northeastern University Press.

Simon, R. J., and Simon, J. D. (1993). Female guards in men's prisons. In R. Muraskin (Ed.) *It's a crime: Women and justice* (pp. 226–241). Englewood Cliffs, NJ: Regents/Prentice Hall.

Smykla, J., and Williams, J. (1996). Co-corrections in the United States of America, 1970–1990: Two decades of disadvantages for women prisoners. *Women & Criminal Justice*, 8, 61–76.

Stohr, M. K. (1997). Noteworthy personnel findings from the women's jail study. *American Jails*, 11, 45–60.

——. (2005). Criminal justice organizations and management. Unpublished manuscript.

Stohr, M. K., Lovrich, N. P., and Mays, G. L. (1997). Service vs. security focus in training assessments: Testing gender differences among women's jail correctional officers. *Women & Criminal Justice*, 9, 65–85.

Stohr, M. K., Lovrich, N. P., and Wood, M. (1996). Service vs. security concerns in contemporary jails: Testing behavior differences in training topic assessments. *Journal of Criminal Justice*, 24, 437–448.

Stohr, M. K., Mays, G. L., Beck, A. C., and Kelley, T. (1998). Sexual harassment in women's jails. *Journal of Contemporary Criminal Justice,* 14, 135–155.

U.S. Department of Justice. (1997). Justice Department reaches agreement with Arkansas corrections system ensuring equal employment opportunities for women. Accessed April 29, 2004 from: *http://www.usdoj.gov.*

Walters, S. (1992). Attitudinal and demographic differences between male and female correctional officers. *Journal of Offender Rehabilitation,* 18, 173–189.

Wright, K., and Saylor, W. G. (1991). Male and female employees' perceptions of prison work: Is there a difference? *Justice Quarterly,* 8, 505–524.

Yates, H. M. (2002). Margaret Moore: African American feminist leader in corrections. *Women & Criminal Justice,* 13, 9–26.

Young, V. D. (2004). All the women in the Maryland state penitentiary: 1812–1869. In M. K. Stohr and C. Hemmens (Eds.), *The inmate prison experience* (pp. 253–268). Upper Saddle River, NJ: Prentice Hall.

Zimmer, L. (1986). *Women guarding men.* Chicago: University of Chicago Press.

——. (1989). Solving women's employment problems in corrections: Shifting the burden to administrators. *Women & Criminal Justice,* 1, 55–79.

Zupan, L. L. (1986). Gender-related differences in correctional officers' perceptions and attitudes. *Journal of Criminal Justice,* 14, 349–361.

——. (1992). The progress of women correctional officers in all-male prisons. In I. L. Moyer (Ed.), *The changing roles of women in the criminal justice system: Offenders, victims, and professionals* (2nd edition), (pp. 323–343). Prospect Heights, IL: Waveland Press.

Cases Cited

Dothard v. Rawlinson, 433 U.S. 321 (1977).

Grutter v. Bollinger et al. 288 F. 3d, affirmed, U.S. 02-241 (2003).

Jordan v. Gardner, 986 F.2d 1521 (9th Cir. 1993).

Pulido v. State of California et al. (Marin County Superior Court Case—1993/1994) involving the issue of sexual harassment in a state prison (San Quentin). Judicial decision for the plaintiff in the amount of $1.3 million in January 1994, appellate court affirmed decision and award in December 1994.

Torres v. Wisconsin Department of Health and Social Services, 48 Fair Employment Practices Cases 270 (8th Cir. 1988).

University of California Regents v. Bakke, 438 U.S. 265 (1978). ✦